Pain and Its Ending

The Four Noble Truths in the Theravāda Buddhist Canon

BUDDHIST TRADITION SERIES

VOLUME 45

Edited by

ALEX WAYMAN

Pain and Its Ending

The Four Noble Truths in the Theravāda Buddhist Canon

CAROL S. ANDERSON

MOTILAL BANARSIDASS PUBLISHERS
PRIVATE LIMITED • DELHI

First Indian Edition : 2001

First Published : UK, 1999
by Curzon Press

ISBN: 81-208-1806-7

Also available at:

MOTILAL BANARSIDASS

236, 9th Main III Block, Jayanagar, Bangalore 560 011
41 U.A. Bungalow Road, Jawahar Nagar, Delhi 110 007
8 Mahalaxmi Chamber, Warden Road, Mumbai 400 026
120 Royapettah High Road, Mylapore, Chennai 600 004
8 Camac Street, Kolkata 700 017 002
Ashok Rajpath, Patna 800 004
Chowk, Varanasi 221 001

Printed in India
BY JAINENDRA PRAKASH JAIN AT SHRI JAINENDRA PRESS,
A-45 NARAINA, PHASE-I, NEW DELHI 110 028
AND PUBLISHED BY NARENDRA PRAKASH JAIN FOR
MOTILAL BANARSIDASS PUBLISHERS PRIVATE LIMITED,
BUNGALOW ROAD, DELHI 110 007

CONTENTS

FOREWORD

Before discussing the contents of this excellent book, let us mention her scriptural reference of SV 420, which stands for Saṃyutta-nikāya, Part V, scripture no. 420. This is one of the four divisions of the Päli canon, with that title normally rendered "The Book of the Kindred Sayings". The Four Noble Truths—the fourth meaning the Eightfold Noble Path—are basic to ancient Buddhism, and their original statement would occupy a small paragraph. It is wonderful to have their expansion to a whole book, well written as is here. The author discusses various ancient scriptures, such as those which have expanded the Four Truths, or do so without mentioning the four.

The author emphasizes the attitude toward those Four, and it is especially "right view" of the four, meaning "pain" [or 'suffering'], its origin, its ending, and the way leading to its ending. Later, "mindfulness" is also praised as having those Four as a foundation, and the famous 12-numbered formula called Dependent Origination is said to explain nos. 2 and 3 of the Four. Starting with her Chapter Four on the Abhidhamma [=S. Abhidharma], there is a somewhat more technical discussion of the Four. It is the fourth Truth, "the way leading to the ending of pain," that is variously explained, implicating the Buddhist theory of three worlds, and the Buddha's Enlightenment.

In Chaps. Six and Seven the author presents the study of those Four in Europe and the United States, and then what various modern authors say about those Four, including the theory that they are the basis of Buddhism. The author is to be congratulated for the precious information here and in the rest of her book.

ALEX WAYMAN
Professor Emeritus of Sanskrit,
Columbia University

PREFACE

I remember vividly the moment when I read Carolyn Augusta Foley's short note to the *Journal of the Royal Asiatic Society of Great Britain and Ireland* entitled "Curious Omissions in the Pāli Canonical Lists." She pointed out that, if certain doctrines (such as the four noble truths) were as central to the Theravāda tradition as they were usually considered to be, then there were critical passages in the canon from which such teachings were missing. I read her comments with a sense of mutual discovery that stretched across the decades; Foley put into words one of the hypotheses with which I had been working on this project. I share her curiosity about the points at which the teaching of the four noble truths appear and the rapidity with which they disappear in the wealth of Buddhist traditions, both textual and lived. While the four noble truths are certainly central in many canonical *sutta*s, they vanish quickly when one turns to the pragmatic discussions in the *Vinaya-piṭaka* of how the *saṅgha* was established and maintained or when one turns to the *paritta* or other contemporary Buddhist rituals. Within the sphere of my interest in broad patterns of soteriology and the path catalyzed by studying the writings of Paul Mus with Frank Reynolds, Foley's observations crystallized my approach to this study.

Alongside my fundamental curiosity about the four noble truths, there are several conversations that lie embedded in the pages of this book, some of which are more explicit than others. The first is a longstanding dialogue with the recent work of scholars committed to the study of doctrines. Certainly, Paul J. Griffiths is among the leading scholars in this endeavor, as demonstrated in his books on the teachings of body and mind and the Buddha in Indian Buddhist traditions; the writings of theologians such as George Lindbeck and William Christian are also present. What I have gained from these scholars are tools with which to describe more precisely what people do with doctrines (primary doctrines, that is) in a religious community. I am most interested in the ways in which doctrines serve explicitly *non*-doctrinal purposes within a community. I am less interested in what is ultimately true, as are the above scholars, than I am fascinated with how teachings that are taken to be true unfold and develop within religious traditions. It is the human religious imagination that intrigues me, and in this I have learned a great deal from David Tracy. His writings and lectures on the history of the theological imagination, together with conversations that I have had with him and with his students, have contributed to any insights I have developed in this area. The argument in this book that seeks to articulate the cosmological settings that contextualize classic doctrines weaves together strands of various exchanges that I have had with Frank Reynolds, Paul Griffiths, and David Tracy.

The second conversation present in the pages of this book is an ongoing interest in untangling some of the implications of Catherine Bell's analysis most recently articulated in *Ritual Theory, Ritual Practice*. In that study of theories and theorists of ritual, she observes that scholars of ritual have long separated "our" theories from the rituals of "those" actors who actually perform the rituals, in an unequal and imbalanced separation of theory from action, with theory elevated over action. She calls on scholars of ritual to consider the ways in which we produce our theories of ritual and rightly points out that the production of knowledge is in itself a ritualized action played out within the halls of academia. Her analysis is not limited to studies of ritual. All academic discourses, I would suggest, rely on the separation of theory from action. In response to Bell's incisive critiques, I have sought to demonstrate in the early chapters of this study how scholars of Buddhism have replicated this separation or, to paraphrase Mary Douglas's language, how we have "wrongly divided human experience." I have attempted to offer an alternative model with which to examine central religious teachings, one that requires us to glean from those teachings a broader frameworks of actions and the practices that surround the doctrines within a religious tradition. What we find when we expand our predilections for textual sources is a complex and intriguing history of the emergence and development of religious ideas, conceptions, and acts of teaching.

This observation leads to a third set of conversations that inform this study, which are largely silent in this book: the exchanges that I have on this topic had with friends, colleagues, and scholars in Sri Lanka. While studying Sinhalese and Pāli with Professor W. S. Karunatillake during the academic year of 1990-1991, I had the great pleasure of participating in an intensive introduction to Sinhalese Buddhist lay life. I was welcomed into many homes and into many conversations about the Buddhism that Sinhalese speakers live. At that time, President Premadasa was waging his war against the LTTE in the north and had just conducted a bloody purge of the JVP movement in the central and southern parts of the Island. Conversations about these events were not separated from discussions of the four noble truths. Since that period, however, the edges of the Sinhalese Buddhist chauvinism that, in part, fuels the war have become more sharply honed. Discussions with a few leading scholars in Sri Lanka have been somewhat less fruitful in recent years than when I first did research on the Island; in part this is due to a tendency among some Sinhalese Buddhist scholars to simplify and sterilize Buddhism in Sri Lanka in order to defend it more readily to critics of the government's policies. My response is the opposite: I wish to offer a more complex and nuanced reading of one of the most readily appropriated teachings of South Asian Buddhism at a time when such readings are resisted in certain quarters in Sri Lanka.

There are many people who have contributed to this study over the years, both directly and indirectly. This project began as my dissertation at the University of Chicago, but it has been revised extensively since my formal colloquium. As a student at the Divinity School, I owe a great debt to Professor John A. Brinkman in the Oriental Institute, who taught me how to read in-between the lines of historical sources without sacrificing the accuracy so essential to historical studies. When I was sketching out the project as a dissertation proposal, John H. Engler was quite generous with his time and his suggestions for framing the questions I wished to pursue. While Charles Hallisey's remarks and puzzled looks spurred me to focus the project more narrowly, David Tracy encouraged me to expand my treatment of the category of doctrines and to make the connections between Catherine Bell's argument and my interest in the pragmatic functions of doctrines. Paul Griffiths has consistently offered his feedback on the manuscript through its various incarnations, and his suggestion that I focus on religious pedagogy has enabled me to integrate various strands of the study. I would like to thank Steven Collins for the time he spent one summer helping me to distill the finer points of the manuscript, as well as for the wealth of insights into the Pāli language that I have learned from him. Throughout the entire process and well beyond the dissertation itself, Frank Reynolds has provided his characteristic unflagging support and reliable criticism. The strengths of this book are due in no small part to these teachers and scholars; any errors are, of course, my own.

I would like to thank Professor W. S. Karunatillake, Kalyani Karunatillake, and their son, W. S. K. Karunatillake for their friendship and generosity since we first met in Ithaca in August of 1990. I have learned a great deal from the Karunatillakes, and I remember fondly the many afternoons that Professor Karunatillake and I spent studying Pāli and Sinhala. I value our on-going collaborations more than I can say in any language.

I must convey my indebtedness to colleagues in Kalamazoo, Michigan whose meticulous attention to detail have strengthened the book: Ellen Caldwell, Annie McCombs, and David Collins. Other people who have propelled and supported me as I have brought this project to completion include R. Amy Elman, Nora Evers, Ralph Deal, Kay A. Read, Susan E. Henking, Betty Bayer, L. DeAne Lagerquist, Ellen K. Wondra, Sandra Lee Dixon, and Jean Elisabeth Pedersen. I thank Jonathan S. Walters for his comments, scholarship, and humor that have come at critical points. My parents, Joann M. Anderson and Robert A. Anderson, have offered their unstinting encouragement and for this I am grateful. Most recently, I appreciate the enthusiasm that Charles Prebish has shown for this study and his most helpful suggestions throughout the editing and publication process. Finally, I would like to acknowledge the financial support I received from the Fulbright program administered by the Institute for International Education in New York and the United States Educational Foundation in Colombo, the American Academy of Religion, and Kalamazoo College.

Carol S. Anderson

TABLES

ABBREVIATIONS

Abbreviations follow those of the Critical Pāli Dictionary.

Texts

A	Aṅguttara-nikāya
As	Atthasālinī (commentary on the Dhammasaṅganī)
Kv-a	Kathāvatthu-pparakarana-atthakathā
Th	Theragāthā
D	Dīgha-nikāya
Dhātuk	Dhātukathā-pakaraṇa
M	Majjhima-nikāya
Moh	Mohavicchedanī
Mp	Manorathapūranī (commentary on the Aṅguttara-nikāya)
Pp	Puggalapaññatti
Paṭis	Paṭisambidhāmagga
Ps	Papañcasūdanī (commentary on the Majjhima-nikāya)
S	Saṃyutta-nikāya
Sp	Samantapāsādikā (commentary on the Vinaya-piṭaka)
Spk	Sārattha(p)pakāsinī (commentary on the Saṃyutta-nikāya)
Sv	Sumaṅgalavilāsinī (commentary on the Dīgha-nikāya)
Vibh	Vibhaṅga-pakaraṇa
Vin	Vinaya-piṭaka
Vism	Visuddhimagga
Yam	Yamaka-pakaraṇa

Secondary Works and Authors

CPD	Critical Pāli Dictionary
HIB	Lamotte, *History of Indian Buddhism*
PED	Pāli-English Dictionary
PTC	Pāli Tipiṭakaṃ Concordance
BHSD	Buddhist Hybrid Sanskrit Grammar and Dictionary

INTRODUCTION

A Historical Context for the Four Noble Truths

But I appeal again to writers on these things – votaries we much leave to a more distant future – to look closer into evidential material now available, and to see Buddhism less as a readymade, if bifurcated, cult and more as a growth with a long history.[1]

Caroline Augusta Foley (1935)

A Beginning

The story of Gautama Buddha's enlightenment is known well to students of Buddhism: it is set in Deer Park at Isipatana near ancient Bārāṇasi, the audience is comprised of five religious seekers with whom the Buddha once travelled in his search for release from the cycle of rebirth and death in saṃṣāra, and it is to these men that the Buddha announced that he had attained enlightenment. The term used by the Pāli canon for this address that the Buddha gave is a talk (*kathā*), although the Pāli word is often translated as 'sermon.' The Buddha begins his talk to Koṇḍañña, Vappa, Bhaddiya, Mahānāma, and Assaji by stating that there are two extremes to be avoided: devotion to sensual pleasures and devotion to mortification of the body. Between these two poles, he continues, lies the middle way which consists of the noble eightfold path: right view, right aim, right speech, right action, right living, right effort, right mindfulness, and right concentration. This middle path leads to 'insight, knowledge, calm, higher knowledge, enlightenment, and *nibbāna*.' The Buddha then states the four noble truths: 'this is pain' (*idaṃ dukkhaṃ*), 'this is the origin of pain' (*ayaṃ dukkha-samudayo*), 'this is the ending of pain' (*ayaṃ dukkha-nirodho*), and 'this is the way leading to the ending of pain' (*ayaṃ dukkha-nirodha-gāminī paṭipadā*). The Buddha tells his former companions that once he realized and knew the four noble truths, he knew that this life was his last rebirth and that he had no more births in the future. Inspired by this talk, Koṇḍañña cultivates a knowledge of the four noble truths and thereby becomes a stream-enterer, which means that he reached the first of four stages of the path to *nibbāna*. At the end of the *sutta* ('discourse' or 'text'), the gods in the heavens and all beings in the cosmos proclaim that the wheel of *dhamma* has been turned and that no one may turn it back. The title of the *sutta* in which this story is told is the '*Sutta* on the Turning of the *Dhamma*-Wheel' (*Dhammacakkappavattana-sutta*).[2]

At the center of this *sutta* are the four noble truths. One of the striking features of the four noble truths is how they reveal a certain set of relationships between religious experience, doctrine, and cosmology. The four truths are the substance of what the Buddha knew as he became enlightened; thus, they are a doctrine that emerges out of a particular religious experience. The Buddha taught the four noble truths as his first *dhamma* talk, which means that they are the first teaching about what is fundamentally right. Finally, the four truths are the means by which the wheel of *dhamma* is turned: when Koṇḍañña realized the truth of the four truths, he became enlightened. This turning is a cosmogonic moment that reverberates throughout the earth and the heavens of the Buddhist cosmos. The relationship between religious experience, doctrine, and the Buddhist cosmos reflected in the four noble truths is the primary subject of this book.

From a different angle, there is a problem in many studies of Theravādan Buddhism that can be traced to the scholarly focus on Buddhist texts as the vehicle through which Buddhism was first introduced to Europe and the United States. It is the question of how canonical and post-canonical Buddhist writings are related to the practices of actual Buddhists. In many studies of Buddhism conducted toward the end of the nineteenth and during the first half of the twentieth centuries, there was an assumption that what was described in the canonical texts was a realistic representation of how Buddhism was actually practiced. Such a generalization is too broad in its scope, and the ensuing difficulties with this approach have been called 'the Buddhism and Society problem' by Steven Collins. Most attempts to resolve this problem conclude that Buddhist canons reflect the realities of monastic life with a relatively high degree of accuracy. Richard Gombrich and Melford Spiro have suggested that there are different types of Theravāda Buddhism, each with a unique relationship to the Theravāda canon. However, there is an unexamined category at work in these studies: how do doctrines, found in canonical literature, function in a religious community that is more encompassing than a monastic order? Related to this question is another: how are doctrines related to particular religious experiences? To answer these questions, this book traces the four noble truths throughout the Theravāda canon with attention devoted to the pedagogical techniques and results that claim to lead to the attainment of *nibbāna*.

In the cosmology of Theravāda Buddhism, the path to *nibbāna* occupies a central position because it is rooted in the cosmos where humans, gods, and creatures of the hells live. The path provides the means by which humans may escape saṃsāra, the cycle of death and rebirth. Gautama

Buddha's teachings are still remembered in the world today, and thus he is known as *the* Buddha of the current eon. Within this eon, progress on the paths described in the Theravāda canon involves practicing two different types of meditation: insight meditation and *jhāni*c (trance) meditation. The Theravāda canon gives different explanations for how the four noble truths are related to the path to *nibbāna* that a follower of the Buddha must take. In some stories about the Buddha's enlightenment, the four noble truths are mentioned in conjunction with insight meditation and the elimination of four corruptions (*āsavā*): sensual desire (*kāmāsavā*), existence (*bhavāsavā*), view (*diṭṭhāsavā*), and ignorance (*avijjāsavā*).[3] These corruptions stand as obstacles to experiencing *nibbāna*. In other stories of how the Buddha attained *nibbāna*, the four noble truths are associated with the meditative states called the *jhāna*s in which a practitioner turns attention inward to attain certain levels. In still another *sutta*, the Buddha describes how he gained enlightenment but makes no mention of realizing the four noble truths. There has been no extended analysis of where the four noble truths are found in stories of the Buddha's awakening, nor has there been a comprehensive study of what results a practitioner might expect in their progress on the path if they acquire a certain knowledge of the truths. Similarly, in studies of the four truths, the cosmological settings for the teachings of Gautama Buddha are often relegated to footnotes, if discussed at all. This is the topic of this book: what the Theravāda canon says about how followers are to cultivate that religious experience by means of the four noble truths and the path within the Buddhist cosmos.

Surprisingly enough, given that the four noble truths are widely known as a fundamental teaching of the Buddha, there has never been a comprehensive study of the teaching throughout the history of scholarship on Buddhism in Europe and the United States. The four noble truths are often discussed in the course of other studies; the esteemed scholar Étienne Lamotte once wrote that the four noble truths were a teaching that encompassed all of the Buddha's teachings contained in the Theravāda canon. Outside the world of academic studies, the four noble truths are nearly synonymous with the Buddha and with his teachings. However, I have found in the course of my research a brief note by Caroline Augusta Foley (known as Mrs. C. A. F. Rhys Davids after her marriage), published in 1935, in which she observed that there are 'curious omissions' in the Theravāda canon when one looks for references to the teachings of the three refuges, the three marks, the four noble truths, and the eightfold path.[4]

> [T]heir occurrence where they should one and all have come, aye, and been given first rank, is curiously intermittent and the reverse of what we should find, had they always occupied that doctrinal centrality of which Hīnayānists and writers on Buddhism are for ever telling us.[5]

She concluded her article by explaining that, in her analysis of these curious omissions, she is 'in a minority of one – an *eka-nipāta*;' and she was correct in her observation. Since 1844, when Eugène Burnouf was the first to discuss the four noble truths in a study of Buddhism published in a European language, the four noble truths have not been studied systematically; they are generally interpreted according to the '*Sutta* on the Turning of the *Dhamma*-Wheel.' Little attention has been paid to Foley's curious omissions.

In the spirit of Foley's observation, I have been fascinated by the many places in which the four noble truths appear, where they do not appear, and the various roles that the teaching plays throughout the Theravāda canon and commentaries. As I noted above, the subject of this study is what the four noble truths teach about the relationship between religious experience and doctrine within the Buddhist cosmos. Like the initial idea of a comprehensive study on the four noble truths, the significance of these themes may appear to be self-evident. After all, one might respond, religious experience is at the heart of any religion, and doctrines are the way that people learn about and cultivate that experience. It is precisely this self-evident assumption that I wish to examine: to return to basic questions of how the Theravāda canon conceives of religious experience, doctrine, and teaching in order to refine the various premises that have shaped our contemporary understandings of the four noble truths. As a starting point, let me point out that the events recounted in the '*Sutta* on the Turning of the *Dhamma*-Wheel' probably do not describe how the Buddha actually became enlightened. The *stories* of how the Buddha became enlightened describe how the redactors of the Theravāda canon remembered the Buddha and his teachings, and they should be read as such.

Chapter One asks an essential question: are the four noble truths a doctrine, as the category is usually employed in the comparative study of religion? There is no single Pāli word that can be translated accurately as 'doctrine,' but the concept of *diṭṭhi* (view) approximates some of the meanings of doctrine. I examine classical studies of Theravāda Buddhism to illustrate how the category of doctrine has been employed, and I also consider what scholars outside of the study of Buddhism have written recently about defining the category of doctrine. The remainder of the chapter explores the nature of 'view' (*diṭṭhi*) and what it means to say that the four noble truths are a view, or, more specifically, a right view. Matters of doctrine are generally considered to be intellectual exercises, and right view (*sammādiṭṭhi*) shares this meaning. However, right view never carries the sense of ossification that doctrine often does. Right view is dynamic by its very nature, and, above all, it is considered to be fundamentally true. One should not grasp or hold right view, the canon explains, but one should seek to understand it thoroughly. Comparing the two categories requires a clarification of what doctrine means within the history of religions.

Chapter Two explores the four noble truths as they appear in stories of the Buddha's enlightenment, with particular attention to the '*Sutta* on the Turning of the *Dhamma*-Wheel.' The four noble truths are an integral component of most – but not all – accounts of the Buddha's awakening. In this regard, the teaching is significant not only as the product of what the Buddha experienced during the night spent under the Bodhi-tree, but also as the means by which other followers may cultivate the same experience. The four truths are recognized in the canon as salvifically efficacious; that is, understanding the teaching when it is taught by the Buddha (or by two of the Buddha's followers, Assaji or Sāriputta) is an effective means for a practitioner to gain access to the path to *nibbāna*. In these biographical accounts of the Buddha, the four noble truths function symbolically. That is, they represent the Buddha's enlightenment and the possibility that others may acquire the same experience. There is no other teaching of the – or *any* – Buddha that functions in this way, and thus the four noble truths are set apart from other teachings such as no-self (*anattā*), dependent arising (*paṭiccasamuppāda*), and the establishment of mindfulness (*satipaṭṭhāna*). In their capacity as a phenomenological description of what the Buddha experienced as he was enlightened and as a symbol of that experience within the Buddhist cosmos, the four noble truths are unique in the Theravāda canon.

In contrast to the centrality of the four noble truths in stories of the Buddha's enlightenment, Chapter Three traces the points at which the four noble truths appear in the context of other teachings of the Buddha in the *Sutta-piṭaka*. One example of this pattern is the teaching of dependent arising (*paṭiccasamuppāda*) that is sometimes used to explain the second and third truths ('this is the arising of pain' and 'this is the ending of pain'). In passages like these, the four noble truths are not pivotal in and of themselves. Rather, they are significant as a means to comprehend other teachings; and, in turn, other teachings are explained as a way to grasp the meaning of the four noble truths. It is precisely this context – a network of teachings – that distinguishes the teaching from its function as a symbol in stories of the Buddha's enlightenment. Here, the teaching is a proposition of right view that would-be Buddhists must recognize initially as worthy of being learned and that they must subsequently understand as fully as possible.

The same network of teachings are analyzed differently in the *Abhidhamma-piṭaka*, and Chapter Four explores the role of the four noble truths in matrices of *abhidhamma* analysis. The teachings of the Buddha are arranged into lists and are analyzed with different categories. The discourse is not contextualized in the *Abhidhamma-piṭaka*; the four noble truths are abstracted from any concrete situation and are examined minutely in terms of how they intersect with other teachings to produce the world in which human beings live. Like the networks in which the four noble truths appear in the *Sutta-piṭaka*, the four truths are not set apart from other teachings in any particular way, nor do they carry any association with the Buddha's enlightenment, his first teaching, or Koṇḍañña's cultivation of enlightenment. In the *Abhidhamma-piṭaka* the four noble truths are propositions whose relationships must be understood in order to comprehend how the cosmos comes into being and how it passes away.

Chapter Five focuses on the pedagogical techniques that surround the teaching: how are the four noble truths taught and how are they learned? The specific path attainments that the canon and commentaries offer as the results of fully comprehending the four noble truths and the pedagogical techniques used to teach the four truths show that there are two distinct models associated with the four noble truths. The first model is linked to the symbolic function of the four noble truths and to a set of four stages of the path: the stream-winner (no more than seven rebirths in the world before becoming enlightened), once-returner (no more than one more rebirth in the world), the non-returner (no more than one rebirth in the heavens), and the *arahat* (who has no more rebirths at all). The second model, however, is rooted in the four noble truths when they function as a proposition for what is ultimately true in the cosmos. Followers are to comprehend the truth of different propositions and understand how they are related to each other. While the reason for learning these propositions is defined consistently as attaining *nibbāna*, no specific path attainment is provided as a guide. Different pedagogical techniques are employed in each model, thus mirroring the distinctions between the two models of how one is to attain enlightenment by learning the four noble truths.

Chapter Six surveys scholarship on the four noble truths that has been conducted in Europe and the United States since the teaching was first described in a western language in the early nineteenth century. These studies of Buddhism, some articles of which focus exclusively on the four noble truths, generally treat the four truths in one of two ways. The four noble truths are either cited as the most important teaching of the Buddha, or they are incorporated into a list of three or four of the most important teachings of Buddhism. I have paid particular attention to the question of whether these scholars explored the implications of the four noble truths for a Theravādan conception of religious experience and doctrine, and it appears that the category of doctrine is used repeatedly as if it were self-evident. In keeping with the assumption that doctrine is an appropriate category for the four noble truths, very few scholars have explored the possibility that the teachings of the Buddha functioned in other, non-doctrinal, ways in the Theravāda canon. With notable exceptions discussed in the chapter, scholarship on the four noble truths has been remarkably consistent throughout the past one hundred and fifty years in Europe and in the United States. The history of scholarship on the four noble truths has reified the four noble truths as they appear in the '*Sutta* on the Turning of the *Dhamma*-Wheel.'

Chapter Seven returns to the first question posed as the primary subject of this book: what do the four truths suggest about how religious experiences were regarded in the Theravāda canon? The argument in this chapter is that there are two models for interpreting religious experience in occidental scholarship on religions that have influenced our readings of the four noble truths. The first is to regard the category of doctrine as belonging to the realm of the intellect, and the second is to employ the category of symbol for a particular kind of immediate and direct experience. This division reflects the evidence that will be found in Chapters One through Four: there are two different ways that the four noble truths function in the Theravāda canon and commentaries. First, the four noble truths represent symbolically the possibility of cultivating a particular religious experience: one seeks an experience of *nibbāna* and release from the cycle of rebirth (saṃsāra). Second, after the Buddha's entry into *parinibbāna*, the four noble truths become a proposition which can be learned only with diligence, memorization, attention, and dedication. However, Chapter Seven concludes this study with a reflection on the comparability of the categories of symbol and doctrine, on the one hand, and the category of rights views (*sammādiṭṭhi*) on the other.

The difference between the two patterns lies in the figure of the Buddha and the construction of a sacred biography in the Theravāda canon: through his abilities as a teacher (that were enhanced by his powers as a Buddha), the Buddha made it possible for others to comprehend immediately the truths that 'this is pain,' 'this is the arising of pain,' 'this is the ending of pain,' and 'this is the way to the ending of pain.' When the Buddha entered *parinibbāna*, the four noble truths appeared in his biography as a symbol of enlightenment; but, after that point in time, the canon regards the four noble truths as one among many. The authority of the four noble truths rests in their incorporation into sacred biographies of the Buddha, the most significant of which is the '*Sutta* on the Turning of the *Dhamma*-Wheel.' This *sutta* establishes the four noble truths as a path out of the Buddhist cosmos and it is only when we look at the four noble truths as one teaching among many that their cosmological role becomes evident. The differences between both functions of the four noble truths – the symbolic within the Buddhist cosmos and the propositional within the world – reveal the cosmological and doctrinal dimensions of a single teaching that emerged at an undetermined point within the development of the Theravāda canon. To paraphrase Foley, the four noble truths were not part of a ready-made Buddhism; they are an integral part of a Buddhism with a long history.[6]

Although the four noble truths function as a symbol of enlightenment within the cosmos on the one hand and as propositions within the world after the Buddha's *parinibbāna* on the other, these two functions cannot be embraced by such a classic category in the history of religion as that of the sacred and the profane. Neither are they similar to Eliade's contrast between cosmos and history. When Mircea Eliade examines the difference between cosmos and history in *The Myth of the Eternal Return*, he suggests that one difference between the two categories of religious experience is that, in the former, one can return to the beginning to create the world anew. However, one cannot return to the beginning in an historical world because time flows only forward – in one direction. Even though Eliade's categories of cosmos and history are ideal types that are theoretically manifested in history in different ways, his approach is basically ahistorical. Here, the difference between the two roles that the four noble truths play is not a difference between a transcendent cosmos that stands beyond history and a mundane world that is bound by history. The difference between the two roles of the four noble truths is grounded in the historical fact of the Theravāda canon. In the canon, there are two distinct patterns of how the canon remembers the role of the four noble truths: one which was in effect during the time when the Buddha lived and taught on earth, and one that emerged after the Buddha's *parinibbāna*. The foundation for both is historical. The fact that there are two different patterns is evidence of the construction of biographies of Gautama Buddha and of the construction of a history of the early community, both within the Theravāda tradition.

Having argued for an historical foundation, it is now necessary to place the four noble truths within such a context. The remainder of this introduction is devoted to the following topics: the nature of the Theravāda canon, its language, historical development, and the place of the four noble truths within the development of the canon.

The Content of Theravāda Canon

The Theravāda canon is the collection of sacred writings of the Theravāda Buddhist tradition that today is practiced widely in Sri Lanka, Thailand, and Myanmar. The authority of the canon rests in the fact that the texts are considered to be the words of the Buddha (*buddhavacana*). When the Theravāda canon was said to have been written down, in the first century B.C.E., the canon was known as *pāli* (canon or text), as opposed to the commentaries (*aṭṭhakathā*), although there was no inherent sense of a canon as closed or fixed at this point in time.[7] The process by which the canon became closed involved the political struggles of the three monastic branches of Theravāda Buddhism in Sri Lanka.[8] Two of the three, the Mahāvihāra and the Abhayagiri, competed with each other for state sponsorship throughout the first millennium in Sri Lanka; the Theravāda canon that we have today is the result of Mahāvihāra monks whose success was ultimately supported by King Parakkamabāhu I in the twelfth century.[9] (The third branch was the Jetavana which emerged in the fourth century; they are not significant in this immediate context.) The Theravāda canon was substantially closed by the early fifth century, when Buddhaghosa compiled his commentaries on the canon. Collins points out that the closed collection of writings that we call the canon of the Theravāda school 'should be seen as a *product* of that school, as part of a strategy of legitimation by the monks of the Mahāvihāra lineage in Ceylon in the early centuries of the first millennium A.D.'[10] It is important to point out that the existence of the canon in actual texts was not always its most significant aspect; Collins suggests that it was the *idea* of a Theravāda canon – and, I would emphasize, the authority that the idea of a canon carried – that was often more important than the actual collection of texts.[11]

The contents of the Theravāda canon are organized according to three *piṭaka*s, from which it derives the title of *Tipiṭaka* (*ti*- is a prefix meaning three).[12] *Piṭaka* is a word that is usually translated as 'baskets,' which refers to a collection of texts within the Buddhist lineage.[13] The first *piṭaka* is the *Vinaya-piṭaka*, which is divided into three sections: the *Suttavibhaṅga*, *Khandaka*, and the *Parivāra*. The *Suttavibhaṅga* contains the rules of discipline for the monastic *saṅgha* of *bhikkhu*s (monks) and *bhikkhunī*s (nuns), with stories that explain the need for specific rules. The *Khandaka* contains a narrative of how the Buddha established the *saṅgha* in its two sections, the *Mahāvagga* and *Cullavagga*. The *Parivāra* is an abbreviated or condensed version of the rules discussed in the *Suttavibhaṅga*.

The *Sutta-piṭaka* is the second *piṭaka*, which is the collection of the Buddha's talks on *dhamma* and, more rarely, talks given by certain followers of the Buddha. There are five *nikāya*s (the term refers to a 'class' or 'group') according to which the *Sutta-piṭaka* is organized: the *Dīgha*- (Long), the *Majjhima*- (Middle Length), the *Aṅguttara*- (By Number), the *Saṃyutta*- (Collected by Topic), and the *Khuddaka-nikāyas* (Short). The first four *nikāya*s have parallels called *āgama*s in the Chinese Buddhist canon, but the *Khuddaka-nikāya* does not. The Theravāda *Khuddaka-nikāya* includes such texts as the *Jātaka* (Birth Stories of the Buddha), the *Theragāthā* and *Therīgāthā* (Hymns of the [male] Elders and [female] Elders), and the *Dhammapada* (Footprint of *Dhamma*).

The third *piṭaka* is the *Abhidhamma-piṭaka*, and it includes material that is usually considered to be more abstract; the term *abhidhamma* means 'further or higher *dhamma*.' There are seven books to the *Abhidhamma-piṭaka*: *Dhammasaṅginī*, *Vibhaṅga*, *Dhātukathā*, *Puggala-paññati*, *Yamaka*, *Kathāvatthu*, and the *Paṭṭhāna*. There was an early distinction in the development of the canon between *abhidhamma* and *vinaya*, which suggests that there was once a significant distinction between *abhidhamma* and discipline (*vinaya*). These books of the Theravāda canon and their commentaries are the sources that I have used for this study of the four noble truths; I have compared those *sutta*s in the Theravāda canon where the four truths appear with the canons of other schools of Buddhism below.

The Language of the Theravāda Canon

Pāli is the name used for the language in which the Theravāda canon is recorded. It is a dialect of Middle Indo-Aryan, falling between Old Indo-Aryan, which is the Sanskrit of the *Veda*s that may date to the end of the second millennium B.C.E., and New Indo-Aryan. New Indo-Aryan consists of the modern languages of northern India and Sinhalese in Sri Lanka.[14] Despite the fact that scholars call the language of the Theravāda canon 'Pāli,' the word *pāli* never actually appears in the Theravāda canon as a name for the language of the canon. Professor K. R. Norman explains that several centuries ago the term *pāli-bhāsā* was interpreted erroneously as the 'language of Pāli,' and *pāli* was interpreted as a particular language instead of translated properly as a word for 'canon or text.'[15] Because this reading of *pāli-bhāsā* was in error, Norman suggests that we should call the Pāli canon by the more accurate term of the Theravāda canon, and I have followed his suggestion here. Nonetheless, the Pāli canon and the Theravāda canon are simply different names for the same group of canonical writings. And, correctly or incorrectly, Pāli is used widely as a name for a conglomerate of Middle Indo-Aryan dialects that were spoken in northern India at the time of the Buddha.[16]

The commentator Buddhaghosa wrote that Māgadhī was the language of the Buddha.[17] Norman explains that it is reasonable that Buddhaghosa referred to the language of the Buddha as Māgadhī when it is understood that Buddhaghosa used the name Māgadhī to refer to a group of dialects used collectively as the administrative language of King Aśoka, ruler of the Mauryan empire in northern India in the third century B.C.E. (We know of the dialects of the Mauryan empire from the edicts on stone pillars that Aśoka had carved in different dialects of Middle Indo-Aryan; many of the edicts can be reliably dated.) However, contemporary scholars reserve the name Māgadhī for a specific dialect spoken in Pāṭaliputra in Magadha, and refer to the larger group of dialects as Middle Indo-Aryan or the Prakrits. Norman suggests that it is likely that the Buddha spoke in several dialects, including Old Māgadhī and Ardha-Māgadhī (the language of the Jain canon).[18] In short, there is no original language of Buddhism or the Buddha: the languages of the prose and verses recited by followers of the Buddha were dialects of Middle Indo-Aryan that have come to be known as Pāli.[19]

In the centuries following the height of the Mauryan empire in the third century B.C.E., Pāli was gradually standardized. Classical Sanskrit emerged as the language of rulers, religion, and literature. Pāṇini wrote a grammar of Sanskrit (c. 400 B.C.E.) which provided a standard for Classical Sanskrit, and the dialects of Middle Indo-Aryan were re-translated (or transposed, as Hinüber suggests) according to the grammatical rules of Sanskrit.[20] This standardization eliminated certain archaic features of the Middle Indo-

Aryan dialects and carried with it all of the potential for mistakes that such rescensions involve (scribal errors, an insufficient knowledge of Sanskrit, and so on).[21] By the time that the Theravāda canon was written down (in the first century B.C.E., according to Theravādan sources), this process of Sanskritization was well underway.[22] The re-translation in the texts that belonged to different schools of Buddhism was done with varying degrees of success, depending on how and the extent to which the texts were Sanskritized. The language of northern Indian Buddhist texts that were re-translated is called Buddhist Hybrid Sanskrit; comparing these texts with the Theravāda canon often produces useful insights into the spread of the Buddha's teachings and canonical material.[23] The Theravāda canon became linguistically fixed when it was written down, although there were further modifications in the later medieval period of Sinhalese history when Pāli grammarians introduced rules for proper grammatical forms. The Theravāda canon that we have today, Norman concludes, is actually a result of the Pāli that was in use during the twelfth century C.E.[24]

The Historical Development of the Theravāda Canon

The process by which the words of the Buddha became a canon begins with the question of when the Buddha passed into *parinibbāna* at the dissolution of his physical body in this world. There are two chronologies offered by scholars as possible answers: the 'long' and the 'short.'[25] The long chronology is based on the dates provided by the Sri Lankan chronicles of the *Mahāvaṃsa* and the *Dīpavaṃsa* (compiled between the fourth and sixth centuries C.E.), which relate that the Buddha entered into *parinibbāna* 218 years before the reign of Aśoka.[26] Calculations from this date lead to 544 (or 543) B.C.E. as the start of the Buddhist era – this date is traditionally accepted throughout South and Southeast Asia.[27] This date is known as the 'uncorrected long chronology.' In his 1837 publication of the *Mahāvaṃsa*, George Turnour arrived at a different date of 486 (or 477) B.C.E. He reached this conclusion in part by comparing names in the list of Indian rulers to Greek sources.[28] Turnour's 'corrected long chronology' is found in nearly all scholarly works on Indian history. Both variants of the long chronology are based on sources from Sri Lanka. On the other hand, the short chronology is based upon the written sources of the Tibetan and Chinese Buddhist traditions, which explain that the Buddha's *parinibbāna* was 100 years before Aśoka's rule. This produces a date of c. 350 B.C.E. for the Buddha's entry into *parinibbāna*. These two dates, 486 (or 477) B.C.E. and 350 B.C.E. provide us with a reasonably accurate span of time within which the Buddha passed into *parinibbāna*.

The Theravāda *Vinaya-piṭaka* provides a consistent narrative of the events that unfolded after the Buddha entered into *parinibbāna*, although the accounts of the first two councils vary in the details throughout the sources from different Buddhist textual traditions.[29] The narrative begins with Mahākassapa (Mahākāśyapa), who was a follower of the Buddha and an *arahat*. He was travelling to Kusinăra (Kuśinagara) with a group of five hundred monks; along the way, an Ājīvaka (ascetic) told him of the Buddha's entry into *parinibbāna*. In order to instill a sense of order among the Buddha's followers after the dissolution of the Buddha's physical body, Mahākassapa asked four hundred and ninety nine *arhats* to join him in reciting the *dhamma* and *vinaya* – Ānanda (the Buddha's cousin and devout attendant) is invited to join them even though he was not yet an *arahat*. The assembled followers agreed to settle at Rājagaha for the monsoon season for the recitation. On the morning of the council, Ānanda became an *arahat*, and thus the session began with five hundred *arahats*. Mahākassapa questioned two of these *arahats* about the content of what the Buddha had uttered throughout his lifetime, asking Upāli about the rules of discipline (*vinaya*) for *bhikkhus* and *bhikkhunīs* and asking Ānanda about the *dhamma*. The remaining monks repeated what Upāli and Ānanda said, and thus the corpus of the words of the Buddha came into existence. This act is traditionally accepted as the first recitation of the Buddhist canon; it is known as the council of Rājagaha that took place immediately after the Buddha entered *parinibbāna*.

The *Cullavagga* of the *Vinaya-piṭaka* describes the second council at Vesālī (Vaiśālī), one hundred years after the Buddha's *parinibbāna*. It was convened over disagreements about ten practices, particularly over the collection of money by *bhikkhus*. The Vajjiputtakas of Vesālī had set a bowl in the center of a table for the donations of gold and silver from *upāsakas* (lay Buddhists). The *arahat* Yasa (who was the sixth *bhikkhu* to join the Buddha) protested this act, convinced the *upāsakas* that this practice was wrong, and eventually the *saṅgha* met in Vesālī to resolve the matter. The council is called a *vinaya-sangīti* (council on the discipline) in the *Vinayapiṭaka*, but the Sinhalese chronicles of the *Mahāvaṃsa* and the *Dīpavaṃsa* (redacted by Sinhalese monastics) call it a *dhammasaṅgaha* (collection of the *dhamma*).[30] Buddhaghosa provides a fuller description, saying that seven hundred *tipiṭatakdharas* (supporters of the *tipiṭaka*) were chosen to rehearse the *dhamma* and the *vinaya* at Vesālī.[31]

The Sinhalese chronicles of the *Mahāvaṃsa* and *Dīpavaṃsa* describe the same events that occurred at the first two councils, provide a lineage of teachers, an account of the reign of King Aśoka, and go on to recount a third council where Moggaliputta led a gathering of one thousand *bhikkhus* after a schism in the order.[32] (Buddhaghosa's description is contained in his commentary to the *Vinaya-piṭaka*.)[33] The *Mahāvaṃsa* relates how Aśoka's son and daughter, Mahinda and Saṅgamittā, joined the monastic order and how they brought Buddhism and a branch of the Bodhi tree to Sri Lanka.[34] After the first two councils, the accounts from different Buddhist canons diverge. This marks the beginning of the sectarian period, which resulted in eighteen different schools of what is known as Hīnayāna Buddhism (a somewhat derogative name that means 'the lesser way' in contrast to Mahāyāna or 'the greater way'). Canons from some of these eighteen schools, which includes the Theravāda school, have survived, and it is possible to compare different versions of the same canonical passages.[35] Dating the sectarian period is difficult, since it depends upon a reliable date for the Buddha's *parinibbāna* and requires evidence outside the different canons to confirm the events that they describe.

The *Mahāvaṃsa* and Buddhaghosa both explain that the canon which was present in Sri Lanka in the fifth century was compiled at the first council and recited again at the second and third councils. The *Dīpavaṃsa* gives an account of how the canon was set in writing during the reign of Vaṭṭagāminī (29–17 B.C.E.) at a monastic center named Alu-vihāra.[36] The language of the Theravāda canon shows features of a Western dialect of Middle Indo-Aryan that was probably spoken in eastern India during the first century B.C.E.[37] Buddhaghosa was a commentator who arrived in Sri Lanka early in the fifth century C.E., during the reign of King Mahānāma (r. 412–434 C.E.).[38] Buddhaghosa came to Sri Lanka to learn the Sinhalese commentarial tradition and to undertake the translation of the body of Sinhalese commentaries into Pāli so that others who did not know Sinhalese could read them. These Sinhalese commentaries are known as the *Sīhalaṭṭhakathā*, and we know of their existence through references in commentarial literature.[39] Buddhaghosa's commentaries on the Theravāda canon provide a date for the period in which the canon existed in a form similar to that which we have today, if not the point when the canon was substantially closed. That date is the early fifth century, the period in which Buddhaghosa wrote and translated his commentaries: between 412 and 434 C.E.

There is evidence outside the texts which supports indirectly the narrative of the Theravādan sources. As discussed earlier, Norman points out that the language of the Theravāda canon was preserved orally in north India in the third century B.C.E., perhaps in Magadha near the border with Kaliṅga.[40] Rupert M. L. Gethin suggests that additional evidence may be found to strengthen the accounts of the Sinhalese chronicles regarding the transmission of the canon to Sri Lanka in Aśoka's thirteenth rock edict. That inscription states that Aśoka's 'conquest by *dhamma*' reached as far as Taṃbapaṃni (Sri Lanka).[41] Gethin concludes that the *Vinaya-piṭaka* and the *Nikāya*s of the *Sutta-piṭaka* probably existed, in a form similar to what is recognized today as canonical, at the time of Aśoka, who began his rule c. 265 B.C.E.[42]

Inscriptional evidence indicates that there were reciters (*bhāṇaka*s) of various portions of material that we identify as canonical by the first century B.C.E. This material was first transmitted orally, memorized by groups of reciters who were responsible for different sections of what was later redacted into the closed Theravāda canon.[43] Inscriptions at the

Buddhist archaeological sites of Bhārhut, Sāñcī, and Kārli show that there were those known as 'reciters' (*bhāṇaka*) or 'ones who know the *Sūtras*' (*sutaṃtika*) early in the first century B.C.E. Newer terms, such as *peṭakin* (one who knows a *piṭaka*), that refer to *trepiṭaka* monks or *trepiṭakā* nuns began to appear alongside the older terms in the first century C.E. at Bhārhut, Sārnāth, Śravātī, and Mathurā.[44] The term *majhimabaṇaka* (reciter of the *majjhima*) has been found in a Brahmi inscription in Sri Lanka that may date to the second century B.C.E.[45]

A description of the Theravāda *bhāṇaka* tradition comes from Buddhaghosa, who stated that at the first council the *Vinaya* was given to Upāli and his students, and that the *Dīgha-*, *Majjhima-*, *Saṃyutta-*, and *Aṅguttara-nikāyas* were delegated to Ānanda, Sāriputta, Mahākassapa, Anuruddha, and their respective students.[46] There are references to the *bhāṇakas* of the first four *nikāyas*, the two *vibhaṅgas*, the *Jātakas*, and the *Dhammapada*.[47] There is only one reference to reciters of the *Khuddaka-nikāya*, found in the post-canonical *Milindapañha* (Questions of King Milinda).[48] The names of those who recited and transmitted *piṭakas* of what became the canon that appeared in the early inscriptions also appear in the commentaries. Those who had charge of the *Sutta-piṭaka* were known as *suttantikā* or *dhammadharā*; those responsible for the *Vinaya-piṭaka* were called *vinayadharā*; and, those who knew the *Abhidhamma-piṭaka* were called *Abhidhammikā*.[49] Those entrusted with the transmission of the commentaries were identified as *aṭṭhakathikā*; there were also reciters who knew all three baskets (*tipiṭakā*) and the four *nikāyas* (*catunikāyikā*).[50] These *bhāṇakas* had their own definitions of which books were canonical and had their own versions about the history of the early *saṅgha*.[51] The appearance of these terms both in the earlier inscriptions and in commentarial literature may indicate that these terms provide an accurate description of how the canonical material was transmitted orally.

Now, in contrast with this evidence from the Sinhalese chronicles, commentaries, Buddhist Sanskrit sources, and inscriptions, Gregory Schopen argues that the chronology that places the writing of the Theravāda canon in the first century B.C.E. is unconfirmed.[52] He points out that even though such terms as *bhāṇaka* appear in early inscriptions, we have no idea what they were reciting. Schopen and others have cited the observation of Professor G. P. Malalasekera, a faculty member of University College in Colombo, who pointed out in 1928 that it is difficult to know precisely *what* was written down at Alu-vihāra in the first century B.C.E.[53] Schopen insists correctly that we have no confirmed way of knowing the textual tradition because we have no direct evidence for what the canon contained before the late fourth century when we have a Chinese translation of two parts of the *Sutta-piṭaka* that can be dated reliably: '[I]t is, in fact, probably not until we arrive at the translations of the *Madhyāgama* and the *Ekottarāgama* by Dharmanandin in the last quarter of the fourth century that we have the first datable sources which allow us to know – however imperfectly – the actual doctrinal content of at least some of the major divisions of the *nikāya/āgama* literature.'[54]

As a point of interest, the earliest Pāli text has been dated recently to the middle or the end of the fifth century C.E. by Janice Stargardt and others. The text is called the Khin Ba Mound Golden Pāli Text, after the mound in which it was found at Śrī Kṣetra in Myanmar (Burma). Śrī Kṣetra was the last capital of the Pyu dynasty. The Golden Pāli Text consists of twenty gold leaves inscribed with canonical Pāli, and it includes eight excerpts from the Theravāda canon.[55] Several additional objects were also found inscribed with Pāli at Śrī Kṣetra, but the Golden Pāli Text is the longest text by far.

The span of time in which the Theravāda canon emerged is bracketed by two dates. The first is the end of the Buddha's life. According to Theravāda sources, the Buddha entered *parinibbāna* in 486/477 B.C.E., and the first council at Rājagaha when the *dhamma* and the *vinaya* were first recited was held immediately after his death. Sources from China and Tibet indicate that the Buddha passed away c. 350 B.C.E. The evidence for the Buddha's *parinibbāna* is inconclusive; it may have been any time between 486 (or 477) B.C.E. and 350 B.C.E. Aśoka's rock edicts provide a stable point of reference in the third century B.C.E., and I believe that Norman may be correct in his conclusion that the Theravāda canon circulated orally in northern India during the third century B.C.E. However, the evidence is at best suggestive, not conclusive. There is no obvious reason to reject the accounts of the Sinhalese chronicles that explain that the Theravāda canon was first written down in the first century B.C.E. (other than the need for verification from sources outside the chronicles). The inscriptions that refer to *bhāṇaka*s and *sutaṃtika*s provide indirect support for the first century B.C.E. as the time at which the canon was first recorded. However, the other end of the range of possible dates is the late fourth century C.E.: this is the only confirmed date for the existence of the Theravāda canon in a form that was similar to what is available today. The existence of the canon in the third century B.C.E. is a possibility that requires further verification.

The Four Noble Truths in Buddhist Canons

The four noble truths are found throughout the Theravāda canon and in the literature of other Buddhist schools. The teaching is found traditionally at two sequences in biographies of the Buddha: first, it is found in stories of the Buddha's enlightenment and as the substance of his first *dhamma* talk, in the *Dhammacakkappavattāna-sutta*; second, it is mentioned in some accounts of the Buddha's entry into *parinibbāna*, in the *Mahāparinibbāna-sutta*.[56] The four noble truths that appear in the sequence of the Buddha's enlightenment and the Buddha's first *dhamma* talk are present in the Buddhist Sanskrit rescensions of the *vinaya* in the following Hīnayāna schools: the *Mahāvastu* of the Mahāsaṅghika-Lokottaravāda,[57] the *Saṅghabhedavastu* of the Mūlasarvāstivāda, the *Catuṣpariṣasūtra* of the Sarvāstivāda, and the *vinaya*s of the Mahīśāsaka and the Dharmaguptaka schools found in the Chinese *Tipiṭaka*.[58] At least one point in the Chinese translation of the *Mūlasarvāstivada-vinaya* notes that the Buddha is known for his teaching of the four noble truths.[59] The four noble truths are part of the biography of the Buddha recorded in the *Lalitāvistara*, a text that belongs to the Sarvāstivāda that was probably composed in the second century C.E.[60] André Bareau identified the four noble truths in the *Sūtra-piṭaka* of the Chinese *Tripiṭaka*: at three points in the *Saṃyuktāgama*, and once in the *Ekottarāgama*.[61] In each of these cases, the four noble truths are found in the account of the Buddha's enlightenment.

The four noble truths also appear in Buddhist Sanskrit *Avadāna* literature (in the *Dīvyavadāna*, the *Sumāgadhāvadāna*, and the *Avadāna-śataka*) and in the *Apadāna*s of the Theravāda *Khuddaka-nikāya*.[62] The four noble truths are neatly deconstructed by Nāgārjuna in his *Mūlamadhyamakakārikaḥ*, and they are said to be empty in the Heart Sūtra.[63] The teaching is not found commonly in the sources of Chinese and Japanese Buddhism, but there are references in Indian Buddhist texts that have been translated into Chinese and Japanese. One such example is in the *Śrimālādevi Sūtra*, in which Queen Śrimālā talks to the Buddha on the nature of the *tathāgatagarbha* and the impermanence of the four noble truths.[64] The four noble truths also appear in a Japanese Nō play of the late fourteenth and early fifteenth centuries, in which the Buddha is remembered in part for his teaching of the four noble truths in Deer Park.[65] This brief survey of where the four noble truths appear in Buddhist literature outside of the canonical sources indicates that the four noble truths were widely recognized as a central teaching of the Buddha by the middle of the first millennium throughout the world of Indian Buddhism, usually in their role as Gautama Buddha's first *dhamma* talk. The teaching continued to be identified as a central tenet of Indian Buddhism throughout Southeast and East Asia as the texts of Indian Buddhism were translated; the reference to the four noble truths in a Nō play in the middle of the second millennium is an indication of their sustained presence, however attenuated.

Because the *Dhammacakkappavattana-sutta* is firmly fixed in the *vinaya* texts of the Theravāda, Mahāsaṅghika-Lokottaravāda, Mūlasarvāstivāda, and Sarvāstivāda schools, scholars have concluded that the four noble truths represent a very early strand of the Buddha's teachings, if not the actual words of the Buddha. Gregory Schopen lays bare the assumption behind this conclusion:

> The cardinal tenet of this criticism states, in effect, if all known sectarian versions of a text or passage agree, that text or passage must be very old; that is, it must come from a presectarian stage of the tradition.[66]

Schopen rightly points out that this assumption does not recognize two fundamental points: first, that we do not know when the sectarian period began; and second, that all of the passages or texts to which this principle applies are relatively late. Taking these points into account, he offers a reformulation of the principle: 'If all known versions of a text or passage agree, that text or passage is probably late; that is, it probably represents the results of the conflation and gradual leveling and harmonization of earlier existing traditions.'[67] In accord with this insight and with evidence discussed below, it is more likely that the four truths are an addition to the biographies of the Buddha and to the *Dhammacakkappavattana-sutta*. These additions were probably made at some point after the earliest versions but early enough within the leveling period that Schopen describes to establish the forms in which the four truths appear.

In his preface to a collection of papers presented at the 7th World Sanskrit Conference in 1987, Schmithausen outlines three types of responses to the question of 'whether and to what extent [Buddhist] texts can be regarded as faithfully preserving the doctrine of the Buddha himself at least *in essence*, ad sensum and, in *some* cases – but which ones? – perhaps even verbatim.'[68] The first approach emphasizes the homogeneity and authenticity of a large body of material found in the *Nikāyas*. The second position offers a highly skeptical answer to the question of retrieving any substantial knowledge of the period of early Buddhism. The third approach taken by scholars applies the principles of textual and higher criticism to smaller bodies of Buddhist canonical materials in the hopes of discovering a 'relative sequence (or sequences) of textual layers and/or sequence (or sequences) of stages of doctrinal development' that cannot, without additional evidence, be assigned a clear date or authorship.[69] This third approach is most appropriate for a discussion of the historical development of the four noble truths.

Norman identifies five different sets in which the four noble truths appear throughout Buddhist canons.[70] The first three of these sets are found in the *Dhammacakkappavattana-sutta*. The first is the introduction set:

> *Idaṃ kho pana bhikkhave dukkham ariyasaccaṃ . . . idaṃ kho pana bhikkhave dukkhasamudayam ariyasaccaṃ . . . idaṃ kho pana bhikkhave dukkhanirodham ariyasaccaṃ. . . idaṃ kho pana bhikkhave dukkhanirodhagāminī paṭipadā ariyasaccaṃ.*[71]
>
> *Bhikkhus*, the noble truth that 'this is pain'; [and,] *bhikkhus*, the noble truth that 'this is the origin of pain'; [and,] *bhikkhus*, the noble truth that 'this is the ending of pain'; [and,] *bhikkhus*, the noble truth that 'this is the way leading to the ending of pain.

In each of the first three sets – the introduction, enlightenment, and the gerundival – the four noble truths are identified with the neuter pronoun *idaṃ*: the noble truth that 'this is pain' (*idaṃ dukkhaṃ ariyasaccaṃ*), and so on.[72] Each of the four items is also consistently called a 'noble truth,' a point to which I will return below. The enlightenment set is found in the *Dhammacakkappavattana-sutta*, when the Buddha first explains that he realized the four noble truths:

> *Idaṃ dukkham ariyasaccan ti me bhikkhave pubbe ananussutesu dhammesu cakkhum udapādi ñāṇam udapādi paññā vijjā udapādi āloko udapādi.*[73]
>
> Thinking, *bhikkhus*, 'the noble truth that "this is pain",' insight arose, knowledge arose, wisdom arose, higher knowledge arose, and light arose in me concerning proper things of which I had not heard before.

The gerundival set appears in combination with four different gerundives (future passive participles) that describe how the Buddha knew what he had to realize:

> *Taṃ kho panidaṃ dukkham ariyasaccam pariññeyyan ti me bhikkhave pubbe ananussutesu dhammesu cakkhum udapādi ñāṇam udapādi paññā vijjā udapādi āloko udapādi. Taṃ kho panidaṃ dukkham ariyasaccam pariññātan ti me bhikkhave pubbe ananussutesu dhammesu cakkhum udapādi ñāṇam udapādi paññā vijjā udapādi āloko udapādi.*[74]
>
> Then again thinking 'the noble truth that "this is pain",' should be known completely, insight arose, knowledge arose, wisdom arose, higher knowledge arose, and light arose in me concerning proper things of which I had not heard before. Again thinking 'the noble truth that "this is pain",' has been known completely, insight arose, knowledge arose, wisdom arose, higher knowledge arose. and light arose in me concerning proper things of which I had not heard before.

This passage is the model for each of the four truths. There are four verbs, one for each truth, that the Buddha uses to describe how he knew what he had to do and to acknowledge the fact that he had done it, and each verb is followed by the formulaic statement that describes what arose from his new-found knowledge (insight arose, and so on): (1) the noble truth 'this is pain' should be known completely/has been known completely (*pariññeyyaṃ/pariññātaṃ*), (2) the noble truth 'this is the arising of pain' should be given up/has been given up (*pahātabbaṃ/pahīnaṃ*), (3) the noble truth 'this is the ending of pain' should be realized for oneself/has been realized for oneself (*sacchikātabbaṃ/sacchikātaṃ*), and (4) the noble truth 'this is the way leading to the ending of pain' should be developed/has been developed (*bhāvitabbaṃ/bhāvataṃ*).[75]

In each of these three sets there is an inconsistency in grammar. The first truth, *dukkhaṃ* (pain), is neuter in gender and is in the nominative singular case. The second and third truths, *samudayo* (arising) and *nirodho* (ending) are masculine nouns and are declined in the accusative singular case. The fourth truth, *paṭipadā* (way or practice), is feminine and is in the nominative singular case. The same neuter singular nominative (or accusative) pronoun (*idaṃ*) is used in relation for each of these terms. Norman asks a logical question: how can a neuter pronoun (*idaṃ*) properly refer to a feminine noun (*paṭipadā*)?[76] His answer is based, in part, on two other formulaic passages that provide the items of the four noble truths with pronouns that are correctly gendered.

The 'basic' set is Norman's fourth set, which differs from the pattern of the first three insofar as it omits the word *ariyasaccaṃ* (noble truth) and each item has the correctly gendered pronoun:

> *idaṃ dukkhan ti yathabhūtaṃ abbhaññāsim,*
> *ayaṃ dukkhasamudayo ti yathābhūtaṃ abbhaññāsiṃ,*
> *ayaṃ dukkhanirodho ti yathābhūtaṃ abbhaññāsiṃ,*
> *ayaṃ dukkhanirodhagāminī paṭipadā ti yathābhūtaṃ abbhaññāsiṃ.*[77]
>
> I understood as it really is: this is pain, this is the origin of pain, this is the ending of pain, this is the path leading to the ending of pain.

The fifth and final set is actually a series of condensed forms of the four noble truths. Norman calls these 'mnemonic sets' because they are abbreviated versions that may hvae served as reminders of the fuller formulations of the four noble truths.[78] He offers three variations of the mnemonic sets: (a) 'the four noble truths: pain, (its) origin, (its) ending, the path'; (b) 'the four noble truths: the truth of pain, the truth of origin, the truth of ending, the truth of the path'; and (c) 'the four noble truths: the noble truth of pain, the noble truth of origin, the noble truth of ending, the noble truth of the path.'[79] There is an additional variation on these sets, not discussed by Norman, in which the four noble truths are simply listed as pain, arising, ending, and the path – without the modifiers of truth (*sacca*) or noble (*ariya*) and endings which are not correctly gendered.[80] The endings of this set agree with the pronoun *idaṃ*, but the pronoun itself has been omitted; the endings of these items do not have the correct gender, and so it is likely that they represent abbreviations of the introduction, enlightenment, and/or gerundival sets – but not the basic set.

Norman concludes that the original form of the enlightenment set was the basic set: *idaṃ dukkhaṃ, ayaṃ dukkhasamudayo, ayaṃ dukkhanirodho, ayaṃ dukkhanirodho-gāminīpaṭipadā.*[81] Each item has the properly gendered pronoun, and each has the approriately gendered ending. He shows that the earliest form of the mnemonic set was *dukkhaṃ samudayo nirodho maggo*, without the addition of *ariya* (noble) or *sacca* (truth). *Ariya* and *sacca* were added gradually to the four items and thus they became identified as 'truths' and as 'noble.' The addition of *ariyasacca*, he suggests, led to an erroneous division in the words that contributed to the use of incorrectly gendered pronouns for *samudayo* (arising) and *nirodho* (ending). Norman identifies *ariyasacca* as a syntactical compound, a type of compound that appeared later in the development of the canon during the process of re-translating the texts according to the rules of Sanskrit.[82] The form of this syntactical compound was misunderstood by the redactors of the Theravāda canon and thus led to the grammatical puzzle that Norman has solved.

These different sets of the four truths indicate that there was not a single fixed grammatical form for the four noble truths; instead, there were first four items that later became identified as 'noble' and as 'truths.' The appearance of the four noble truths in the introduction, enlightenment, and gerundival sets in the *Dhammacakkappavattana-sutta* provide evidence for Norman's correct conclusion that the teaching was probably not part of the earliest version of the *Sutta*. However, the consistency of the three sets indicates that the doctrine was inserted into the *Sutta* early enough in its history to fix the three grammatical forms of the four noble truths without further variation.

Where the four noble truths appear in stories about the Buddha's enlightenment, they fall into a category that Étienne Lamotte has called the 'biographical fragments incorporated in the *Sūtra*s.' Lamotte identifies these fragments as the first of five layers in the development of Śākaymuni's biography: (1) biographical fragments incorporated into the *sutta*s and *sūtra*s, (2) biographies, whole or partial, in the *Vinaya*s, (3) 'Lives' of the Buddha elaborated by various Buddhist schools at the beginning of the Christian era, (4) the complete biography of the *Mūlasārvāstivāda-vinaya*, and (5) the *Nidānakathā* and an outline of annals compiled in the fifth century by Sinhalese commentators.[83] Norman's evidence, however, demonstrates that the four noble truths were not part of the earliest form of the *Dhammacakkappavattana-sutta*. Bareau has also concluded that the four noble truths were not among the earliest components of the Buddha's biography. Bareau notes that the *Dhammacakkappavattana-sutta* within the Pāli *Vinaya-piṭaka* and *Sutta-piṭaka* are nearly identical, particularly when compared to other versions of the *Dhammacakkappavattana* found in Chinese translations.[84] Even though Bareau's extensive study of the biographies of the Buddha is rooted in the tenet critiqued by Schopen – that different versions which agree with each other must be early – his conclusion that the *Dhammacakkappavattana-sutta* is a later addition to the biographies of the Buddha seems correct.

Peter Skilling offers confirmation of Bareau's argument. In the course of his study of Tibetan translations of thirteen Theravādin texts, Skilling traces several different versions of the *Dhammacakkappavattana-sutta*. Skilling compares the Tibetan and Theravādin versions with the *Dharmacakrapravartana-sūtra* of the Mūlasarvāstivāda (in the *Saṅghabhedavastu*) and the Mahāsaṅghika-Lokottaravāda (in the *Mahāvastu*). The terms in the Theravādin versions that the Buddha uses to describe his insight ('insight arose, knowledge arose, wisdom arose, higher knowledge arose, and light arose') differ both in number and in the specific words of the Mūlasarvāstivāda and Mahāsaṅghika-Lokottaravāda versions.[85] The version of the *Sutta* found in the Theravāda *Mahāvagga* in the *Vinaya-piṭaka* is nearly identical to the *Dhammacakkappavattana-sutta* in the *Saṃyutta-nikāya*, particularly in contrast to the variations found in the other versions. Skilling's comparison supports Bareau's conclusion: the *Dhammacakkappavattana-sutta* and the *Mahāvagga* versions in the Theravāda canon were probably redacted at a later date so that they agreed with each other.

Schmithausen draws attention to evidence throughout the body of Buddhist literature that indicates that the four noble truths are sometimes used as the definition for liberating insight, and are replaced by other teachings elsewhere in the literature.[86] Both Schmithausen and Bronkhorst conclude that because the four noble truths do not appear have been part of the earliest strata of the *Dhammacakkappavattana-sutta*, it is likely that the four noble truths were not as central in the earlier periods of Buddhism's history as they were in later periods.[87] Norman's analysis of the grammatical forms of the four noble truths indicate that the teaching was not among the earliest components of the *Dhammacakkappavattana-sutta*, and the parallels between the two versions of the *Sutta* in the Theravāda canon suggests a later redaction designed to bring the two versions into agreement. This evidence demonstrates that the four noble truths were probably not part of the earliest strata of what came to be recognized as Buddhism, but that they emerged as a central teaching in a slightly later period that still preceded the final redactions of the various Buddhist canons.

Conclusion

The following chapters seek to establish the thesis that the four noble truths are significant for more reasons than their appearance in the '*Sutta* on the Turning of the *Dhamma*-wheel.' As the teaching that Koṇḍañña understood when the Buddha uttered his first *dhamma* talk, the four noble truths are a vehicle for the establishment of the Buddha's teachings (*sāsana*) in the cosmos – and they come to symbolize the moment of enlightenment that is possible for anyone who follows the Buddha's teachings. In this capacity, the teaching is an account of how the Theravāda canon remembered the Buddha – and all Buddhas – as actors within the cosmos. As an account of what the Buddha experienced as he attained enlightenment and as the subject of what he taught, the four truths are a doctrine. And, in this context, the four noble truths are recorded in the Theravāda canon as a teaching that must be learned the hard way by humans: as propositions. In both capacities the Theravāda canon claims that four noble truths lead to enlightenment, but the paths are rather different.

Notes

1 C. A. F. Rhys Davids, 'Curious Omissions in the Pāli Canonical Lists,' *Journal of the Royal Asiatic Society of Great Britain and Ireland* (1935): 723—724.
2 S V 420 and also Vin I 10. All citations are in Pāli with the exception of some titles of Buddhist Sanskrit *sūtras*. I have occasionally provided Sanskrit names in parentheses. Sanskrit terms that are widely used in English and proper names in either Sanskrit or Pāli have not been italicized. All translations from the Pāli are my own.
3 e.g. D II 81, 84, 91. There is also a set of three corruptions which eliminates *diṭṭhāsavā*.
4 The three refuges are the Buddha, *dhamma*, and the *saṅgha* (order); the three 'marks' are the three characteristics of *saṃsāra/sankhāra* (the realm of rebirth): *anicca* (impermanence), *dukkha* (pain) and *anattā* (no-self).
5 C. A. F. Rhys Davids, 'Curious Omissions,' 723.
6 C. A. F. Rhys Davids, 'Curious Omissions,' 723–724.
7 See K. R. Norman, 'Pāli Language and Scriptures,' in *Collected Papers*, 6 vols. (Oxford: Pāli Text Society, 1990–1996), 4:103 and K. R. Norman, *Pāli Literature, including the Canonical Literature in Prakrit and Sanskrit of all of the Hīnayāna Schools of Buddhism* (Wiesbaden: Otto Harrowitz, 1983), 1; for the terms *piṭaka* and *pāli* as terms that came to be interpreted as 'canon,' see Steven Collins, 'On the Very Idea of the Pāli Canon,' *Journal of the Pāli Text Society* 15 (1990): 90–95.
8 Collins, 'Pāli Canon,' 95–101.
9 Collins, 'Pāli Canon,' 96.
10 Collins, 'Pali Canon,' 89.
11 Collins, 'Pāli Canon,' 104.
12 How the Theravāda canon has been classified is a complex topic. Norman provides a thorough summary of the various portions of the Theravāda canon and includes a comparison with other canonical writings in Buddhist Hybrid Sanskrit and, at some points, the Chinese Buddhist canon. See Norman, *Pāli Literature*.
13 Collins, 'Pāli Canon,' 92–93. Collins comments that there is no need to look for an underlying metaphor in the translation of 'basket,' such as a container to hold texts (because it makes no sense if the texts were transmitted orally). He suggests instead that *piṭakaṃ* be interpreted as 'collection' and understood as the means by which the Buddhist tradition was transmitted from teacher to student.
14 K. R. Norman, 'The Origin of Pāli and its Position among the Indo-European Languages,' in *Collected Papers*, 3:225.
15 Norman, *Pāli Literature*, 1 and K. R. Norman, 'The Pāli Language and Scriptures,' in *Collected Papers*, 1993), 4:103–104.
16 K. R. Norman, 'The Dialects in which the Buddha Preached,' *Collected Papers*, 1991), 2:145. See other articles by Norman on this topic: on Pāli and other dialects in the Pāli textual tradition, see K. R. Norman, 'Pāli and the language of

heretics,' in *Collected Papers*, 1:238–245; 'The Role of Pāli in Early Sinhalese Buddhism,' in *Collected Papers*, 2:30–51; and 'The language in which the Buddha Taught,' in *Collected Papers*, 2:84–93.

17 Sp 1214

18 The variations are of three kinds: the Māgadhī dialect used the ending -e for the nominative singular, -l- for all -l- and -r- sounds, and recorded all sibilants as ś. In comparison, Pāli rarely uses -e in the nominative singular (-o is the accepted form), rarely substitutes -l- for -r- sounds, and never uses ś for s. Norman concludes that Pāli was at the borders of the area in which Māgadhī was spoken. Norman, 'The Dialects,' in *Collected Papers* 2:136–137 and Norman, 'The Origin of Pāli,' in *Collected Papers* 3:233–234.

19 Norman, 'The Dialects,' in *Collected Papers* 2:144.

20 See O. von Hinüber, 'Pāli as an Artificial Language,' *Indologica Taurinensia* 10 (1982): 133–140. For a response to this argument see Norman, 'The Pāli Language,' in *Collected Papers* 4:106.

21 Norman, 'The Origin of Pāli,' in *Collected Papers* 3:238–240 and Norman, 'The Pāli Language,' in *Collected Papers* 4:102–104.

22 Norman, 'The Origin of Pāli,' in *Collected Papers* 3:235–236.

23 Norman, 'The Origin of Pāli,' in *Collected Papers* 3:238–239.

24 At several places in his collected papers, Norman credits Helmer Smith for this observation that the Pāli used in the canon is the result of twelfth century redaction. See Helmer Smith, ed. *Saddanīti: La grammaire palie d'Aggavamsa* (Lund: C. W. K. Gleerup, 1928), vi. For his references, see Norman, 'The Influence of the Pāli Commentators and Grammarians on the Pāli Tradition,' in *Collected Papers*, 3:107; Norman, 'The Origin of Pāli,' in *Collected Papers* 3:243; and Norman, 'The Pāli Language,' in *Collected Papers*, 4:112.

25 For a comprehensive treatment of the issue, see Heinz Bechert, ed. *The Dating of the Historical Buddha*, 2 vols., Abhandlungen der Akademie der Wissenschaften in Göttingen Philologische-Historische Klasse Dritte Folge, Nrs. 189 and 194 (Göttingen: Vandenhoeck & Ruprecht, 1991); Heinz Bechert, 'The Date of the Buddha Reconsidered,' *Indologica Taurinensia* 10 (1982): 29–36; Heinz Bechert, 'A Remark on the Problem of the Date of Mahāvīra,' *Indologica Taurinensia* 11 (1983): 287–290; and Heinz Bechert, 'Remarks on the Date of the Historical Buddha,' *Buddhist Studies (Bukkyō Kenkyū)* 17 (1988): 97–117.

26 Mhv III 21

27 For a fascinating discussion of the activities surrounding the *Buddhajayanti* (the 2,500-year anniversary of the Buddha) in Sri Lanka during the 1950s, see George D. Bond, *The Buddhist Revival in Sri Lanka: Religious Tradition, Reinterpretation and Response*, Studies in Comparative Religion Series (Columbia: University of South Carolina Press, 1988).

28 Bechert, *The Dating of the Historical Buddha*, 1:2–3 and George Turnour, 'An examination of the Páli Buddhistical Annals, No. 2,' *Journal of the Asiatic Society* 6, part 2, no. 69 (September 1837): 713–717.

29 Vin II 284–308; see Buddhaghosa's version of the same event at Sp 14–15. For a discussion of the different accounts of the councils, see Lamotte, *HIB*, 124–140 and André Bareau, *Les premiers conciles bouddhiques* (Paris: École française, d'Extrême-Orient, 1955). See also Norman, *Pāli Literature*, 7–14 for his overview of the Pāli sources on the development of the Pāli canon.

30 Mhv IV 63; Dīp V 28

31 Sp 16–22, 34

32 Mhv III, IV, V 244–282; cf. Dīp IV 1–26, 47–53; V 1–54; VII 39–40, 57–59

33 Sp 18–19, 34, 61

34 Mhv III 194–211; XV–XIX

35 On the councils and the Hīnayāna schools, see: Janice J. Nattier and Charles S. Prebish, 'Mahāsāṃghika Origins: The Beginnings of Buddhist Sectarianism,' *History of Religions* 16 (1977): 237–272; Charles S. Prebish, 'A Review of Scholarship on the Buddhist Councils,' *Journal of Asian Studies* 33 (1974): 239–254; Charles S. Prebish, *A Survey of Vinaya Literature* (London: Curzon Press, 1994); André Bareau, *Les sectes bouddhiques du petit véhicule* (Paris: École française d'Extrême Oriente, 1955); E. Frauwallner, *The Earliest Vinaya and the Beginnings of Buddhist Literature*, Serie orientale Roma no. 8 (Rome: Instituto Italiano per il Medio ed Estremo Oriente, 1956); Heinz Bechert, 'The Importance of Aśoka's So-called Schism Edict,' in *Indological and Buddhist Studies: Volume in Honor of Professor J. W. de Jong on his Sixtieth Birthday* (Canberra: Faculty of Asian Studies, 1982), 61–68; and K. R. Norman, 'Aśoka's 'Schism' Edict,' in *Collected Papers*, 3:191–224.

36 Dīp XX 21–21; Mhv XXXIII 100–101. For a discussion of how the development of writing influenced the Theravāda canon, see K. R. Norman, 'The Development of Writing in India and its Effect upon the Pāli Canon,' in *Collected Papers*, 5:247–261.

37 Norman, 'The Pāli Language,' in *Collected Papers*, 4:100.

38 For a comprehensive account of the sources and information on the person of Buddhaghosa, the *Visuddhimagga*, and his commentaries, see Bhadantācariya Buddhaghosa, *The Path of Purification (Visuddhimagga)*, trans. Bhikkhu Ñāṇamoli (Colombo: R. Semage, 1956), x–xxvii.

39 See E. W. Adikaram, *Early History of Buddhism in Ceylon or State of Buddhism in Ceylon as Revealed by the Pāli Commentaries of the Fifth Century* (Colombo: M. D. Gunasena, 1946) and Sodō Mori, 'Chronology of the 'Sīhala Sources' for the Pāli Commentaries,' *Buddhist Studies (Bukkyō Kenykū)* 17 (1988): 119–167.

40 Norman, 'The Pāli Language,' in *Collected Papers*, 4:100 and Norman, 'The Dialects,' in *Collected Papers* 2:136–137.

41 R. M. L. Gethin, *The Buddhist Path to Awakening: A Study of the Bodhi-Pakkhiyā-Dhammā* (Leiden: E. J. Brill, 1992), 8. For the inscriptions, see Jules Bloch, *Les Inscriptions d'Asoka* (Paris: Société d'Édition 'Les belles lettres,' 1950), 129–130; see also Romila Thapar, *Aśoka and the Decline of the Mauryas* (Oxford: Oxford University Press, 1961), 48–49. She states that there is no 'necessary connection between the Buddhist missions and the embassies of Aśoka. The 13th Rock Edict was issued in 256–255 B.C. and the embassies must have been sent before this date' (49). We know of the Buddhist missions from the *Mahāvaṃsa* (XII 108), which says that monks of good repute were sent out to other regions at the end of the Third Council. See also Jonathan S. Walters, *Rethinking Buddhist Missions* (Ph. D. diss., University of Chicago, 1992).

42 Gethin, *Buddhist Path*, 15.

43 See L. S. Cousins, 'Pāli Oral Literature,' in *Buddhist Studies: Ancient and Modern*, Collected Papers on South Asia no. 4 (London: Curzon Press, 1983), 1–11.

44 For an overview of the inscriptional evidence, see Lamotte, HIB, 149–150; where Lamotte's chronology is unclear, see Gregory Schopen, 'Two Problems in the History of Indian Buddhism: The Layman/Monk Distinction and the Doctrines of the Transference of Merit,' *Studien zur Indologie und Iranistik* 10 (1985): 9–14; reprinted in Schopen, *Bones, Stones and Buddhist Monks: Collected Papers on the Archaeology, Epigraphy, and Texts of Monastic*

Buddhism in India (Honolulu: University of Hawaii, 1997), 23–25; see also O. von Hinüber, 'On the Tradition of Pāli Texts in India, Ceylon and Burma,' *Buddhism in Ceylon and Studies in Religious Syncretism in Buddhist Countries*, ed. H. Bechert, Abhandlungen der Akademie der Wissenschaften in Göttingen Philologische-Historische Klasse, Dritte Folge, no. 108 (Göttingen: Vandenhoeck and Ruprecht, 1978), 48–49.

45 W. S. Karunaratne, 'Unpublished Brāhmī Inscriptions of Ceylon,' *Epigraphia Zeylanica* 7 (1984); Norman cites Karunaratne, and for Norman's discussion of this inscription, see Norman, 'On the Role of Pāli in early Sinhalese Buddhism,' in *Buddhism in Ceylon and Studies in Religious Syncretism*, ed. H. Bechert, Abhandlungen der Akademie der Wissenschaften in Göttingen Philologische-Historische Klasse, Dritte Folge, no. 108 (Göttingen: Vandenhoeck and Ruprecht, 1978), 34, n. 4. See also S. Paranavitana, *Inscriptions of Ceylon* (Ceylon, 1970), 1:civ, cvi, cited by Norman, 'The Languages of Early Buddhism,' in *Collected Papers*, 5:149, n. 5.

46 Sv 2–13, 15, 23–24

47 Adikaram, *Early History*, 24.

48 Mil 342

49 Adikaram, *Early History*, 25.

50 Pj 1 151 and Adikaram, *Early History*, 25.

51 Norman, *Pāli Literature*, 9 and 31; Adikaram, *Early History*, 25–32.

52 Schopen, 'Two Problems in the History,' 9–10.

53 G. P. Malalasekera, *The Pāli Literature of Ceylon* (London: Royal Asiatic Society of Great Britain and Ireland, 1928), 44. For Schopen's citation, see 'Two Problems,' 9; for Collins' citation, see 'Pāli Canon,' 96.

54 Schopen, 'Two Problems,' 14.

55 Janice Stargardt, 'The Oldest Known Pāli Texts, 5th–6th Century; Results of the Cambridge Symposium on the Pyu Golden Pāli Text from Śrī Kṣetra, 18–19 April 1995, ' *Journal of the Pāli Text Society* 21 (1995): 199–213.

56 The four noble truths in the *Mahāvastu* appear in the *Dharmacakrapravartana-sūtra*; the *Mahāvastu* is part of the *vinaya* of the *Mahāsaṅghika-Lokottaravādin* school. See Emile Sénart, ed., *Mahāvastu* (Paris: Imprimerie Nationale, 1897), 3:330–334. See Winternitz, *Indian Literature*, 2:240 for a discussion of the Mahāsaṅghika Lokuttaravādin school and the *Mahāvastu*; for a critical study of the work, see Bhikkhu Telwatte Rahula, *A Critical Study of the Mahāvastu* (Delhi: Motilal Banarsidass, 1978).

57 Raniero Gnoli, ed. *The Gilgit Manuscript of the Saṃghabhedavastu Being the 17th and Last Section of the Vinaya of the Mūlasarvāstivādins*, 3 vols. (Rome: Instituto Italiano per il Medio ed Estremo Oriente, 1977), 1:137–139. The *Saṅghabhedavastu* is in the *vinaya* of the now-extinct Mūlasarvāstivāda branch of Hīnayāna, and the text is is the same as the *Catuṣpariṣa-sūtra* of the Sarvāstivāda school.

58 André Bareau, *Recherches sur la biographie du Buddha dans des Sūtrapiṭaka et les Vinayapiṭaka anciens*, 2 vols. (Paris: Ecole française d'Extrême-Orient, 1963 and 1970), 2:173f. For a discussion of Bareau's claims for the four noble truths, see Johannes Bronkhorst, *Two Traditions of Meditation in Ancient India*, 2nd. ed. (Delhi: Motilal Banarsidass, 1993), 107. For a much earlier discussion of these versions of the four noble truths in Sanskrit, Tibetan, and Pāli, see Léon Feer, 'Études bouddhiques: Les quatre vérité et la prediction de Bénarèes (Dharma-cakra-pravartanaṃ),' *Journal asiatique*, 6ᵉ série, 15 (Mai-Juin 1870): 346, 350–351. Feer discussed the relationship between the eighteen schools of Hīnayana Buddhism and the teaching of the four noble truths.

59 J. Takakusu and K. Watanabe, ed., *Taishō shinshū daizōkyō* (Tokyo, 1924–29) no. 1448, 24:38c, cited and translated in John Strong, *The Experience of Buddhism: Sources and Interpretations* (Belmont, California: Wadsworth Press, 1995), 60; for a alternate translation, see Jean Przyluski, 'Le Nord-ouest de l'Inde dans le Vinaya des Mūla-Sarvāstivādins et les textes apparentés,' *Journal asiatique* 4 (1914): 500–502. Gnoli points out that the Chinese *Mūlasarvāstivāda-vinaya*, translated by I-ching between 700 and 712, is an aggregate work made up of sources from different periods and is not as complete as the Tibetan translation done between the end of the eighth century and the beginning of the ninth century. Gnoli, *Saṃghabhedavastu*, xx and xxiii.

60 The *Lalitavistara* was translated from Sanskrit into Tibetan in the ninth century. For a discussion of the dates that may be attributed to the work, see Winternitz, *Indian Literature*, 2:248, 254.

61 Bareau, *Recherches sur la biographie* 1:178f.

62 P. L. Vaidya, ed., The *Divyāvadana*, Buddhist Sanskrit Texts, no. 20 (Darbhanga: Mithila Institute, 1959), 248–52; see Eugène Burnouf, *Introduction à l'histoire du Buddhisme Indien*, 2nd ed. (Paris: Maisonneuve et Cie, 1876), 258 and 568 for his references to the *Sumāgadhāvadana* and *Avadānaśataka*; and Mary E. Lilley, ed. *The Apadāna of the Khuddakanikāya* (London: Pali Text Society, 1927), 2:529–543. For a fine analysis of the *Gotamī-apadāna*, see Jonathan S. Walters, 'A Voice from the Silence: The Buddha's Mother's Story,' *History of Religions* 33 (1994): 358–379.

63 On Nāgārjuna's treatment of the four noble truths, see J. W. de Jong, ed., *Mūlamadhyamakakārikaḥ* (Adyar: Adyar Library and Research Centre, 1977), 34–40; see also Roger Corless, 'The Chinese Life of Nāgārjuna,' in *Buddhism in Practice*, ed. Donald S. Lopez, Jr. (Princeton: University of Princeton Press, 1995), 525–531. Corless describes briefly a biography of Nāgārjuna that follows the traditional biographies of the Buddha. For the *Heart Sūtra*, see Edward Conze, ed., 'The Prajñāpāramitāhṛdaya-sūtra,' in *Thirty Years of Buddhist Studies* (London: Bruno Cassirer, 1967), 148–167.

64 J. Takakusu and K. Watanabe, eds., *Taishō shinshū daizōkyō* (Tokyo, 1924- 29), no. 353, 12:221c–222a, 221c and 222b, cited and translated in Strong, *Experience of Buddhism*, 186. For an alternate translation, see Alex Wayman and Hideko Wayman, *The Lion's Roar of Queen Śrimālā* (New York: University of Columbia Press, 1974), 98–106.

65 Robert Morrell, 'Passage to India Denied: Zeami's Kasuga Ryūjin,' *Monumenta Nipponica* 37 (1982): 194.

66 Schopen, *Bones, Stones, and Buddhist Monks*, 26.

67 Schopen, *Bones, Stones, and Buddhist Monks*, 27.

68 Lambert Schmithausen, 'Earliest Buddhism,' in *Earliest Buddhism and Madhyamaka*, ed. David Seyfort Ruegg and Lambert Schmidthausen (Leiden: E. J. Brill, 1990), 1.

69 Schmithausen, 'Earliest Buddhism,' 2.

70 The following section is a synopsis of the arguments that Norman presents in K. R. Norman, 'The Four Noble Truths,' in *Collected Papers*, 2:210–223.

71 Vin I 11f.; S V 421f.; K. R. Norman, 'The Four Noble Truths,' 212.

72 Vin I 10; S V 420; K. R. Norman, 'The Four Noble Truths,' 212.

73 S V 422

74 S V 422; Vin I 12

75 Peter Skilling has noted that the final insight of the four noble truths (that they have been mastered) is missing from a Tibetan version of the *Dhammacakkappavattana-sutta*; he concludes that it must be from 'a faulty manuscript or

translation: since the insights are an essential part of the sutta, their omission cannot be deliberate or redactional.' Peter Skilling, 'Theravadin Literature in Tibetan translation,' *Journal of the Pāli Text Society* 19 (1993): 104.

76 Norman notes that the Pāli tradition did not always render the pronoun for *paṭipadā* in the same way, which may indicate some degree of uncertainty about the grammatical inconsistency between genders of the neuter *idaṃ* and the feminine *paṭipadā*. Norman, 'The Four Noble Truths,' 213.

77 M I 23; Norman, 'The Four Noble Truths,' 213.

78 Norman, 'The Four Noble Truths,' 213.

79 (a) *cattāri ariya-saccāni . . . dukkhaṃ samudayo nirodho maggo*; (b) *cattāri saccāni: dukkhasaccaṃ samudayasaccaṃ nirodhasaccaṃ maggasaccaṃ*; and (c) *ariyasaccāni dukkhaṃ ariyasaccaṃ dukkhasamudayāriyasaccaṃ dukkhanirodhāriyasaccaṃ, dukkhanirodhagāminīpaṭipadā ariyasaccaṃ*. Examples of each are found at Th 492, Pp 2, and D III 277, respectively. Vism 494 has *-gāmini-* in the fourth truth, which Norman says 'probably represents the attempt to write the stem form of *gāminī* in a compound.' Norman, 'The Four Noble Tuths,' 213.

80 M I 379–380

81 Norman, 'The Four Noble Truths,' 214 and M I 23.

82 For his discussion of such compounds, see K. R. Norman, 'Syntactical Compounds in Middle-Indo-Aryan,' in *Collected Papers*, 4:218–225. Norman also examines the meaning of the compound *ariyasaccāni*. He concludes that 'those persons who first translated the compound *ariyasaccāni* into English could have translated 'the noble's truths', or 'the nobles' truths', or 'the truths for nobles', or 'the noblising truths', or 'the noble truths', but they could have only one of the translations. . . .' He finds the noble truths to be the least satisfactory of all these possible renditions. K. R. Norman, 'Why are the Four Truths called 'Noble'?' in *Collected Papers*, 4:171–175.

83 Lamotte, HIB, 648ff.

84 Bareau, *Recherches*, 1:173–180.

85 Skilling, 'Theravādin Literature,' 104–105 and 194.

86 Lambert Schmithausen, On Some Aspects of Descriptions of Theories of 'Liberating Insight' and 'Enlightenment' in Early Buddhism,' in *Studien zum Jainismus und Buddhismus* (Weisbaden: Franz Steiner, 1981), 211–219.

87 Bronkhorst, *Two Traditions*, 107 and Schmithausen, 'On Some Aspects,' 203.

CHAPTER ONE

Cultivating Religious Experiences: Doctrine and *Diṭṭhi*

The more intractable puzzles in comparative religion arise because human experience has thus been wrongly divided.[1]

Mary Douglas (1966)

Introduction

Since the European discovery of Buddhism toward the end of the eighteenth century, studies of Buddhism in Europe and in the United States have been conducted largely through the examination of Buddhist textual material. Collections of Buddhist sacred texts were brought back to Europe by diplomats, missionaries, and travellers in the first half of the last century; and, as chairs were established in European universities for the study of Sanskrit and other languages, a majority of scholarly attention was focused on the evidence located in these textual sources.[2] This attention was not restricted entirely to scholars. Missionaries such as Daniel J. Gogerly, who worked for the Wesleyan mission in Sri Lanka, published a number of articles on Buddhist rituals and beliefs between 1837 and 1876. Similarly, Bishop Paul Ambrose Bigandet published a study of Buddhism in 1858 that was based on texts that he had received in Burma; the book went through four editions by 1912.[3] In general, first-hand accounts of rituals observed in South and Southeast Asia did not inform the emerging corpus of scholarship on Buddhism: scholars in Europe and in the United States were engaged in untangling the wealth of information contained in the texts.

One of the legacies of this textual emphasis in the history of the study of Buddhism is the question of the relationship between the Buddhism that is contained in the texts and the Buddhism that people actually practice in South and Southeast Asia. Steven Collins and others have identified this problem as the 'Buddhism and Society' problem. In short, this question asks how the Buddhist canons, the Pāli *Tipiṭaka* in particular, is related to the actual behavior of Buddhists. The classic studies of Melford Spiro and Richard Gombrich on Burmese and Sinhalese Buddhism, respectively, explore the relationship that was presumed to exist between the teachings of the Buddha – his doctrines – and his followers. In *Buddhism and Society: A Great Tradition and Its Burmese Vicissitudes* (1970) and in *Precept and Practice: Traditional Buddhism in the Rural Highlands of Ceylon* (1971), Spiro and Gombrich examine the relationship between the Buddhist canon and the practices of Buddhists. Spiro explains that he wishes to pursue the 'interaction between the doctrines found in . . . texts and conceptions found in the heads of religious devotees. . . .'[4] He also states that his study focuses on the beliefs of Buddhists and the doctrines of Buddhist texts.

Both Spiro and Gombrich conclude that the relationship between practice and text is much more complex than a simple emulation of what was recorded in the texts. Spiro proposes 'three systems of Theravāda Buddhism': *nibbānic, kammatic*, and apotropaic. *Nibbānic* Buddhism refers to the ideal practices and doctrines that lead to escape from the cycle of rebirth as recorded in the Theravāda canon; *kammatic* Buddhism focuses upon a more favorable rebirth through the accumulation of merit and the principles of *kamma* and apotropaic Buddhism is concerned with protection from dangers such as illness, drought, and demons. Spiro recognizes that these systems are inextricably intertwined in living Buddhism and cannot be extracted into separate packages.[5] In a similar vein, Gombrich proposes two categories: cognitive religion and affective religion. These categories reflect the distinction 'between what people say they believe and say they do' and 'what people really believe and really do.'[6] What people really do, Gombrich says, is religious behavior, and 'it is the religion of the heart, not the head.'[7] Gombrich suggests that his two categories are representative of two syndromes that exist in Buddhism in Sri Lanka, one which denies the world and the other which affirms the world. The conclusions of both of these studies underscore two crucial points in the study of Buddhism: first, that the relationship between text and practice is multilayered, and, second, that 'Buddhism' cannot be defined solely in terms of the canonical and postcanonical writings.

Collins has taken answers to this question one step further. He shows that Buddhist doctrine itself takes social reality into account by incorporating imagery that reflects the lived social experiences of Buddhists. Collins explores images of house and home, vegetation, and streams or rivers, demonstrating how each of these images are used to elucidate certain Buddhist concepts. For example, the image of a seed and fruition is used to illustrate the notion of consciousness; the image of the house represents the body, which gives force to the image of homelessness. He demonstrates that the concepts of Buddhism are woven together with the perceptions of the social world and human behavior into a cultural whole of Theravāda Buddhism. 'Not only does the intellectual tradition take account of what it imagines to be the social and psychological reality of actual Buddhists,' he writes, 'but also it is precisely this dimension which gives us the key structures by which we will understand the Pāli canon account of personality and continuity as it was developed, given the initial postulate of the denial of self.'[8] It is in the intellectual tradition of the Theravāda canon, Collins shows, that we find the structures that incorporate social reality into the Theravāda canonical teachings on no-self.

What is at stake in each of these studies is the relationship between what the sacred texts say and what Buddhists 'do'. The historical focus on the recorded Theravāda canon has given rise to a portrait of Theravāda Buddhism that closely reflects what the canon says. The relative lack of sources outside the canon to support or refute the claims of the canon makes this portrait of Buddhism somewhat problematic; the studies of Spiro and Gombrich seek to discover, in part, what role the Theravāda canon has in the lives of Buddhists. Collins focuses on the reverse, asking what experiences the Theravāda canon took into account in its formulation of the doctrine of no-self (*anattā*). This is a perennial question in the study of religions: what are the various relationships between sacred texts and the actual behaviors of religious practitioners? This question hinges in part on what sacred texts are considered to be, and in the study of Buddhism, the sacred texts are regarded largely as a repository of doctrines. Thus for the study of Buddhism, the question becomes: what is the relation between Buddhist doctrines and what Buddhists actually do? This is an inquiry into doctrine and practice, under which lies a distinction between thought and action, where doctrines and sacred texts are considered to occupy the realm of the intellect and thought and what Buddhists do – in rituals and in daily life – constitutes the realm of action. The separation of thinking from acting in studies of ritual has been analyzed extensively by Catherine Bell in *Ritual Studies, Ritual Practice*, and her observations are relevant to the ways in which scholars of Buddhism have employed the category of doctrine.

Robert Buswell, Jr. and Robert Gimello, editors of an excellent volume entitled *Paths to Liberation: The Mārga and Its Transformations in Buddhist Thought*, recognize the preoccupation with matters of the intellect in studies of Buddhism: there is, they write, a 'longstanding tendency within religious studies to focus interpretive attention on doctrines, ie., on certain cardinal concepts or model propositions to which adherents of particular traditions are believed to give their intellectual assent.'[9] This concern with doctrine is a concern with the ideal as opposed to the actual. In his classic study of Burmese Buddhism, Spiro characterizes doctrine as ideal and normative, as opposed to what is real and existential. Once Spiro distinguishes the two dimensions of the ideal and the real, he describes three ways in which doctrines may interact with the actual behaviors of Buddhists: doctrines can become the actual beliefs of Buddhist actors; doctrines can be ignored or rejected by these actors; or, other doctrines can be assimilated to non-normative or anti-normative beliefs to give those beliefs legitimacy.[10] Spiro concludes that doctrines do, in fact, influence the behaviors of Burmese Buddhists; however, in reaching this conclusion, he considers doctrine to be a matter of the intellect that is set apart from actions of Buddhists. This separation of thinking from acting is identified by Bell, who suggests that this delineation of thought from action has disguised the fact that the production of thought is, in itself, a human activity.

More recently, scholars of doctrine *qua* doctrine outside of the study of Buddhism have sought to define more precisely what doctrine is. George Lindbeck's *The Nature of Doctrine: Religion and Theology in a postliberal Age* is an argument for a cultural-linguistic approach to the study of doctrines. In his study, he proposes three possible definitions of doctrine: religious doctrines may be propositions; they may be 'noninformative and nondiscursive' symbols that express inner feelings, attitudes, or orientations; or, doctrines may be rules that lay out the parameters for how a religious community makes certain claims about the sacred and about religious behavior.[11] Put differently, a doctrine may be a truth-claim about objective reality; it may be a symbol of a certain inner religious experience; or, it may provide a set of rules that reflect the structures of the religious world of a community. While Lindbeck rejects the propositional and symbolic definitions of doctrines for his own theological purposes, his three definitions are useful because they allow us to define more precisely how a doctrine *might* function in any given religious community.

In studies of Buddhism, doctrines are generally understood as propositions – 'propositions to which adherents of particular traditions are believed to give their intellectual assent.' However, when Lindbeck discusses the possibility that a doctrine may also be a symbol, he draws attention to a crucial dimension: the role of religious experience. Lindbeck and Paul Griffiths each explain that doctrines provide the structure for a religious community to define certain kinds of religious experiences. In Griffiths' words: 'God cannot address or be heard by the experiencing subject unless that subject already knows how to hear God and how to identify what is heard as God's voice. Schleiermacher should be stood on his head: the engagement of the religious affections is possible only when there already exists an appropriately developed doctrinal context.'[12] Lindbeck makes a similar point when he defines religion: 'religions are seen as comprehensive interpretive schemes, usually embodied in myths or narratives and heavily ritualized, which structure human experience and understanding of self and world.'[13] These scholars both draw our attention to the structural dimension of doctrines and its role in shaping religious experience. The problem they draw our attention to is how inner religious experiences are cultivated in relation to the external structures of religion and doctrines.

Largely because of the emphasis on textual sources and doctrines within Buddhist texts in studies of Buddhism, most understandings of the four noble truths portray the doctrine as the most comprehensive statement of the Buddha's teachings. This view of the four noble truths presumes that followers of the Buddha imitate the model of the Buddha, seeking to realize for themselves the truth-claims of the four noble truths first realized by the Buddha. The source of this interpretation lies in a rather straightforward model of the relationship between doctrine and practice: doctrines provide the instructions which are then to be enacted in real life. But our understanding of the four noble truths should not be so simple. As Griffiths has phrased it, and as Spiro, Gombrich, and Collins have shown: 'there is an exceedingly complex symbiotic and reciprocal relationship between religious experience and doctrine-expressing sentences.'[14]

If, as I have suggested above, scholars of Buddhism have separated doctrine from practice as thought has been separated from action, and if, as scholars of doctrine have suggested, doctrines provide a context within which religious experiences are cultivated in religious communities, then it is crucial to examine what the Theravāda canon has to say about the interaction between doctrine (thought), religious practices (action), and religious experiences. The category of *diṭṭhi* or 'view' provides the framework for this exploration. *Diṭṭhi* is much the same as the category of *darśana* in other Indian philosophical systems; both refer to recognizable bodies of reflection, both theoretical and practical, that share various characteristics with what western scholars would call philosophical schools. However, *darśana* and *diṭṭhi* cannot readily be distinguished from theological traditions, and thus blur the distinction between philosophy and theology that characterizes European and American intellectual traditions. Within the Theravāda tradition, Collins has suggested that distinguishing the difference between right views (*sammādiṭṭhi*) and wrong views (*micchādiṭṭhi*) is the first step in cultivating an experience of enlightenment. 'Right view' is a Pāli term that is akin to the notions of doctrine insofar as both doctrine and *diṭṭhi* are categories which, by definition, are propositions that express the central claims of a religious community. *Diṭṭhi* and doctrine are also comparable insofar as the process of fully learning the propositions involve established practices; while intellectual assent to *diṭṭhi* or doctrine is certainly required of a religions's practitioners, we will see that recognizing and learning right views is a process that is considered to be a form of proper conduct that involves actions that, in turn, influence one's future incarnations. However, doctrine and *diṭṭhi* are not wholly equivalent; one essential dimension of 'right view' (*sammādiṭṭhi*) that distinguishes it from doctrine is the claim that right view actuates religious transformation when learned as a component of the path.

The Category of *Diṭṭhi* in the *Tipiṭaka*

There is no single Pāli term which can be translated unequivocally as doctrine. For example, Buddhadatta provides *buddhavacana* (word[s] of the Buddha), *vacana* (word), *sāsana* (teaching or order), *buddhasāsana* (teachings of the Buddha) and *diṭṭhi* (view) as translations for doctrine.[15] The *Pāli-English Dictionary* offers a similar set of selections, defining *sāsana* and *buddhasāsana* as 'the doctrine of the Buddha' as well as 'order, message, teaching.'[16] *Dhamma*, however, is the word most commonly rendered as 'doctrine' in the English translations of the Theravāda canon, as illustrated by the definition of *dhamma* as doctrine, in opposition to *vinaya* (discipline) and *abhidhamma* (further or higher *dhamma*).[17] Both *dhamma* and *sāsana*, when used as synonyms for *dhamma*, denote the entire scope of the Buddha's life, teachings, and actions – indeed, the entire world correctly seen, known, realized, and experienced. Right view (*sammādiṭṭhi*) comes much nearer to doctrine as belief or even dogma, because the term is more restricted in scope than either *dhamma* or *sāsana*. The classification of views as right (*sammā*) and wrong (*micchā*) opens up the possibility of analyzing the claims of specific teachings or doctrines. *Diṭṭhi* is also identified as the teachings of the Buddha and thus shares the sense of authoritative teachings with doctrine, as well as with the terms *vacana*, *dhamma* and *sāsana*. Despite the fact that *diṭṭhi* is the term that comes closest to the English meaning of doctrine, it has been translated most frequently as 'view', although there are other ways to translate *diṭṭhi* which range from view or belief to dogma, doctrine, theory, speculation, or opinion. Each of these translations is reasonably accurate, depending upon the context in which the term is used. While there are several Pāli terms that have been commonly translated as doctrine, *diṭṭhi* is the term which comes closest to the English term doctrine because of its specificity in relation to the broader terms of *dhamma*, *vacana*, and *sāsana* its connotation of ideas and propositions; and, the status of right view (*sammādiṭṭhi*) as an authoritative teaching. *Diṭṭhi* also carries with it the same dual connotation that the term doctrine derives from Latin: it refers, upon occasion, to the content of a teaching as well as the act of teaching itself.[18]

There are two fundamental kinds of *diṭṭhi* in the Theravāda canon: right (*sammādiṭṭhi*) and wrong (*micchādiṭṭhi*). The differentiation between right and wrong view is consistent throughout the canon and the commentaries; it is the mechanism which introduces the basic components of Buddhist teachings. Even when *diṭṭhi* is used without the adjective 'right' or 'wrong,' view connotes either right or wrong views; very few passages offer a neutral interpretation of view.[19] If the canonical text is ambiguous, the commentaries clarify the meaning.[20] Right view (*sammādiṭṭhi*) is proper or correct view or belief. Wrong view (*micchādiṭṭhi*) carries the connotation of erroneous speculation which is rejected by the Buddha. Thus, it is appropriate to translate *micchādiṭṭhi* as false opinion or speculative view. Occasionally, *micchādiṭṭhi* has been rendered as heresy, although the rigid overtones of that term are not generally reflected by the Pāli word. The passages that I discuss in the remainder of this chapter represent a comprehensive survey of the major passages in which *diṭṭhi* appears in the literature of the four *Nikāya*s of the *Sutta-piṭaka* and their commentaries.[21] This material shows the range of meanings and interpretations for both senses of *diṭṭhi* as well as how right view is the appropriate Pāli category for our study of the four noble truths.

Collins has outlined three types of right view in his study of no-self (*anattā*).[22] The first is fundamentally a 'pro-attitude' toward the basic ideas of karma and saṃsāra; while a practitioner has not yet personally experienced the truth of the teachings of which the Buddha speaks in the *Tipiṭaka*, he or she should be favorably inclined to believe in the accuracy of those teachings. The second type is a familiarity with right view as the first component of the eightfold path (*aṭṭhaṅgiko maggo*) together with basic doctrines, such as the four noble truths and the sequence of dependent origination (*paṭiccasamupāda*) – what Collins paraphrases as 'acquaintance with Buddhist doctrine.'[23] The third type of right view is that of liberating insight, which is the highest realization of right view, the wisdom and insight which lead to release. This structure demonstrates that there is a process to right view (*sammādiṭṭhi*): right view begins with an attitude which is favorably inclined toward the basic Buddhist teachings and culminates with the realization and knowledge of liberation itself. Knowing what right views are is necessary to become more familiar with the Buddha's teachings.[24]

Distinguishing Right Views from Wrong

Wrong view (*micchādiṭṭhi*) is most commonly identified as two basic views: that the self and/or the world exist(s) permanently (*bhavadiṭṭhi*) or that the self and/or the world do/es not exist(s) (*vibhavadiṭṭhi*). *Bhava* means existence; and, with the prefix *vi-*, *vibhava* means non-existence (*vi* in this instance carries a sense of reversing the meaning of the verb to which it is affixed). Buddhaghosa provides eternal (*sassato*) as a synonym for the view of existence (*bhavadiṭṭhi*), which clarifies the meaning of permanent existence. Buddhaghosa also gives annihilation (*uccheda*) as a synonym for the view of non-existence (*vibhavadiṭṭhi*).[25] Mahācunda asks the Buddha at one point how a *bhikkhu* comes to reject such views about the self (*diṭṭhiyo attavādapaṭisaṃyuttā*) or the world (*diṭṭhiyo lokavādapaṭisaṃyuttā*). The Buddha replies that these views dissipate when one sees them 'as they are' (*yathābhūtaṃ*) through right wisdom (*sammāpaññā*).[26] In the commentary on this passage, Buddhaghosa explains that 'views about the self' mean that one 'regards form as self' (*rūpaṃ attato samanupassati*), implying that views about the self mean that one mistakes form for an existing self. Buddhaghosa also explains that 'views about the world' mean that one understands that 'self and world are eternal' (*sassato attā ca loko cā*).[27]

To further clarify the definition of views about the self and the world, Buddhaghosa provides a list of eight wrong views about the self and the world that are based on the pair of terms eternal (*sassato*) and finite (*antavā*).[28] Similar discussions appear in a passage about a certain Brahmā who held erroneous views (*pāpako diṭṭhigato*) about the nature of the self, i.e., he believed that the self is eternal and permanent (*ahaṃ nicco'mhi sassato ti*).[29] The commentary explains that there are two views: the view of theories (*laddhidiṭṭhi*) and the view that the self and the world are eternal (*sassatadiṭṭhi*). Buddhaghosa explains that such views are eradicated in followers of the Buddha

> Here, views and theories are destroyed in one who has seen the Tathāgata and the followers of the Tathāgata. The Blessed One delivered an important *dhamma* talk on this. The fruit of a stream-winner was established in the Brahmā by the end of the talk. The view of eternalism is abandoned by the path.[30]

The stream-winner (or stream-enterer) is one who has entered the path at the first stage. There are different definitions of a stream-winner, but the most familiar is the claim that a stream-winner will be reborn no more than seven times in this world before s/he attains *nibbāna*. As in the discussion with Mahācunda, Buddhaghosa states that wrong view is understood as the view that things exist permanently and that the elimination of views is accomplished by following the path.

Wrong views are further identified in a set list of ten (or occasionally eight) views that are known as the 'Unanswered Questions'. In the 'Talk to Vacchagotta on Fire' (*Aggivacchagotta-sutta*), Vacchagotta asks the Buddha if he is of the view (*diṭṭhi*) that the world is eternal.[31] The Buddha replies that he does not hold such a view. Vacchagotta asks about a number of other views, each of which the Buddha refutes. Vacchagotta then inquires whether the Buddha holds any of the following views:

(1) the world is eternal (*sassato loko*);
(2) the world is not eternal (*asassato loko*);
(3) the world is finite (*antavā loko*);
(4) the world is not finite (*anantvā loko*);
(5) the body and life are the same (*taṃ jīaṃ taṃ sarīraṃ*);
(6) the body and life are different (*taṃ jīvaṃ aññaṃ sarīaṃ*);
(7) the Tathāgata exists after dying (*hoti tathāgato param maraṇā*);
(8) the Tathāgata does not exist after dying (*na hoti tathāgato param maraṇā*);
(9) the Tathāgata both exists and does not exist after dying (*hoti ca na hoti tathāgato param maraṇā*); and
(10) the Tathāgata neither exists nor does not exist after dying (*n'eva hoti na na hoti tathāgato param maraṇā*).[32]

The first four views are composed of the pairs of permanent existence and absolute non-existence and finite or infinite, which we have already seen in Buddhaghosa's commentaries.[33] When Vacchagotta asked the Buddha about these ten views, the Buddha responded that these ten views lead to 'grasping views, holding views, the wilds of views, the scuffling of views, the struggling of views, to the fetters, suffering, distress, disturbance, fever, and they do not lead to indifference, dispassion, stopping, calming, the higher knowledges, awakening, nor to *nibbāna*.'[34] The list of modifiers that describes what experiences the ten unanswered questions produce inverts a standard description of the path to *nibbāna*: the path leads to indifference, dispassion, stopping, calming, the higher knowledges, awakening, to *nibbāna*.[35] The *Aggivacchagotta-sutta* explains that wrong views inhibit progress toward *nibbāna*, and lists the views which should be abandoned.

Other lists of wrong views are variations of claims about the permanent existence or non-existence of the self and/or the world. The *Sabbāsava-sutta*[36] explains that one of six views arise in one who does not pay careful attention (*ayoṇiso manasikaroto*):

(1) the self exists for me (*atthi me attā*);
(2) there is no self for me (*natthi me attā*);
(3) I recognize a self by self (*attanā va attānaṃ sañjānāmi*);
(4) I recognize no-self by self (*attanā va anattānaṃ sañjānāmi*);
(5) I recognize self by not-self (*anattanā va anattānaṃ sañjānāmi*); and
(6) whatever this self that speaks and knows is for me, that experiences the fruit of actions that are variously good and bad, it is this self that is permanent, stable, eternal, not subject to change for me, that will stand firm as if it were eternal (*yo me ayaṃ attā vado vedeyyo tatra tatra kalyāṇapākānaṃ kammānaṃ vipākaṃ paṭisaṃvedeti, so kho pana me ayaṃ attā nicco dhuvo sassato avipariṇāmadhammo sassatisamaṃ tath' eva ṭhassatiti*).[37]

One who does not pay careful attention (*ayoṇiso manasikaroto*) is censured for holding these views. As in the *Aggivacchagotta-sutta*, taking refuge in these views is described as going to views, holding on to views, the wilds of views, scuffling of views, and struggling of views. Bound by views in this way, the passage continues, an ordinary person is not set free from birth, from old age and death, from grief, from sorrow, from suffering, from tribulation.[38] (This last phrase is familiar from the *Dhammacakkappavattana-sutta* as an explanation of the first noble truth.) Wrong views are again understood in terms of the views of permanent existence or non-existence, and the Buddha details the costs of holding to such erroneous views by inverting the well-known benefits of the path to *nibbāna*.[39]

The term *diṭṭhigataṃ* (resorting to, holding, or having a view) refers to the claim that views should not be grasped. Again in the *Aggivacchagotta-*

sutta, we find that the Buddha no longer 'holds on to views' when the Buddha teaches Vacchagotta about the aggregates (*khandhā*), explaining the arising and passing away of form (*rūaṃ*), feeling (*vedanā*), perception (*saññā*), and so on. The *sutta* explains the difference between *diṭṭhigataṃ* (holding views) and *diṭṭhi* (view): the Buddha does not hold views, but he does have his own views which one should understand properly.[40] The phrase 'holding views' refers to views in their sense of wrong views, even though 'holding' (*-gataṃ*) may be simply a term that denotes 'resorting to' or 'referring to'. 'Holding' is associated with the adjectives 'bad' (*pāpako*) or 'wicked' (*lāmikā*). Buddhaghosa glosses 'bad holding to views' (*pāpakaṃ diṭṭhigataṃ*) as 'wicked eternalism' (*lāmikā sassatadiṭṭhi*).[41] Budddhaghosa defines 'holding views' in two ways: (1) as 'resorting to even one theory' (*laddhimatta diṭṭhigataṃ*), and (2) as views of eternalism in the *Mahātaṇhāsaṅkhaya-sutta*.[42] There is a slight distinction between the phrase 'holding on or resorting to views' (*diṭṭhigataṃ*), which denotes views in their negative sense, and right views (*sammādiṭṭhi*), which the tradition identifies as the Buddha's teachings. The basic Buddhist rejection of grasping (*upādāna*) also means that one should not hold views. In the *Sammādiṭṭhi-sutta*,[43] grasping is defined as fourfold (*cattaro upādānā*): grasping sense-pleasures (*kāmupādānaṃ*), rituals (*sīlabbatupādānaṃ*), views (*diṭṭhupādānaṃ*), and theories of the self (*attavādupādānaṃ*). The Theravāda canon rejects grasping as a legitimate reason to hold views and thus further distinguishes *diṭṭhigataṃ* (holding views) from *sammādiṭṭhi* (right view).

However, no views – right or wrong – should be grasped. As discussed earlier, the first stage of right view is a general sense of affirmation toward the teachings of the Buddha (a pro-attitude) and the second stage is a greater familiarity with the tenets of Buddhist doctrine. At neither of these stages, nor at the third stage of liberating insight, should views be grasped or held. In the *Dīghanakha-sutta*,[44] Dīghanakha approached the Buddha and explained that his view was that nothing was acceptable to him. The Buddha responded, saying that one should neither say that 'everything is acceptable to me' (*sabbaṃ me khamati*) nor that 'nothing is acceptable to me' (*sabbaṃ me na khamati*); it is not even appropriate to say that 'some things are acceptable while other things are not' (*ekaccaṃ me khamati, ekaccaṃ me na khamati*) because in each case, conflict and disputes will arise. One who sees that arguments will come out of such positions will, the *sutta* continues, put them away and abandon them. Instead, one should realize that the body is impermanent, and, realizing this, one should cultivate dispassion:

> And so, Aggivessana, a *bhikkhu* whose mind is liberated in this way will not take sides with anyone and will not dispute with anyone; he uses the language of the world without grasping it.[45]

The Buddha covers all of the options in this *sutta*: one should not agree with everything, or nothing, or agree on some points and not on others, because each position carries with it the potential for strife. Dīghanakha is enjoined to use words and views but not to adhere to them; views are always a means to the end of liberation, never an end in themselves. After hearing this talk, Dīghanakha took refuge as a lay follower (*upāsako*).

In the *Pañcattaya-sutta*,[46] the Buddha discusses five erroneous views concerning the future, the past, and the experience of *nibbāna* in the present. He cautions his audience not to grasp even positive meditative states. After each theory, there is a refrain in which the Buddha explains:

> That is constructed and coarse, but there is an ending to constructions. Having known 'there is this', the Tathāgata – seeing an escape from all that – has gone beyond that.[47]

In other words, what the Buddha knows is that there is an end to the constructions. The point to deconstructing these views is that those who assume certain things about existence or non-existence of the self in the future, past, or in the present do not fully understand the absence of grasping and are thus deluded as to their attainments. One who meditates should not be attached to views about the past (*pubbantānudiṭṭhiṃ*), to views about the future (*aparantānudiṭṭhiṃ*), to fetters of sensual pleasure (*kāmasaṃyojanaṃ*), to the state of joy of solitude (*pavivekaṃ pītiṃ*), to disinterested happiness[48] (*nirāmisaṃ sukhaṃ*), or to feelings that are neither painful nor pleasant (*adukkhamasukhaṃ vedanaṃ*). Toward the end of the *sutta*, the Buddha warns his audience about clinging to the notion of the self during the practice of meditation, even if they have rejected all of the problematic views about the future or the past. The Buddha explains that, if while meditating one reflects on any of the joyous or peaceful states, thinking 'this is calm, this is excellent' (*etaṃ santaṃ etaṃ paṇītaṃ*), then grief arises when the meditative state has ended. The meditative state is like the sun, and its ending is like the shade, and grief arises when the meditative state has come to an end. One should not to think 'I am calm, I am at peace, I am beyond grasping' (*santo 'ham asmi, nibbuto 'ham asmi, anupādāno 'ham asmī*).[49] Such a person still grasps because the statement is phrased in terms of 'I' (*aham asmi*) and one still possesses a form of attachment. The way to eliminate such grasping is to know what is constructed and to know that one can end the constructions. Knowing how things come to be constructed is the knowledge that one should gain in order to do away with wrong views about the past and future, and therefore, grasping.

The *Cūlasuññatā-sutta*[50] offers a similar teaching. The Buddha explains to Ānanda how it is that one should recognize and abide in emptiness. Focusing his comments on the eight meditative levels of *jhāni*c meditation, the Buddha explains that after each of the eight stages, one should reflect on the stages:[51]

> Thus one regards what is not there as empty; but one knows that what remains there exists, (thinking) 'this exists'.[52]

In other words, one should see clearly what is empty and what remains present; the goal is to see things as they are (*yathābhuccā*) with no attachment or grasping, even to the idea of the path or to views of any sort.[53]

To summarize, wrong views are identified as theories about the permanent existence or the non-existence of the self or the world. The permanent existence or the permanent non-existence of selves or the world is not conducive to recognizing the Buddha's teaching that the world and selves are constructed, that they exist but always in a state of change. Belief in such wrong views does not lead to release; instead, belief in these views binds one to rebirth and to suffering. One should not be attached to views – either wrong views or right views – because attachment does not lead to *nibbāna*. Even attachment to positive experiences leads to loss when the experience comes to an end. In the general Buddhist attitude of dispassionate observation of the constructed nature of that which exists from moment to moment, one should employ views but not grasp them. The Buddha concluded the *Pañcattaya-sutta* with these words: there is release without grasping.[54] Recognition and the subsequent rejection of wrong views is the first step necessary for learning rights views.

Learning Right Views

Within Collins' framework, this section examines those propositions that constitute right views alongside the ways in which one is said to learn right views. Right view is most familiar as the first constituent of the eightfold path (*aṭṭhaṅgiko maggo*). In the *Dhammacakkappavattana-sutta*, the Buddha explains that right view is the first 'limb' of the eightfold path and is thus one of the factors which 'leads to vision and knowledge, calm, higher knowledge, awakening, *nibbāna*.'[55] The following passage from the *Magga-saṃyutta* explains how one should cultivate the eightfold path, including right view.

> And how, *bhikkhu*s, does a *bhikkhu* who is a friend of that which is beautiful develop the noble eightfold path and devote himself to the noble eightfold path? Here, *bihikkhu*s, a *bhikkhu* cultivates right view, which produces reliance upon detachment, reliance on dispassion, reliance on ending, resulting in relinquishing, and so on. . . . He cultivates right concentration, which results in the restraint of passion, which produces reliance upon detachment, reliance on dispassion, reliance on ending, resulting in relinquishing, and so on.

> In this way, *bhikkhus*, a *bhikkhu* who is a friend of that which is beautiful develops and devotes himself to the noble eightfold path.[56]

The same formulaic description is used to explain the compound 'accomplishments of (right) view' (*diṭṭhisampadā*) later in the same section. Buddhaghosa defines *diṭṭhisampadā* as the attainment of knowledge (*ñāṇasampatti*).[57] The *Dhammacakkappavattana-sutta* and the *Magga-saṃyutta* give us two examples of how right view is understood in relation to the eightfold path, and both *sutta*s show that right view, like the other seven factors of the path, should be cultivated – not simply positively regarded but fully developed, practiced and learned.

In the *Mahācattārīsaka-sutta*, right view is defined as twofold. First, there are right views associated with the corruptions (*sāsavā*), which are on the side of merit (*puññābhāgiyā*), and which leads to new birth (*upadhivepakkā*). Second, there are right views which are noble (*ariyā*), not associated with the corruptions (*anāsavā*), transcendent (*lokuttarā*), and a factor or 'limb' of the path (*maggaṅgā*).

> And what, *bhikkhus*, is right view which is associated with the corruptions, has a share in merit, and which results in attachment? There is giving, offering, and sacrifice; there is the ripening of the fruit of *kamma* of good or bad actions; there is this world and the world beyond; there is mother and father; there are beings who have been reborn spontaneously; there are in this world perfected and properly disposed recluses and brahmans who proclaim this world and the world beyond, having personally experienced them by higher knowledge; *bhikkhus*, this is right view which is associated with the corruptions, on the side of merit, and which leads to new birth.

> And what, *bhikkhus*, is right view which is noble, not associated with the corruptions, transcendent and a factor of the path? Whatever, *bhikkhus*, is wisdom, the faculty of wisdom, the strength of wisdom, the factor of enlightenment that is investigation into things, the right view that is a factor of the path in one who, developing the noble path, is of noble thought, thought without the corruptions, familiar with the noble path; *bhikkhus*, this is a right view that is noble, not associated with the corruptions, transcendent, and a factor of the path.[58]

Right view that leads to rebirth refers to a range of activities: giving, in the sense of religious donations (*dāna*), offerings, and sacrifice. There are also various kinds of beings, karma, and merit, all of which are associated with attachment and future rebirth. In the second kind of right view which leads to release, there is wisdom, investigation, the noble path, and the view is transcendent (*lokuttarā*) with no corruptions (*āsavā*).[59]

Collins points out that right view is developed gradually. It begins with a generally favorable attitude toward the doctrines, moves toward a greater familiarity with and knowledge of the Buddha's teachings, and culminates with the comprehension of right view in terms of liberating insight, which is the second type of right view described above. At some points in the canon, these three types of right view can correspond to three types of people described in later parts of the Theravāda canon and commentaries: the one who is ordinary (*puthujjano*), the learner (*sekho*), and the adept (*asekho*).[60]

According to the commentary on the *Sammādiṭṭhi-sutta*,[61] the ordinary person is said to be 'outside' (*bāhirako*) the teachings or Buddhism, while the learner and the adept belong to the teachings of the Buddha (*sāsaniko*). The ordinary one falls outside the teachings because he 'one who is influenced by views of (a) self' (*attadiṭṭhiparāmāsakattā*) even though he is a believer in *kamma* (*kammavādin*). The ordinary one and learner are classified as this-worldly (*lokiyā*) while the adept possesses other-worldly right view (*lokuttarā*). The adept is one who has the insights necessary for entry into one of the four levels of the path: the stream-winner, who will experience only a limited number of rebirths; the once-returner, who will be reborn only one more time; the non-returner, who will not be reborn as a human again but who will be reborn into one of the heavens; and the *arahat* who has attained *nibbāna* in this life and who will not be reborn again in any form.[62] To develop *sammādiṭṭhi*, then, is to develop an understanding of the concept gradually and to move from outside the teachings of the Buddha to entry into the path.

The commentaries consistently define right view in terms of right seeing, wisdom, insight, and entry into the path. Buddhaghosa explains that *sammādiṭṭhi* is right seeing.[63] Right view is also twofold: right view regarding insight (*vipassanāsammādiṭṭhi*) and right view regarding the path (*maggasammādiṭṭhi*).[64] Buddhaghosa further explains that the right view concerning insight (*vipassanāsammādiṭṭhi*)[65] is connected to the path (*maggasampayuttā*);[66] and, more specifically, he identifies right view as the view of stream entry (*sotāpattimaggadiṭṭhi*).[67] He draws the same connection between view, insight and wisdom, and the path: 'Wisdom through the effort of view,' he explains, 'means through insight and wisdom, through bodily and mental effort which is connected to insight and the right view of the path.'[68] Knowing through views (*diṭṭhiyā suppaṭividdha*) is also explained in terms of wisdom: 'Knowing through views means knowing the meaning and the action with wisdom.'[69] Wrong views are eliminated by seeing things as they really are through right wisdom.[70] Buddhaghosa explains that 'knowing through views' (*diṭṭhiyā pi suppaṭividdhāṃ hoti*) means knowing the causes of the world with wisdom (*lokiyapaññā*) and that 'not knowing through views' (*diṭṭhiyā pi appaṭtividdhaṃ hoti*) means that there is no clarity regarding views that are to be understood.[71] This distinction makes the point that knowledge that is to be learned through right views is not always understood clearly – and it should be. In the commentaries as well as in the canon definitions of right view are closely linked to wisdom and insight as well as the path.

Right view is defined with explicit references to *nibbāna* and to the four noble truths. Right view is linked with *nibbāna*, for example, in the enumeration of eight conditions which lead to *nibbāna* and with the explanation that 'well aimed right view' leads to *nibbāna*.[72] In the *Saccavibhaṅga-sutta*, right view consists of the four noble truths:

> What, *bhikkhus*, is right view? Right view, *bhikkhus*, is explained as knowledge of pain, knowledge of the arising of pain, knowledge of the ending of pain, knowledge of the way that leads to the ending of pain.[73]

Buddhaghosa adds that right view is classified according to the eightfold path in this teaching.[74] There is a different relationship between view and the four noble truths in the *Sacca-saṃyutta*. View appears in the compound 'endowed with view' (*diṭṭhisampanno*), which is identified as a characteristic of a noble follower (*ariyasāvako*); a noble follower is one who has fully understood the four noble truths 'as they really are (*yathābhūtaṃ*).'[75]

In the *Dīghanakha-sutta*, the renouncer Dīghanakha asks the Buddha if he holds the view that 'all is not acceptable to me' (*sabbaṃ me na khamati*). In a lengthy deliberation, the Buddha replies that he does not adhere to that particular view. In his commentary on this passage, Buddhaghosa explains that the *diṭṭhi* to which Dīghanakha refers should be understood as annihilation (*ucchedavāda*). In the remainder of the passage, the Buddha details his points of difference with those who hold the view that all is eternal and with those who hold that all does not exist. After listening to the Buddha's talk, the follower Sāriputta freed himself of the corruptions (*āsavā*) and became an *arahat*. At the same time, Dīghanakha cultivated the *dhamma*-eye (*dhammacakkhu*) and, the commentary explains, attained the first level of the path, that of a stream-winner. The connection between analyzing the error of wrong views and realizing right views and an individual's entry into or advancement along the path is rarely as explicit as it is in the *Dīghanakha-sutta*.

We saw that right view is defined in terms of the four noble truths; other *suttas* state that knowledge of the four noble truths leads to entry into the path. The *Sabbāsava-sutta*[76] explains that wrong view is eliminated by means of the four noble truths. While the ordinary person is bound by birth, old age and death, one who is skilled in *dhamma* is said to be able to properly attend to the corruptions (*āsavā*). One way of doing so is to properly attend to the corruptions by observing 'this is pain,' 'this is the arising of pain,' 'this is the ending of pain,' and 'this is the way to end pain.'[77] This practice results in the decline of three fetters (*saṃyojanāni*): wrong view regarding the belief in a self (*sakkāyadiṭṭhi*), doubt (*vicikicchā*), and adherence to rites and ceremonies (*sīlabbataparāmāso*).[78] Elimination of the view regarding the existence of a self (*sakkāyadiṭṭhi*) is identified elsewhere as a function of the path,[79] and holding on to the view of a self is said to be antithetical to the attainment of *nibbāna*.[80] Understanding the four noble truths is one way to eliminate the first three fetters, one of which is the wrong view regarding the existence of a self; thus, understanding the four noble truths enables one to become a stream-winner. The Buddha points out elsewhere that right view consists of the four noble truths.[81] The *Sabbāsava-sutta* makes the same claim as that of the *Dīghanakha-sutta*: right view leads to entry into the path. However, where the *Sabbāsava-sutta* explains right view in terms of the four noble truths and states that elimination of the first three fetters leads to entry into the path, in the *Dīghanakha-sutta*, when Sāriputta and Dīghanakha hear the Buddha's talk on eliminating wrong views, they respectively attain the states of an *arahat* and a stream-enterer.[82] Right views are consistently associated with reaching and advancing along the path, but not always with reference to the four noble truths.

There are a few references that define view by distinguishing it from other kinds of opinions or arguments. Buddhaghosa clarifies the difference between opinion (*adhivuttipadaṃ*) and view at one point, saying that the common use of 'view' was 'opinion', and that 'view' refers to 'opinions' about existence, but not to existence as it really is.[83] As expected, opinions and wrong views refer to the theories of a fixed existence or non-existence in popular use. Right view is what separates (right) views from opinions: right views are 'taught or held by the Buddha', and wrong views are opinions. The *Dīghanakha-sutta* explains how to eradicate wrong views by employing vernacular language without holding on to the common meaning.[84] This passage indicates that right view consists of using the vernacular but without grasping the particular genre of speech.

The difference between those teachings held by the Buddha and wrong views (as in opinions) or views erroneously held by others is explicitly made by the Buddha in the *Aggivacchagotta-sutta*.

> For, Vaccha, this dhamma is deep, difficult to see, difficult to understand, peaceful, excellent, beyond logic, subtle, intelligible to the wise; but it is hard for you who are of another view, another allegiance, another objective, of a different observance, and under a different teacher.[85]

Dhamma and right views are what the Buddha taught; other views are held by other teachers. View is not defined with exclusive reference to substantive propositions; opinions or teachings other than the Buddha's are views, but they are not right views. Right views are unambiguously the teachings of the Buddha which should be cultivated and learned.

There are consistent definitions of right view in the commentaries and in the canonical writings. First, it is right seeing – seeing 'just as it is.' Second, right view is consistently defined in terms of insight and wisdom and with other teachings of the Buddha, including the four noble truths. Here, right view involves different types of activities – giving, offerings, sacrifice, and the practice of wisdom and the attainment of release. Third, right view is linked explicitly to *nibbāna*, the path, and to the entry of the path as a stream-winner. Buddhaghosa's explanation that the practice of wisdom and insight involve both bodily and mental effort also indicates that right view is not solely an intellectual exercise. His commentary that one should know both the meaning and action illustrates the point that right view involves more than the learning of propositions.

Right Views as Efficacious

In the 'Greater Teachings on Undertaking *Dhamma*' (*Mahādhammasamādāna-sutta*),[86] the Buddha includes wrong and right views as factors in rebirth. He discusses an ignorant person who does not see the relationship between present actions and their results in the future, and compares such a person to a wise person who does see the connection. One who possesses wrong views may experience either pain or happiness in the present world but will be reborn into one of the hells in the future. (There are usually four hells identified in the *Tipiṭaka: niraya* (purgatory), *tiracchāna-yoni* (rebirth as an animal), *petā* (rebirth as a ghost), *asurā* (rebirth as a demon). The *Jātaka*s, or Birth Stories of the Buddha, contain many references to other hells and states of suffering.) In contrast to one who holds wrong views, one who possesses right views may experience either pain or happiness in the present life but will enjoy happiness in future rebirths.[87] If, the *sutta* continues, one takes what is not given and engages in other misconduct (including the possession of wrong views), even though one is happy in the present life, then such a person is reborn in one of the hells. Similarly, if one engages in misconduct and possesses wrong views, and is unhappy, one is still reborn into one of the hells. But if one behaves properly, possesses right views and is either unhappy or happy in the present, one is reborn into one of the heavens. The point is that views, behavior, and one's emotional state are interrelated factors when it comes to an individual's rebirth, and adherence to wrong views or right views are determining factors in one's rebirth that override a particular emotional state in the present. Emotional happiness or unhappiness does not determine one's rebirth: one's views and actions do.

Similar passages are found elsewhere in the *Nikāya*s. Those who adhere to wrong views will be reborn into hell or a place of suffering (*vinipātaṃ nirayaṃ upapannā*), but those who hold right views will enjoy a birth in one of the heavenly worlds, having gained the *kamma* that is the fruit of right view.[88] Right and wrong view are causal factors in the process of *kamma*, and in combination with one's actions, views determine one's rebirth. The Buddha makes the same point at length the 'Great Discourse on the Analysis of *Kamma*' (*Mahākammavibhaṅga-sutta*).[89] In the Buddha's discourse to Ānanda about various relationships between actions, views and rebirth, he explains that actions and views determine one's rebirth, and that if one who abstains from wrong action and holds right views in the present is reborn into one of the hells, it is because of some past wicked action – in other words, *kamma*. Finally, the Buddha draws attention to the significance of view as a causal factor in the *Aṅguttara-nikāya*: 'I know of nothing so likely, *bhikkhu*s, when the body breaks up after death, to cause rebirth of beings into a place of suffering (*apāya*), a difficult road (*duggati*), destruction (*vinipāta*), or purgatory (*niraya*) as wrong view.'[90] Right view is likewise identified as the factor most likely to produce rebirth in the heavens.

The *Mahādhammasamādāna-sutta* includes views in a list of various kinds of appropriate or inappropriate conduct. The list includes those who take life (*pāṇātipātī*), who take what is not given (*adinnādāyī*), who misbehave with regard to matters of sexual desire (*kāmesu micchācārī*), who lie (*musāvādī*), who slander (*pisuṇāvāco*), who speak harshly (*pharusāvāco*), who speak trivially (*samphappalāpī*), who are envious (*abhijjhālu*), who have malevolent thoughts (*byāpannacitto*), and possess wrong views (*micchādiṭṭhi*).[91] Appropriate behavior, of course, involves abstaining from all of these forms of misconduct and possessing right view (*sammādiṭṭhi*). Furthermore, there is a casual relationship established between conduct, which includes one's views, and one's rebirth. The first case sets the pattern for the remainder of the passage:

> In this case, *bhikkhus*, someone who becomes one who destroys life, even with suffering and grief, experiences suffering and grief because of that destruction of life. . . .[92]

The relationship between what one does and what one experiences is delineated with compounds created with the suffix 'cause' (*-paccaya*). That compound is constructed with all of the factors listed in this passage, including right and wrong view. Locating views in a list of other appropriate behaviors indicates that having right view is a factor that influences one's future. The specific causal relationship established between behavior and rebirth provides a foundation for the more extensive associations between right and wrong views and actions as factors in the determination of one's rebirth and access to the path.

A similar passage on views and action is found in the *Madhura-sutta*, which is an exchange between the king of Madhurā and Mahākaccāna about the caste system and brahmans. In the course of the debate, the king asks Mahākaccāna the same set of questions raised in the *Mahādhamma-samādāna-sutta* discussed in the paragraph above. The king's question is whether a noble person, regardless of caste, who refrained from engaging in misconduct, would be reborn in to a heavenly world. Mahākaccāna replies that yes, such a person would be reborn in one of the heavens. Mahākaccāna provides an authority for his answer: 'This is how it seems to me,' the passage concludes, 'and have I heard it this way from perfected ones.'[93] In this exchange, right view is accompanied by the same behaviors as in the *Mahādhammasamādāna-sutta* above and establishes the same relationship between conduct, right view, and rebirth. An interesting variant on this set of relations is found in the *Cakkavattisīhanāda-sutta*.[94] The *sutta* contains a story about a king whose kingdom is in gradual decline and explains that the result of holding on to wrong views is that fathers will see the lifespan of their sons reduced from one thousand years to five hundred years. In turn, wrong views are listed along with other wrong doings, such as stealing, wrong speech, not giving alms, and so on.[95] The *Mahādhammasamādāna-*, *Madhura-* and *Cakkavattisīhanāda-sutta*s each explain that one's views and actions determine one's future rebirths.

Right view is compared with wrong view in recitation lists which enumerate certain ways of acting which should be avoided or cultivated. Thus, in the *Saṅgīti-sutta*[96] and the *Dasuttara-sutta*,[97] wrong view is listed in the following groups: the six roots of contention (*vivāda-mūlāni*);[98] the ten poor ways of acting (*akusalakammapathā*);[99] and the eight (and ten) things to be eliminated (*dhammā pahātabbā*).[100] Alternatively, right view is found among the six gracious states (*sārāṇīyā dhammā*);[101] the ten good ways of acting (*kusalakammapathā*);[102] and the eight, nine, and ten things which should be cultivated (*dhammā bhāvetabbā*).[103] Buddhaghosa says little about view in these recitations, although he explains the compound 'one who has the view of a renouncer' (*diṭṭhisāmaññagato*) by referring to the four paths.[104] He also explains wrong view as greed and delusion,[105] and list three kinds of wrong view: nihilists (*natthikavādī*), those who hold that there is no cause (*ahetukavādī*), and those who hold that there are no results (*akiriyavādī*).[106] In these passages, view is once again considered as a type of behavior to be avoided (in the case of wrong view) or cultivated (in the case of right view).

In the *Dasuttara-sutta*, Sāriputta enumerated ten lists of ten qualities (*dhammā*) to be learned for the attainment of *nibbāna*. In that list, he explains that wrong view is eliminated by right view.

> What are the ten *dhammas* to be fully learned? The ten bases of decay. Wrong view is destroyed by right view. Whatever various bad or poor qualities caused by wrong views arise – those are destroyed, and various good qualities caused by right view are cultivated and brought to perfection.[107]

The *Sallekha-sutta*[108] points out that wrong views dissipate with the proper seeing of right wisdom and careful attention. The *Dīghanakha-sutta*[109] explains how to eradicate wrong views: by learning that the constituent parts of the body decay and by learning that there are three kinds of feeling (pleasant, painful, and neither pleasant nor painful), one is able to refute wrong views. One who does so is called an 'instructed follower of the noble ones' (*sutavo ariyasāvako*). It appears that not only is right view associated with certain behaviors that should be developed and with specific actions that should be practiced; right views also destroy wrong views as well as poor behaviors caused by wrong views.

These passages that define right view in terms of conduct and behavior reveal the efficacy of right view. Where we saw above that right views are considered to lead the ultimate liberating insight, this material indicates that views lead to actions that determine one's rebirth. At points, the canon seems to define the holding of any views at all as a type of behavior or action in itself. Views are thus cast as central factors in the maintenance or destruction of one's continued existence in saṃsāra. Collins defines the third stage of right view as liberating insight; we have seen here that this dimension of right views is related to a broader conception of the efficacy of *any* views at all. The act of holding either right or wrong views is a type of action that can release one from or further link one to the unending cycle of existence.

Conclusions

This foray into what the category of *diṭṭhi* means in the Theravāda canon and commentaries has uncovered several features of *diṭṭhi* which makes it comparable in certain ways to the more familiar category of doctrine. First, *diṭṭhi* refers to any view that can be either right or wrong, but we have seen that distinguishing right view from wrong view is the initial step to identifying right view and learning it in greater detail. In the broadest sense, wrong view consists of variations on two doctrines: that either there is permanent existence of a self or the world, or that there is no existence of the self or the world at all. Recognizing the fallacy of both of these positions means that a follower of the Buddha's teachings would have some sense of the conditioned nature of existence; that is, things do exist, but they exist dependent upon other things, and they exist only for a limited period of time.

Second, one is encouraged by the canon and commentaries to *learn* right views. One should know the place of right view in the eightfold path; one should know with insight and with wisdom; and, one should know the kinds of right view and their results. One must know right view (*pajānāti*), practice right view (*bahulīkaroti*), cultivate right view (*bhāveti*), experience right view (*paṭisaṃvedeti*), and thus know things just as they are (*yathābhūtaṃ*). One should put forth both bodily and mental effort to know right view. Right views involve certain actions, such as giving (*dinnaṃ*), offerings (*yiṭṭhaṃ*), sacrifice (*hutaṃ*), and one's duties to one's parents. Buddhaghosa explains that views (*diṭṭhi*) influence actions (*kamma*), and we have seen that views and actions, both past and present, determine one's future rebirth. Right views, in this equation, have the potential to eliminate wrong views and to shape one's actions, thus making a more favorable rebirth possible. While right views involve certain actions, and while learning right views involves both bodily and mental effort, they are not the same as action (*kamma*). Views and action interact with each other to influence one's future. Learning right views is a necessary act that makes it possible for one to experience enlightenment, but learning is not simply an intellectual exercise.

Third, right views, when understood thoroughly and completely, *are* liberating insight. That is, when one knows right views with wisdom, insight, and knowledge, one experiences freedom from the cycle of rebirth. This last dimension of right views is the feature that sets *diṭṭhi* apart from doctrine: the claim that right view, when properly and fully known, is the transcendent knowledge of enlightenment. Right view ushers in the religious experience and knowledge that places one on the path to *nibbāna*; it also eliminates the fetters (*saṃyojanāni*) and the corruptions (*āsavā*) that prevent one from attaining the status of an *arahat*. In contrast, wrong views result in further rebirths within saṃsāra in possibly less fortunate circumstances; both right and wrong views are central factors that, in combination with other factors, determine one's enlightenment or continued rebirths. Right views are thus ultimately effective insofar as the claim is made that they can destroy wrong views and the concomitant results of improper actions.

To look at particular teachings of the Buddha as *diṭṭhi* means considering the teaching as something more than a proposition or a doctrine in the usual way that we think of religious teachings as doctrines – generally as a matter of the intellect. Views are doctrines, but they are doctrines within a particularly Buddhist framework. Right views provide (as Griffiths explains for doctrine) the foundation for a particular religious experience – the experience of release from the endless cycle of rebirth in the Buddhist cosmos. In other words, enlightenment is not possible without one's recognition that certain propositions are not conducive to that experience (wrong views) and without learning right views. In this Buddhist framework, the Theravāda canon explains that right views are transformative in and of themselves: they eliminate wrong views, they influence one's actions, and they are the means by which one experiences and gains knowledge within the path. Doctrinally, right views are to be recognized, learned, and learned fully and completely in order to attain release from saṃsāra.

I suggested at the outset of this chapter that because the categories of thought and action have been separated in studies of Buddhism, we should examine closely the relationship between doctrine, actions, and experiences in the content of the Theravāda canon. Through this survey of the category of *diṭṭhi*, it has become necessary to reconfigure Collins' three stages of understanding right views (pro-attitude toward right views, learning Buddhist teachings, and right view as liberating insight). First, recognizing right from wrong view and developing a positive regard for right views *is* largely an intellectual matter, but not exclusively so. Second, learning right views is far more than an intellectual endeavor; the process involves, as we have seen, both exertion and certain actions. Third, the Theravāda canon claims not only that right views can be an experience of liberating insight, but that these right views can eradicate wrong views and the results of improper actions.

When Mary Douglas wrote that 'the more intractable puzzles in comparative religion arise because human experience has thus been wrongly divided,' she was referring to Sir James George Frazer's separation of magic from religion, and to his assertion that ethics had no place in the worlds of 'primitive' cultures.[110] Her point is that we ought not divide human experience, but that we should examine underlying structures for any larger explanations that make clear the anomalies that appear to scholars to be out of place. As a doctrine, the four noble truths are an anomaly: they appear in various places throughout the canonical texts, they disappear at other points, and are extolled as necessary in still other places. As *sammādiṭṭhi*, however, the four noble truths are not out of place. Because we have traditionally defined doctrine as propositions to which practitioners must grant intellectual assent, the practices and actions closely associated with right view appear to be extraneous in previous studies of right views. When we place the four noble truths in their proper context of right views, the propositional role of the teaching emerges as thoroughly enmeshed with the ethical actions and behaviors that are conductive to recognizing right views, learning them, and knowing them as liberating insight. As *sammādiṭṭhi*, propositions initially require an intellectual agreement. But beyond that, developing a familiarity with the teachings and knowing them as liberation involves more than the mind. In turn, the Theravāda canon demonstrates that views are efficacious in and of themselves, influencing one's actions and success along the path. The play between types of human action in the category of *diṭṭhi* is the pattern that structures the appearance and disappearance of the four noble truths.

Notes

1 Mary Douglas, *Purity and Danger: An Analysis of Concepts of Pollution and Taboo* (London: Routledge & Kegal Paul, 1966; Binghamton, New York: Routledge & Kegan Paul, 1980), 28.

2 For a more detailed examination of this phenomenon, see Philip C. Almond, *The British Discovery of Buddhism* (Cambridge: Cambridge University Press, 1988); Thomas A. Tweed, *The American Encounter with Buddhism, 1844–1912: Victorian Culture and the Limits of Dissent* (Bloomington: Indiana University

Press, 1992); Schopen, *Bones, Stones, and Buddhist Monks*, 1–22; Charles Hallisey, 'Roads Taken and Not Taken in the Study of Theravāda Buddhism' in *Curators of the Buddha: The Study of Buddhism under Colonialism*, ed. Donald Lopez, Jr. (Chicago: University of Chicago Press, 1995).

3 Paul Ambrose Bigandet, *The Life or Legend of Gaudama: The Buddha of the Burmese*, 2nd edition (1858; London: Kegal Paul, Trench & Trübner, 1866), 203. The book was issued in four editions by 1911 (1858, 1866, 1880, 1911), and was most recently reprinted in Varanasi in 1979.

4 Melford Spiro, *Buddhism and Society: A Great Tradition and Its Burmese Vicissitudes* (New York: Harper & Row, 1970), 3–4.

5 Spiro, *Buddhism and Society*, 12.

6 Richard Gombrich, *Precept and Practice: Traditional Buddhism in the Rural Highlands of Ceylon* (Cambridge: Cambridge University Press, 1971), 322–326.

7 Gombrich, *Precept and Practice*, 5.

8 Steven Collins, *Selfless Persons: Imagery and Thought in Theravāda Buddhism* (Cambridge: Cambridge University Press, 1982), 166.

9 Robert E. Buswell, Jr. and Robert M. Gimello, *Paths to Liberation: The Mārga and Its Transformations in Buddhist Thought*, Studies in East Asian Buddhism, vol. 7 (Honolulu: University of Hawaii Press, 1992), 4.

10 Spiro, *Buddhism and Society*, 4.

11 George A. Lindbeck, *The Nature of Doctrine: Religion and Theology in a Post-Liberal Age* (Philadelphia: Westminster Press, 1984), 16–18.

12 Paul J. Griffiths, *On Being Buddha* (Albany, NY: State University of New York Press, 1994), 19.

13 Lindbeck, *Nature of Doctrine*, 32.

14 Griffiths, *On Being Buddha*, 18.

15 A. P. Buddhadatta Mahāthera, *Enlish-Pali Dictionary* (London: Pāli Text Society, 1970), s.v. 'doctrine.'

16 PED, s.v. *sāsana*

17 PED, s.v. *dhamma* (C)

18 Paul J. Griffiths, 'The Doctrine of Buddhahood,' unpublished manuscript, 5–6.

19 These two senses of *diṭṭhi* have produced a variety of English translations, including a literal translation of the term based on the root meaning of *dassati* 'to see'. For example, in her translation of the *Aggivacchagott-sutta* in the *Majjhima-nikāya*, I. B. Horner rightly translated *ditthigataṃ* with a negative sense as 'going to "speculative view".' In the following line, where *diṭṭhi* refers to the teachings that the Buddha holds, she rendered *diṭṭhi* literally as 'has been seen.' See M I 486 and *The Middle Length Sayings* (*Majjhima-nikāya*), 3 vols., trans. I. B. Horner (London: Pāli Text Society 1954–1959), 2:164. Similarly, Woodward translated the compound *diṭṭhisampanna* as 'blessed with vision.' See *The Book of Kindred Sayings* (Saṃyutta-nikāya), trans. F. L. Woodward (London: Pāli Text Society, 1965), 385. The term is rendered as vision or with its literal meaning 'to see' when it is used in its sense as right vision or view, but as view or opinion when the term is used in its negatoive sense as wrong view.

20 There is one point at which *diṭṭhi* is defined descriptively in terms of how it arises in relation to the elements (*dhātu*), recognition (*saññā*), and reasoning (*vitakka*). 'Because of an element, *bhikkhus*, recognition arises, view arises, initial thought arises' (*Dhātuṃ bhikkhave paṭicca uppajjati saññā uppajjati diṭṭhi uppajjati vitakka ti*) (S II 153).

21 Collins, *Selfless Persons*, 88–95.

22 Collins, *Selfless Persons*, 90.

23 The survey is based on sources from the Pāli Text Society edition of the Pāli canon, but I have used the commentaries throughout to further understand the meanings found in the canon. The commentaries are not always accurate nor do they always agree with each other or the canonical passage; nonetheless, the commentators were historically closer to the canon than the twentieth century and should thus be consulted whenever possible.

24 S II 17ff.

25 Ps II 10 (on M I 65). Buddhaghosa explains that the phrase 'clinging to the view of existence' *bhavadiṭṭhiṃ allīna* should be understood as 'clinging to the view that (all) is eternal because of views and craving' (*taṇhādiṭṭhivasena sassatodiṭṭhiṃ allīnā*). Ps III 197 has the same gloss.

26 *etaṃ yathābhūtaṃ sammappaññāyapassato evam etāsaṃ diṭṭhīnaṃ pahānaṃ hoti* (M I 40).

27 Ps I 182

28 *Tā aṭṭha honti sassato asassato sassaato ca asassato ca n'eva sassato nāsassato antavā anantavā anatavā ca anantavā ca n'eva antavā nāntavā attā ca loko cā ti evaṃ pavattā* (Ps I 182).

29 S I 142–144

30 Spk I 213

31 The *Aggivacchagotta-sutta* is found at M I 481–489.

32 M I 484. Buddhaghosa adds little to the text in his commentary; he simply notes that the text refers to those who hold views of eternalism (*sassatadiṭṭhiko*) and annihilation (*uccedadiṭṭhiko*) (Ps III 197). The full list of the unanswered questions is also found in the *Avyākata-saṃyutta* of the *Saṃyutta-nikāya* (S IV 391), where Vacchagotta asks Moggallāna the same questions, and Moggallāna replies that the Buddha has not answered these ten inquiries. A parallel passage is found in *Vacchagotta-saṃyutta*, where the Buddha says that these views arise out of an ignorance of the body, its arising, ending and the way of its ending (S III 258). See Collins, *Selfless Persons*, 131–138 for an extended discussion of the unanswered questions and *anattā*.

33 cf. Ps I 182

34 *Sassato loko ti kho Vaccha diṭṭhigataṃ etaṃ diṭṭhigahanaṃ diṭṭhikantāraṃ diṭṭhivisūkaṃ diṭṭhivipphanditaṃ diṭṭhisaṃyojanaṃ sadukkhaṃ savighātaṃ saupāyāsaṃ saparilāhaṃ na nibbidāya na virāgāya na nirodhāya na upasamāya na abhiññāya na sambodhāya na nibbānāya saṃvattati* (M I 485).

35 See, for example, D I 189, S V 82, A III 83, and elsewhere.

36 M I 6–12

37 M I 6–12. The relationship between one who pays proper attention (*yoniso manasikaroto*) and right view, and between one who does not pay proper attention (*ayoniso manasikaroto*) and wrong view is also found at Mp II 23.

38 On the 'ordinary person' (*puthujjano*), see Collins, *Selfless Persons*, 92–95.

39 This point is further emphasized in the commentary on this passage, where Buddhaghosa glosses 'the self exists for me' (*n' atthi me attā*) as (*c' ettha sassatadiṭṭhi sabbakālesu attano atthitaṃ gaṇhāti*) and 'the self doesn't exist for me' (*n'atthi me attā*) with a reference to the view of annihilation (*ucchedadiṭṭhi*) and non existence (*vibhava*) (Ps I 70).

40 This difference was recognized by I. B. Horner who translated *diṭṭhigato* as 'holding onto "speculative view".' *Diṭṭhigato* has also been translated as 'evil opinion.' On the translation of *diṭṭhigato*, see also Collins, *Selfless Persons*, 103f.

41 Spk I 208. A similar explanation is found in his commentary on a passage in the *Aṅguttara-nikāya: diṭṭhi hi bhikkhave pāpikā ti yasmā tassā puggalassa diṭṭhi pāpikā lāmakā* (Mp II 24).

42 M I 256–271; commentary at Ps II 305. The commentary on the *Mahātaṅhāsaṅkhaya-sutta* refers to the *Alagaddūpama-sutta* (M I 130–142), which takes up six wrong views; on the nature of the views refuted in the *Alagaddūpama-sutta*, see K. R. Norman, 'A note on *attā* in the *Alagaddūpama-sutta*,' in *Collected Papers*, 2:200–209.
43 M I 51; cf. M I 66
44 M I 497–501
45 M I 500
46 M II 228–238; Collins, *Selfless Persons*, 121–123.
47 M II 230–237
48 This happiness is detached (*nirāmisa*), free from the sense-pleasures, and the opposite of physical pleasure.
49 M II 237
50 M III 104–109
51 For more on the *jhānas*, see Chapter Two.
52 M III 105. The meditative stages discussed in the *Cūlasuññatā-sutta* are the eight levels of *jhāna* meditation. On *jhāna* meditation, see Paul J. Griffiths, 'Buddhist Jhāna: A Form-Critical Study,' *Religion* 13 (1983): 55–68; Paul J. Griffiths, 'Concentration or Insight: The Problematic of Theravāda Buddhist Meditation-Theory,' *The Journal of the American Academy of Religion* 44 (1981): 605–624; L. S. Cousins, 'Buddhist Jhāna: Its Nature and Attainment According to the Pāli Sources,' *Religion* 3 (1973): 115–131; and Winston L. King, *Theravāda Meditation: The Buddhist Transformation of Yoga* (University Park: Pennsylvania University State Press, 1980).
53 See also M I 134, 147, 260.
54 *anupādā vimokko ti* (M II 238).
55 *ayam kho sā bhikkhave majjhimā paṭipadā Tathāgatena abhisambuddhā cakkhukaranī ñāṇakaraṇī upasamāya abhiññā sambodhāya nibbānāya saṃvattati* (S V 421). This is a standard formula used throughout the canon. *Abhiññā* is a term which means further, or higher knowledges, and at some points refers to a specific set of transpersonal powers. Bhikkhu Bodhi and Gethin both translate the term as 'direct knowledge,' which could potentially be misleading when one considers that there is a technical distinction between indirect and direct analysis. I. B. Horner translated the term in this passage as 'super-knowledge.' *The Middle Length Discourses of the Buddha: A New Translation of the Majjhima-nikāya*, trans. Bhikkhu Ñāṇamoli and Bhikkhu Bodhi (Boston: Wisdom Publications, 1995), 935; *Middle Length Sayings*, 3:115. Gethin, *Buddhist Path*, 84.
56 S V 30
57 Spk III 133
58 M III 72. There is also *micchādiṭṭhi* which is the opposite of these qualities at M III 71. The same passage is found at M I 287, 401; III 22, 52; D I 55.
59 Bhikkhu Bodhi suggests that another difference between these two types of right view is that the first type consists of a 'conceptual comprehension of the four truths' and the second consists of a 'direct penetration' of the four truths. He presumably (but does not say so) bases his comments on Buddhaghosa's gloss of *dhammavicayasambojjhaṅgo* in this passage as 'having gotten the factor of enlightenment is investigation of the four-truths-*dhamma* (*catusaccadhamme*) (Ps IV 13). Bhikkhu Bodhi refers to a different passage in the *Majjhima-nikāya* where right view is said to consist of the four noble truths; this explanation of right view is found at S V 8–9; also at M I 46 ff., III 251f. (Bhikkhu Bodhi cites M III 251f.). *Middle Length Discourses*, 1322, n. 1103.

60 cf. Collins, *Selfless Persons*, 88–94.
61 M I 46–55 and Ps I 196
62 This notion of a fourfold path is discussed at greater length in Chapter Four, where I discuss Manné's analysis of the variations on the particular stages.
63 *sammādiṭṭhī ti yaṃ paṇḍitā devamanussā tesu tesu thānesu sammādassanaṃ vadanti, sabbam pi taṃ dvīhi padehi sankhipitvā pucchati* (Spk II 32); and *ettāvatā kho, kaccāna, sammādiṭṭhi hotī ti evaṃ satta-saññāya pahīnattā ettakena sammādassanaṃ nāma hoti ti missaka-sammādiṭṭhiṃ āha* (Spk II 34).
64 Ps IV 131 (on M III 71, the *Mahācattārīsaka-sutta*).
65 Ps II 307 and Ps IV 131
66 Ps II 401
67 Ps II 401
68 *Paññā viriyena diṭṭhiyā ti vipassanāpaññāya c'eva vipassanāsampayuttena kāyakacetasikaviriyena ca maggasammādiṭṭhiyā ca* (Mp IV 49).
69 *Diṭṭhiyā suppaṭividdhā ti atthato ca kāraṇato ca paññāya suppaṭividdhā* (Mp III 29, 170).
70 *Etaṃ yathābhūtaṃ sammappaññāya passato evam etāsaṃ diṭṭhīnaṃ pahānaṃ hoti* (M I 40).
71 Mp V 53
72 S V 11
73 S V 8–9; also at M I 46 ff., III 251.
74 Spk III 123–124
75 *Evam eva kho bhikkhave ariyasāvakasa diṭṭhisampannassa puggalassa abhisametāvino etad eva bahutaraṃ dukkhaṃ yad idam parikkhīṇam pariyādinnam appamattakam avasiṭṭhaṃ saṅkham pi na upeti upanidham pi an upeti kalabhāgam pi na upeti. purimaṃ dukkhakkhandham parikkhīṇam pariyādinnam upanidhāya yad idaṃ sattakkhattum paramatā. yo idaṃ dukkhan ti yathābhūtam pajānāti . . . la . . . ayaṃ dukkhanirodhagāminī paṭipadā ti yathābhūtam pajānāti* (S V 458–465, *passim*). Buddhaghoṣa does not comment on this passage.
76 M I 6–12
77 M I 9
78 M I 9
79 M I 299; S III 159, IV 260
80 S IV 175
81 M III 251; Ş V 8–9
82 M I 497–501
83 *athavā bhūtamattaṃ abhibhavitvā yathāsabhāvato agahetvā vattanato adhivuttiyo ti diṭṭhiyo vuccanti, ądhivuttīnaṃ padāni adhivuttipadāni, diṭṭhidīpakāni vacanāni ti attho; tesaṃ adhivuttipadānaṃ diṭṭhivohārānaṃ* (Mp I 18).
84 *Evaṃ vimuttacitto kho Aggivessana bhikkhu na kenaci saṃvadati na kenaci vivadati, yañ ca loke vuttaṃ tena voharati aparāmasan ti* (M I 500–501). The same phrase is found at S I 14 and D I 202. The latter passage is cited at Ps III 208.
85 M I 487. The phrase '*aññadiṭṭhikena aññkhantikena aññarucikena aññatravogena aññathācarivakena*' also appears at M II 43; D I 87, III 35.
86 M I 309–317
87 M I 313–315
88 M I 348, II 21; A I 27 (commentary at Mp II 23); D I 82; III 52. The commentary on D III 52 explains *micchādiṭṭhika* as one who does not give (alms) (*n'atthi dinnan*) (Sv III 839).
89 M III 207–215

90 A I 31; see also S II 153–154.
91 M I 313
92 M I 313. Buddhaghosa devotes his commentary on this passage to clarifying *somanassa* and *domanassa* and does not gloss either *micchādiṭṭhi* or *sammādiṭṭhi* (Ps II 376).
93 *Evaṃ me ettha hoti, evañ ca pana me etaṃ arahataṃ sutan ti* (M II 87). There is no commentary on this passage.
94 D III 70f.
95 Buddhaghosa defines one who holds wrong views as the one who does not believe in giving alms (Sv III 839, 853; also Ps I 202).
96 D III 207–271
97 D III 272–292
98 D III 246
99 D III 269
100 D III 286–290
101 D III 245
102 D III 269. The commentary explains that there are two roots for right view, *alobhā dosavasena* (Sv III 1051).
103 D III 287, 288, 291
104 *Diṭṭhisāmaññagato iminā pana padena kosambakasutte paṭhama-maggo kathito. Idha cattāro pi magga* (Sv III 1035). Elsewhere, Buddhaghosa glosses *diṭṭhisāmaññagato* as 'one who, having developed right view, resides' (*sammādiṭṭhi-bhāvaṃ upagato hutvā viharati*) (Ps II 401).
105 *Tathā vyāpādo micchādiṭṭhi lobha-moha-vasena dvi-mūlāti* (Sv III 1050).
106 Sv III 1036 (on D III 246). The same three wrong views are also explained at Ps IV 136: *Ahetuvādā ti 'n'atthihetu n'atthi paccayo sattānaṃ visuddhiyā' ti evam ādivādino. Akiriyavādā ti 'karoto na kirīyati pāpan' ti evam kiriyapaṭikkhepavādino. Natthikavādī ti 'n'atthi dinnan' ti ādivādino; te imesu tīsu pi dassanesu okkantaniyāmā ahesuṃ.* There are a number of parallel passages listed in the commentary for these terms, including the *Apaṇṇaka-sutta* where the Buddha explains that these views should be abandoned. See also Collins, *Sefless Persons*, 89.
107 D III 291
108 M I 40–46
109 M I 497–501
110 Douglas, *Purity and Danger*, 22–28. Frazer made this distinction as early as 1890.

CHAPTER TWO

Stories and a Symbol of the Buddha's Enlightenment

The fact is, most people in those neighborhoods we drove through, tryin' to live decent and they do it in part by living on symbols. Religious symbols, freedom symbols, legal symbols, and now holiday symbols. They are all but worthless at the bank, but sometimes black folks don't try to cash them there. Know what I mean?[1]

Derrick Bell (1992)

Introduction

As the content of the Buddha's first talk on *dhamma*, the four noble truths are recognized as perhaps the most important teaching of the Buddha.[2] The passages examined in this chapter reveal that when the four noble truths are regarded in the canon as the first teaching of the Buddha, they function as a view or doctrine that assumes a symbolic function. Where the four noble truths appear in the guise of a religious symbol in the *Sutta-piṭaka* and the *Vinaya-piṭaka* of the Pāli canon, they represent the enlightenment experience of the Buddha and the possibility of enlightenment for all Buddhists within the cosmos. The four noble truths are a important part of the Buddha's biography that is recorded partially in the Pāli *Tipiṭaka* as well as in the *Tripiṭaka* recorded in Buddhist Hybrid Sanskrit. All of these features with which the four noble truths are associated show us that the four noble truths were at the center of a specific set of teaching about the Buddha, his teachings, and the path.

However, the four noble truths do not always appear in stories of the Buddha's enlightenment where we might expect to find them. This feature may indicate that the four noble truths emerged into the canonical tradition at a particular point and slowly became recognized as the first teaching of the Buddha. Speculations about early and late teachings must be made relative to other passages in the Pāli canon because of a lack of supporting extratextual evidence. Nonetheless, it is still possible to suggest a certain historical development of the four noble truths within the Pāli canon. What we will find is a doctrine that came to be identified as the central teaching of the Buddha by the time of the commentaries in the fifth century C.E.

There are different grammatical forms in which the four noble truths appear throughout the canonical corpus; there is no one formula for the four noble truths. Even though the four noble truths do not appear in a single fixed grammatical form throughout the canon, it is possible to identify a limited number of established patterns or formulas with which the teaching was recorded and passed on. The pattern of presence and absence of the four noble truths within canonical accounts about the enlightenment of the Buddha, his decision to teach, and his first *dhamma* talk, makes it possible to discern that one strata of the Pāli canonical tradition considered the four noble truths to be an integral part of the Buddha's biography and that the commentator Buddhaghosa also recognized the four noble truths as perhaps the most important teaching of the Buddha by the fifth century C.E.

When the four noble truths appear in the stories of the Buddha's enlightenment they function differently than they do elsewhere in the canon. They serve both as a symbol of the Buddha's awakening and as the means for followers of the Buddha to cultivate the same religous experience. To identify the symbolic function of the four noble truths in the canon is to elicit the range of associations that the Theravāda canon establishes for the four noble truths; it is not to claim that the four noble truths are a symbol that evokes a dimension of human experience that can only be approached through symbols. The pattern and consistency of references to the four noble truths in these stories display a tightly organized conception of how the Buddha reached enlightenment, how he taught, how his followers became enlightened, and how the path to that enlightenment was configured. This pattern establishes a set of associated events that are evoked by the four noble truths when they function as a symbol.

In the Pāli canon, the Buddha's experience of enlightenment is fully described in three set passages in the *Nikāya*s of the *Sutta-piṭaka*: (1) the 'Teachings on Fear and Terror' (*Bhayabherava-sutta*), (2) the 'Teachings on the Noble Search' (*Ariyapariyesana-sutta*), and (3) the 'Sayings on the Truths' (*Sacca-saṃyutta*) that contain the *Dhammacakkappavattana-sutta*. To this list from the *Sutta-piṭaka*, we need to add the account of the Buddha's enlightenment found in (4) the *Mahāvagga* of the *Vinaya-piṭaka*. These passages parallel and diverge from each other at specific points. For example, the *Bhayabherava-sutta* contains the Buddha's own description of the three watches of the night and his realization of the four noble truths. It does not describe how the Buddha came to his enlightenment, nor does it describe how he decided to teach. Those details are found in the *Ariyapariyesana-sutta* and in the *Mahāvagga* version. The *Dhammacakkappavattana-sutta* on the four noble truths is found in the *Sacca-saṃyutta*

('Sayings on the Truths'), but it does not contain any discussion of how the Buddha arrived at his decision to teach the four noble truths; these details are again found in the *Ariyapariyesana-sutta* and in the *Mahāvagga*. The analysis of these interlocking passages shows that there are different versions of the Buddha's enlightement experience and different descriptions of what he taught in his first talk on *dhamma*. The four noble truths are arranged with primary reference to the Buddha's enlightenment and his first talk in the canonical passages; the commentaries insert the four noble truths into the canon in those places where the four noble truths are not explicitly mentioned.

Bhayabherava-sutta

The setting for this *sutta* is Jeta's Grove in Anāthapiṇḍika's monastery near Sāvitthī. Here, the Buddha responds to a question by a brahman who is called by his title of Jāṇussoni, which Buddhaghosa explains means 'chief priest' (*purohita*).[3] This Jāṇussoni asks the Buddha whether it is a distraction to meditate in the thick of the jungle; the Buddha replies that those who are not purified in body are, in fact, filled with fear and terror by the wild animals and the rustle of the wind in the trees. The Buddha explains that he did not walk, stand, or sit until he had subdued his fear of being alone in the thick of the jungle and that now he is no longer deluded: he is calm and his mind is focused. Then, he tells his audience about his experience of enlightenment, beginning with his entry into the first level of enstatic trance meditation (*jhāna*).

The *jhāna*s are a series of eight levels of meditation which one enters into by shutting out the distractions and disturbances of the senses, first from the outside and then from internal sources; Eliade called this type of inward meditation enstatic to distinguish it from the outward-directed ecstatic religious experiences.[4] The first four levels are called the *jhāna*s of form, and the second group of four are the *jhāna*s of the formless states. In the first *jhān*ic level, a practitioner is separated from desire (*kāma*) and negative states of mind (*akusalā dhammā*) and achieves and remains in a state that: has reasoning (*vitakko*) and deliberation (*vicāro*), emerges out of detachment (*vivekaja*), and involves both joy (*pīti*) and happiness (*sukhaṃ*).[5] The second *jhāna* eliminates reasoning and deliberation and develops inner tranquility or concentration (*samādhi*) and one-pointedness of mind (*cetaso ekodibhāva*). In the third *jhāna*, a practitioner becomes detached from joy but still experiences physical happiness. In the fourth *jhāna* joy, happiness, and sorrow are all left behind, and a practitioner resides in 'the purity of mindfulness called equanimity' (*upekhāsatiparisuddhi*). The fifth through eighth levels are, respectively, the spheres of infinite space (*ākāsāñcāyatanaṃ*), infinite consciousness (*viññāṇañcāyatanaṃ*), nothing at all (*ākiñcaññāyatanaṃ*), and neither recognition nor non-recognition (*nevasaññānāsaññāyatanaṃ*).[6] The *Mahāparinibbāna-sutta* describes how the Buddha rose from the first to the eighth *jhāna* and experienced the state of the cessation of recognition and sensation (*saññāvedayitanirodho*), descended to the first, and finally rose again to the fourth level, from which level he entered *parinibbāna*.[7]

In the *Bhayabherava-sutta*, the Buddha says that when he reached the fourth *jhāna*, he directed his memory to his previous births. His recollections, as he resided in the fourth *jhāna*, constituted the first knowledge that arose in him during the first watch of the night. The second knowledge during the middle watch was the memory of the passing and arising of all beings. The third and final knowledge that the Buddha realized during the last watch was the knowledge of the four noble truths and the destruction of the corruptions (*āsavā*) by understanding the corruptions (*āsavā*) in accordance with the four noble truths.

> I understood as it really is: 'this is pain,' 'this the arising of pain,' 'this is the ending of pain,' 'this is the way leading to the ending of pain.' I understood as it really is: 'these are the corruptions,' 'this the arising of the corruptions,' 'this is the ending of the corruptions,' 'this is the way leading to the ending of the corruptions.'[8]

The description of the third watch concludes with a standardized refrain:

> This, brahman, was the third knowledge I attained in the last watch of the night; insight arose, knowledge arose, wisdom arose, higher knowledge arose, and light arose even as I remained alert, ardent, and self-determined.[9]

After describing the three watches and his experience of the first four *jhānic* stages, the Buddha tells the Jāṇussoni that there are two reasons to meditate in the jungle: pleasant abiding here and now, and out of compassion for future generations. The *sutta* concludes with the Jāṇussoni's acceptance into the *saṅgha* as a lay follower.

The four noble truths are an integral part of this *sutta* and the Buddha's description of his enlightenment. The grammatical form of the four noble truths in this passage is that of the basic set, with the properly gendered pronouns, and the adjectives 'noble truths' are not used. (The basic set is the one that Norman identified as the correct form and suggested that this was the earliest form in which the four noble truths appeared in the Pāli canonical tradition.) The passages that parallel the *Bhayabherava-sutta* have the same grammatical form: the *Mahāsaccaka-sutta*,[10] The *Suttavibhaṅga* of the *Vinaya-piṭaka*,[11] and the *Aṅguttara-nikāya*.[12] The description of the third knowledge – the destruction of the corruptions according to the truths – is found *verbatim* in the *Chabbisodhana-sutta*.[13] The same description of the third knowledge is found in the *Aṅguttara-nikāya*, but it describes how a person who has entered into the *jhāna*s is able to eradicate the corruptions – not the Buddha himself.[14]

The *Bhayabherava-sutta* and its parallel passages give one version of how the Buddha became enlightened: the story of the three watches, the role of the *jhāna*s, and the part that the four noble truths played in the last of the three periods of the night during which the Buddha was enlightened This is a classical part of the story of how the Buddha reached enlightenment. However, not all versions of the Buddha's biography agree with that of the *Bhayabherava-sutta*. There are variations on what the Buddha realized during the three watches of the night; further, the three watches themselves are missing in other stories of how the Buddha became enlightened.

Ariyapariyesana-sutta

The setting for this *sutta* is the same as that for the *Bhayabherava-sutta*: Jeta's Grove in Anāthapiṇḍika's monastery near Sāvitthī. The Buddha went out for his alms-round and upon his return said to Ānanda that they would go to the Eastern Park, to the palace of Migāra's mother for the day. Ānanda had already been approached by other monastics who had asked to hear the Buddha give a *dhamma* talk, and so they went to the palace of Migāra's mother. The Buddha waited until another group of *bhikkhu*s had finished their discussion on *dhamma* and then began his talk on the two searches or quests (*pariyesanā*): one that belongs to the noble ones and one that does not. The search of the noble ones (*ariyapariyesana*) is the quest of 'one who is subject to birth, who knows the danger in that which is equally subject to birth, who searches for *nibbāna* where there is no birth [and is] the greatest respite from efforts.'[15] This person – who knows the dangers of aging, illness, death, grief, and stain – searches for *nibbāna* 'where there is no old age' (*ajaraṃ*), 'where there is no illness' (*abyādhiṃ*), 'where there is no death' (*amataṃ*), 'where there is no grief,' (*asokaṃ*), and 'where there is no stain' (*asaṃkiliṭṭhaṃ*).[16] This *sutta* provides a different description of the Buddha's search for *dhamma* that leads to the ending of pain, one in which the four noble truths are not mentioned.[17] The description of the goal of the search of the noble ones – the search for *nibbāna* where there is no birth, and so on – is the same one used to explain the first truth in the *Dhammacakkappavattana-sutta*, but the four noble truths themselves do not appear in the *Ariyapariyesana-sutta*. The commentaries supply the missing four noble truths.

The narrative of the *Ariyapariyesana-sutta* begins with the Buddha's description of how he left his home, put on yellow robes, and met Āḷāra the Kālāma. The Buddha tells his audience how he studied with Āḷāra the Kālāma and that he arrived at the same knowledge that Āḷāra the Kālāma had – the knowledge of the eighth *jhāna*, the sphere of nothing at all (*ākiñcaññāyatanaṃ*). The Buddha realized, however, that this *dhamma* led only to the plane of nothing at all, not to *nibbāna*.

> Then it occured to me, *bhikkhus*: this *dhamma* does not lead to weariness, dispassion, stopping, calm, higher knowledge, enlightenment, or to *nibbāna*, but only as far as the plane of nothing at all. So, *bhikkhus*, I disregarded and turned away from this *dhamma*, not getting enough from this *dhamma*.[18]

This description of the path to *nibbāna* as leading to weariness and so on is common and connotes the desired state of being tired literally of the world and desiring escape.[19] The teachings of Āḷāra the Kālāma, the Buddha concluded, led only to the plane of nothing at all and no further. His next teacher was Uddaka, Rāma's son, who taught the plane of neither cognition nor non-cognition (*nevasaññāsaññāyatanaṃ pavedesi*); the Buddha turned away from that *dhamma* for the same reason.[20] As his search continued, the Buddha found a grove near the Nerañjarā River, with a village nearby, and sat down thinking that 'this is appropriate for [my] endeavor.'[21] The text of the *sutta* tells us that the Buddha described his enlightenment with the same passage as he used to describe the noble search: knowing the dangers of aging, illness, death, grief, and stain, the Buddha sought *nibbāna* 'where there is no birth,' 'where there is no old age,' 'where there is no illness' 'where there is no death,' 'where there is no grief' and 'where there is no stain.'[22] The *sutta* explains that the Buddha attained *nibbāna* and proclaimed:

> Knowledge and vision arose in me: release is unshakable for me, this is the last birth, there is no more becoming.[23]

As he said this, the *sutta* continues, the Buddha explained that he knew that he had found a *dhamma* that was difficult to understand and that it would be tiring if he were to teach it to those who were not able to understand.

> Then it occurred to me, *bhikkhus*: This *dhamma* that I have reached is profound, hard to see, hard to understand, calm, sublime, beyond superficial reasoning, subtle, and may be known by the learned.[24]

The only mention of the four noble truths in the commentary is found at this point in the *sutta*, when Buddhaghosa explains that *dhamma* refers to the four noble truths.[25] The Buddha continues his talk, saying that humans (*pajā*) delight in sensual pleasure, are delighted by sensual pleasure, and rejoice in sensual pleasure.[26] For such humans, he explains, dependent arising is difficult to see and the calming of the activities, renouncing attachment and destroying craving, dispassion, stopping, and *nibbāna* are equally hard to understand. Thinking of how difficult it would be to teach this, and how frustrating it would be for people to not understand, the *sutta* says that the Buddha was not particularly inclined to teach *dhamma*. At this point in the *sutta*, Brahmā Sahampati appeared to him, saying that the world was lost because the Buddha had not put forth much effort and does not teach *dhamma*.[27]

The exchange between the Buddha and Brahmā Sahampati is found at three other points in the canon: in the *Mahāvagga*,[28] in the *Brahmā-saṃyutta*,[29] and in the *Mahāpadāna-sutta*.[30] In the latter, the Buddha is not Gautama but Vipassin, a Buddha who was the first Buddha and who reigned ninety-one eons ago.[31] Structurally, however, the sequence is identical in all four versions. The commentaries on each of these versions define *dhamma* as the four truths (*catu-sacca-dhamma*), with the exception of the *Mahāvagga*.[32] This identification of *dhamma* as the four noble truths in the commentaries shows that Buddhaghosa saw the four noble truths as connected closely with the first teachings of the Buddha where the canonical account of the noble search did not.

The *Ariyapariyesana-sutta* tells us that the Buddha responded to Brahmā Sahampati's entreaty to teach *dhamma* once he saw that there were beings in the world who would understand his teachings. He surveyed the world with the 'eye of an awakened one' (*buddhacakkhu*) and saw:

> As I was looking at the world, *bhikkhus*, with the eye of an awakened one I saw beings with little dust in their eyes, with a lot of dust in their eyes, with sharp faculties, with dull faculties, of good qualities, of bad qualities, those who are easy to teach, and those who are hard to teach, and very few who dwell seeing because of fear of things to be avoided and of the other world.[33]

The text compares the Buddha's seeing of these different kinds of beings to different colored lotuses growing in various ponds: 'Even as in a pond of blue lotuses or in a pond of red lotuses or in a pond of white lotuses, a few red and blue and white lotuses are born in the water, grow in the water, do not rise above the water but thrive while entirely immersed.' Other lotuses reach the surface and still others rise above the water. The Buddha says that he saw the many different kinds of beings in the world in the same way. Realizing that there were beings in the world who would understand his teachings, the Buddha decided to teach, and Brahmā Sahampati left. The Buddha then thought about to whom he should first teach what he had learned.

The *Ariyapariyesana-sutta* describes how the Buddha considered his two teachers, Āḷāra the Kālāma and Uddaka, Rāma's son, but realized that they had recently passed away; the Buddha then decided to find the group of five renouncers who had accompanied him earlier.[34] The group of five companions are not mentioned earlier in this *sutta*, nor are they mentioned in other versions of this story in the *Saṃyutta-nikāya*[35] or in the *Mahāvagga* of the *Vinaya-piṭaka*.[36] With his divine eye (*dibbacakkhu*) he saw that the group of five were residing at Isipatana, and he set out to find them. On the way, he met an ascetic named Upaka, who asked the Buddha who his teacher was. The *sutta* says that the Buddha replied in verse that he knows for himself and that he is on his way to turn the wheel of *dhamma*.[37] When the Buddha says that he 'goes to beat the drum of that which does not die' in the last stanza of his answer, the phrase refers to the popular image of making an announcement by walking through the city streets beating a drum to gain attention.[38] Upaka, the *sutta* says, shook his head, wished the Buddha well, and left down another road. As the Buddha approached his five former companions, they first shunned him, rejecting him because he had broken his fast. The Buddha, however, spoke to them about the nature of a *tathāgata*.

> I, *bhikkhus*, am a fully enlightened one, a *tathāgata*. Listen, *bhikkhus*, that which does not die has been found; I (will) instruct, I (will) teach *dhamma*. Practicing what has been taught, by realizing here in this world by your own direct knowledge you will quickly enter and reside in the highest goal of the *brahmacariya*, the reason for which young men of good families rightly go forth from the home into homelessness.[39]

The five ask the Buddha how it was that he came to such knowledge when he lives a life of abundance, observing that he did not arrive at it by practicing austerities. The Buddha explains that he does not live in abundance, and he repeats that he has found the deathless and the reason for taking the robes. The Buddha asks the group if he has ever spoken to them like this before, and they reply that he has not. Eventually, the Buddha was able to convince the group.

At this point, the *sutta* says that three of the five monks made rounds for food, while the Buddha taught the remaining two. Then, the two went begging for food while the Buddha taught the remaining three, so that all five monks were duly instructed. As a result of the Buddha's teachings, the *sutta* continues, the five followers attained the same state of *nibbāna* that is without birth, aging, decay, death, sorrow, and stain as did the Buddha. Like the Buddha, the monks acknowledged their attainment with the phrase: 'Then knowledge and insight arose in me, the release of my mind was unshakable; this is the last birth and there is no more becoming.'[40] The text makes it clear that the Buddha's teachings led to this knowledge:

> Then, *bhikkhus*, I enjoined and instructed the group of five *bhikkhus*, and, being subject to birth themselves, knowing the dangers in that which is equally subject to birth, searching for *nibbāna* where there is no birth and which is the greatest respite from efforts, they reached *nibbāna*.[41]

After the five companions attained the same experience as the Buddha, the *sutta* provides an analysis of the five strands of sensual pleasures (*pañca kāmaguṇā*), which Buddhaghosa explains belong to the path that is not noble. The Buddha explains that those who enjoy these strands of sensual pleasures and are trapped by them are subject to Māra, but those who enjoy the strands of sensual pleasure and are not infatuated by them are not trapped by Māra. The metaphor of being trapped by or outwitting Māra in the search for *nibbāna* continues throughout the enumeration of the eight *jhāna* levels which conclude the *Ariyapariyesana-sutta*.

In comparison with the *Bhayabherava-sutta*, the Buddha does not explain that he entered the four *jhāna*s when he was enlightened, nor does he explain what he experienced in terms of dependent arising or the four noble truths. Neither does the Buddha make any reference to three watches. There is a reference to the *jhāna*s in the commentary, where Buddhaghosa explains that of the two sorts of talks (*dhamma* and the noble silence or silence of a noble one, *ariyo vā tuṇhībhāvo*) recommended by the Buddha in the introductory portions of this *sutta*, the silence of a noble one is actually the second *jhāna*.[42] Buddhaghosa also inserts the four noble truths in his explanation of the *dhamma* that the Buddha said that he realized during his conversation with Brahmā Sahampati. There are two other references in the commentary to events that are narrated in the *Dhammacakkappavattana-sutta*; the first is to identify Koṇḍañña by the name given to him by the Buddha: 'Koṇḍañña who Knows.'[43] This is a reference to the fact that Koṇḍañña is the first one to cultivate the *dhamma* eye, and thus he is the first person in the world to experience *nibbāna* as a result of the Buddha's teachings. Buddhaghosa's second reference is to the turning of the *dhamma* wheel. When the Buddha says in this *sutta* that he was able to convince the five companions of the truth of his teachings, Buddhaghosa explains that the Buddha gave the *sutta* on the turning of the *dhamma* wheel that brought about Koṇḍañña's full knowledge of the body after he himself had known (literally 'caused to know') the majesty of a buddha.[44] The commentary thus places this *sutta* into a larger cosmological context by explaining the significance of the Deer Park at Isipatana where the Buddha spoke to the five renouncers and when the Buddha first wondered about to whom he should first speak about *dhamma*. The commentary presumes that the audience is familiar with the *Dhammacakkappavattana-sutta* and reminds us that the *dhamma* realized by the Buddha consisted of the four noble truths, but it does not belabor the point in any way.

The absence of the four noble truths from the *Ariyapariyesana-sutta* is unusual. An indication of how often scholars assume that the four noble truths are always found in all of the stories of the Buddha's enlightenment lies in an error made by Professor Étienne Lamotte, who asserted that the Buddha did teach the four noble truths to his companions in this *sutta*, when, in fact, the Buddha did not.[45] Contrary to our expectations, the *Ariyapariyesana-sutta* shows that certain redactors of the canon conceived of the Buddha's act of teaching without the four noble truths. The Buddha's injunctions to the five companions, his teaching in accordance with what he himself realized, and the fact that his companions reached the same *nibbāna* as he did all fit with other passages on the Buddha's teachings. The middle portion of this *sutta* is identical with the sequence in the *Mahāvagga* of the *Vinaya-piṭaka* which describes the Buddha's conversation with Brahmā Sahampati and his decision to teach *dhamma*. The *Ariyapariyesana-sutta* provides us with a different description of what the Buddha experienced during his enlightenment, what he taught, and what others should search for: *nibbāna* where there is no birth, no old age, no illness, no death, and no grief. The path to *nibbāna* is not defined in this *sutta* in terms of the four noble truths, although we have seen that Buddhaghosa inserts the reference into his commentary.[46]

Dhammacakkappavattana-sutta

In contrast to the absence of the four truths in the *Ariyapariyesana-sutta* and the presence of the doctrine in the *Bhayabherava-sutta* and its parallel passages detailing the three watches, the four noble truths are the pre-eminent subject of the *Dhammacakkappavattana-sutta*.[47] The *dhamma*-talk is found in both the *Mahāvagga* of the *Vinaya-piṭaka* and the *Saṃyutta-nikāya*, where it is the second chapter of the section on the *Sacca-saṃyutta*. The biographical details about the Buddha's search for enlightenment are not found in the *Saṃyutta-nikāya* version, and no reference is made to how the Buddha gained enlightenment. The talk stands on its own in the *Saṃyutta-nikāya*, in the context of other teachings on the truths.

> Thus did I hear. One time, the Blessed One was staying in the Deer Park at Isipatana near Bārāṇasī.
>
> There the Blessed One spoke to a group of five *bhikkhus*: There are, *bhikkhus*, two extremes which should not be followed by those who have gone forth. What two?
>
> The low, common practice of clinging to happiness through pleasure in desire that belongs to the ordinary person, not to the noble ones, and that is not worth pursuing; and the practice of exhausting oneself that is pain(ful), that does not belong to the noble ones, and that is not worth pursuing. The middle way, fully realized by the Tathāgata, does not lead to either of these extremes, *bhikkhus*, but does lead to insight, knowledge, calm, higher knowledge, enlightenment, and nibbāna.
>
> And which one, *bhikkhus*, is the middle way, fully realized by the *Tathāgata*, that leads to insight, knowledge, calm, higher knowledge, enlightenment, and nibbāna? This is the eightfold path of the noble ones which is: right view, right intention, right speech, right action,

right livelihood, right effort, right mindfulness, and right concentration. This, *bhikkhu*s, is the middle way, fully realized by the *Tathāgata*, that leads to insight, knowledge, calm, higher knowledge,[48] enlightenment, and *nibbāna*.

This, *bhikkhu*s, is the noble truth that is pain. Birth is pain; old age is pain; illness is pain; death is pain; sorrow and grief; physical and mental suffering, and disturbance are pain. Association with things not liked is pain, separation from desired things is pain; not getting what one wants is pain; in short, the five aggregates of grasping are pain.

This, *bhikkhu*s, is the noble truth that is the arising of pain. This is craving that leads to rebirth, is connected with pleasure and passion and finds pleasure in this or that; that is, craving for desire, existence, and the fading away of existence.[49]

This, *bhikkhu*s, is the noble truth that is the ending of pain. This is the complete fading away and ending of that very craving, giving it up, renouncing it, releasing it, and letting go.

This, *bhikkhu*s, is the noble truth that is the way leading to the ending of pain. This is the eightfold path of the noble ones: right view, right intention, right speech, right action, right livelihood, right effort, right mindfulness, and right concentration.

Thinking, *bhikkhu*s, 'the noble truth that is pain,' insight arose, knowledge arose, wisdom arose, higher knowledge arose, and light arose in me concerning proper things of which I had not heard before. Then again thinking 'the noble truth that is pain,' should be known completely, insight arose, knowledge arose, wisdom arose, higher knowledge arose, and light arose in me concerning proper things of which I had not heard before. Again thinking 'the noble truth that is pain,' has been known completely, insight arose, knowledge arose, wisdom arose, higher knowledge arose, and light arose in me concerning proper things of which I had not heard before.

Thinking, *bhikkhu*s, 'the noble truth that is the arising of pain,' insight arose, knowledge arose, wisdom arose, higher knowledge arose, and light arose in me concerning proper things of which I had not heard before. Then again thinking 'the noble truth that the arising of pain' should be given up, insight arose, knowledge arose, wisdom arose, higher knowledge arose, and light arose in me concerning proper things of which I had not heard before. Again thinking 'the noble truth that is the arising of pain' has been given up, insight arose, knowledge arose, wisdom arose, higher knowledge arose, and light arose in me concerning proper things of which I had not heard before.

Thinking, *bhikkhus*, 'the noble truth that is the ending of pain,' insight arose, knowledge arose, wisdom arose, higher knowledge arose, and light arose in me concerning proper things of which I had not heard before. Then again thinking I should realize 'the noble truth that is the ending of pain' for myself, insight arose, knowledge arose, wisdom arose, higher knowledge arose, and light arose in me concerning proper things of which I had not heard before. Again thinking I have realized 'the noble truth that is the ending of pain' for myself, insight arose, knowledge arose, wisdom arose, higher knowledge arose, and light arose in me concerning proper things of which I had not heard before.

Thinking, *bhikkhus*, 'the noble truth that is the way leading to the ending of pain,' insight arose, knowledge arose, wisdom arose, higher knowledge arose, and light arose in me concerning proper things of which I had not heard before. Then again thinking 'the noble truth that is the way leading to the ending of pain' should be developed, insight arose, knowledge arose, wisdom arose, higher knowledge arose, and light arose in me concerning proper things of which I had not heard before. Again thinking 'the noble truth that is the way leading to the ending of pain' has been developed, insight arose, knowledge arose, wisdom arose, higher knowledge arose, and light arose in me concerning proper things of which I had not heard before.

As long as I had not completely purified these four noble truths according to the three parts and twelve modes just as they were and with knowledge and insight, *bhikkhus*, I was not fully enlightened with the proper and highest enlightenment in the world with gods, with Māras, with Brahmās, with renouncers, brahmans, and descendents, with gods and human beings: I acknowledged this.

But when I had completely purified these four noble truths according to the three parts and twelve modes just as they were and with knowledge and insight, *bhikkhus*, I was fully enlightened with the proper and highest enlightenment in the world with gods, with Māras, with Brahmās, with renouncers, brahmans, and descendents, with gods and human beings: I acknowledged this. Then knowledge and insight arose in me, the release of my heart was unshakable; this is my last birth and there is no more existence.

The Blessed One said this. Pleased, the group of five *bhikkhus* was delighted with the Blessed One's speech. While this discourse was

> being given, *dhamma*-eye, dustless and stainless, arose in the venerable Koṇḍañña: whatever has the nature of arising, all that has the nature of ending.
>
> When the Blessed One turned the *dhamma*-wheel in this way, the gods of the earth made a loud noise: the *dhamma*-wheel has been turned by the Blessed One in the Deer Park at Isipatana near Bārāṇasī, and cannot be turned back by any renouncer, brahman, god, Māra or Brahmā or by anyone in the world.
>
> Hearing the noise of the gods of the earth, the four divine kings (*cātummahārājikā*) made a noise: the *dhamma*-wheel has been turned by the Blessed One in the Deer Park at Isipatana near Bārāṇasī, and cannot be turned back by any renouncer, brahman, god, Māra or Brahmā or by anyone in the world.
>
> Hearing the noise of the *cātummahārājikā* gods, the thirty-three gods, *yāmā*, *tusitā*, *nimmānaratī*, *paranimmitta-vasavatti*, and *brahma-kāyikā* made a noise: the *dhamma*-wheel has been turned by the Blessed One in the Deer Park at Isipatana near Banaras, and cannot be turned back by any renouncer, brahman, god, Māra or Brahmā or by anyone in the world.
>
> At that moment, at that second, at that instant the noise rose as far as the Brahmā world; the ten thousand worlds trembled, shook, and quaked and a immeasurable great light that surpassed the divine majesty of the gods became visible in the world.
>
> Then the Blessed One breathed these solemn words: 'Kondanna knows, Kondanna truly knows.' So it was that venerable Koṇḍañña was named 'Koṇḍañña who Knows.'[50]

This *sutta* contains the definition of the four noble truths and their most common formula that Norman calls the introduction set: the noble truth (that is) pain (*dukkham ariyasaccaṃ*), the noble truth (that is) the arising of pain (*dukkhasamudayaṃ ariyasaccaṃ*), the noble truth (that is) the ending of pain (*dukkhanirodhaṃ ariyasaccaṃ*), and the noble truth (that is) the way leading to the ending of pain (*dukkhanirodhagāminī paṭipadā ariyasaccaṃ*). The enlightenment and gerundival sets are also found in this *sutta*. The enlightenment set is this formula, repeated for each of the four truths: 'Thinking, *bhikkhus*, 'the noble truth that is pain,' insight arose, knowledge arose, wisdom arose, complete knowledge arose, and light arose in me concerning proper things of which I had not heard before.' The gerundival set follows immediately after the enlightenment set and is also repeated for each of the four truths, but with gerundives for each truth:

> Then again thinking 'the noble truth that is pain,' should be known completely, insight arose, knowledge arose, wisdom arose, higher knowledge arose, and light arose in me concerning proper things of which I had not heard before. Again thinking 'the noble truth that is pain,' has been known completely, insight arose, knowledge arose, wisdom arose, higher knowledge arose, and light arose in me concerning proper things of which I had not heard before.

The introduction set, enlightenment set, and gerundival set each wrongly employ the neuter pronoun for each of the four truths; and, as I discussed in the Introduction, Norman's analysis shows that the syntactical compound of 'noble' and 'truth' led the redactors to wrongly divide the compound, which led them to employ the incorrectly gendered pronouns for the 'arising' (*samudayo*), 'ending' (*nirodho*), and 'way' (*paṭipadā*). These grammatical errors indicate that the four truths were probably added after the earliest version of this *sutta*.[51]

Dukkha is the first of the four noble truths, and it is defined in this *sutta* (where it was not in the *Bhayabherava-sutta*). *Dukkha* (pain) is birth, old age, disease, and death. The following line, that pain is 'sorrow and grief, mental distress and physical distress, and unrest is pain' expands on the sorts of things which are classified as pain: sorrow (*soka*), grief (*parideva*), pain (*dukkha*), physical and mental distress (*dukkhadomanassa*),[52] and unrest (*upāyāssa*).[53] The last line concludes the definition: 'Association with things not liked is pain, separation from desired things is pain; not getting what one wants is pain; in short, the five aggregates of grasping are pain.' The last phrase, the five aggregates of grasping are the *pañc' upādānakkhandhā*, in which *upādāna* means grasping or holding on (it also means, more literally, fuel or provision) and *khandhā* refers to a mass or accumulation, rendered here as 'aggregate.' They are: the aggregate of holding onto the body (*rūpūpādānakkhandho*), feelings (*vedanūpādānakkhandho*), perceptions (*saññūpādānakkhandho*), formations (*saṃkhārūpādānakkhandho*), and consciousness (*viññāṇūpādānakkhandho*).[54] Taken together, these five aggregates of grasping represent the various ways that people come to the conclusion that there is an independent and permanent self or an 'I.' And all of these ways – clinging to the body, feelings, perceptions, volition, and consciousness – are pain. In other words, the sentences describing *dukkha* cover a variety of possible kinds of pain, from bodily pain to the mental anguish which results from clinging to the idea that an 'I' exists.

The second truth is the 'arising of pain' (*dukkhasamudayo*), which is further explained as 'craving' or 'thirst,' (*taṇhā*); the third truth is the 'ending of pain' (*dukkhanirodho*). There are three kinds of craving enumerated in this passage: craving for desire (*kāmataṇhā*), craving for existence (*bhavataṇhā*), and craving for existence to fall away (*vibhavataṇhā*).[55] The complete and absolute ending of craving is the solution to the problem of pain: 'The ending of that craving, without any passion remaining; abandoning it, surrendering it, releasing it and releasing all pleasure in it'. *Samudayo* (arising) and *nirodho* (ending) are opposing terms; this is evident not only from definition of the four noble truths in the *sutta* above but also from the formulaic expression of the realization which arose first in Koṇḍañña: 'Whatever has the nature of arising, all that has the nature of ending' (*yaṃ kiñci samudaya-dhammaṃ sabban taṃ nirodhadhamman ti*).[56] This phrase that describes Koṇḍañña's enlightenment is one of the more familiar phrases throughout the canon.

The fourth truth is the 'way leading to the ending of pain' (*dukkhanirodhagāminī paṭipadā*) and consists of the noble eightfold path. The range of meanings for *paṭipadā* include path, way, means, method, mode of progress, practice, or course. It is often taken as a synonym for *magga* (path).[57] The significance of the term is that it carries a sense of pragmatism and direction: it is the practice or means which leads to the ending of pain. The means are the eight steps of right view (*sammādiṭṭhi*), intention (*sammāsaṅkappo*), speech (*sammāvācā*), action (*sammākammanto*), livelihood (*sammājīvo*), effort (*sammāvāyāmo*), mindfulness (*sammāsati*), and concentration (*sammāsamādhi*).

Each of these steps are explained at different places in the canon and commentaries.[58] The commentator Buddhaghosa followed one canonical arrangement in the *Majjhima-nikāya* which classified the eightfold path into three stages of virtue (*sīlaṃ*), concentration (*samādhi*), and wisdom (*paññā*), with right speech, action, and livelihood grouped under virtue (*sīlaṃ*), right effort, mindfulness, and concentration under concentration (*samādhi*), and right view and intention under wisdom (*paññā*).[59] The progress through these eight stages is intended to be interdependent instead of linear; for example, the remaining seven steps are occasionally listed as requisites for right concentration.[60] While descriptions of the eightfold path may vary, the fourth truth remains the means or the way which leads to the ending of pain. The fourth truth is not always explained, but when it is, it is consistently explained in terms of the eightfold path. However, the four noble truths are not associated with measurable levels of path attainment. Even though the eightfold path is the way to *nibbāna*, the results that a practitioner might expect are not often defined explicitly. This point is taken up at length in Chapter Five.

There are several features of the *Dhammacakkappavattana-sutta* that set it apart from other stories about how the Buddha became enlightened: knowing the four truths by the threefold and the twelvefold ways, Koṇḍañña's awakening, and the subsequent turning of the wheel of *dhamma*.

The Buddha described his experience of enlightenment here in a way that is unique in the Pāli canon. The Buddha explains in this *sutta* that he had to realize them according to the three parts (*tiparivaṭṭaṃ*) and the twelve modes (*dvādasākāraṃ*). The three parts are composed of (1) an initial recognition of the four truths, (2) an awareness that identifies them as something that should be learned (signified by a gerundival form of the verb), and (3) the knowledge that they have been mastered (denoted with a past participle). These three parts are applied to each of the four truths and the entire analysis is called the twelve modes. There are four verbs that describe how each truth is to be learned, one for each truth:

> 'the noble truth that "this is the way leading to the ending of pain" should be known completely/has been known completely (*pariññeyyaṃ/pariññātaṃ*)
>
> 'the noble truth that "this is the arising of pain" should be given up/ has been given up (*pahātabbaṃ/pahītaṃ*)
>
> 'the noble truth that "this is the ending of pain" should be realized for oneself/has been realized for oneself (*sacchikātabbaṃ sacchikataṃ*)
>
> 'the noble truth that "this is the way leading to the ending of pain" should be developed/has been developed (*bhāvitabbaṃ/bhāvataṃ*).[61]

The three parts and twelve modes leads to 'seeing the truths as they really are,' to full enlightenment, and to the ending of the cycle of rebirth. This threefold and twelvefold analysis is not foundational throughout the canon in the same way as are the four noble truths themselves.

The cosmological events that unfold in the *Dhammacakkappavattana-sutta* are signficant. The turning of the wheel of *dhamma* and the fact that various *deva*s of the heavens as well as the hells recognized the significance of the event set this *sutta* apart from other points in the canon where the four truths appear. The gods who witness this event – the gods of the earth, the four divine kings, and so on – occupy the deva worlds; the list of gods is found in later texts as the list of gods who are born into their divine state (*upapattidevā*) as opposed to conventional gods (*sammutidevā*) or beings who reach that state by virtue of their purity, such as *arahat*s or Buddhas (*visuddhidevā*).[62] The list of gods denotes the gods who occupy, respectively, the six levels of the deva heavens, which in turn is the fifth level of the realm of desire (*kāmadhātu*). The realm of desire consists of the hells, which are usually located under the earth; the animals which are most often represented as occupying the water; the pretas which are either under the surface of the earth or just on top of it; and human beings who live on the continents of the earth. The devā heavens are located above the earth but below the Brahmā heavens which occupy the realm of form (*rūpadhātu*) The sound that reached as far as the Brahmā worlds (the *Brahmakāyikā* gods occupy the first of the Brahmā heavens), then, echoed throughout the realm of desire (*kāmadhātu*) and reached the realm of form (*rūpadhātu*).[63]

The noise (*saddaṃ*) that reached into the Brahmā worlds is akin to a particular kind of cosmological uproar (*kolāhalāni*), which is heard throughout the worlds of form at five specific points in time. The uproar marks the announcement of five specific events: the end of an age (*kappa*-), the establishment of a world-king (*cakkavatti*-), a Buddha (*buddha*-), a Buddha's pronouncement of something auspicious or favorable (*mangala*-), and the point when a *bhikkhu* asks the Blessed One about the highest wisdom (*moneyya*-).[64]

The commentary explains the significance of this *dhamma* talk in cosmological terms. 'The Deer Park at Isipatana,' Buddhaghosa begins, 'is so-named because it is safe to give gifts to the animals in the wood.'[65] He says that the park is also named Isipatana because it is at this place where all-knowing seers (*isiyo*) both descend from Anotatta Lake to gather for *uposatha* and rise up to fly to Gandamādana Mountain. Isipitana is the place where all Buddhas give their first *dhamma* talks, as in the *Mahāpadāna-sutta*, where Vipassin Buddha (the first Buddha) gave his first talk on *dhamma*. Isipatana is a place in the Buddhist cosmology that links the earth with the heavens.

The moment at which the wheel of *dhamma* is turned occurs when Koṇḍañña develops his eye of *dhamma* and becomes a stream-enterer. This is the point at which the Buddha's teaching bears fruit. The succession of events that begins with the Buddha's decision to seek his own enlightenment, the moment of his enlightnment, his decision to teach, and his first *dhamma* talk, culminates with Koṇḍañña's enlightenment. The final events in this sequence – the Buddha's delivery of the four truths and Koṇḍañña's cultivation of the *dhamma*-eye – are repeated throughout the canon in various ways, and establish one pattern for how the four noble truths produce measurable results on the path. The *Dhammacakkappavattana-sutta* identifies the four noble truths as the content of what the Buddha realized during his enlightenment experience and makes clear that knowing this doctrine is the means for others to cultivate the same experience of awakening. In short, when Koṇḍañña realized the truth of the four truths, he too was awakened, and his enlightenment was witnessed by the gods and beings of the ten-thousand world systems as the moment at which the wheel of *dhamma* is irrevocably set in motion.

In each of the *sutta*s examined up to this point, there are three different portraits of the Buddha's enlightenment. The *Bhayabherava-sutta*, the *Ariyapariyesana-sutta*, and the *Dhammacakkappavattana-sutta* differ in terms of content as well as in the phrases used to describe the Buddha's enlightenment experience. In the descriptions of the three watches the *Bhayabherava-sutta* relates the story of how the Buddha entered into the first and then the fourth *jhāna*, where he contemplated his own previous existences and the past and future lives of all beings, and finally eradicated the corruptions by knowing them according to the four noble truths. While the *Dhammacakkappavattana-sutta* is devoted to the four truths, it does so with different ways of knowing them as well as different grammatical formulas; neither the three watches nor the *jhānas* make an appearance. After he had grasped the four noble truths, the Buddha recites the phrase found in the *Ariyapariyesana-sutta*, but not in the *Bhayabherava-sutta*: 'Then knowledge and vision arose in me, release is unshakable for me; this is my last birth, there is no more becoming.'[66] The *Ariyapariyesana-sutta* tells us that the Buddha described his experiences in terms of the noble search, having realized the dangers of those things which are subject to birth, decay, death, and so on; it makes no mention of the four noble truths. In the *Dhammacakkappavattana-sutta* and in the *Mahāpadāna-sutta* the cosmological imagery and description of the significance of the Buddha's first sermon accompany the four truths. What we have at this point is a series of interlocking narratives, each of which has at least one component in common with another narrative but none of which are identical to the others.

Mahāvagga

This section contains more references to the four noble truths than anywhere else in the *Vinaya-piṭaka*; they are mentioned only once in the *Suttavibhaṅgha*. There are three sections in the *Vinaya-piṭaka*: the *Suttavibhaṅga*, the *Khandaka*, and the *Parivāra*. The core of the *Suttavibhaṅga* is the *Pātimokkha* which contains the detailed rules for *bhikkhus* and *bhikkhunīs* in the *Mahāvibhaṅga* and *Bhikkhunīvibhaṅga*, respectively. The *Khandaka* is composed of two parts, the *Mahāvagga* and the *Cullavagga*, where the bulk of references to the four truths are found. The *Mahāvagga* and *Cullavagga* contains parts of the Buddha's biography as well as a number of rules which are arranged by topic within the context of the narrative of how the order of *bhikkhus* and *bhikkhunīs* came into existence. Both the *Mahāvagga* and the *Cullavagga* are assembled from various sources found within the Theravāda tradition as well as within the South Asian Buddhist milieu.[67]

The *Khandaka* and the *Suttavibhaṅga* embed the rules within stories about the Buddha's life and the lives of his followers to provide a context for understanding the circumstances in which the rules are thought to have been set down.[68] The third section, the *Parivāra*, is a lengthy appendix which summarizes much of the material found elsewhere in the *Vinaya-piṭaka*. Norman has speculated that the *Parivāra* may serve the same cataloguing function as the *mātikā* lists of the *Abhidhamma-piṭaka*, a point which is discussed further in Chapter Four.[69] In the *Vinaya-piṭaka*, the four noble truths appear most often in the *Mahāvagga* in the narrative of how the *saṅgha* (order) was established that begins with the biography of Gotama Buddha.

The *Mahāvagga* opens with the time that the Buddha spent sensing the joy that followed his enlightenment. He first stayed at Uruvelā under the Bodhi-tree for seven days, 'experiencing the happiness of freedom.'[70] At the end of those seven days the Buddha observed the chain of dependent arising, both directly and in the reverse, during each of the three watches of the night.[71] He moved on to the foot of a type of banyan tree, then to the base of a Mucalinda tree, spending seven days at each tree. Under the Mucalinda tree, the Buddha was protected from a thunderstorm by a snake king and, in response, gave a short talk on the greatest happiness (*paramaṃ sukhaṃ*). The Buddha moved to the base of another tree, a royal tree (*rājāyatana*) for another seven days. Two merchants, Tapussa and Bhallika, were told by a *devatā* (a female deity who was a relation in the past, Buddhaghosa explains) to take food to the Buddha. The Buddha had no alms-bowl in which to receive the offerings, and the four kings presented him with an alms-bowl made of rock crystal. (These are the same four divine kings [*cātummahārājikā*] who appear in the *Dhammacakkappavattana-sutta*. They are the first of seven kinds of *uppattidevā* – beings born as gods, not as kings, *arahat*s, or *buddha*s – who live in the heavens.) Having given the Buddha a type of rice cake and balls of honey in his new alms-bowl, the merchants became the first lay disciples to ask for admission into the order with the two-word formula: 'I take refuge in the Buddha' and 'I take refuge in the *dhamma*.' (This formula is known as the two-word formula in contrast to taking refuge with the three words of the *Buddha*, *dhamma*, and *saṅgha*). After the exchange with Tapussa and Bhallika, the Buddha continued on to another banyan tree.

This entire span of time is characterized in the *Mahāvagga* as the time when the Buddha was reluctant to teach *dhamma*. As the Buddha sits under the last tree, the passage depicts him as thinking about how difficult and complex *dhamma* is and how hard it would be if people did not understand his teachings.[72] In the midst of these contemplations, Brahmā Sahampati appeared from the Brahma world and appealed to the Buddha: 'Blessed One, may the Blessed One teach *dhamma*, may the one who goes well (*sugato*) teach *dhamma*; there are beings with few obstacles who, not hearing *dhamma*, are fading away, and who, hearing *dhamma*, would prosper.'[73] The Buddha acquiesced to this request after surveying the world with the vision (or eye) of an awakened one and seeing that, indeed, there were people who could learn what he had to teach. The exchange between Brahmā Sahampati and the Buddha is familiar; it is the same as that of the *Ariyapariyesana-sutta*.[74] Also as in that *sutta*, the Buddha's next concern is to whom he should first teach what he now knows. He decides that his five former companions would serve; and, as we have already seen, the five renouncers eventually recognized the Buddha's authority and listened to his first talk, which in the *Mahāvagga* is identical with that of the *Dhammacakkappavattana-sutta* in the *Saṃyutta-nikāya*.

Buddhaghosa explains that when Brahmā Sahampati uses the word *dhamma* in his appeal to the Buddha, *dhamma* means the four noble truths. His explanation makes the *Mahāvagga* consistent with the *Dhammacakkappavattana-sutta* in that the four noble truths are central in both accounts.[75] Again like the *Dhammacakkappavattana-sutta*, the *Mahāvagga* concludes with the Buddha's explanation of what he experienced, Koṇḍañña's cultivation of the same experience, and the turning of the wheel of *dhamma*:

> But when I had completely purified these four noble truths according to the three parts and twelve modes just as they were and with knowledge and insight, *bhikkhus*, I was fully enlightened with the proper and highest enlightenment in the world with gods, with Māras, with Brahmās, with renouncers, brahmans, and descendents, with gods and human beings: I acknowledged this. Then knowledge and insight arose in me, the release of my heart was unshakable; this is my last birth and there is no more existence. The Blessed One said this. Pleased, the group of five *bhikkhus* was delighted with the Blessed One's speech. While this discourse was being spoken, the undefiled, unstained dhamma-eye arose in the venerable Koṇḍañña: whatever has the nature of arising, all that has the nature of ending.
>
> When the Blessed One turned the *dhamma*-wheel in this way, the gods of the earth made a loud noise: the *dhamma*-wheel has been turned by the Blessed One in the Deer Park at Isipatana near Bārāṇasī and cannot be turned back by any renouncer, brahman, god, Māra or Brahmā or by anyone in the world.[76]

The remainder of the passage follows the *Dhammacakkappavattana-sutta* precisely, through the naming of Koṇḍañña as 'Koṇḍañña who Knows.' As Bareau noted, the consistency between these two versions of the Buddha's enlightenment is an indication that the redactors of the Theravāda canon probably brought the two accounts into agreement with each other at a relatively late point in the formation of the canon.[77] Léon Feer had already suggested in 1870 that the versions of the four noble truths found in the *sūtras* and *suttas* were derived from the *vinaya* rescensions in the larger body of Buddhist literature; Bareau's conclusion builds on this claim.[78]

The *Mahāvagga* version continues on beyond the point at which the *Dhammacakkappavattana-sutta* ends. After the cataclysmic turning of the *dhamma* wheel, Koṇḍañña requests ordination from the Buddha.

> Then the respected 'Koṇḍañña who Knows,' having seen *dhamma*, mastered *dhamma*, known *dhamma*, was immersed in *dhamma*, who was free from doubt, who had dispelled uncertainty, and who had

> gained complete confidence, not dependent upon others for the teachings of the teacher, said this to the Blessed One: 'May I, Blessed One, be received with the Blessed One; may I receive ordination (*upasampadā*)?'[79]

The Buddha responds with the standard acceptance:

> 'Come, *bhikkhus*,' the Blessed One said, '*Dhamma* is spoken well, live as a *brahamacariya* to bring about a proper ending of pain.' Thus he received (*upasampadā*) ordination from him who is respected.[80]

Buddhaghosa adds that this ordination meant that the *bhikkhus* had experienced the fruit of stream-winners, accompanied by the sounds of a large number of gods on the full moon in the month of Äsala (July–August).[81] Koṇḍañña sought and received the *upasampadā* ordination.

This ordination sequence is not found in the *Ariyapariyesana-sutta*, although that *sutta* explains that all five reached *nibbāna* and succeeded in their noble search; as we saw, Koṇḍañña is not singled out, there is no turning of the wheel of *dhamma*, nor is the eye of *dhamma* mentioned. The *Mahāvagga* provides more detail, describing how the Buddha gave a *dhamma* talk to the remaining four companions after Koṇḍañña understood the four noble truths. Vappa and Bhaddiya are the first of the four to become stream-winners; and, their understanding is described with the same phrases as Koṇḍañña's. The same thing occurs with the last two companions, Mahānāma and Assaji:

> Then the Blessed One taught and instructed the remaining monks with a *dhamma* talk. While they were being taught and instructed by the Blessed One with a *dhamma* talk, a *dhamma*-eye, dustless and stainless arose in the respected Vappa and to the respected Bhaddiya that 'whatever has the nature of arising, that has the nature of ceasing.'[82]

The commentary on this passage makes it clear that the reason that the texts talk about the five followers (*pañcavaggiyā*) is because they have each developed the eye of *dhamma*; Vappa was first, Buddhaghosa explains, followed by Bhaddiya, Mahānāma and then Assaji.[83] The way that these five followers attained enlightenment locates the four noble truths as the entry-point for the first three stages of the path. The four noble truths enable a follower of the Buddha to understands the truth of what the Buddha says, cultivates the eye of *dhamma*, and thus enters at least the first level of the path as a stream-winner (see Table 2.1 for a detailed comparison of all of these *suttas*).

Buddhaghosa explains what the eye of *dhamma* (*dhammacakkhu*) means in his commentary on the *Vinaya-piṭaka*:

Table 2.1 The Four Noble Truths in Enlightenment Stories

	Description of Enlightenment	Decision to Teach	Content of Teaching	Audience and Result
Dhammacakka-ppavattana-sutta (S V 420)	four noble truths (introduction set) (enlightenment set) (gerundive set)	none	four noble truths (introduction set) (enlightenment set) (gerundive set)	Koṇḍañña Vappa Bhaddiya Mahānāma Assaji *dhamma*-eye
Ariyapariyesana-sutta (M I 160)	noble quest (*ariyapariyesana*)	Brahmā Sahampati	noble quest (*ariyapariyesana*)	Koṇḍañña Vappa Bhaddiya Mahānāma Assaji *nibbāna*
Bhayabherava-sutta (M I 22)	four noble truths (basic set) destruction of corruptions (*āsavā*) during third watch (*ratti pacchima*)	none	none	none
Mahāvagga (Vin I 1)	dependent origination (*paṭiccasamuppāda*) during all three watches	Brahmā Sahampati	four noble truths (basic set)	Koṇḍañña Vappa Bhaddiya Mahānāma Assaji *dhamma*-eye
Mahāpadāna-sutta (D II 32) (Vipassin)	dependent origination (*paṭiccasamuppāda*) five aggregates (*upādāna khandhā*)	Brahmā	graduated talk (*anupubbikathā*)	Khanda Tissa *dhamma*-eye

> 'The arising of a *dhamma*-eye' means the arising of any stream-enterer, any once-returner, or any non-returner; these three paths are said to be the *dhamma*-eye.[84]

If one experiences the *dhammacakkhu*, then one has entered the path as a stream-enterer, once-returner, or non-returner. What distinguishes these first three levels from that of an *arahat* is the destruction of the corruptions (*āsavā*). The corruptions are destroyed in the five renouncers after they hear a second *dhamma* talk. After the *dhamma*-eye arises in Koṇḍañña, it is awakened in his friends; and, upon hearing a second talk on the nature of the aggregates (*rūpaṃ*, *vedanā*, *saññā*, *saṃkhārā*, and *viññāṇaṃ*), all five renouncers eliminate the corruptions and are now full *arahat*s who will no longer be reborn.[85]

Conclusion

This comparison of stories of the Buddha's enlightenment in the *Bhayabherava-*, *Ariyapariyesana-*, *Dhammacakkappavattana-sutta*s, and in the *Mahāvagga* reveals three important points. First, the four noble truths are not identified consistently in the Theravāda canon as the content of what the Buddha realized when he became enlightened. Not only are the four noble truths absent from the *Ariyapariyesana-sutta*, but the sequence of the three watches and the description of what the Buddha learned during each watch are not found in the *Dhammacakkappavattana-sutta* nor in the *Mahāvagga*. If we add these observations to the previous work done by K. R. Norman, André Bareau, Feer, and the contributions of Schmithausen, Bronkhorst, and Skilling, it is reasonable to suggest that these different stories of the Buddha's enlightenment show a development of one version of what the Buddha realized. The relationship between the *Mahāvagga* version in the *Vinaya-piṭaka* and the *Dhammacakkappavattana-sutta* of the *Saṃyutta-nikāya* indicates that it is likely that the four noble truths were introduced into Buddhist *sūtra/sutta* literature from *vinaya* collections. The four noble truths quickly came to occupy a central position among the body of teachings attributed to Gautama Buddha.

George D. Bond has shown that the four noble truths are a hermeneutical tool in the post-canonical *Netti-pakaraṇa* to determine whether any given statement is the word of the Buddha.[86] To briefly summarize his conclusions, the *Netti-pakaraṇa* explains that a claim that something was taught by the Buddha must agree with the four noble truths for the claim to be considered seriously as the word of the Buddha (*buddhavacana*). The absence of the four noble truths from certain versions of how the Buddha became enlightened, the grammatical indicators that mark the slightly later insertion of the four noble truths into the *Dhammacakkappavattana-sutta*, the agreement of the Pāli stories in the

Dhammacakkappavattana-sutta and the *Mahāvagga*, particularly in contrast to the Sanskrit and Tibetan variations of the same *sutta*, all support the conclusion that the four noble truths emerged into the Theravādin tradition at some point when the canon was being formed but not at its earliest stages. The pre-eminence of the four noble truths in the post-canonical *Netti-pakaraṇa* attests to their growing significance in the Theravāda tradition, particularly when contrasted to their absence elsewhere in the canon.

Secondly, where the four noble truths are present, they are linked unavoidably to the Buddha's enlightenment experience. In the *Bhayabherava-sutta* and its parallels, they are the substance of what the Buddha realized in the third watch of the night; they are also the means by which the Buddha analyzed the nature of the corruptions to gain his release. The *Dhammacakkappavattana-sutta* and the *Mahāvagga* describe how the Buddha analyzed the four noble truths in three different modes, for a total of twelve ways, on the night that he was enlightened.

The four noble truths are not only inextricable from the Buddha's awakening in these latter stories, but they are also the means by which others are able to cultivate the same experience. The sequence of: hearing the talk on the four noble truths, cultivating the *dhamma*-eye, requesting ordination, and then eliminating of the corruptions after hearing a second talk on *dhamma* is present in both narratives of the *Dhammacakkappavattana-sutta* and the *Mahāvagga*. It differs from the *Bhayabherava-sutta*, where the Buddha does not mention his development of the eye of *dhamma* and where he eradicates the corruptions according to the four truths. That the four truths are nearly synonymous with the Buddha's enlightenment is further confirmed by Buddhaghosa's commentaries, where he inserts the four noble truths when they are missing from the canonical story in the *Ariyapariyesana-sutta*.

Where the four truths appear in the canonical stories of the Buddha's enlightenment, the doctrine functions as a symbol. In those passages, the four noble truths are associated consistently with the Buddha's enlightenment and his decision to teach. The four noble truths are set apart and regarded by the canon as a distinct teaching. The symbolic nature of the four noble truths lies in their reference to a particular religious experience which must be cultivated and learned. Here the four noble truths refer concretely to the Buddha, his enlightenment, and to the fact that anyone can – theoretically – enter into the path by understanding the teaching of the four noble truths.

The third point is that, as a symbol, the four noble truths are set in a cosmological setting. It is not simply a rhetorical flourish on the part of the authors of the *Dhammacakkappavattana-sutta* to go into the details of how the gods and all beings in the cosmos responded to the turning of the *dhamma* wheel. We are taken through the levels of the cosmos: hearing the gods of the earth, the four kings (*cātummahārājikā*) made a noise; hearing the noise of the *cātummahārājikā* gods, the thirty-three gods, *yāmā*, *tusitā*, *nimmānaratī*, *paranimmitta-vasavatti*, and *brahmakāyikā* made a noise. Then we are told: 'At that moment, at that second, at that instant the noise rose as far as the Brahmā world; the ten thousand worlds trembled, shook, and quaked and a immeasurable great light that surpassed the divine majesty of the gods became visible in the world.' All of these gods are beings who are born as gods, but even as gods, they are subject to death and rebirth. They have not yet escaped saṃsāra, and thus the news of the Buddha's *dhamma* must reach into the highest heavens. The same cosmological reference is found in the *Ariyapariyesana-sūtta*, when the Buddha replies to Upaka that he is on his way to the city of Kāsi (where the Deer Park at Isipatana is located) to turn the wheel of *dhamma* and to 'beat the drum of the deathless.' The reference to turning the *dhamma* wheel in the *Ariyapariyesana-sutta* is worth noting particularly because there is no other reference to the four noble truths elsewhere in the *sutta*.

When the four noble truths function symbolically, either in the setting of the Buddha's lifetime on earth or in the broader cosmos, they are not a symbol that represents a prelinguistic, non-discursive, or non-informative inner religious experience, as George Lindbeck asserts.[87] Rather, they are an encapsulation of a particular body of claims about the Buddha and his teachings. Kay Read has argued correctly that discourse does not belong only to written or spoken forms of language; images, she suggests, are also forms of discourse.[88] The four noble truths embed a distinctive soteriological experience into their layers of meaning, the formation of which we have traced in this chapter. The doctrine conveys a fixed set of related events in the canonical tradition by their repeated association with the person of the Buddha and his enlightenment. The context of these associations expands the literal meaning of the terms. Those meanings are both informative and discursive when analyzed within the context of the sacred texts of a particular religious tradition.

When I suggest that a doctrine functions as a symbol of a particular religious experience, I do not wish to leave the impression that I agree that all symbols participate in another dimension that might be called the 'sacred,' in a way that Paul Ricour or Mircea Eliade may have used.[89] I also wish to stop short of saying that the four noble truths are *themselves* a particular religious experience.[90] The key element to the symbolic function of the four noble truths is their multivalency. The four noble truths point beyond themselves, although that to which they point may not be defined unqualifiedly as 'the sacred' without a more specific set of definitions for what we mean by 'sacred.' The truths denote more than the four enumerated truths; as a unit, they denote how the Theravāda canon has remembered the Buddha's enlightenment and how the canon has recorded the means by which others may enter the path by acquiring of the *dhamma*-eye.

The meaning of the four noble truths is something more than the sum of the four truths: they evoke the possibility of enlightenment for all beings. Law professor Derrick Bell touches on the sense of possibility that symbols contain in an fictional exchange that he has with a black limousine driver named Mr. Jesse B. Semple who is chauffering Bell to a wealthy community outside New York City to give the second of three lectures in connection with the birth day of Martin Luther King, Jr. Symbols, Semple says, are sometimes the substance of what people draw on to live their lives – even though 'they are all but worthless at the bank, sometimes black folks don't try to cash them there.'[91]

The passage cited from Derrick Bell's *Faces at the Bottom of the Well* highlights what symbols do; this point is taken up again in Chapter Seven. Bell highlights the fact that symbols are not readily reducible to a 'bottom-line analysis'. The very nature of symbols rests in their multivalency. To reduce symbols to one level of analysis is to misinterpret the function of symbols. That is to say, it is a mistake to reduce Martin Luther King, Jr. Day to its direct impact upon the economic development of African Americans in the United States. In the same conversation with Semple, Bell points out that is equally mistaken to exempt the impact of symbols from an economic analysis. In the same way, we need to understand how it is that the four noble truths function both at the center of a set of symbolic associations about the Buddha, enlightenment, and the cosmos and how they function within the propositional networks of other teachings of the Buddha without reducing the teaching to either role. This chapter has sketched out the context in which the four noble truths are understood to be the content of the Buddha's enlightenment, the substance of his first talk, and the means by which the heavens resounded when Koṇḍañña cultivated the *dhamma* eye. The following two chapters suggest that there are many points in the *Nikāya*s of the *Sutta-piṭaka* and in the *Abhidhamma-piṭaka* where the four noble truths are taught in direct relation to other teachings, where the four noble truths are regarded as propositions about reality – not primarily as a symbol.

Notes

1 Derrick Bell, *Faces at the Bottom of the Well: The Permanence of Racism* (New York: Basic Books, 1992), 24.
2 Vin 1 10; S V 420
3 Ps I 108. A *purohita* acts in consort with the king to mediate the sacrifice that is necessary for the king's rule. See Ronald Inden, *Imagining India* (Cambridge, Massachusetts: Blackwell, 1990), 202.
4 Mircea Eliade, *Yoga: Immortality. and Freedom*, 2nd ed., trans. Willard R. Trask (Princeton: Bollingen Foundation, 1969), 76–79
5 S V 307
6 D III 234
7 D II 156

8 M I 23
9 M I 23
10 M I 249. The *Mahāsaccaka-sutta* (M I 237–251) contains the same story of how the Buddha became enlightened as the *Bhayabherava-sutta* (M I 249). In the *Mahāsaccaka-sutta* the Buddha says to Aggivessana that he teaches to all and then returns to his state of concentration, in which his mind is fixed within the 'sign of concentration' (*samādhinimitta*). Buddhaghosa explains that the Buddha resides in that concentration by virtue of 'concentration on the fruit of emptiness' (*suññataphalasamādhi*) (Ps II 292).
11 Vin III 3–5
12 A IV 177–179
13 M III 36
14 A II 211. M I 23, A II 36, and A IV 179 mention only three corruptions (*āsavā*). Vin III 4 has four.
15 M I 163. The adjectives modifying *nibbānaṃ, ajātaṃ anuttaraṃ yogakkhemaṃ* have a range of meanings. For a new angle on *ajātaṃ* and *amataṃ* see Norman, 'Mistaken Ideas about Nibbāna,' *Collected Papers*, 6:18–24. *Yogakkhemaṃ* is a compound found throughout Sanskrit literature that means work and rest. Norman points out that this is an old *dvandva*, found in the *Ṛg-veda*, that was later understood as a *tatpurusa* that was identical with *nibbāna*: rest from work. There are four types of *yogas* – *kāma-*, *bhava-*, *diṭṭhi-*, and *avijjā-* – that detail release from different kinds of work or that are attachments to the world (A II 10 and D III 230). *The Elders' Verses*, 2 vols., trans. K. R. Norman (London: Pāli Text Society, 1995), 1:128. The compound has been translated as the 'uttermost security from bonds' and 'supreme security from bondage.' See *The Middle Length Sayings*, 1:207; *The Middle Length Discourses*, 255.
16 M I 162–163
17 M I 160–175
18 M I 165
19 For example, M I 484.
20 M I 165f.
21 *So kho ahaṃ bhikkhave tath'eva nisīdiṃ, alam idaṃ padhānāyāti* (M I 167).
22 M I 167
23 M I 167
24 M I 167
25 Sp II 174
26 *Ālayarāmā kho panāyaṃ pajā ālayaratā ālayasammudā* (M I 167).
27 M I 168
28 Vin I 7
29 S I 136–138
30 D II 32–34
31 Gautama Buddha is the seventh buddha. The *Mahāpadāna-sutta* (D II 2) provides a list and short description; T. W. Rhys Davids has tabulated these in his translation. *Dialogues of the Buddha (Dīgha-nikāya)*, 3 vols., trans. T. W. Rhys Davids (1910; London: Luzac & Co., 1966), 2:6–7.
32 Ps II 174 (on M I 160ff.); Spk I 195 (on S I 136–138); Sv II 464 (on D II 29ff.); Sp V 961 (on Vin I 4) does not comment on *dhamma*.
33 M I 169. The commentary explains the last phrase: *Ye paralokañ c'eva vajjañ ca bhayato passanti, te paralokavajjabhayadassāvino nama*, Sp II 179.
34 Jonathan S. Walters, 'Four Approaches to the *Sermon on the Noble Quest (Ariyapariyesana-sutta)*,' *History of Religions*, forthcoming.

35 S V 420. The version in the *Saṃyutta-nikāya* is not identified as the first *dhamma* talk on the four truths, nor is it prefaced with the story of the Buddha's quest. See Table 2.1.
36 Vin I 7,11. The exchange with Brahmā Sahampati found in the *Ariyapariyesana-sutta* is identical to the passage in the *Vinaya-piṭaka*.
37 M I 171. When the Buddha says 'he knows for himself' (*sayaṃ abhiññāya*), the phrase takes on a certain emphasis because it is repeated in his speech to the five companions about the nature of a *tathāgata*.
38 M I 171. See Norman, 'Mistaken Ideas,' *Collected Papers*, 6:21.
39 M I 171–172
40 M I 173
41 M I 173. The verbs of teaching in this phrase are *ovadati* and *anusāsati*, which both carry the same range of meanings, 'to give advice, exhort, instruct or admonish.'
42 Ps II 169
43 Ps II 187
44 Ps II 192 on M I 193
45 Lamotte, HIB, 650.
46 John Ross Carter makes no distinction between the canon and commentaries on this point. He identifies the *Ariyapariyesana-sutta* as the *locus classicus* for the Buddha's teaching of *dhamma*. As the analysis of this chapter shows, I find that this position obscures the various ways that the four truths were located within the Buddha's experience of enlightenment and his teachings. See John Ross Carter, *Dhamma: Western Academic and Sinhalese Buddhist Interpretations – A Study of a Religious Concept* (Tokyo: The Hokuseido Press, 1978), 72ff.
47 For an extended commentary on the symbolism of the wheel in this title, see Carter, *Dhamma*, 74, n. 44. Briefly, he suggests that the wheel represents a sense of conquering authority, possibly derived from the wheel of a chariot or a discoid weapon. He also provides a summary of the literature on this question.
48 The commentary glosses 'higher knowledge' (*abhiññā*) as the four noble truths (Spk III 297).
49 I. B. Horner notes in her translation of the *Mahāvagga* passage that *vibhavataṇhā* means wealth or prosperity, non-becoming, and more becoming. I agree with her intepretation that here *vibhavataṇhā* means the longing for sensations to fall, and rise again. See *The Book of the Discipline (Vinaya-piṭaka)*, 6 vols., trans. I. B. Horner (London: Pāli Text Society, 1971), 4:16.
50 S V 420–23. This passage is also found at Vin I 9, and the portion of the middle way also at M I 15 and S IV 330. The commentary on Vin I 9 (VA 965) refers to the commentary on M I 15 (Ps I 104f.).
51 Norman, 'The Four Noble Truths,' 222f.
52 The two terms, *dukkhadomanassa*, are also found paired together at A I 157, 216; II 149; III 207; IV 406; S II 69, IV 198, 343; S V 141; M II 64; It 89. In this pair, *dukkha* can be taken as physical pain as opposed to *cetasikaṃ domanassaṃ*, mental distress or suffering. This distinction is also found at Nett 12, where two kinds of suffering are distinguished: mental and bodily, *domanassaṃ* and *dukkhaṃ*.
53 This formula is also found at D I 136; M II 64; A V 216f.; It 89.
54 S III 47, 100; M III 16. For more references to the *upādānakkhandhā*, see PED, s.v. *khandha*.
55 These three kinds of craving are listed also at Vin I 10f., and in these passages: D II 61, 308; D III 216, 275; S III 26, 158; It 50; Ps I 26, 39; Ps II 147; Vbh 101,

365; Nett 160. There is another set of three cravings listed at D III 216 and Vbh 395: *kāmataṇhā*, *rūpataṇhā*, and *arūpataṇhā*.

56 Also found at Vin I 11; D I 110; S IV 47, 107; M III 280. Buddhaghosa's explanation of both terms is in Vism 495.

57 *Paṭipadā* is specified as *dukkhanirodhagāminī paṭipadā* at D I 84, 189; III 136; S V 426f.; A I 177; Ps I 86, 119 and Dhs 1057. It is also defined as *āsavanirodhagāminī paṭipadā* at D I 84. It is found paired with *magga* at Vin I 10; D I 157, D III 219; M II 11, M III 251, 284; S I 24; A I 295f.

58 At A V 55, 174 the eightfold path is explained as the means to bring about the end of suffering, and also at M I 301 and Vism 509, 511. The first book of the final section of the *Saṃyutta-nikāya* is entitled *Magga-saṃyutta* (Sayings on the Path), and contains eight chapters on different aspects of the eightfold path, and S V 8–10 lays out the details of each step. It is worth noting that the definition of the first step, *sammādiṭṭhi* (right view) is knowledge of the four truths (same definition also at A II 196; M I 46f., M III 251; S II 17, S V 8). Other discussions of the eightfold path can be found in the *Mahācattārīsaka-sutta* (M III 71–78), and in the *Mahāsattipaṭṭhāna-sutta* (D II 311–314). Alternatively, one sees the noble truths through right wisdom (*ariyasaccāni sammāppaññāya passati*, S II 185; It 17; A III 10). At M I 292–298 (*Mahāvedalla-sutta*) one gains wisdom (*paññā*) through the four truths. The remainder of the *sutta* distinguishes between consciousness (*viññāṇa*) and wisdom (*paññā*).

59 M I 301 and Vism 514 (which cites M I 301).

60 D II 216–217 explains how the stages are interconnected: right intention supports right views, right speech maintains right intentions, and so on. But right knowledge (*sammāñāṇa*) and right freedom (*sammāvimuttiṃ*) are added to the list, for a total of ten steps. This list of ten is also found at M I 42 and A II 222. At M III 71, the list is headed by right concentration.

61 Peter Skilling has noted that the final insight of the four noble truths (that they have been mastered) is missing from a Tibetan version of the *Dhammacakkappavattana-sutta*; he concludes that it must be from 'a faulty manuscript or translation: since the insights are an essential part of the sutta, their omission cannot be deliberate or redactional.' Skilling, 'Theravādin literature,' 104.

62 For the classification, see Nd 307. For other lists, see D I 216; A I 210;

63 William Montgomery McGovern, *A Manual of Buddhist Philosophy* (1923; Lucknow, India: Oriental Reprinters, 1976), 60–68.

64 PED, s.v. *kolāhala*; SnA 480 and KhA 120ff.

65 Spk III 296

66 *Ñāṇañca pana me dassanam udapādi akuppā me cetovimutti ayam antimājāti natthidāni punabbhavo ti* (S V 423). M I 167 has *vimutti* instead of *cetovimutti*.

67 For example, the historical information found in the Pāli *Mahākhandaka* (which contains part of the Buddha's biography) is also found in the Mūlasarvāstivādin *Saṃghabedhavastu* of the *Skandhaka*. The *Mahāvastu* is another text, based upon a *Vinaya* recension belonging to the Mahāsaṅghika-Lokotaravādin school which is roughly similar to the *Mahāvagga* of the Pāli *Vinaya*. The *Mahāvastu*, however, contains few disciplinary regulations and has far more Jātaka and Avadāna stories. There are also portions found in the Mūlasarvāstivādin *Kṣudrakavastu* which are missing from the Pāli *Mahāvagga*. See Norman, *Pāli Literature*, 23–24. Holt also points out that much of the *Khandaka* material is also drawn from other parts of the canon. See John C. Holt, *Discipline: The Canonical Buddhism of the Vinayapiṭaka* (Delhi: Motilal Banarsidass, 1983), 107, n. 1.

68 Norman, *Pāli Literature*, 22.

69 Norman, *Pāli Literature*, 27.
70 *vimuttisukhapaṭisaṃvedī*, Vin I 1
71 As Table 2.1 shows, the three watches are not found in the *Dhammacakkappavattana-sutta* (S V 420), but two versions of the three watches are found at other points in the *Nikāyas* and *Vinaya-piṭaka*. The first is the one that appears here, and the second includes the four truths during the third watch (see Vin III 3–6).
72 Vin I 4–5. *Iti ha bhagavato paṭisañcikkhato appossukkatāya cittaṃ namati no dhammadesanāya.*
73 Vin I 5
74 Vin I 6–7 and parallel at M I 167.
75 Sp V 962, but one Burmese manuscript omits *'ti catusaccadhammaṃ*.
76 Vin I 11–12
77 Bareau, *Recherches*, 1:178–181 and 2:173f. See also Bronkhorst, *Two Traditions*, 107.
78 Feer, 'Études bouddhiques,' 360–361.
79 Vin I 12
80 Vin I 12
81 Sp V 965
82 Vin I 12
83 Sp V 965
84 Sp V 971
85 Also at S III 66
86 George D. Bond, *The Word of the Buddha: The Tipiṭaka and Its Interpretation in Theravāda Buddhism* (Sri Lanka: M. D. Gunasena, 1982), 33–99.
87 Lindbeck, *Nature of Doctrine*, 16 and Griffiths, 'An Apology for Apologetics,' 65.
88 Kay A. Read, 'Binding Reeds and Burning Hearts: Mexica-Tenochca Concepts of Time and Sacrifice,' Ph. D. dissertation (University of Chicago, 1991), 62–72.
89 Paul Ricoeur, 'The Symbol . . . Food for Thought,' *Philosophy Today* 4 (Fall 1960): 196–207; Paul Ricoeur, *Interpretation Theory: Discourse and the Surplus of Meaning* (Fort Worth: Texas Christian University Press, 1976); Paul Ricoeur, *The Symbolism of Evil* (Boston: Beacon Press, 1967); and Mircea Eliade, 'Methodological Remarks on the Study of Religious Symbolism,' in *History of Religions: Essays in Methodology*, ed. Mircea Eliade and Joseph M. Kitagawa (Chicago: University of Chicago Press, 1959).
90 For example, see Joachim Wach, *Types of Religious Experience: Christian and Nonchristian* (Chicago: University of Chicago Press, 1951), 38.
91 Bell, *Faces at the Bottom of the Well*, 24.

CHAPTER THREE

Analyzing the Four Noble Truths

Why is it the central teaching, and what does it teach? The 'truths' are just the same and just as fundamental in the Sāṅkhya, the Yoga, the Nyāya systems and in medical science. There is very little Buddhistic in them.[1]

F. I. Shcherbatskoi (1932)

Introduction

I have pointed out that the four noble truths are not always a fundamental symbol of the Buddha's teachings in the *Tipiṭaka*. In contrast to their central role in most biographies of the Buddha, the four noble truths are set in relation to a variety of teachings at other points in the canon – teachings that include the four bases of mindfulness, dependent arising, the aggregates of grasping, the corruptions, the spheres of sense, and, in some places, *nibbāna*. Where the four truths appear within these networks of teachings, they have a notably different role than their symbolic function. The four truths are not linked as explicitly to the Buddha's enlightenment, nor do they produce an experience of stream-entry through the acquisition of the *dhammạ* eye.

Within the networks of the Buddha's teachings, the four noble truths are one doctrine among others and are not particularly central. The four noble truths and other doctrines are propositions that, when taken together, establish a map of how the cosmos exists. Doctrines – or right views – chart reality; and, in doing so, they locate the individual within the world by setting one teaching in relation to another. Even though right views delineate the world in which humans live, the world they lay out is never fixed or static. One of the fundamental principles of *abhidhamma* ('further or higher *dhamma*') analysis is that all things (*dhammā*) are causally related. The purpose of *abhidhamma* is to understand reality directly through various causal relationships. In this type of analysis, the four noble truths function as all doctrines function in the books of the *Abhidhamma-piṭaka*: as teachings which must be fully analyzed and understood through established questions and answers. The four noble truths are located within certain matrices found in the *Abhidhamma-piṭaka* and in portions of the *Sutta-piṭaka*; and, they are analyzed according to the same standards as other doctrines. The emphasis in *abhidhamma* is understanding, knowing the possible causal relations that produce the world in which humans live; the underlying principle is that there is no unchanging or fixed reality.[2] Defining the points of articulation between the Buddha's teachings is the goal of *abhidhamma* analysis.

As a proposition, the four noble truths map out the construction and the accompanying deconstruction of reality. They are employed in such a way that a practitioner must comprehend how the cosmos comes into existence within the Buddhist analysis of cause and result; when a practitioner understands the place of the four noble truths within the Buddha's teachings, she or he understands how the cosmos and the individual comes to be, and thus how the individual can cease to exist. The way in which the four noble truths are taught emphasizes detail, particularity, and fluidity, which is rather different than their role as a symbol for enlightenment and, by extension, as a symbol of the whole of the Buddha's *dhamma*. When the four noble truths are set in relation to another doctrine, they no longer serve as a symbol for all *dhamma* or even enlightenment; instead, the four noble truths become part of the entire *dhamma* matrix. For example, in the *Mahāsatipaṭṭhāna-sutta*, the four noble truths are one of four means by which a practitioner may grasp the true nature of mental objects (*dhammā*). The immediate goal is perceiving and understanding the nature of *dhammā* as fully as possible. There is no single way of understanding the teachings: one teaching may be used to explain another in one passage; the relationship may be reversed or altered in other talks. The reality that the teachings reveal is fluid and shifting because reality is continually constructed and re-constructed; the doctrines are used in different combinations to analyze this continuous construction of reality. Perhaps the best known example of this is found in the relationship between the four noble truths and *paṭiccasamuppāda* (dependent arising), where the twelvefold chain of dependent arising is understood as a magnification of the movement between the second and third truths.[3] In short, the different functions of the doctrine of the four noble truths represent *dhamma* differently. Within the networks of the Buddha's teachings, the four noble truths are part of an analysis of reality that unravels the dynamic construction of the cosmos; where, as a symbol, they represent holistically the possibility of release from saṃsāra and the entirety of *dhamma*.

The underlying principle in these networks of propositions is knowing specific right views and how they produce the world in which humans live. These right views are to be understood in order to move forward along the path; and, a practitioner is to comprehend how specific conditions or states produce – and are produced in – the cosmos. By setting the four noble truths in relation to other doctrines within a network and learning the doctrines in that network, a practitioner learns how the various teachings intersect with each other. The teaching of the four noble truths within networks of doctrines is found in both the *Sutta-piṭaka* and the *Abhidhamma-piṭaka*. Beginning with the four bases of mindfulness, I will trace the points at which the four noble truths appear and explore the salvific purposes for which they are taught.

Mahāsatipaṭṭhana-sutta

The relationship between the four noble truths and the *sutta*s on the setting up of mindfulness is laid out in the *Mahāsatipaṭṭhāna-*, *Satipaṭṭhāna-*, *Saccavibhaṅga-sutta*s, and the *Vibhaṅga*.[4] *Sati* is the Pāli term for mindfulness, based on the Sanskrit root for 'remember' (*smṛ*); *paṭṭhāna* is usually translated as 'establishing' or 'setting up.' The establishment of mindfulness is thus the subject of the first two *sutta*s. The third, the *Saccavibhaṅga-sutta*, is a *sutta* that contains material which overlaps with the other two *sutta*s but does not discuss how to establish mindfulness. The fourth point at which the four noble truths are set in relation to the practice of mindfulness is in the *Vibhaṅga* of the *Abhidhamma-piṭaka*. The same formulaic descriptions used to explain the four noble truths in the *Dhammacakkappavattana-sutta* appear again in these *sutta*s, thus indicating some degree of continuity in how the four truths were defined. However, the four truths are explained only briefly in the *Dhammacakkappavattana-sutta* when compared to the analysis to which they are subjected in these *sutta*s. The same types of analysis applied to the four noble truths are found in both the *Sutta-piṭaka* and the *Abhidhamma-piṭaka*. The fact that the four noble truths are analyzed in precisely the same ways in both *piṭaka*s points to an analytic style that underlies both the *Sutta-piṭaka* and the *Abhidhamma-piṭaka*. This is a point that Gethin has suggested in his extensive study of the thirty-seven factors of enlightenment. I will begin with the parallels between the *Mahāsatipaṭṭhāna*-and *Satipaṭṭhāna-sutta*s.

The first part of the *Mahāsatipaṭṭhāna-sutta* explains the bases for the establishment of mindfulness (*sati*). The Buddha presents the four ways to establish mindfulness so that his followers may attain *nibbāna* and eliminate pain. The four ways are through the body (*kāyo*), feelings (*vedanā*), mind (*cittaṃ*), and mental objects (*dhammā*). The last basis, mental objects (*dhammā*), is further subdivided into the five hindrances (*nīvaraṇāni*), the five aggregates (*upādāna-kkhandhā*), the internal and external spheres of sense (*ajjhattikạ-bāhira-āyatanaṃ*), the seven enlightenment factors (*bojjhaṅgā*), and the four noble truths (*ariyasaccāni*). A practitioner should mindfully and attentively contemplate the body, feelings, mind, or mental objects, so that envy and grief in the world may be controlled.[5] How should mental objects be considered from the point of view of the four noble truths?

> Now, *bhikkhus*, a *bhikkhu* fully understands 'this is pain'; fully understands 'this is the arising of pain'; fully understands, 'this is the ending of pain'; fully understands 'this is the way to the ending of pain.'[6]

The four noble truths are applied to mental objects insofar as the four noble truths are the topics to which a practitioner should direct her or his attention and reflection. After knowing what the truths are, one contemplates mental objects. One should consider whether mental objects (i.e., the four noble truths) belong to the internal or external sense spheres or to both; one should reflect upon the arising or ending of mental objects, or both; or, one should establish the awareness that 'there are mental objects.' This second set of instructions on how one should consider mental objects is repeated after each of the ways that one can establish mindfulness; there is nothing unique in the set that follows the four noble truths. Up until the introduction of the four noble truths in the basic set, the *Mahāsatipaṭṭhāna-* and the *Satipaṭṭhāna-sutta*s are identical (see Table 3.1).[7] The description of how one should consider mental objects follows the four noble truths only in the *Satipaṭṭhāna-sutta*.

We should note two points regarding the four noble truths as they appear in both the *Mahāsatipaṭṭhāna-* and the *Satipaṭṭhāna-sutta*s. The first concerns the basic set in which the four truths appear: the four noble truths are not described with the adjectives 'noble' or 'truths,' and they have the properly gendered pronouns. Because Norman suggests that the basic set is the earliest form of the teaching, it is possible that the four noble truths were not yet considered to be either 'noble' or 'truths' at the point in history when the *Mahāsatipaṭṭhāna-* and *Satipaṭṭhāna-sutta*s were formulated. The second point is that it is not unusual to find the four truths included in a list that contains the five hindrances, the five aggregates of grasping, the six sense spheres, and the seven enlightenment factors. These items are incorporated as components of a longer list of thirty-seven factors that are conducive to enlightenment (*sattatiṃsa bodhipakkiyā dhammā*): four bases of mindfulness, four right efforts, four bases of success, five faculties, five powers, seven enlightenment factors, and the eightfold path. As the following chapter discusses, these thirty-seven factors of enlightenment are related to different lists found throughout the canon, most notably in the *Abhidhamma-piṭaka*. The appearance of the four noble truths in the longer list is typical of one kind of analysis to which the teaching is subjected.

The second section of the *Mahāsatipaṭṭhāna-sutta* contains a more detailed analysis of the four noble truths than we encountered in the *Dhammacakkappavattana-*, *Bhayabherava-*, or *Ariyapariyesana-sutta*s. Parts of the second section of the *Mahāsatipaṭṭhāna-sutta* are found in

Table 3.1 The Four Noble Truths and the Establishment of Mindfulness

	Dhammacakka-ppavattana-sutta (S V 420)	*Mahāsatipaṭṭhāna-sutta* (D II 290)	*Satipaṭṭhāna-sutta* (M I 55)	*Saccavibhaṅga-sutta* (M III 248)	*Vibhaṅga* (Vbh 99)
Teacher	Buddha	Buddha	Buddha	Buddha Sāriputta	none
Audience	Koṇḍañña Vappa Bhaddiya Mahānama Assaji	unnamed group of *bhikkhus* at Kammāsaddhamma in the country of the Kurus	unnamed group of *bhikkhus* at Kammāsaddhamma in the country of the Kurus	unnamed group of *bhikkhus* at Deer Park in Isipatana near Bārāṇasī	none
Result	*dhamma*-wheel turned and all developed *dhamma*-eye	if mindfulness practiced for at least seven days, fruit of knowledge or state of non- returner	if mindfulness practiced for at least seven days, fruit of knowledge or state of non- returner	*dhamma*-wheel turned	none
Content	four noble truths: introduction set 'birth is pain' set enlightenment set gerundival set	four bases of mindfulness (*sati*): body (*kāyo*) feelings (*vedanā*) mind (*cittaṃ*) mental objects (*dhammā*): hindrances (*nīvaranā*) aggregates (*khandā*) spheres of sense (*āyatanāni*) enlightenment factors (*bojjhaṅgā*) noble truths (*ariyasaccāni*) (basic set)	four bases of mindfulness (*sati*):	four noble truths	*sutta*-analysis *abhidhamma*-analysis interrogation of the four noble truths

the *Saccavibhaṅga-sutta*, but none of it appears in the *Satipaṭṭhāna-sutta.*[8] The *Mahāsatipaṭṭhāna-sutta* opens with the same question and answers found in the *Dhammacakkappavattana-sutta* that define each of the four noble truths:

> What, *bhikkhus*, is the noble truth '[this is] pain'? Birth is pain; old age is pain; disease is pain; death is pain; sorrow and grief, mental distress and physical distress, and unrest is pain; not getting what one wants is pain; in short, the five aggregates of grasping are pain.[9]

It is useful to call this passage the *jāti pi dukkhā* ('birth is pain') set because it appears in more or less the same form in four out of the five passages that are examined here: the *Mahāsatipaṭṭhāna-*, *Saccavibhaṅga-*, *Dhammacakkappavattana-sutta*s, and in the *Vibhaṅga.* The items in the 'birth is pain' set are all found in the *Dhammacakkappavattana-sutta*, but sorrow (*soko*) is missing from two Sinhalese manuscripts and from one Burmese manuscript.[10] The list of items in the 'birth is pain' set vary in the *Saccavibhaṅga-sutta*.and in the *Vibhaṅga*; illness, association with things not liked, and separation from desired things are not found in the *Vibhaṅga*, and they are also omitted from the list of questions found in the *Mahāsatipaṭṭhāna-* and *Saccavibhaṅga-sutta*s, and the *Vibhaṅga.* The grammatical form of the four noble truths in this formula shows that they have been combined with *ariyasaccaṃ*, thus indicating that the four truths were, at the time of their incorporation into the second section of the *Mahāsatipaṭṭhāna-sutta*, considered to be both noble and truths.

The *Mahāsatipaṭṭhāna-sutta*, *Saccavibhaṅga-sutta*, and *Vibhaṅga* have more extended analyses of each characteristic of the 'birth is pain' set. Here are the explanations of the first two items, birth and old age:

> And what, *bhikkhus*, is birth? Birth is the production, the entry, the coming-to-be, the appearance of the aggregates (*khandhā*), [and] the acquisition of the spheres of sense (*āyatanāni*) of every being in each class of beings; this, *bhikkhus*, is what is called birth.
>
> And what, *bhikkhus*, is old age? Old age is decay, having broken teeth, gray hair and wrinkled skin, the shrinking of life and the maturing of the sense-faculties (*indriyāni*) of every being in each class of beings; this, *bhikkhus*, is what is called old age.[11]

The analysis continues in the *Mahāsatipaṭṭhāna-sutta*, explaining in detail how death (*maraṇaṃ*), sorrow and grief (*soko* and *paridevo*), physical and mental distress (*dukkhaṃ* and *domanassaṃ*), unrest (*upāyāso*), not getting what one wants (*yam p'icchaṃ na labhati tam pi dukkhaṃ*), and the five aggregates of grasping (*pañcupādānakkhandhā*) are pain. These detailed descriptions of each kind of pain are found in both the *Mahāsatipaṭṭhāna* and the *Saccavibhaṅga-sutta*s, but not in the *Dhammacakkappavattana-sutta.*

The *Mahāsatipaṭṭhāna-sutta* expands the explanations of the second, third, and fourth truths beyond those found in the *Dhammacakkappavattana-sutta*. The second and third truths are defined with the same explanation as in the *Dhammacakkappavattana-sutta*:

> And what, *bhikkhus*, is the noble truth that is the arising of pain? This is craving that leads to rebirth, is connected with pleasure and passion and finds pleasure in this or that; that is, craving for desire, existence, and the fading away of existence.[12]

> And what, *bhikkhus*, is the noble truth that is the ending of pain? This is the complete fading away and ending of that very craving, giving it up, renouncing it, releasing it, and letting go.[13]

The extended answer to the question 'what is the truth that is the arising of pain?' explains that craving arises and resides in the material things (*rūpaṃ*) of the world that are dear and pleasant. What are these things? The answer is a list of ten sets, the first of which are the six sense-organs: eye (*cakkhuṃ*), ear (*sotaṃ*), nose (*ghānaṃ*), tongue (*jivhā*), body (*kāyo*), and mind (*mano*). The second set is made up of the objects of the senses: forms (*rūpā*), sounds (*saddā*), smells (*dandhā*), tastes (*rasā*), tangible objects (*phoṭṭhabbā*) and mental objects (*dhammā*). The remaining sets are subdivided into the same six classes: consciousness (*viññāṇaṃ*), contact (*samphasso*), feeling born of contact (*samphassajā vedanā*), recognition (*saññā*), volition (*sañcetanā*), craving (*taṇhā*), reflection (*vittako*), and deliberation (*vicāro*).[14] Each of these ten sets is followed with the refrain that 'here this craving, arising, arises; dwelling here, [it] dwells.' The ten sets also make up the extended analysis of the third truth, but the refrain is 'here this craving, being abandoned, is abandoned; being destroyed here, [it] is destroyed.'[15] These extended analyses of the second and third truths are found in the *Vibhaṅga*, but not in the *Saccavibhaṅga-sutta*.

The *Mahāsatipaṭṭhāna-* and *Saccavibhaṅga-sutta*s both have longer descriptions of the eightfold path as the definition of the fourth truth. Each of the eight limbs of the path is explained, instead of simply listed as they are in the *Dhammacakkappavattana-sutta*. Right view is explained in terms of the four noble truths. The three kinds of right thought are those of desirelessness, non-hatred, and an absence of cruelty. Right speech consists of avoiding false speech, slander, divisive speech, harmful speech, and gossip. Right action means refraining from taking life, taking what is not given, and sexual misconduct. Right livelihood is explained as 'giving up wrong livelihood and making a living by right livelihood.' The explanation for right effort is more lengthy; briefly, right effort consists of putting forth effort to control one's mind in order to: (1) prevent the arising of unwholesome states (*dhammā*) that have not yet arisen, (2) eliminate those that have arisen, (3) cultivate wholesome states that have not yet arisen, and (4) firmly establish wholesome states that have arisen. Right mindfulness consists of the four foundations of mindfulness; and right concentration is identified as the first four levels of the *jhānas*.[16]

The second section of the *Mahāsatipaṭṭhāna-sutta* provides a more extensive analysis of the four noble truths. The substantive definitions of the *Dhammacakkappavattana-sutta* are expanded and are given more detail, but remain basically the same. What is different in the *Mahāsatipaṭṭhāna*-and *Satipaṭṭhāna-sutta*s is the goal that a practitioner might expect to reach by understanding the four noble truths. The *Mahāsatipaṭṭhāna-* and *Satipaṭṭhāna-sutta*s include this statement close to the end of each *sutta*:

> Now if anyone, *bhikkhus*, should develop these four bases of mindfulness in this way for seven years, one fruit of two is expected for him: knowledge now in this world, or if there are remainders of grasping, the state of non-return.[17]

The period of time for how long a practitioner should develop mindfulness in this passage decreases by the end to seven days: one who develops mindfulness for seven days should expect either the fruit of knowledge now in this world or the state of non-return. These *sutta*s make explicit a different structure of the path than that found in the *Dhammacakkappavattana-sutta*. Here, one who practices the four bases of mindfulness – if only for seven days – will experience the fruit of knowledge or will achieve the state of a non-returner. In the *Dhammacakkappavattana-sutta*, the commentary explains that one should expect to attain one of the first three paths.

The purpose for which mindfulness (and the four noble truths) are taught concludes both *sutta*s.

> There is one way, *bhikkhus*, for the purification of beings, for overcoming sorrows and griefs, for the destruction of pain and misery, for finding the right way, for realizing *nibbāna*; that is, the four bases of mindfulness . . .[18]

This passage is found at the beginning and the end of both the *Mahāsatipaṭṭhāna-* and *Satipaṭṭhāna-sutta*s; Gethin identifies this as the *ekayāna* ('one way') formula.[19] The reason for these teachings is clear: they are taught for the attainment of *nibbāna*, with the results of one's practice clearly described.

The *Saccavibhaṅga-sutta* uses the same the 'birth is pain' formula to explain the first noble truth, as do the two *sutta*s on mindfulness. There are additional parallels between the *Saccavibhaṅga-sutta* and the *Dhammacakkappavattana-sutta* that are not found in either of the *Satipaṭṭhāna-sutta*s. In the *Saccavibhaṅga-sutta*, the four noble truths are taught because the wheel of *dhamma* was turned by the Buddha and cannot be turned back

– they are not taught only as one basis for the setting up of mindfulness. This passage from the *Saccavibhaṅga-sutta* is the same as that from the *Dhammacakkappavattana-sutta*:

> The Buddha spoke: The matchless wheel of *dhamma* set rolling by the *Tathāgata*, the perfected one, fully awakened one in the deer park at Isipatana near Benares cannot be rolled back by a recluse or brahmin or *deva* or Māra or Brahmā or by any being in the world. That is to say, it was a proclamation of the four noble truths, a teaching, a laying down, establishing, opening up, analyzing and making them clear. Of what four? It was a proclamation, a teaching, a laying down, establishing, opening up, analyzing and making clear of the noble truth 'this is pain.'[20]

The *Saccavibhaṅga* continues with an admonishment to follow Sāriputta and Moggallāna, comparing Sāriputta to a mother and Moggallāna to a foster-mother. Sāriputta, the Buddha explains, is able to establish followers as stream-enters, and Moggallāna can instruct followers to become *arahats*; Sāriputta is the one who can teach the four noble truths. Sāriputta then takes up the *sutta* and delivers a talk on the four noble truths. His talk employs the same explanations of the first three truths from the *Dhammacakkappavattana-sutta* but uses the extended description of the eightfold path found in the *Mahāsatipaṭṭhāna-sutta* for the fourth truth. Sāriputta carried on the teaching of the four noble truths and is given this authority by the Buddha himself. The explicit reason for teaching the four noble truths in the *Saccavibhaṅga-sutta* is for the ending of the truth that 'this is pain.'

The parallels between the *Saccavibhaṅga-* and the *Dhammacakkappavattana-suttas* draw explicit connections between the different features of the four noble truths in their symbolic role. The four noble truths are recorded as the means by which both Sāriputta and Moggallāna became stream-enterers in the *Mahāvagga*; the commentaries on the four noble truths explain that knowledge of the four noble truths enables one to become at least a stream-enterer; and, we saw that Koṇḍañña's cultivation of the *dhamma* eye was the catalyst for the turning of the wheel of *dhamma*. This set of features associated with the four noble truths indicates that in the *Saccavibhaṅga-sutta* the four truths are operating as a symbol. The analyses of the four truths in that *sutta* indicate that, even in their symbolic function, the four noble truths were subject to further analysis.

In the two *suttas* on developing mindfulness, the four noble truths are one set of analytic tools to be used for a specific purpose. We find no statements that set the four noble truths apart from the other teachings that may be used to develop mindfulness. The fact that they were the means by which the Buddha turned the *dhamma* wheel is not mentioned, nor is their significance for Sāriputta and Moggallāna noted. In the first section of the

Mahāsatipaṭṭhāna-sutta, the four noble truths are not qualitatively different from the hindrances, the five aggregates, or the seven enlightenment factors. Practicing the four bases of mindfulness for various lengths of time, the *sutta* declares, will result in various degrees of advancement along the fourfold path or in the acquisition of certain fruits of the path. The four noble truths, then, are identified as one tool among others to be used in a meditative practice designed for the attainment of *nibbāna* through a full understanding of mental objects even as they are understood to be symbolic of the Buddha's awakening.

The significance of the four noble truths is demonstrated by the fact that the four noble truths are singled out in the *Mahāsatipaṭṭhāna-sutta* in a way that none of the other factors are. They are explained in more detail in the second section than anywhere else, except in the *Vibhaṅga* of the *Abhidhamma-piṭaka*. The style is quite similar to a commentarial style, with a word-for-word commentary; it seems clear that the four noble truths are considered to be set apart in some way that is remiscent of the approach found in the *Dhammacakkappavattana-sutta*. The same phrases also appear in the *Saccavibhaṅga-sutta*, highlighting the unique status of the four noble truths. The pattern is laid out in Table 3.2.

Paṭiccasamupāda

Dependent arising (*paṭiccasamuppāda*) consists of twelve steps or 'limbs' (*nidāna*) in which each component leads to the next. If one limb is destroyed, the one that precedes it is also destroyed. Thus, each step of the twelvefold cycle is dependent, or co-dependent, on the remaining eleven. The usual *paṭiccasamuppāda* formula reads:

> And what, *bhikkhu*s, is dependent arising? From ignorance, *bhikkhu*s, comes (mental) formations; from formations come consciousness; from consciousness comes name-and-form; from name-and-form come spheres of sense; from spheres of sense comes contact; from contact comes feelings; from feelings comes craving; from craving comes clinging; from clinging comes being; from being comes (re-)birth; from birth comes old-age-and-death, sorrow and grief, mental and physical distress, and unrest; such is the arising of this entire mass of pain.[21]

This sequence explains the production of pain (*paccaya*, 'cause'); and, when deconstructed in reverse order, it leads to the ending of pain. When the sequence describes the destruction of pain, it follows the same order but substitutes *nirodha* (cessation or ending) for *paccaya* (cause): from the cessation of ignorance comes the cessation of (mental) formations and so on. From the last phrase, 'such is the arising of this entire mass of pain,' the relationship between *dukkha* and dependent arising is made explicit.

Table 3.2 Analyses of the Four Noble Truths I

	Dhammacakkappavattana-sutta (S V 420)	*Mahāsatipaṭṭhāna-sutta* (D II 290)	*Satipaṭṭhāna-sutta* (M I 55)	*Saccavibhaṅga Sutta* (M III 248)	*Vibhaṅga* (Vbh 99)
First truth	birth old age illness death sorrow-grief physical & mental pain association with things not liked separation from desired things not getting what one wants five aggregates of grasping	birth death [illness] death sorrow-grief physical & mental pain [association with things not liked] [separation from desired things] not getting what one wants five aggregates of grasping	none	= *Mahāsatipaṭṭhāna-* bracketed items included	= *Mahāsatipaṭṭhāna-* bracketed items omitted
		What is birth? What is old age? What is death? What is sorrow? What is grief? What is pain? What is physical pain? What is mental pain? What is not getting what one wants? What are the five aggregates of grasping?		= *Mahāsatipaṭṭhāna-sutta*	= *Mahāsatipaṭṭhāna-sutta*

Table 3.2 continued

	Dhammacakkappavattana-sutta (S V 420)	*Mahāsatipaṭṭhāna-sutta* (D II 290)	*Satipaṭṭhāna-sutta* (M I 55)	*Saccavibhaṅga Sutta* (M III 248)	*Vibhaṅga* (Vbh 99)
Second truth	leads to rebirth, connected with pleasure and passion; craving for desire, craving for existence, and for the fading away of existence.	same as *Dhammacakka-ppavattana-sutta*, adds: sense-faculties objects of senses consciousness contacts feelings volitions recognitions cravings reflections deliberations 'Here craving arises'	none	= *Dhammacakka-ppavattana-sutta*	= *Mahāsatipaṭṭhāna-sutta*
Third truth	ending of passion and craving; giving it up, renouncing, releasing, letting go.	same as *Dhammacakka-ppavattana-sutta*, adds: sense-faculties objects of senses consciousness contacts feelings volitions recognitions cravings reflections deliberations 'Here craving ends'	none	= *Dhammacakka-ppavattana-sutta*	= *Mahāsatipaṭṭhāna sutta*
Fourth truth	eightfold path list only	eightfold path extended explanation	none	= *Mahāsatipaṭṭhāna-sutta*	= *Mahāsatipaṭṭhāna-sutta*

Through the twelve limbs of the cycle, pain comes into being; and, when the cycle is broken, pain ceases to exist.

One way of linking dependent arising with the four noble truths is by substitution, as shown in a passage from the *Aṅguttara-nikāya*. The *sutta* appears in the collection that is ordered according to the number three and follows three ways that the Buddha refutes various wrong views.[22] After the Buddha explains in three ways what one should do to get rid of wrong views, he states that 'I teach this *dhamma*,' and he gives a short exposition on the elements, contact, the eighteen applications of mind, and the four truths. The four noble truths are prefaced with a short explanation of how the elements, birth, name and form, the sense spheres, contact, and feeling are related to the four truths. The Buddha says that he teaches the four truths to one who experiences feelings.[23] The first and fourth noble truths are explained as they are in the *Dhammacakkappavattana-sutta*, but dependent arising appears as the explanation of the second and third truths.[24] The second truth ('this is the arising of pain') is explained according the twelve limbs in their direct order (how they produce pain), and the third truth ('this is the ending of pain') is in reverse order (how pain can be destroyed). The *paṭiccasamuppāda* formula is substituted for the explanations we have encountered in the *Dhammacakkappavattana-*, *Mahāsatipaṭṭhāna*, *Satipaṭṭhāna-sutta*s, and *Vibhaṅga*.

Paṭiccasamuppāda and the four noble truths are brought together differently in the *Mahāhatthipadopama-sutta*.[25] In this *sutta*, Sāriputta explains that all wholesome states of mind are included among the four noble truths. He uses the expected explanation of the first truth in response to the question 'what is pain?' (*jāti pi dukkhā*) 'birth is pain' and so on), but then he goes on to analyze the components of the first aggregate of grasping, which is form (*rūpa*). By analyzing each of the four major elements (*cattāro mahābhutā*) of form, one sees the aggregates of grasping with perfected wisdom and is thus able to achieve a state of equanimity. This *sutta* focuses exclusively on the analysis of the aggregates of grasping (*panc' upādānakkhandhā*) that conclude the *jāti pi dukkhā* (birth is pain) formula. It is only toward the end of the *sutta* that Sāriputta says 'The Blessed One has said this: Whoever sees dependent arising sees *dhamma*, whoever sees *dhamma* sees dependent arising. And [the limbs of] dependent arising are these five aggregates of grasping.'[26] Instead of the substitution of the *paṭiccasamuppāda* sequence for the second and third truths as in the *Aṅguttara-nikāya* noted above, the association is made here through the aggregates of grasping.

Paṭiccasamuppāda and the four noble truths are tied together in still another way in the *Sammādiṭṭhi-sutta*.[27] The purpose of this *sutta* is to lay out the various ways in which *sammādiṭṭhi* (right view) may be acquired. The general goal for attaining right view is an understanding of *dhamma*, but the *sutta* concludes with an explanation of how the corruptions may be eliminated according to the four noble truths and, by implication, how one becomes an *arahat*. However, the latter point is not made explicitly in the *sutta*. Sāriputta gives the talk on right view in the Jeta Grove in Anāthapiṇḍika's monastery. He explains that one should know: what is unwholesome and the unwholesome roots (*akusalamūlāni*), what is wholesome and the wholesome roots (*kusalamūlāni*); sustenance; and then the arising, ending, and the way to ending each of these items. If one has this knowledge, that follower comes to be of right view. The next topic in Sāriputta's teachings are the four noble truths, although they are not identified as such. When asked the formulaic question 'might there not be another method by which a follower comes to be of right view,' Sāriputta answered

> There might be, friends. In a different way, friends, a follower of the noble ones comprehends pain, the arising of pain, the ending of pain, and the way to the ending of pain. To that extent, friends, a noble follower is of right view, and is one whose view is upright, one who is possessed of stable confidence in *dhamma*, one who has come into this good *dhamma*.[28]

Each of the truths is then explicated with the same answers as we found in the *Dhammacakkappavattana-sutta*: (1) birth is pain (*jāti pi dukkhā*); (2) this is craving (*yāyaṃ taṇhā*) and the three kinds; (3) this is the complete ending of the passion of that craving (*yo tassā yeva taṇhāya asesavirāganirodho*); and (4) the way to the ending of pain is by means of the noble eightfold path (*ariyo aṭṭhaṅgiko maggo*). These four truths will establish a follower in right view and in the good *dhamma*.

The remaining way that one may gain right view is an understanding of the twelve links of dependent arising, with the addition of the corruptions (*āsavā*): old age and death (*jarāmaraṇaṃ*), birth (*jāti*), being (*bhavo*), grasping (*upādānaṃ*), craving (*taṇhā*), feeling (*vedanā*), contact (*phasso*), spheres of sense (*saḷāyatanaṃ*), name-and-form (*nāmarūpaṃ*), consciousness (*viññaṇaṃ*), formations (*saṅkhārā*), and ignorance (*avijjā*). The analysis embedded in the four noble truths is used to dissect each item in this list, but the analysis is not called that of the four noble truths in the canonical passage. For example, Sāriputta explains that one should know old age and death, that one should know the arising, ending, and means to the ending of old age and death.[29] The same analysis is applied to each of the twelve items in the sequence of *paṭiccasamuppāda* (dependent arising). This differs from the *Aṅguttara-nikāya*, discussed above, where the second and third noble truths were explained in terms of *paṭiccasamuppāda* (dependent arising). But here, *paṭiccasamuppāda* is accompanied first by the four noble truths (explained with the usual statements) as ways to cultivate right view; and then, each limb of the sequence is analyzed in terms of knowing the item, its arising, ending, and the way to its ending.

The four noble truths are said to constitute a fourfold method of analysis (*catuparivattaṃ*) in the *Khandhavāgga* of the *Saṃyutta-nikāya.*[30] The Buddha asks his audience about the five aggregates of grasping (*upādāna-kkhandha*) and lists the five. He explains that it was only when he fully understood these aggregates of grasping as they really are and the fourfold series that he became fully enlightened 'in the world with its Māras, Brahmās, recluses and brahmans, devas and men.'[31] The fourfold analysis is the same method as found in the four noble truths: knowing a thing according to what it is, how it comes to be, how it ceases to be, and the means by which it ceases to be. The Buddha then applies the fourfold analysis to the following items: form (*rūpaṃ*), sustenance (*āhāro*), feeling (*vedanā*), recognition (*saññā*), formations (*saṅkhārā*), and consciousness (*viññāṇaṃ*). The *Sāmaññaphala-*, *Bhayabherava-*, and *Chabbisodhana-sutta*s all use the fourfold analysis in relationship to the corruptions (*āsavā*): knowing them, knowing their arising, ending, and the means to their ending. However, in these *sutta*s that understand and thus eliminate the corruptions by knowing the four noble truths, the application of the analytic sequence found in the four noble truths is not called a separate fourfold analysis (*catuparivattaṃ*). The reference to being enlightened in the world with Māra and Brahmā faintly echoes the *Dhammacakkappa-vattaṅa-sutta*.

The commentary on the *Saṃyutta-nikāya* passage glosses *catuparivaṭ-ṭaṃ* in terms of the four aggregates and explains that the analysis of form should be understood as analysis according to the four noble truths.[32] In both the *Saṃyutta-nikāya* example and the *Sammādiṭṭhi-sutta* above, knowledge is obtained by applying the analytical sequence used in the four noble truths, which the commentary recognizes as linked explicitly to the four noble truths. Should this fourfold analysis should be considered as a dimension of the four noble truths in the canon? Looking at how the same term 'fourfold analysis' appears in the *Bahudhātuka-sutta* in the *Majjhima-nikāya* requires that we not define 'fourfold analysis' solely in terms of the four noble truths. At the end of his talk, the Buddha adjures Ānanda to remember what he has said by different titles:

> Therefore, Ānanda, remember this *dhamma* analysis as the 'many elements,' remember this as the 'fourfold analysis,' remember this as the 'mirror of *dhamma*,' remember this as 'beating the drum of that which does not die,' and remember it as the 'incomparable victory in battle.'[33]

As we can see, in the *Bahudhātuka-sutta* 'fourfold analysis' refers not to the four noble truths – they do not appear in the talk at all – but to the eighteen elements, the sense spheres, dependent origination, and what is possible and what is not possible (*ṭhānāṭṭhānaṃ*). Despite the fact that the commentator on the *Saṃyutta-nikāya* passage explained the fourfold analysis in terms of the four noble truths, it appears that the meaning of 'fourfold analysis' was not fixed throughout the canon.

The associations between the four noble truths and *paṭiccasamuppāda* are made in several ways. The first is the same as we found in the *sutta*s that link the four truths with the establishment of mindfulness; namely, the same formulaic statements that define each of the truths appear in combination with discussions of dependent arising. Second, the sequence of dependent arising in direct and reverse order is substituted for the usual explanations of the second and third truths. Third, there is a connection made through an analysis of the aggregates of grasping that appear in the *jāti pi dukkhā* (birth is pain) formula. Fourth, the analysis embedded in the four truths – knowing a thing, its arising, ending, and the way to its ending – is applied to either the twelve limbs of dependent arising or to other teachings. Table 3.3 describes these relationships.

The *Aṅguttara-* and *Saṃyutta-nikāyas*

The four noble truths appear in the the *Aṅguttara-* and *Saṃyutta-nikāya*s in ways that are similar to their appearance in the *Majjhima-* and *Dīgha-nikāyas.* We have already examined one passage from the *Aṅguttara-nikāya*, in which the four truths appear in a list of the Buddha's *dhamma.* The *Aṅguttara-* and *Saṃyutta-nikāya*s are composed of lists, perhaps designed to provide a comprehensive treatment of all of the Buddha's teachings. Gethin writes that the *Saṃyutta-nikāya* 'takes a particular list and attempts to assemble all the significant treatments and discussions of it from the available stock of material, while the [*Aṅguttara-nikāya*], by means of a system of numerical progression from one to eleven, arranges its material according to the number of items or divisions involved.'[34] These two sorts of lists are complementary, Gethin explains; the *saṃyutta* method was designed to lay out the basic themes of early Buddhist thought, while the numerical *aṅguttara* method provided a way to catch any items that may have slipped through the broader *saṃyutta* net.[35] We saw above that there are a standardized list of thirty-seven *dhammā*s that lead to awakening. This list forms the basic organizational structure of the *Saṃyutta-nikāya*, as well as one of the *mātikā* in the *Abhidhamma-piṭaka.* The inclusion of the four noble truths in a longer list based on the thirty-seven factors of awakening is our point of departure for a comparison of the four noble truths in the lists of the *Saṃyutta-nikāya* and the *Abhidhamma-piṭaka.*

The first of the four noble truths appears in the *Aṅguttara-nikāya* in a list of 'six sixes.'[36] The section consists of a series of questions according to which one should understand *dukkha. Dukkha* appears in a list given in a *dhamma* talk that is described as a discriminating discourse (*nibbedhika-pariyāya*).[37] This form of discourse is different than the usual forms of

Table 3.3 Analyses of the Four Noble Truths II

	A I 176–177	*Mahāhatthipadopama-sutta* (M I 184–191)	*Sammādiṭṭhi-sutta* (M I 46–55)	S III 58
Introduction of truths	elements birth name and form sense spheres contact feeling four noble truths	simile of the elephant's foot 'all wholesome states can be included in the four noble truths' (Sāriputta)	what is unwholesome and unwholesome roots, what is wholesome and wholesome roots sustenance know it, its arising, ending, and way (way is always eightfold path) another way to right view: four noble truths	aggregates of grasping: body feelings recognition formations consciousness by *catuparvaṭṭam* (fourfold analysis)
First truth	= *Dhammacakkappavattana-sutta*	'birth is pain' what are the aggregates of grasping? form feelings recognitions formations consciousness what is form? earth, water, fire, air	= *Dhammacakkappavattana-sutta* 'birth is pain'	no mention
Second truth	*paṭiccasamuppāda* direct order	no mention	= *Dhammacakkappavattana-sutta*	no mention
Third truth	*paṭiccasamuppāda* reverse order	no mention	= *Dhammacakkappavattana-sutta*	no mention
Fourth truth	= *Dhammacakkappavattana-sutta*	no mention	= *Dhammacakkappavattana-sutta*	knowing the way to the ending of each item is by means of the eightfold path as in the *Dhammacakka-ppavattana-sutta*
Following topic	none	'One who sees dependent arising sees *dhamma*, one who sees *dhamma* sees dependent arising.'	another way: know each limb of dependent arising, its ending, and the way to its ending (eightfold path)	ones who know in this way are freed without grasping (*arahats*)

discourse that we have encountered so far; it refers to an analysis that pays detailed attention to the definitions of the items explored in the discourse. Desire (*kāmā*), feelings (*vedanā*), recognitions (*saññā*), corruptions (*āsavā*), actions (*kammā*), and pain (*dukkhaṃ*) should all be known according to six categories. These categories begin with the simple injunction that, for example, desire is to be known (*veditabbaṃ*). Desire is then to be known according to its source of origin (*nidānasambhava*), different kinds (*vemattatā*), results (*vipakā*), ending (*nirodho*), and finally according to the way leading to cessation (*nirodhagāminī paṭipadā*). Pain is first to be known according to the standard formula of the *Dhammacakkappavattana-sutta*; the *jāti pi dukkhā* (birth is pain) formula. We find the standard explanations of the remaining truths – this is craving (*yāyaṃ taṇhā*); this is the complete ending of the passion of that craving (*yo tassā yeva taṇhāya asesavirāganirodho*); and, the way to the ending of pain is by means of the noble eightfold path (*ariyo aṭṭhaṅgiko maggo*). In this list, however, the four noble truths are analyzed with different questions. The formulas explaining the truths are exactly the same as those that we have traced through the various *sutta*s from the *Dhammacakkappavattana-sutta*, but they are interrogated as to their origin, type, result, ending, and by the way to their ending. The four noble truths are inserted into the analysis and definition of pain.

The 'Collection on Truth' (*Sacca-saṃyutta*) in the *Saṃyutta-nikāya* arranges the four noble truths in lengthy and varied combinations. There are one hundred and thirty-one passages divided into eleven chapters (*vaggo*), and each is about the four noble truths.[38] The content of these chapters vary from the Buddha's *Dhammacakkappavattana-sutta* to different topics which should be understood according to the four noble truths. There are also a number of parables which use various similes to demonstrate the greatness of the four noble truths. With few exceptions, each of the one hundred and thirty-one sayings end with this admonition:

> Therefore, *bhikkhu*s, an effort should be made to realize 'this is pain,' an effort should be made to realize 'this the arising of pain,' an effort should be made to realize 'this is the ending of pain,' an effort should be made to realize 'this is the way leading to the ending of pain.'[39]

Very briefly, the first chapter of the *Sacca-saṃyutta* is on *samādhi* (concentration).[40] In different sections, the Buddha explains that those who know *samādhi* (concentration) and *paṭisallāṇa* (seclusion) know the four noble truths; that men of good families who have gone forth from the home into homelessness (*kulaputtā sammāgārasmā anagāriyam pabbajitā*), recluses, and brahmans (*samaṇā vā brāhmaṇā*) know the four noble truths; and that the four noble truths are useful when turning away from unprofitable reasoning (*akusale vittake*), unprofitable thoughts (*akusalā cittā*), bickering (*viggāhikakathā*), and gossip (*tiracchānakathā*). The second chapter opens with two recitations of the *Dhammacakkappavattana-sutta* and also explains the aggregates of grasping (*upādānakkhanda*) and the spheres of sense (*āyatana*) in terms of knowing the four noble truths. The remainder of the second chapter discusses how to remember (*dhāreti*) the four noble truths and explains that ignorance (*avijja*) is not knowing the four noble truths, that knowledge (*vijjā*) is knowing the four noble truths, that there are endless ways of explaining (*saṅkāsanā*) the four noble truths, and that the four noble truths are true – not false or changeable (*tathā*).[41]

Chapters three, four, and five contain talks given by the Buddha at Koṭigāma, at the Siṅsapā Grove in Kosambī, and in Rājagaha; the talks cover diverse topics that include those found in the first two chapters: the fact that a fully awakened one (*sammāsambuddho*) and *arahats* know the four noble truths; and, parables on the greatness of the four noble truths. The parables range from comparing the futility of holding water in a basket made of the leaves of an acacia tree to the futility of ending pain without knowing the four noble truths[42] to a comparison between seven pieces of gravel and Mount Sineru – which is like the difference between the pain that remains to one who understands the four noble truths and the pain that remains to one who does not understand the four noble truths.[43] The last six chapters of the *Sacca-saṃyutta* continue in this vein, enumerating various wrong behaviors that result from not understanding the four noble truths and the number of beings who exist in the various hells because they do not comprehend the four noble truths.[44]

This collection on the four noble truths in the *Saṃyutta-nikāya* is perhaps the most compelling example of the way in which the truths are explained with a discourse that is rooted in the experiences of living in the world. The discourse is naturalized insofar as there is no effort to dissociate the propositional truth of the four noble truths from daily experiences. The parables follow familiar patterns of comparison between one who knows the four noble truths and one who does not. For example, the Buddha takes up a bit of dust on his finger and asks his followers which is greater, the dust on his finger or the earth? The answer, of course, is that the earth is greater. Just so, the Buddha replies, is the amount of pain that is destroyed by one who has comprehended the four noble truths greater than the amount of pain that remains.[45] In all cases, an effort should be made to realize the four noble truths. The varied and diverse ways that the Buddha urges his audience to comprehend the four noble truths are characteristic of all of the collections in the *Saṃyutta-nikāya*, which employ parables, stories, metaphors, and similes to convey the importance of knowing and understanding various points of doctrine. The *Saṃyutta* follows the basic *mātikā* list (which is taken up at greater length in the next chapter): path, enlightenment factors, mindfulness, faculties, right efforts, powers, bases of success, *anuruddha*, meditation, in-breathing and out-breathing, stream-attainment, and truths.[46] Unlike the *mātikā* lists in the *Abhidhamma-piṭaka*, however, the *Saṃyutta-nikāya* uses naturalized and concrete language to teach the various doctrines, of which the four noble truths are one.

Nibbāna and the Four Noble Truths

There are a few passages in the canon outside of the *Saṃyutta-nikāya* where the four noble truths are concretely said to be a means to the attainment of *nibbāna*. When the four noble truths are analyzed and set in detailed relation to other teachings of the Buddha, the purpose for which they are taught is not usually explained. However, there are a few points at which the the four truths are taught simply for the purpose of attaining *nibbāna*. The teaching is not invoked with any of the associations with enlightenment, with the Buddha's biographies, or the *dhamma* eye, as it is in its symbolic role.

In the *Pāsādika-sutta* Ānanda is asked: 'What, friends, was taught by the recluse Gautama?' His reply is that the Buddha taught 'this is pain,' 'this is the origin of pain,' 'this is the cessation of pain,' and 'this is the way to the cessation of pain.' Why, the text continues, did the Buddha teach this? The answer is that those who ask why the Buddha taught this should be told:

> This, friends, is endowed with profit, is endowed with *dhamma*, this belongs to the higher *brahmacariya*, this leads to dissatisfaction, dispassion, to destruction, to perfect wisdom, to *nibbāna*. This is what the Buddha has taught.[47]

The four noble truths, according to this *sutta*, are taught for the attainment of *nibbāna*. This passage has parallels in the *Poṭṭhapāda-sutta*[48] and in the *Dasuttara-sutta*.[49] The context for the *Pāsādika-* and *Poṭṭhapāda-sutta*s is the same: after the Buddha refuses to respond to the unanswered questions (*avyākata*), he answers the question 'what is taught?' with the four noble truths, which, he responds, are taught for the attainment of *nibbāna*. The four noble truths stand against the unanswered questions because the four noble truths alone, these *sutta*s imply, are profitable and result in the acquisition of knowledge.

Sāriputta teaches *dhamma* in groups from one to ten in the 'Talk on the Tenfold Series' (*Dasuttara-sutta*). The stated purpose for teaching the series is the attainment of *nibbāna*.

> I will proclaim *dhamma* in groups from one to ten so that *nibbāna* may be won, so that pain may be ended and so that every bond may be set free.[50]

Within this series, the four noble truths are found among a list of other teachings of the Buddha that can be classified according to the number four.

Where the four noble truths were taught in the *Pāsādika-* and *Poṭṭhapāda-suttas* as independent units which stood against the 'unanswered questions,' here the four noble truths are taught as one set among a list of fours within a much larger group that runs from one to ten. While these are relatively minor references to the attainments that one might enjoy by virtue of knowing the four noble truths, they are significant because in each of these *suttas*, the four truths appear as one in a list of a number of propositions that lead to *nibbāna* – not in either of the well defined formulas that we have identified above. However, the passages do not explain just how it is that the four noble truths lead to *nibbāna.*

Conclusion

The material examined in this chapter has demonstrated how thoroughly the four noble truths were integrated into the analytic categories of the Buddha's teachings. When F. I. Shcherbatskoi wrote that the four noble truths had nothing particularly Buddhistic about them because they appear in other schools of Indian philosophical thought, he was referring to the type of analysis that we have just explored. It it evident that in these passages, the four noble truths are not particularly set apart; they are not extracted from other teachings; and, the point is to understand how the teachings intersect and produce the world in which human beings live. We have seen that the four truths are placed in relation to other teachings in a variety of ways. The teaching of dependent arising is used to explain the four truths and the four truths are used to explain dependent origination. The formulaic descriptions of each of the four truths serve as a thread that is woven throughout the network of the Buddha's teachings. The analysis embedded in the four noble truths is extracted and called the 'fourfold analysis.' The analysis of the four noble truths according to the categories of *abhidhamma* are also found in the *Sutta-piṭaka*. Taken together in these contexts, the four truths are regarded as propositions which should be learned for the purposes of attaining *nibbāna*, but propositions made in concrete and natural language.

Notes

1 F. I. Shcherbatskoi, 'The Doctrine of the Buddha,' *Bulletin of the School of Oriental Studies*, 6 (1932): 892.

2 Rupert M. L. Gethin, 'The *Mātikās*: Memorization, Mindfulness, and the List,' in *In the Mirror of Memory: Reflections on Mindfulness and Remembrance in Indian and Tibetan Buddhism*, ed. Janet Gyatso (Albany: State University of New York Press, 1992), 167.

3 See Susan Stalker's comments on this point in the second chapter of her dissertation, where she has provided a clear discussion of interpretations of dependent origination offered by Oldenberg, Senart, Oltramare, La Valleé

Poussin, Lamotte, and others. Susan C. Stalker, 'A Study of Dependent Origination: Vasubandhu, Buddhaghosa, and the Interpretation of Pratityasamutpada' (Ph.D. diss., University of Pennsylvania, 1987), 47–86.

4 D II 290–315; M I 55–63, III 248–252; Vbh 99–121. On the relationship between these *sutta*s, see Gethin, *Buddhist Path*, 44ff.

5 D II 290; M I 55. *Idha bhikkhave bhikkhu kāye kāyānupassī viharati ātāpī sampajāno satimā vineyya loke abhijjhādomanassaṃ*, and so on.

6 D II 304; M I 55

7 M I 55–63

8 This fact has led Norman to suggest that the two suttas are two versions, the *Mahāsatipaṭṭhāna* being the greater (*mahā*) and the *Satipaṭṭhāna* being the *cūla*, or shorter, version. This speculation is rooted in the fact that many of the *sutta*s have *mahā* and *cūla* versions, as for example, in the *Majjhima-nikāya*, where there are seventeen paired *sutta*s prefaced by *mahā-* or *cūla-*. The *Mahāsatipaṭṭhāna-sutta* is classified in the second group of the *Dīgha-nikāya* called the *Mahāvagga*, or 'Great Chapter.' Norman also notes that this second group of *sutta*s in the *Dīgha-nikāya* reflect a later date than the first group and should be called legends instead of discourses. The *sutta*s of this second group, he has written, have features 'which show them to be later than the *sutta*s of the first vagga where the Buddha is only a man, alive or recently dead.' Norman, *Pāli Literature*, 32–36.

9 D II 305

10 S V 421, n. 2. Similarly, one Sinhalese manuscript and one Burmese manuscript of the *Mahāsatipaṭṭhāna-sutta* omit 'illness' (*vyādhi*) but insert 'association with things not liked' and 'separation from desired things' (*apiyehi sampayogo dukkho piyehi vippayogo dukkho*). See D II 305, notes 2 and 3.

11 D II 305

12 D II 308

13 D II 310

14 D II 308–309. This list of ten items is a bit unusual; they are similar to the twelve limbs of dependent arising, but are not identical. Each of the sets recur throughout the canon, but the combination of the various sets is what sets this explanation apart from other explanations.

15 D II 310

16 D II 312–313. See Gethin, *Buddhist Path*, 190–226 on the eightfold path.

17 D II 314

18 M I 56,63; D II 290,315

19 Gethin, *Buddhist Path*, 46.

20 M III 248

21 S II 1

22 The views refuted are those found in the *Devadaha-sutta* (M II 214).

23 The commentary actually explains the term found in the passage: *vediyamānasso* is one who knows that one experiences feelings (Mp II 282 on A I 176). The commentary has an extensive discussion of how the four truths are appropriate for such a person. The commentary repeats a short section found in the *Mahāsatipaṭṭhāna-sutta* on how one should consider feelings (D II 298 = Mp II 282).

24 A I 176–177

25 M I 184–191

26 M I 191

27 M I 46–55; cf. *Mahāhatthipadopama-sutta* (M I 184–191)

28 M I 48

29 *Yato kho āvuso ariyasāvako jarāmaraṇañ ca pajānāti jarāmaraṇasamudayañ ca pajānāti jarāmaraṇanirodhañ ca jarāmaraṇanirodhagāminipaṭipadañ ca pajānāti, ettāvatā pi kho āvuso añño pi pariyāyo yathā ariyasāvako sammādiṭṭhi hoti ujugatā 'ssa diṭṭhi dhamme aveccappasādena samannāgato āgato imam saddhammam ti* (M I 49).
30 S III 58
31 S III 59
32 Spk II 276 (on S III 58)
33 M III 67
34 Gethin, *Buddhist Path*, 20.
35 Gethin, *Buddhist Path*, 22.
36 A III 411–417
37 *Nibbedhikapariyāyaṃ vo bhikkhave dhammapariyāyaṃ desessāmi, taṃ suṇāthasādukkhaṃ manasikarotha, bhāsissāmī ti* (A III 410).
38 S V 414–478
39 S V 414
40 S V 414–420
41 S V 420–431
42 S V 438f.
43 S V 457f.
44 S V 468–476
45 S V 460
46 S V 478; see also Gethin, *Buddhist Path*, 21.
47 D III 137
48 D I 189
49 D III 277
50 D III 272

CHAPTER FOUR

Abhidhamma Analysis of the Four Noble Truths

In what sense is it a mātikā? In the sense of being like a mother. A mātikā is like a mother just as a face is like a lotus. As a mother gives birth to different kinds of sons, and then protects them and raises them, so too does a mātikā give birth to various kinds of dhammā and meanings, and then protects them and raises them so that they do not perish.[1]

Kassapa of Coḷa (c. 1200 C.E.)

Networks of *Mātikā*s in the *Abhidhamma-piṭaka*

The previous chapter demonstrated that the four noble truths were thoroughly integrated into the same analysis to which other teachings of the Buddha are subjected. The four noble truths appear as explanations for the foundations of mindfulness, dependent arising explains the second and third truths, and the formulas that define each truth appear in a variety of places. The four noble truths are used to analyze desire, feeling, recognition, actions, and the corruptions. In those passages, the four noble truths function as propositions rather than as a symbol of the Buddha's enlightenment. They are not identified as the central teaching of the Buddha, although there are allusions to their role in the Buddhist cosmology.

In this chapter, I wish to examine a question that emerges in the course of this detailed examination of how the four noble truths are analyzed: is there any particular order to how the four noble truths appear in the canon, outside of their symbolic guise as in the *Dhammacakkappavattana-sutta*? My initial answer is both yes and no. There is an order, but it is so broad and scattered that it may often appear as no order at all because of its expansiveness. In fact, this observation helps us to further clarify how the four noble truths function throughout the entire canon. The symbolic role of the four noble truths is characterized by its tightly structured explanations, its associations with the Buddha's enlightenment stories that form a central theme in his biographies, and its location in the Buddhist cosmos. In sharp contrast, when the four noble truths appear as propositions within the network of the Buddha's teachings, there is no definitive order that shapes where we find them: when extracted from the center that they occupy as a symbol, the four noble truths become ubiquitous. The setting for the four truths as propositions is nothing less than the entire corpus of the Buddha's teachings throughout the canon. We saw the results of this in the *Sutta-piṭaka* in the previous chapter; in this chapter, the four truths are simply one integral dimension of *abhidhamma* analysis in the *Abhidhamma-piṭaka*.

Gethin has suggested that the *mātikā*s (lists or matrices of doctrines) may have been a form of textual transmission that aided in both memorization and recitation as well as in the analysis of *dhamma*. He hypothesizes that the *mātikā* lists emerged within the expanding body of Buddhist literature and that they are found in the *Sutta-piṭaka* as well as in the *Abhidhamma-piṭaka*. Gethin proposes that a core list of teachings that organizes the *Saṃyutta-nikāya* is one of two *mātikā*s (the second being the list of triplets and couplets used in the *Abhidhamma-piṭaka*). When both of these *mātikā*s are taken together, they provide the order for the *Vibhaṅga* (one of the seven books of the *Abhidhamma-piṭaka*). Instead of accepting the common claim that both the *mātikā*s and the *abhidhamma* literature emerge late in the tradition, Gethin suggests that the *mātikā*s were an earlier development of transmitting and teaching texts which later grew into the canonical *Abhidhamma-piṭaka* works.[2] 'It would appear, then,' Gethin writes, 'that a *mātikā* can be any schedule or table of items or lists – but especially one built up according to a system of numerical progression – that acts as a basis for further exposition.'[3] He shows that the *mātikā*s should be understood as a series of building blocks that can create 'a palace that is much larger in extent than the sum of the parts' instead of a condensation of teachings.[4]

*Mātikā*s are basic to the seven books of the *Abhidhamma-piṭaka* and commentaries and also to the *Aṅguttara-nikāya* and *Saṃyutta-nikāya*. The feature that the lists share is the enumeration of teachings while setting one teaching in relationship to another. They are not designed to develop an all-encompassing theory of the cosmos, but rather they specify how states (*dhammā*) arise and pass away in the world. The principle that structures this network of teachings, and the place of the four noble truths within these networks, is the laying out of *dhamma* – laying it out 'bare and revealing its inner workings,' as Gethin phrases it. Exposing the working of *dhamma* involved showing how things that appear to exist permanently in the world exist only in dependence upon one another. These lists do not constitute a universal accounting of all things which exist (however temporarily) in the world, but provide a framework within which one might trace the causal relationships that account for how the world is continually changing. Gethin suggests that to know how these lists fit together is to know the inner structure and dynamic of *dhamma*.[5] The building blocks of the *mātikā*s reveal *dhamma*, which the canon describes repeatedly as 'beautiful in the beginning, beautiful in the middle, beautiful in the end.'

In contrast to the concrete language of the *Sutta-piṭaka*, the denaturalized discourse of *abhidhamma* 'make[s] available to users what really exists' through the form of the matrices (*mātikā*).[6] The four noble truths are analyzed in four of the seven *Abhidhamma-piṭaka* texts; a close reading of those passages reveals a method which defines, enumerates and analyzes the causal relations which the Theravāda canonical tradition understands to constitute reality. The matrices that structure *abhidhamma* analysis are organized as networks. The lists in the *Abhidhamma-piṭaka* do not provide a comprehensive description of the universe; instead, they are structured as networks of doctrinal propositions which lead infinitely lead to other propositions within the web. For example, a person enters a matrix at a specific point; the analysis of that point leads to another point, which in turn leads to another, *ad infinitum*. C. A. Foley alluded to these networks in the introduction to her translation of the *Dhammasaṅgaṇī*: 'The object is not so much to extend knowledge as to ensure mutual consistency in the *in*tension of ethical notions, and to systematize and formulate the theories and practical mechanism of intellectual and moral progress scattered in profusion throughout the Suttas.'[7]

The subject matter analyzed in the *abhidhamma* texts is drawn largely from the *Sutta-piṭaka*. But, the fundamental principle which supports the *Abhidhamma-piṭaka* begins with the proper understanding of

> any given item, [knowing] it in all relations, under all the aspects recognized in the philosophy and the practical doctrine and discipline of Buddhism. Therefore the same material is sought to be classified in different ways and from different points of view. This explains why in the *Dhammasaṅgaṇī* and other *Abhidhamma pakaraṇa*s, one encounters interminable lists of classifications. Although they may appear as repetitive and therefore monotonous, yet they serve a useful purpose. For they bring into relief, not only the individual characteristics of each *dhamma*, but also its position in relation to other *dhamma*s.[8]

The four noble truths are set in this network of doctrinal propositions, and their relations to other doctrines are outlined according to a specific *abhidhamma* methodology. They function here as all doctrines function in the *Abhidhamma-piṭaka* – as items of knowledge to be learned and set in a larger web of interconnected teachings which show how reality is divided and arranged in a multitude of ways.

There are two fundamental lists (*mātikā*s) found in the *Abhidhamma-piṭaka*: the lists of the *tika*s (threes) and *duka*s (twos), and the groups of *dhammā* which include the aggregates (*khandhā*), spheres of sense (*āyatanāni*), elements (*dhātuyo*), and so on. (The lists of controversial topics in the *Kathāvatthu* are not a *mātikā*, although Buddhaghosa defines them as such.) The first list consists of the *tika*s and *duka*s, to which an additional forty-two *suttantika duka*s are sometimes added. The *tika*s are a list of twenty-two 'threes' or 'triplets,' the first of which is: how many are good? how many are bad? how many are neither good nor bad? The *duka*s are a list of one hundred 'twos' or 'couplets,' such as: what are the roots? what are not roots? The *tika*s and *duka*s are presented in the *Dhammasaṅgaṇī*, the first book of the *Abhidhamma-piṭaka*. Because of the placement of these lists in the *Dhammasaṅgaṇī* and because they also form the basis of the *Paṭṭhāna* (the last of the seven books), the *tika*s and *duka*s are often interpreted as being the 'fundamental *mātikā*.'[9] The *tika* and *duka* lists are identical throughout the *Abhidhamma-piṭaka*, and are different from the groups of *dhammā*. The lists of the *khandhāyatanadhātu* (aggregates, spheres of sense, elements, and so on) vary widely throughout the collection of *abhidhamma* texts, but they provide the organizational framework for four of the seven books: the *Vibhaṅga*, *Dhātukathā*, *Puggalapaññatti*, and *Yamaka*. Each of these books lists a *mātikā* at the beginning of the text; the *Vibhaṅga* and *Dhātukathā mātikā*s are the most comprehensive of the four. The *Puggalapaññatti* lists six designations (*paññatti*): aggregates (*khandha-*), spheres of sense (*āyatana-*), elements (*dhātu-*), truths (*sacca-*), sense-faculties (*indriya-*), and persons (*puggala-*). The *Yamaka* lists ten pairs (*yamaka*): root (*mūla-*), aggregates (*khandha-*), elements (*dhātu-*), truths (*sacca-*), formations (*sankhāra-*), inclinations (*anusaya-*), mind (*citta-*), states (*dhammā-*), and sense-faculties (*indriya-*). The four noble truths belong to the second matrix of *dhammā*; thus, they appear in the four books of the *Abhidhamma-piṭaka* that are based on this matrix.

The work of A. K. Warder stands as the foundation for studies of the *mātikā*s, although his proposals are flawed by his attempt to provide a chronology for the *mātikā*s found in various Buddhist schools.[10] However, if we set aside his historical claims, his observations on the unique nature of the Theravāda *mātikā* are useful.[11] Warder compared the Theravāda and Sarvāstivāda lists, concluding that the 'Pali lists make no attempt at comprehensiveness, they deal only with particular questions and frequently end with *ye vā pana . . . aññe pi. . . .* (this is one . . . this is another).'[12] He explained that because a category may vary from context to context, the Pāli lists suggest a system of relations instead of a comprehensive 'plurality of elements.' The Sarvāstivāda schools listed seventy-five *dhamma*s which could be classified according to certain groups of aggregates (*skandha*). The seventy-five *dhamma*s can also be classified according to their spheres of sense (*āyatana*) and elements (*dhātu*), as *āśrava* and *anāśrava*, or according to the four noble truths (*satya*).[13] On the other hand, the Theravāda lists are more extensive.

Warder's comparison of *abhidhamma* lists shows that the Theravāda school significantly rearranged the lists and included a number of additional categories which are found in the *Sutta-piṭaka*.[14] The commentary on the *Dhammasaṅgaṇī* added still more. Because of the fluidity of the Theravāda lists, Warder wrote that the Theravāda tradition did 'not aim at the exhaustive description of the elements of the Universe which seem to be implied by the Sarvāstivāda seventy-five *dharmas*.' Instead, he continued, the Theravāda schools took up 'only such categories as seem relevant from some unspecified source (fluid tradition?).'[15] Warder leaves his parenthetical question unaswered, but points out that because the categories used in the Theravāda tradition vary from context to context, the Theravāda *abhidhamma* constitutes a 'system of relations in which, having taken any questions for study, one may go on indefinitely reviewing connected phenomena from that standpoint.'[16]

In addition to a useful critique of Warder's chronologies for the *mātikās*, Gethin suggests that the *mātikās* aided memorization of the teachings because they ordered the material in a particular way and because they provided a 'map' of the Buddha's teachings. He also states that 'the recitation and repetition of the lists of the Abhidhamma constituted a meditation exercise in itself,' although the support for this position is scant.[17] Gethin proposes that the *mātikās* were the basis for further exposition of the Buddha's teachings and that the *mātikās* were particularly designed to show the interrelationship of all aspects of the teachings of the Buddha.

The following analysis of the doctrine of the four noble truths supports the position that the Theravāda *abhidhamma* books form a network of doctrines instead of a comprehensive catalogue. The four noble truths are part of the *khandhāyatanadhātu mātikā* which are then analyzed according to the *tika* and *duka* lists. Gethin poses these two *mātikās* as two axes on a grid, both as essential and vital to the analysis and neither more fundamental than the other.[18] The remainder of this chapter explores the analysis of the four noble truths in four of the *Abhidhamma-piṭaka* texts: the *Vibhaṅga*, *Dhātukathā*, *Puggalapaññati*, and the *Yamaka*. The *khandhāyatanadhātu mātikā* structures these four books, and thus the four noble truths are an integral part of these texts, unlike the *Dhammasaṅgaṇī* and the *Paṭṭhāna*, which are organized according to the *tikas* and *dukas*, or the *Kathāvatthu*. Linguistically, the four noble truths appear in each of the *Abhidhamma-piṭaka* books in some form of the mnemonic sets identified by Norman. In these four books, the four noble truths are indeed set into a network of related phenomena and are analyzed from different angles in each text. The categories of analysis overlap with each other, yet they are used with precision and accuracy. These precise definitions are the purpose of the analysis – the delineation of terms and categories, together with the relationship between states (*dhammā*).

The *Vibhaṅga*

The *Vibhaṅga* is the second book of the *Abhidhamma-piṭaka*; it analyzes the *khandhāyatanadhātu mātikā* according to three kinds of inquiry: *suttantavibhaṅga* (analysis according to the *sutta*s), *abhidhammavibhaṅga* (*abhidhamma* analysis), and the *pañhāpucchaka* (interrogation). Generally, the contents of the *sutta* analysis reflect the definitions and descriptions found in the *Sutta-piṭaka*. For example, the *sutta* analysis for the four noble truths is the same as that found in the *Mahāsatipaṭṭhāna-sutta*. The *abhidhamma* analysis of the four noble truths consists of further definitions, employing the categories of impurities (*kilesā*), states (*dhammā*), roots (*mūlāni*), corruptions (*āsavā*), and results (*vipākā*). Finally, the *pañhāpucchakā* (interrogation) section is made up of the *tika*s and *duka*s. This analysis provides a clear example of how the two *mātikā*s are often combined. Here, the *tika*s and *duka*s are the categories used to further categorize the list of doctrines (*khandhāyatanadhātu*); in the *Dhātukathā*, for example, the *tika*s and *duka*s are simply appended to the list of doctrines.

The contents of the *Vibhaṅga* follow the *khandhāyatanadhātu* list, discussed above, with eighteen items analyzed:

5 *khandhā* (aggregates)
12 *āyatanāni* (spheres of sense)
6 *dhātuyo* (elements)
4 *saccāni* (truths)
22 *indriyāni* (sense-faculties)
12 *paṭiccasamuppāda* (dependent arising)
4 *satipaṭṭhānā* (bases of mindfulness)
4 *sammāppadhānā* (right effort)
4 *iddhipādā* (bases of psychic power)
7 *bojjaṅgā* (enlightenment factors)
8 *maggaṅgāni* (limbs of the path)
4 *jhānāni* (trance states)
4 *appamaññā* (illimitables)
5 *sikkhāpadā* (precepts)
4 *paṭisambhidā* (analytic insights)
ñāṇā (knowledge)
khuddakavatthuyo (small items)
dhammahadaya (heart of the teachings).

The *Saccavibhaṅga* (Analysis of Truths) is conducted according to the standard threefold analysis that is used throughout the *Vibhaṅga*: (1) according to the discourses (*suttantabhājaniya*), (2) according to *abhidhamma* (*abhidhammabhājaniya*), and (3) according to the triplet (*tika*) and couplet (*duka*) lists (*pañhāpucchaka*, interrogation). The analysis according to the *suttas* employs the same definitions and comparisons found in the *Mahāsatipaṭṭhāna-*, *Satipaṭṭhāna-*, and *Saccavibhaṅga-suttas*, and elsewhere in the *Sutta-piṭaka.*[19] The analysis according to the triplets and couplets sets the four noble truths within the network of other teachings. The networks of the *sutta* analysis and the interrogation (*pañhāpucchaka*) section are fairly straightforward; they are much the same as those discussed above. It is interesting to note that the four truths are not 'noble' when defined with *abhidhamma* analysis in the second of the three types of analyses. Taken together, the three sections of the *Saccavibhaṅga* explain the four noble truths with three different kinds of discourse and analysis.

Abhidhamma analysis in the *Vibhaṅga* breaks down the first three truths according to the impurities (*kilesā*), states (*dhammā*), roots (*mūlāni*), corruptions (*āsavā*), and results (*vipākā*). Craving is also included as a definition. The fourth truth, however, is defined in terms of the *jhāna* levels and the eight components of the path. A detailed answer is given for each of the four noble truths, and the above five analytical categories are used to explain the first two truths. The third truth is defined as abandoning craving. The fourth is explicated in terms of the eightfold path and the trance states of the *jhānas*. What is noteworthy about this analysis are the ways in which the definitions shift from one set to the next. There are a total of nine sets of answers to four questions: what is pain?, what is the arising of pain?, what is the ending of pain?, and what is the way to the ending of pain? In the first five sets, the answer to 'what is the way to the ending of pain?' remains the same while the answers to the first three questions shifts slightly in each of the first five sets. In sets six through nine, the answers to the first three questions are minor variations on those found in the first five sets while the answer to the fourth question varies. Table 4.1 lays out these variations; the pattern is most readily discerned from the tables, not by means of a prose explanation.

The first full explanation of the first three truths is:

> The four noble truths are: pain, the arising of pain, the ending of pain, the way leading to the ending of pain.
>
> There, what is the *arising of pain*? Craving. This is called the arising of pain.
>
> There, what is *pain*? The remaining impurities, the remaining bad states, the three good roots that are the objects of the corruptions, the remaining good states that are objects of the corruptions, the results of good and bad states that are objects of the corruptions, whatever inoperative states that are neither good nor bad nor the results of action, and all material qualities. This is called pain.
>
> There, what is the *ending of pain*? The abandoning of craving. This is called the ending of pain.[20]

Table 4.1 Analysis of the Four Truths in the *Vibhaṅga*: Sets 1–9 (Vibh 106–113)

Set 1.	What is the arising of pain?	craving
	What is pain?	remaining impurities
		remaining bad states
		three good roots
		remaining good states
		the results of good and bad states that are the objects of the corruptions whatever inoperative states there are, and so on
	What is the ending of pain?	abandoning craving
	What is the way leading to the ending of pain?	entry into first *jhāna* with eightfold path
Set 2.	What is the arising of pain?	craving
		remaining impurities
	What is pain?	remaining bad states
		three good roots
		remaining good states
		the results etc.
	What is the ending of pain?	abandoning craving
		abandoning remaining impurities
	What is the way leading to the ending of pain?	entry into first *jhāna*
Set 3.	What is the arising of pain?	craving
		remaining impurities
		remaining bad states
	What is pain?	three good roots
		remaining good states
		the results etc.
	What is the ending of pain?	abandoning craving
		remaining impurities
		remaining bad states
	What is the way leading to the ending of pain?	entry into first *jhāna*
Set 4.	What is the arising of pain?	craving
		remaining impurities
		remaining bad states
	What is pain?	three good roots
		remaining good states
		the results, etc.
	What is the ending of pain?	abandoning craving
		remaining impurities
		remaining bad states
		three good roots
	What is the way leading to the ending of pain?	entry into first *jhāna*

Table 4.1 continued

Set 5.	What is the arising of pain?	craving remaining obstacles remaining bad states three good roots remaining good states
	What is pain?	results, etc.
	What is the ending of pain?	abandoning craving remaining obstacles remaining bad states three good roots remaining good states
	What is the way leading to the ending of pain	entry into first *jhāna*
Set 6.	What is the arising of pain? What is pain? What is the ending of pain?	Same as Set 1
	What is the way leading to the ending of pain?	entry into first *jhāna* entry with five constitutent path
Set 7.	What is the arising of pain? What is pain? What is the ending of pain?	Same as Set 5
	What is the way leading to the ending of pain?	entry into first *jhāna* with five constitutent path
Set 8.	What is the arising of pain? What is pain? What is the ending of pain?	Same as Set 1
	What is the way leading to the ending of pain?	entry into first *jhāna* and no path constituents
Set 9.	What is the arising of pain? What is pain? What is the ending of pain?	Same as Set 5
	What is the way leading to the ending of pain?	entry into first *jhāna* and no path constituents

When examining the execution of these questions and answers in Table 4.1, in the first set the first question has one answer and the second question has five. By the fifth set, however, the answer to the first question has five and the second question has one. This shift is based on a logic that does not permit an answer to belong to more than one category; that is, that the answers to'what is the arising of pain?' are mutually exclusive of the answers to the question 'what is pain?' The answers to the third question continue to reverse the answers to the first question. The point is that (a) there are different answers to the questions 'what is the arising of pain?' and 'what is pain?' and (b) these different answers are patterned in a particular way. The arising of pain is not the same as pain, although different responses are possible. The ending of pain consists of the elimination of what is defined as pain: if pain is craving and the remaining obstacles, then the ending of pain is abandoning craving and the remaining obstacles. The set shifts by moving definitions from the second truth to the first and by identifying what should be eradicated (i.e., what pain is) in the definition of the third truth.

The analysis of the fourth truth shifts accordingly. The definition of the fourth truth is constant throughout the first five sets.

> There, what is the way leading to the ending of pain?
>
> Here, when a *bhikkhu* develops the transcending *jhāna* which tends toward release and destroys rebirth, for the abandoment of (wrong) views, for the attainment of the first stage, detached from sense pleasures . . . attains and dwells in the first *jhāna* that is difficult to practice and knowledge that is hard to acquire; at that time the eightfold path exists, i.e., right view . . . right concentration.[21]

The fourth truth is defined as entrance into the first level of *jhāna* level, where all eight limbs of the path exist. Each limb of the path is defined in detail in this first round of definitions, but in later rounds may simply be enumerated as present in the first *jhāna*. The combination of the *jhāna*s with the four noble truths in the *Vibhaṅga* continues the same kind of networking function that we have seen above: one set of teachings is used to define another.

Where the *jhāna*s appeared in stories of the Buddha's enlightenment in conjunction with the four noble truths, they were described phenomenologically as the Buddha experienced them. Here, however, the relationship between the four noble truths, the eightfold path, and the *jhāna*s in the first set of answers is more precisely laid out, as one might expect of the *Vibhaṅga*. The first *jhāna* is composed of either the eightfold path (sets 1–5), the fivefold path (sets 6–7), or the path with no parts at all (sets 8–9). The eight limbs of the path are those that we would naturally expect to find: right view, right right thought, right speech, right action, right livelihood, right effort, right mindfulness, and right concentration. In sets six and seven, the fourth truth is still defined in terms of the first *jhāna*, but with five limbs of the path instead of eight: right speech, action, and livelihood are eliminated from the eightfold path to proudce the fivefold version. In sets eight and nine, no mention is made of the limbs of the path at all, and the description of the first *jhāna* is expanded with an analysis which is also found in the *Dhammasaṅgaṇī* definitions of the stages of *jhāna*.[22] The first *jhāna* in the last two sets contain contact, feeling, recognition, volition, thought, application, sustained thinking, zest, ease, and self-collectedness – the usual set of experiences that define the first *jhāna* elsewhere in the *Tipiṭaka*. This extended description of the first *jhāna* is not included in the descriptions of the first *jhāna* when it is combined with the fivefold or the eightfold path.[23]

But what does it mean that, in the first set of questions, the answer to the fourth question consists of the eightfold path, and in sets six and seven, the answers contain the fivefold path, and in sets eight and nine, no limbs of the path exist at all? Like the answers to the first three questions, there are certain answers which are the same (the first *jhāna* is always described the same way) and others are variable. The point is the variability, but always within certain parameters. In the case of the fourth truth, other descriptions of the path in the *Vibhaṅga* (e.g., the *Jhānavibhaṅga* and the *Maggavibhaṅga*) provide a range of possible answers. Different sets of analysis found within the *Vibhaṅga* determine the variety of answers which are possible, and the point to any particular analysis is the relationship which *may* be established between the different sets of analyses.

There is a clear explanation for how to eradicate the factors that cause suffering that depends on what factors cause suffering. Unlike the analysis of the four truths in the *Sutta-piṭaka*, the *vibhaṅga* analysis provides a concise definition of what constitutes the path in relation to what factors are the cause of pain. As the factors that cause pain shift, so does the definition of what should be eliminated. Furthermore, there is a pattern to the definitions provided in sets six through nine. Sets one through five provide all of the possible options for how the first two truths can be defined. Pain can be, at a minimum, craving (set one) or, at the maximum, it can be defined as every factor except the results of good and bad states that are the objects of the corruptions, and so on (set five). Sets two through four lie between these two extremes. With regard to how the path is defined, sets one through five provide all of the possible options, given that the path is defined as entry into the first *jhāna* and the eightfold path. But, sets six and seven just detail the end of each range of options that may accompany the fivefold path; sets eight and nine do the same for the path that consists only of entry into the first *jhāna*. The clarity of definition for each truth seems to be the goal here, given a range of possible definitions and ways of analyzing each truth.

What conclusions can be drawn from this arrangement? First, there is a well-defined set of analytic categories: the first three truths are analyzed according to impurities (*kilesā*), states (*dhammā*), roots (*mūlāni*), corruptions (*āsavā*), and results (*vipākā*). The fourth truth is defined in terms of the *jhāna* levels and the eight components of the path. The categories used to examine the four noble truths do not vary throughout the nine sets. Second, the *abhidhamma* analysis offers exclusive – not inclusive –

combinations. Each set is unique insofar as each uses established definitions in different combinations. There is no single definition of the four noble truths. The analysis demonstrates how one set of categories intersects with others. The nine sets enumerate certain combinations within the parameters of the analytic categories employed. The categories used in this analysis are similar to those that we have encountered in the *Sutta-piṭaka*. The relationship between the *jhāna*s, the four truths, and eliminating the corruptions is extended here to include the impurities (*kilesā*), states (*dhammā*), roots (*mūlāni*), and results (*vipākā*).

The *Dhātukathā*

The second book in which the four noble truths appear is the *Dhātukathā*, the third book of the *Abhidhamma-piṭaka*. Although the *dhātu*s (elements) are examined in the *Dhātuvibhaṅga* of the *Vibhaṅga* and in the *Dhātuyamaka* of the *Yamaka*, the *Dhātukathā* is an in-depth inquiry into the nature of the *dhātu*s. *Dhātu*s have their own intrinsic nature that cannot be tranformed or changed. But the *dhātu*s do not endure, nor do they possess substance. They are the products of both animate and inanimate things. The states (*dhammā*) are the only things that exist, and they are classified under the categories of aggregates, spheres of sense, and elements – none of which possess substantiality or 'self'.[24] The formula of the four noble truths is the mnemonic set (b): *cattāri saccāni: dukkha-saccaṃ samudaya-saccaṃ nirodha-saccaṃ magga-saccaṃ*.[25] The word 'noble' is missing from this form. This formulation is also different from that used in the *sutta* analysis of the *Vibhaṅga*, where the truths are both 'noble' and 'truths'; here, the truths are simply identified as truths as they are in the *abhidhamma* analysis of the *Vibhaṅga*.

The *mātikā* begins with the aggregates (*khandhā*), spheres of sense (*āyatanāni*), elements (*dhātuyo*), truths (*saccāni*), sense-faculties (*indriyāni*), dependent arising (*paṭiccasamuppāda*), and so on.[26] The text states that the list is the *mātikā* of the *Dhammasaṅgani* and the *Dhātukathā*. The first six categories match the *mātikā* of the *Vibhaṅga*, although the list of states included under dependent arising is a collection of the remaining states analyzed in the *Vibhaṅga*. The triplets and couplets follow the core *khandhāyatanadhātu mātikā*; and, the truths in the *Dhātukathā* appear in the same location as in the *Vibhaṅga*, in order, according to the core *mātikā*. There are a total of 371 states (*dhammā*) analyzed in the *Dhātukathā* according to whether they can be (a) classified (*saṃgaha*) or unclassified (*asaṃgaha*) under the aggregates, spheres of sense, and elements, or (b) associated with (*sampayoga*) or dissociated from (*vippayoga*) the aggregates, spheres of sense and elements, or (c) classified and associated with, or classified and dissociated from, and so on.[27] There are fourteen chapters in the *Dhātukathā* which are separated into three groups according to (a), (b), and (c), above.[28] The truths are analyzed according to how they are related to the aggregates, spheres of sense, and elements. The arrangement is based on twos (chapters 1–5 are according to classified and unclassified; chapters 6–10 are based on associated with or dissociated from) and threes (chapters 11–14 are based on associated with or dissociated from the classified or unclassified); the threes are derived from combinations of the categories of twos. The *Dhātukathā* uses the first three items from the core *mātikā* – the aggregates (*khandhā*), spheres of sense (*āyatanāni*), and the elements (*dhātuyo*) – to analyze the remaining items of the core *mātikā* and the twenty-two triplets and one hundred couplets.[29]

Classified, unclassified, associated with, and dissociated from, all refer to other teachings to which the specific item in question is related. For example:

> According to how many aggregates, according to how many spheres of sense, according to how many elements is the truth that is pain classified?
>
> The truth that is pain is classified according to five aggregates, according to twelve spheres of sense, and according to eighteen elements.[30]

The remainder of the chapter analyzing the truths details how each truth is categorized in a variety of numerical arrangements, e.g., by ones, twos, threes and fours.[31] The truths are examined out of order, if the sequence of *dukkha*, *samudaya*, *nirodha*, and *magga* is taken as the usual sequence. For example, the first chapter details *dukkhasacca* (the truth of pain), *samudayasacca* (the truth of arising), *maggasacca* (the truth of the path) and then the third truth, which is *nirodhasacca* (the truth of ending).[32] The same sequence of all four noble truths (with *nirodha* at the end) is found only in chapters 1 and 14.[33] The pair of *samudaya* and *magga* is treated alone in four chapters,[34] and the triad of *samudaya*, *magga*, and *nirodha* is analyzed in four different chapters.[35] Each chapter arranges a combination of each individual truth according to whether they may be classified, unclassified, associated with or dissociated from the aggregates, spheres of sense, and elements. In other words, the four noble truths, which belong to the core *khandhāyatanadhātu mātikā*, are analyzed according to pairs of analytic terms and are compared to the first three items of the core *mātikā* (the aggregates, spheres of sense, and elements) in various numerical arrangements.

Each truth is not analyzed in every chapter. For example, the second chapter categorizes the states which may be classified under the same aggregate and the same sense-sphere, but not the same element.[36] There are forty-two states examined in that chapter, and thirty-five of them belong to the matter aggregate (*rūpakkhandhā*). The remaining states belong to the consciousness aggregate (*viññāṇakkhandhā*) and sphere of sense (*dhammāyatano*). Another example: the truth of arising (*samudayasaccaṃ*), the truth of ending (*nirodhasaccaṃ*), and the truth of the path (*maggasaccaṃ*) are grouped together under the same sense-sphere (*dhammāyatanāni*) and element (*dhammādhātuyo*), but are classified under different aggregates in the third chapter.[37] This pattern continues throughout the remaining chapters, where the truths are analyzed according to their various relationships to the aggregates, spheres of sense, and elements.[38]

The separation of the four noble truths into different combinations in relation to the aggregates, spheres of sense, and elements shows that the four noble truths, like the entire *mātikā*, do not have any permanent existence in the world. The numerical arrangements are not designed to provide a comprehensive map of the world; they illustrate that what exists in the world is temporary and shifting, each state that arises in the world dependent upon another factor. The four noble truths are analyzed in terms of the aggregates, spheres of sense, and elements and, as in the *Vibhaṅga*, the truths are analyzed as states which have no enduring existence or substance because they are defined in terms of other categories which have no substance. They exist only within a matrix of states which come into existence and pass out of existence.

Gethin has described this fluid categorization: '[t]ry to *grasp* the world of the *Dhammasaṅgani*, or the *Paṭṭhāna*, and it runs through one's fingers. In short, the indefinite expansions based on the *mātikā*s continually remind those using them that it is of the nature of things that no single way of breaking up and analyzing the world can ever be final.'[39] The *Dhātukathā* provides an example of how the *mātikā*s may be used to explore the nature of this insubstantial and fluid world. Where the *Vibhaṅga* uses *suttanta-vibhaṅga* (*sutta* analysis), *abhidhamma-vibhaṅga* (*abhidhamma* analysis), and the couplets and triplets to analyze the core *khandhāyatanadhātu mātikā*, the *Dhātukathā* uses the first three items of the core *mātikā* to analyze the remaining core *mātikā* as well as the triplet and couplet *mātikā*. The four noble truths are thus explained in relation to the aggregates, spheres of sense, and elements.

The Puggalapaññatti

This is the third book in which the truths are analyzed, and it consists of an extended analysis (*paññatti*) of various kinds of persons (*puggalā*). *Puggala* is not used in the sense of an essential personality (like *attā*), but in the sense of a person or individual. *Paññatti* means explanation, showing, and explaining; thus, the *Puggalapaññatti* is thus an explanation of persons or individuals. Because *puggala* does not denote an essential personality as it does in the *Kathāvatthu* or the *Milindapañha*, T. W. Rhys Davids' postulation, that the text may be one of the earliest *Abhidhamma* books, may be correct.[40] While it is now recognized as hazardous to propose a date for any given text on the basis of an Orientalist history of ideas, his observation remains that the *Puggalapaññatti* has been considered by scholars of Buddhism to be a slightly unusual *Abhidhamma-piṭaka* text.

The *mātikā* provided at the beginning of the book is similar to those encountered in the *Vibhaṅga* and *Dhātukathā*. The author explains that there are six explanations (*paññatti*): five aggregates (*khandhā*), twelve internal and external spheres of sense (*āyatanāni*), eighteen elements (*dhātuyo*), four noble truths (*saccāni*), twenty-two sense-faculties (*indriyāni*), and persons (*puggalā*). Except for the last item, the list is the same as the one used in the two texts discussed above. The *puggala*s are the only topic analyzed in the *Puggalapaññatti*. The text enumerates the first five *paññatti*s, and there are no surprises. But, the *puggala*s are grouped into ten groups which begin with groups of one. Because the *puggala*s are the only subject examined in this text, the four noble truths are discussed insofar as they describe certain kinds of individuals.

The *Puggalapaññatti* analyzes only one item of the core *khandhāyatanadhātu mātikā*, although it lists the core *mātikā* as the context for the analysis of the *puggalā*. This style is also used in the *Aṅguttara-nikāya* and in the *Saṅgīti-sutta*.[41] The network in which the four noble truths are placed is a simple one: it is used as one way to identify certain individuals, those who 'have (a) view' (*diṭṭhippatto*) and those who are 'freed by faith' (*saddhāvimutto*).[42] The four noble truths appear four times throughout the *Puggalapaññatti*, in both the basic set identified by Norman and in the mnemonic set (b). The four noble truths appear once in their mnemonic set, at the start of the book: *cattāri saccāni: dukkha-saccaṃ samudaya-saccaṃ nirodha-saccaṃ magga-saccaṃ*.[43] The four noble truths are found in the basic set throughout the rest of the text. At one point, the four noble truths are cited precisely in the same language as in the *Bhayabherava-sutta*, where the *sutta* recounts how the Buddha realized the four noble truths just as they are (*yathābhūtaṃ*) and then saw the corruptions (*āsavā*) in the same manner.[44] The same passages are used for those individuals who are compared to soldiers, where a description of a monk entering the *jhāna* trances is included.[45] The connection between the four noble truths and the destruction of the corruptions is found in the remaining references to the four noble truths, although the connection with the *jhāna*s is not.

The four noble truths appear consistently in the description of those persons who have (a) view (*diṭṭhippatto*) and who are freed by faith (*saddhāvimutto*).[46] Such individuals are discussed in the groups of one, seven, and nine. The passages read:

> How does an individual have (a) view? Here, an individual understands as it really is 'this is pain,' 'this is the arising of pain,' 'this is the ending of pain,' 'this is the way to the ending of pain.' Here a person

fully understands that this is pain, that this is the arising of pain, that this is the ending of pain, and that this is the path leading to the ending of pain.' [He] sees and practices with wisdom the teachings taught by the Tathāgata, and having seen with wisdom some of his corruptions are completely destroyed. This is one who has (a) view.[47]

How is an individual freed by faith? Here, an individual understands as it really is 'this is pain,' 'this is the arising of pain,' 'this is the ending of pain,' 'this is the way to the ending of pain.' Here a person fully understands that this is pain, that this is the arising of pain, that this is the ending of pain, and that this is the path leading to the ending of pain.' [He] sees and practices with wisdom the teachings taught by the Tathāgata, and having seen with wisdom some of his corruptions are completely destroyed, but not as in one who has (a) view: this is one who is freed by faith.

The only variation between those who 'have (a) view' (*diṭṭhippatto*) and those who are 'freed by faith' (*saddhāvimutto*) lies in the ways in which their corruptions (*āsavā*) are destroyed. The relationship between realizing the four noble truths and destroying the corruptions is the same as that identified in the *Bhayabherava-sutta* and elsewhere in the *Nikāyas*.

In the *Puggalapaññatti*, the four noble truths are linked explicitly to the *jhānas* and to the corruptions (*āsavā*). The truths are thus networked in much the same way as they are in both the *Sutta-piṭaka* and in other books of the *Abhidhamma-piṭaka*, but with yet a different focus on the sorts of people who require different access to the path. The passages used to describe the four noble truths, the *jhānas*, and the corruptions are the same passages as those found elsewhere in the canon. The four noble truths remain part of the core *mātikā* whose standardized textual descriptions are the building blocks which are used to construct the analysis of individuals.

The *Yamaka*

This is the last book of the *Abhidhamma-piṭaka* that analyzes the four noble truths. It is called the 'Book of Pairs' because each phenomena is defined in terms of a thesis and its antithesis (*yamaka* carries the sense of double or opposite).[48] Jayatilleke explains that the *Yamaka* is an exercise in precise definition: '[T]he purpose of the book . . . is intended to convey to the reader the exact logical boundaries of important concepts in the light of their actual technical usage.'[49] There are ten chapters called *yamakas* in the text. There is no *mātikā* provided at the start of the *Yamaka*, but the commentary and the later *Mohavicchedanī* take the chapters as a *mātikā*.[50] There are ten kinds of pairs (*yamaka*): roots (*mūla-*), aggregates (*khandha-*), spheres of sense (*āyatana-*), elements (*dhātu-*), truths (*sacca-*), formations (*sankhāra-*), inclinations (*anusaya-*), mind (*citta-*), states (*dhammā-*), and sense-faculties (*indriya-*). The kinds of pairs are derived from the core *khandhāyatanadhātu mātikā*. Each pair is analyzed in three sections, the *paṇṇattivāra*, *pavattivāra* and *pariññāvāra*. The first section (*paṇṇattivāra*) sets out the limits of the term and its definition. The second section (*pavattivāra*) takes up the problem of where and as what an individual will be reborn. The third section (*pariññāvāra*) examines the degree to which a given class of beings comprehends the category under consideration. The analysis of the four noble truths follows this pattern. The four noble truths are introduced with the 'mnemonic' set (b): *cattāri saccāni: dukkhasaccaṃ samudayasaccaṃ nirodhasaccaṃ maggasaccaṃ.*[51]

The questions asked of the various teachings analyzed in the *Yamaka* are designed to precisely classify the components of the teachings. The *paṇṇattivāra* of the *Saccayamaka* begins with the following questions:

> Is pain the truth that is pain? Yes. Is the truth that is pain pain? Except for physical and mental pain, the rest of the truth that is pain is the truth that is pain, not pain. Physical and mental pain is both pain and the truth that is pain.[52]

These questions are the only ones that define the components of each of the four noble truths in relation to each other. The first section of the *Yamaka* analysis defines the truths first in relation to their component parts: Is pain the truth that is pain? Is pain the truth? It is interesting to note that the questions asked of the four truths here in the *Yamaka* seek to explain the relationship between realizing the truth that the world is characterized by pain and realizing pain itself. This is an ambiguity in the four noble truths that is not resolved in the *Sutta-piṭaka*.

The second section (*pavattivāra*) analyzes the situation of one who is reborn or passes away in a certain state. It is divided into three subjects: arising (*uppādavāra*), ending (*nirodhavāra*), and both birth and ending (*uppādanirodhavāra*). The four noble truths are asked how each truth arises, ends or both arises and ends in relation to other truths. The same analysis is conducted for arising, ceasing, and both arising and ceasing in the present, in the past, and in the future. The questions begin with the question: 'Of that [in which] the truth that is arising arises, of what does the truth that is pain arise?' (*yassa dukkhasaccaṃ uppajjati, tassa samudaya-saccaṃ uppajjatīti?*).[53] The pattern is intricate; there are questions within questions. The questions are formulated in pairs; then, the pairs are combined. For example, the question 'Of that [in which] the truth that is arising arises, of what does the truth that is pain arise?' is asked with the interrogative 'where' (*yattha*) and then with both interrogatives 'what' and 'where,' Similarly, the inquiries of the present, past, and future are all combined with each other. As in the *paṇṇattivāra* above, these questions and answers delineate the parameters of each truth. This section, like the analysis in rest of the *Yamaka*, defines the doctrine in relation to how each component emerges and when it passes away.

The subject of the third and final division (*pariññāvāra*) is the degree to which one knows the topic in question. The main verb is *parijānāti*, 'to know accurately' or 'to comprehend.' The pattern follows the same temporal sequence found in the second division: present, past, and future. The first two truths are analyzed in relation to each other throughout the section, and the remaining two are not discussed. The first question is a model: is the truth of arising eliminated by one who knows the truth of pain well? Is the truth of pain known well by one who has eliminated the truth of arising?[54] Once again, this method produces a set of precise meanings for the first two of the four noble truths: both answers to the queries are 'yes.'

This analysis of the four noble truths is unique in the *Abhidhamma-piṭaka*. In the *Vibhaṅga* and the *Dhātukathā*, examination of the four noble truths defines them in relation to other teachings. Here, in the *Yamaka*, the four noble truths are analyzed not in relation to other doctrines but in terms of their relation to each other, in pairs of terms. Where the *Dhammasaṅganī* is a text 'not to be read, but to be performed,'[55] the *Yamaka* is not such a book. It is terse and not designed to be recited. It is symmetrical and repetitive; the analysis of the four noble truths follows a set of questions are indeed patterned. While the *Yamaka* does not appear to have been intended for recitation, it is a reference work that contains a number of analytical possibilities. Similar to Gethin's suggestion for the *mātikā*s themselves, Foley suggested that the *Yamaka* could function as a 'thesaurus of theses, from which a teacher may select, and by which he may expound, like a preacher with his 'text'.'[56] The point for such expository talks is to show that nothing, in the final analysis, exists permanently. The *Yamaka* and the other *Abhidhamma* texts all express the fundamental principle that everything is transitory and that there is no stable or fixed map of the cosmos. Mapping the cosmos is an ongoing act, a process one should be capable of performing at any given moment.

The *Abhidhamma* books show that analyzing the relationships which fabricate each passing moment is a comprehensible endeavor. Various combinations are possible, yet each combination of events may be known, and known in its entirety. Gethin has suggested that the *Dhammasaṅganī* or the *Paṭṭhāna* analyses slip away as soon as one tries to grasp them and that the point to such analyses is the possibility of indefinite expansions of the *mātikā*s.[57] The analyses of the *Abhidhamma* books are not dispensible; Gethin suggests that the distinctions themselves are 'pedantic' or 'artificial' and suggests that perhaps this is the point to the analyses.[58] I would suggest instead that the distinctions are made and drawn to show that, in fact, the cosmos may be analyzed and analyzed precisely and accurately. The *mātikā*s and their use in the *Abhidhamma-piṭaka* do demonstrate that there is no single way of analyzing the cosmos, but the multiple ways that the cosmos may be analyzed or mapped are significant in and of themselves. The analysis of the four noble truths in the *Yamaka* demonstrates that nothing exists permanently in the cosmos; yet, the truths are components of the cosmos that may be mapped over and over again in each moment of passing time.

Conclusions

The four noble truths are a doctrine which belongs to the core *khandhāyatanadhātu mātikā*, the matrix that forms the basis of the *Saṃyutta-nikāya* as well as the four *Abhidhamma-piṭaka* texts in which the four noble truths appear. In this chapter, I have followed Gethin's suggestion that *mātika*s were not intended to be comprehensive outlines of what existed in the world, but, instead, are creative analyses capable of producing ongoing examinations of things that exist insubstantially in the world. The *mātika*s are generative, and they illustrate the principle is that the world is impermanent; nothing exists for long. Thus, the different relationships and the network within which the four noble truths are analyzed show that reality is fluid and changing according to the principle of cause and effect: reality is not static and fixed. The appearance of the four noble truths in the *Vibhaṅga*, the *Dhātukathā*, the *Puggalapaññatti*, and the *Yamaka* show how the doctrine is defined in relation to other teachings or analytical categories. The four noble truths are integral to the *khandhāyatanadhātu mātikā* and thus to the insubstantial reality analyzed by the *mātika*s in the *Abhidhamma-piṭaka*.

The status of the four noble truths in the *Abhidhamma-piṭaka* texts is worth considering. In the *Dhammacakkappavattana-sutta*, the four noble truths represent a particular religious experience that is remembered to have been accessible to those who heard the Buddha talk on the four noble truths; those who hear the Buddha teach the four noble truths experienced the reality of those truths by acquiring the *dhamma*-eye and thus by entering the path. In that *sutta*, the four noble truths are a catalyst for an ardent practitioner to attain entry into the path by cultivating the *dhamma*-eye and can be said legitimately to function as a symbol that evokes the Theravāda tradition's recollection of the Buddha's own enlightenment experience. On the other hand, the core *khandhāyatanadhātu mātikā* is a propositional analysis of things which appear to exist in the world but which do not exist permanently. By their inclusion in the core *mātikā*, the four noble truths are propositions which, if true, have the appearance of existing in the world but which in reality have no permanent substance.

Paul Griffiths suggests that *abhidharma* is a form of denaturalizing discourse: a form of discourse that is normative, may be universal, and abstract.

> In sum: formally, a denaturalized discourse is one that, in its ideal-typical form, shows no evidence of rooting in any sociocultural context; exhibits no essential connections with any natural language; and is completely unambiguous. Functionally, a denaturalized discourse is aimed primarily at making available to its users what really exists, a function that, from the view point of a user of such discourse, cannot be performed by ordinary, nondenaturalized, discourse.[59]

In an article on *abhidharma* as denaturalized discourse, Griffiths' goal is to define the nature of philosophical discourse in order to understand *abhidhamma* analysis and discourse; he argues that there is a discourse which may be called philosophical or denaturalized in all of the Buddhist schools. *Abhidharma*, he concludes, 'considered as a discourse, an intellectual practice, is a splendid instance of denaturalized discourse. While *abhidharma* expresses a metaphysic that is quite different from that of the propositional mythos that fostered denaturalized discourse in the West, its function is the same: to make available to its users what there really is, and, in so doing, to make claims about what there really is that are universalizable.'[60] As a form of denaturalized discourse, the Theravāda canon shows that *abhidhamma* discourse is firmly rooted within the life of the Theravādin community. Gethin suggests that the lists that comprise *abhidhamma* literature, in fact, 'were seen as encapsulating the essence of the Dhamma; as such, they were also seen as sources for the further exposition of the Dhamma.'[61] *Abhidhamma* is thus a form of denaturalized discourse that rests at the heart of how the Theravāda canon came to conceptualize the teaching and learning of *dhamma*; the four noble truths are a doctrine that expresses a proposition about what is true in the cosmos within *abhidhamma* discourse.

As propositions, the four noble truths must be learned as one learns other teachings of the Buddha. There is no immediate cultivation of the *dhamma* eye or instantaneous path entry upon hearing the four noble truths. In all of the passages examined in this chapter, the point for the practitioner is to learn how the four noble truths intersect with other teachings. Just as the networks of the *mātika*s in the *Abhidhamma-piṭaka* provide an analysis of reality that articulates certain significant points but do not provide a comprehensive analysis of the cosmos, so too is there a limit to the associations between the four noble truths and other teachings. In contrast to the function of four noble truths as a symbol of the Buddha's enlightenment and the subsequent awakening of all sentient beings, when the four noble truths are regarded as propositions, they are limited in their associations and the ways in which they are analyzed. In short, in the analytic networks of the *Tipiṭaka*, the four noble truths are no more or less important than any other relevant teaching of the Buddha. As propositions of doctrine, the four truths are learned with effort and labor, and the path is gained in various ways.

Notes

1 Moh 2. Gethin cites this passage in his article on the *mātikā*, and offers a slightly different translation. See Gethin, 'The Mātikās,' 161.
2 Gethin, 'The *Mātikās*,' 156–164.
3 Gethin, 'The *Mātikās*,' 160.
4 Gethin, 'The *Mātikās*,' 161.
5 Gethin, 'The *Mātikās*,' 155.
6 Paul J. Griffiths, 'Denaturalizing Discourse: *Ābhidhārmikas*, Propositionalists, and the Comparative Philosophy of Religion,' in *Myth and Philosophy*, ed. Frank E. Reynolds and David Tracy (Albany: State University of New York Press, 1990), 65.
7 *A Buddhist Manual of Psychological Ethics* (*Dhammasaṅgaṇī*), 3rd ed., trans. C. A. F. Rhys Davids (London: Pāli Text Society, 1974), xxxiii.
8 Y. Karunadasa, *Buddhist Analysis of Matter* (Colombo: Department of Cultural Affairs, 1967), 176.
9 *Mohavicchedanī*, xix; see also Gethin, 'The *Mātikās*,' 162–164.
10 Buddhadatta and Warder, *Mohavicchedanī*, xxii. Warder's final sketch of the history of the Theravāda *mātikā* is as follows: (1) the thirty-seven *bodhipakkhiyā dhammā* in seven groups; (2) stages of Buddhist life, training and meditation; (3) the *khandhāyatanadhātuyo* gradually elaborated into the theory of types of consciousness, *kusala* and *akusala*, the four *sacca*s and *paṭiccasamuppāda*, the collection of *puggala*s; (4) the topics of the *kathāvatthu*; (5) analysis of topics such as *kusala/asusala/avyākata dhamma*s as *tika*s (twenty-two) and *duka*s (one hundred), with the miscellaneous *suttanta duka*s (42) added later; (6) the general theory of causation (twenty-four *paccaya*s) elaborated in combination with the *tika* and *duka* analysis (xxvii). Note, these conclusions form the essence of Watanabe's discussion about the development of *abhidhamma* philosophy. Despite the fact that his analysis includes *abhidhamma* lists found in the Chinese *Āgama*s, Watanabe does not move much beyond Warder's developmental outline. Fumimaro Watanabe, *Philosophy and Its Development in the Nikāyas and Abhidhamma* (Delhi: Motilal Banarsidass Press, 1985), 46ff.
11 Gethin argues that Warder's claim that the extended *khandhāyatanadhātu mātikā* was the original *mātikā* is incorrect. He draws attention to findings by J. S. Jaini that the *tika/duka mātikā* is not unique to the Pāli canon. Gethin adds to this evidence by finding that certain triplets are already found in the earlier sections of the Pāli canon. He concludes that 'it would seem that the kernel of the triplet/couplet *mātikā* may be very ancient, and to regard either the core *mātikā* beginning with the five aggregates or the triplet/couplet *mātikā* as more fundamental than the other is to misunderstand the basic principle that determines the way in which the Abhidhamma develops out of the *mātikās*.' Gethin, 'The *Mātikās*,' 163.
12 Buddhadatta and Warder, *Mohavicchedanī*, xxvi. Warder also noted that the later Theravāda writers provided a complete list of *cetasika*s which included the *yevāpana(ka)-dhamma*s.
13 *Mohavicchedanī*, xxiii.
14 *Mohavicchedanī*, xxiii–xxv.

15 *Mohavicchedanī*, xxvi.
16 *Mohavicchedanī*, xxvi.
17 Gethin, 'The *Mātikās*,' 165–167.
18 Gethin, 'The *Mātikās*,' 163.
19 D II 290–315; M I 55–63, III 248–252. The comparison of the *Saccavibhaṅga* in the *Vibhaṅga* with the *Saccavibhaṅga-sutta* in the *Majjhima-nikāya* supports Gethin's conclusion that the core *mātikā* (of *khandhāyatanadhātu*) is fundamental to portions of the *Sutta-piṭaka* as well as the *Abhidhamma-piṭaka*. See Gethin, *Buddhist Path*, 16–25.
20 Vibh 106
21 Vibh 106
22 Dhs 1, 277
23 The same definitions are also found in the *Jhānavibhaṅga*, although in combination with the fivefold path. (Vibh 266–268).
24 Thien Nyun, 'Preface,' in *Discourse on Elements* (*Dhātu-Kathā*), trans. U Nārada (London: Pāli Text Society, 1977), xxii–xxix.
25 Norman, 'The Four Noble Truths,' 213.
26 Dhātuk 2
27 There are 105 internal states (derived from the *khandhāyatanadhātuyo* list) and 266 external states (22 *tikas* [22 × 3 = 66] and 100 *dukas* [100 × 2 = 200]) which total 371 possible states.
28 Dhātuk 1
29 Gethin, 'The *Mātikās*,' 164.
30 Dhātuk 8–9
31 Dhātuk 9–10
32 Dhātuk 9
33 Dhātuk 8–10, 99
34 Dhātuk 39f., 67, 83f., 86
35 Dhātuk 36, 42, 52, 73f.
36 Dhātuk 8–10
37 Dhātuk 36–37
38 Dhātuk 39f., 42, 52, 67, 73f., 83–86, 99, 113
39 Gethin, 'The *Mātikās*,' 165.
40 T. W. Rhys Davids, *Buddhist India: The Story of the Nations* (New York: G. P. Putnam's Sons, 1903), 188.
41 Norman has pointed out that portions of the *Puggalapaññatti* are quite similar to those of the *Saṅgīti-sutta* and the *tika-*, *catukka-*, and *pañcaka-nipātas* of the *Aṅguttara-nikāya*. These comparisons are also made by Gethin, who argues that the *mātikās* were integral to both the *Sutta-piṭaka* and the *Abhidhamma-piṭaka*. Norman, *Pāli Literature*, 102f; Gethin, 'The *Mātikās*,' 160–164.
42 Gethin translates *saddhā* as confidence; there is a relatively large body of literature on the subject. See Gethin, *Buddhist Path*, 106, n. 7.
43 Pp 2; see Norman, 'The Four Noble Truths,' 213.
44 M I 23
45 Pp 68
46 See A I 120 and M I 177 for similar analyses of those who are 'freed by faith' (*saddhāvimutto*).
47 Pp 15, 72, 74
48 PED, s.v. *yamaka*; BHSG, s.v. *yamaka*.
49 J. N. Jayatilleke, *Early Buddhist Theory of Knowledge* (London: George Allen & Unwin, 1963), 309f. Jayatilleke established that the *Yamaka* provided precise technical definitions for significant terms in part to refute Foley's assertion that

the book demonstrates the ways in which terms could be exchanged and converted.

50 Norman, *Pāli Literature*, 105.
51 Yam I 173
52 Yam I 174
53 Yam I 178
54 *Yo dukkhasaccaṃ parijānāti, so samudayasaccaṃ pajahatīti? Yo vā pana samudaya saccaṃ pajahati, so dukkhasaccaṃ parijānātīti?* (Yam 227–228)
55 Gethin, 'The *Mātikās*,' 166.
56 *Yamaka* I:x
57 Gethin, 'The *Mātikās*,' 165.
58 Gethin, 'The *Mātikās*,' 165.
59 Griffiths, 'Denaturalizing Discourse,' 65.
60 Griffiths, 'Denaturalized Discourse,' 80. For a useful critique of some aspects of Griffiths' category, see Charles Hallisey, 'In Defense of Rather Fragile and Local Achievement: Reflections on the Work of Gurulugomi,' in *Religion and Practical Reason: New Essays in the Comparative Philosophy of Religions*, ed. Frank E. Reynolds and David Tracy (Albany: State University of New York, 1994), 136–141.
61 Gethin, 'The *Mātikās*,' 167.

CHAPTER FIVE

The Four Noble Truths and the Path

And I want to show that the four worthy true things (ariyasaccāni) were not throughout necessarily regarded as the four truths of Ill, but that they may sometimes have been taken to stand for these four Ways, and sometimes for another concept.[1]

Isaline Blew Horner (1936)

Structures of the Path

Throughout the Theravāda canon, there are various sequences that followers of the Buddha are enjoined to follow in order to gain an experience of *nibbāna* and thereby end the cycle of rebirth and death. These sequences are often irreconcilable, existing side by side with different arrangements and teachings. There are sets that recur frequently, such as the fourfold path that begins with the level of the stream-enterer and culminates with the attainments of an *arahat*. Buddhaghosa's comprehensive volume written in the early fifth century C.E., *The Path of Purity* (*Visuddhimagga*), is the earliest attempt to synthesize all of the varied teachings of the Buddha found in the Theravāda canon. George Bond has suggested that the notion of the gradual path as an explicit hermeneutical device emerged in the postcanonical texts of the *Netti-pakaraṇa* and *Peṭakopadesa*. These two texts deliberately classify people into three types (the ordinary person, the learner, and the adept) and according to temperament; various *sutta*s are then correlated with these types of people.[2] The hermeneutical exercise of these two texts is an attempt to stratify the teachings of the Buddha in a way that was all-inclusive and synthetic; and, as Bond points out, it reflects a later historical period in the development of Buddhism when it became important to organize the teachings of the Buddha. These early syntheses of the path offered by Buddhaghosa, the *Netti-pakaraṇa*, and the *Peṭakopadesa* illustrate a feature of the Theravāda canon that has long been recognized: the absence of an overarching and comprehensive structure of the path to *nibbāna*.[3]

Regardless of the lack of a single unified path to *nibbāna* outlined in the canon, the notion of the path is indisputably central to the teachings of the Buddha. Robert Buswell, Jr. and Robert Gimello make this point in the introduction to their volume on the Buddhist path, when they write that the *mārga/magga* (path) 'incorporates, underlies, or presupposes everything else in Buddhism, from the simplest act of charity to the most refined meditative experience and the most rigorous philosophical argument.'[4] It is therefore appropriate to analyze the structures of the path in which the four noble truths appear, in order to gain a fuller sense of the functions of this teaching throughout the canon. This chapter explores two bodies of evidence: the features of different paths in which the four noble truths play a role, and the pedagogical techniques used to attain and make progress along the path, however it is construed. As a doctrine, the four noble truths are not simply a theoretical proposition to which followers must grant 'intellectual assent';[5] the pedagogical techniques of meditation, analysis, reflection, debate, hearing, and talking are all embedded – explicitly and implicitly – in the passages which describe the four noble truths.

In the *Mahāvagga* of the *Vinayapiṭaka*

The different functions of the four noble truths that have been explored in the previous two chapters accompany different structures of the path to enlightenment throughout the Theravāda canon. In the *Mahāvagga*, the path remains the same for the first thousand or so members of the Buddha's *saṅgha*, and the four noble truths occupy a central position as a symbol which catalyzes the *dhammacakkhu* (vision of *dhamma* or *dhamma* eye), that in turn enables a practioner to attain the first stage of the fourfold path to *nibbāna* – that of a stream-enterer (*sotāpanno*). We have already analyzed the first section of the *Mahāvagga* in Chapter Two, in which the Buddha experiences enlightenment, decides to teach, and teaches the middle path and the four noble truths to his five former companions: Koṇḍañña, Vappa, Bhaddiya, Mahānāma, and Assaji. The same sequence of the Buddha giving a *dhamma* talk on the four truths, the would-be follower who cultivates a vision of *dhamma* (*dhammacakkhu*), the declaration that 'all that has the nature of arising has the nature of ending,' and the announcement of the follower's new status are found throughout the initial series of enlightenment stories in the *Mahāvagga*.

The narrative structure of the *Mahāvagga* begins with groups of those followers who are awakened according to the pedagogical sequence described above. The first is the noble Yasa, who has a dream about the physical disintegration of five women who had been entertaining him in his suite of rooms. The Buddha teaches Yasa the significance of his dream, and Yasa concludes his awakening with a request to become a *bhikkhu*. The next group to be enlightened are Yasa's father, mother, and his wife – all of whom came to the Buddha in search of Yasa. These three people become, respectively, the first three lay members of the *saṅgha*; Yasa's father is named as the first lay man (*upāsako*) and Yasa's mother and wife become the first lay women (*upāsikā*). After Yasa and his family, the next group to be enlightened are a group of four of Yasa's friends: Vimalo, Subāhu, Puṇṇaji, and Gavampati; following them is a large group of fifty. Each of these episodes that concludes with a follower attaining the status of an *arahat* concludes with the observation that now there are *x arahats* in the world.

The remaining enlightenment stories are about a group of thirty friends of high standing who appear in the grove on their way to Uruvelā, three ascetics and their followers, King Bimbasāra of Maghada, and the leading followers Sāriputta and Moggallāna. These stories about how these curious inquirers attain some measure of the enlightenment experience are interspersed with descriptions of how the Buddha overcame Māra,[6] how he asked his followers to teach,[7] how he decided to ordain his followers,[8] and other pragmatic decisions about the structure of the emerging *saṅgha*. After Sāriputta and Moggallāna become *arahats*, the remainder of the *Mahāvagga* takes up a detailed description of how newly ordained *bhikkhus* are to be taught within the *saṅgha*. It is not until the second section of the *Vinaya-piṭaka* (the *Cullavagga*) that we discover that women were admitted as *bhikkhunīs* into the order – with an accompanying warning of the cost to the order. The point to be gleaned from the narrative structure of the *Mahāvagga* and *Cullavagga* is that the stories of how the *saṅgha* was established are integrated into stories about how followers of the Buddha cultivated an experience of enlightenment. The four noble truths have an integral role in the pattern of these enlightenment stories.

The enlightenment stories all contain the following segments, with slight variations noted below. The first is the *anupubbikathā* (graduated talk) sequence, which contains the four noble truths and an often-repeated metaphor that compares the way that a clean cloth immediately picks up dirt to the way that these followers absorbed the Buddha's teaching. The second is a description of the knowledge that a practitioner has gained as a result of the *dhamma* eye. The third is the formal request for admission into the order – either as a lay follower or as a fully ordained *bhikkhu* or *bhikkhunī*. The fourth segment is a description of a second talk given to certain followers during which they eliminate the corruptions (*āsavā*). The fifth segment is the refrain that now there are *x arahats* in the world.

(1) The graduated talk and the arising of the *dhammacakkhu* (*dhamma*-eye):

> The Blessed One gave a graduated talk: that is, he gave a talk on giving, a talk on virtue, and a talk on heaven; he explained the

dangers, depravity and defilement of sensual pleasures, and the advantages of release. When the Blessed One knew that [Yasa of a good family's] mind was ready, tender, free from the hindrances, happy, and devoted, then he gave a standard *dhamma*-talk of the Buddhas: pain, its arising, its ending, and the path. Just as a clean cloth with all black spots removed will easily pick up dirt, so too, as [Yasa of a good family] sat in the very same seat, the *dhamma*-eye, dustless and stainless, arose in him: whatever has the nature of arising, all that has the nature of stopping.[9]

(2) Knowing *dhamma*:

[She], who had seen *dhamma*, mastered *dhamma*, known *dhamma*, was immersed in *dhamma*, who was free from doubt, who had dispelled uncertainty, and who had gained complete confidence, not dependent upon others for the teachings of the teacher, said this to the Blessed One:[10]

(3) Request for ordination or acceptance as a lay follower and the Buddha's response:

'Sir, may I be received into homelessness with the Blessed One, may I receive ordination (*upasampadā*)?' Then, *bhikkhus*, the Blessed One said '*Dhamma* is spoken well, live as a *brahmacariya* to bring about a proper ending of pain.' And this was the ordination of the noble one.[11]

(4) A second *dhamma* talk:

Then, *bhikkhus*, the Blessed One advised and instructed [them] with a *dhamma* talk. Thus advised and instructed by the Blessed One's *dhamma* talk, [their] minds were unattached, freed from the corruptions.[12]

(5) The status of an *arahat*:

And now there are [*x*] *arahats* in the world.[13]

Table 5.1 provides a summary of the structure of the first enlightenment stories in the *Mahāvagga*. The enlightenment stories in which these formulaic statements appear in the *Mahāvagga* reveal a basic structure for how the first members of the *saṅgha* became followers of the Buddha. They encounter the Buddha; he assesses their state of mind, gives them a graduated talk on giving, virtue, and on the heavens; and, 'he explained the dangers, depravity and defilment of sensual pleasures, and the advantages of release.' When the Buddha knew that his audience was ready, he gave a talk on the four noble truths, which is identified as a *dhamma* talk that is praised by Buddhas (*yā buddhānaṃ sāmukkaṃsikā dhammadesanā*).

Table 5.1 The Four Truths in the *Mahāvagga* (Vin I 1–18)

	Vin I 9–12	Vin I 12–14	Vin I 15–16	Vin I 16–18
Teacher	Buddha	Buddha	Buddha	Buddha
Audience	Koṇḍañña Vappa Bhaddiya Mahānāma Assaji	Yasa	Yasa's father	Yasa's mother Yasa's former wife
First Teaching	*Dhammacakka-appavattana-sutta*	graduated talk four truths	graduated talk four truths	graduated talk four truths
Result	*dhamma*-eye request for ordination acceptance	*dhamma*-eye request for ordination acceptance	*dhamma*-eye first *upāsaka*	*dhamma*-eye first *upāsikā*
Second Teaching	on the aggregates (*khandhā*)	overhears *dhamma* talk to father	none	none
Result	corruptions destroyed *arahat*s	corruptions destroyed *arahat*	none	none

Table 5.1 (continued) The Four Truths in the *Mahāvagga* (Vin I 19–35)

	Vin I 18–19	Vin I 20	Vin I 23–24	Vin I 24–35
Teacher	Buddha	Buddha	Buddha	Buddha
Audience	Vimala Subāhu Puṇṇaji Gavampati (Yasa's householder friends of good families)	a group of fifty of Yasa's householder friends of good families	a group of thirty young men of high birth	Uruvelakassapa Nadīkassapa Gayākassapa and 1000 followers
First Teaching	graduated talk four truths	graduated talk four truths	graduated talk four truths	five wonders (*pañcamaṇ paṭihāriyaṃ*)
Result	*dhamma*-eye request for ordination acceptance	*dhamma*-eye request for ordination acceptance	*dhamma*-eye request for ordination acceptance	no mention request for ordination acceptance
Second Teaching	unnamed talk ('advised and instructed')	unnamed talk ('advised and instructed')	no mention	*Ādittapariyāya* ('Discourse on Burning')
Result	eliminated corruptions *arahat*s	eliminated corruptions *arahat*s	no mention	eliminated corruptions no mention of *arahat* status

Table 5.1 (continued) The Four Truths in the *Mahāvagga* (Vin I 35–44)

	Vin I 35–39	Vin I 39–44	Vin 41–44
Teacher	Buddha	Assaji	Sāriputta
Audience	King Bimbisāra of Magadha and his retinue	Sāriputta	Moggallāna
First Teaching	graduated talk four truths	'the cause of things that arise from a cause and their ending'	'the cause of things that arise from a cause and their ending'
Result	*dhamma*-eye request for *upāsakā* status silent response	*dhamma*-eye request for ordination acceptance	*dhamma*-eye request for ordination acceptance
Second Teaching	no mention	no mention in *Vinaya-piṭaka* overhears talk to Aggivessana (described in M I 497–501)	no mention in *Vinaya-piṭaka*
Result	no mention	eliminated corruptions *arahat* (described in M I 497–501)	

The response to the Buddha's graduated talk and talk on the four noble truths is that those who hear the talk are able to cultivate the *dhamma* eye or vision; the commentary makes it clear that this results at least in the status of a stream-enterer. In the story of the awakening of the group of thirty friends of high birth, the commentary provides the following gloss for the phrase 'the *dhamma*-eye arose' (*dhammacakkhuṃ udapādi*):

> The arising of the *dhamma*-eye is the arising of any stream-winner, once-returner, or non-returner; the arising of the *dhamma*-eye means these three paths.[14]

This commentary indicates that the cultivation of the *dhamma*-eye refers to the first three stages of the path. The commentaries on *sutta*s that parallel these enlightenment stories in the *Sutta-piṭaka* explain that the *dhamma*-eye (*dhammacakkhu*) denotes the four paths and the four fruits; that is, the paths and benefits (fruits) of a stream-enterer (*sotāpanno*), a once-returner (*sakadāgāminī*), a non-returner (*opapātiko* or *anagāminī*), and an *arahat*.[15] *Dhammacakkhu* is also explained as the first three paths;[16] as the destruction of the corruptions for an *arahat*;[17] but, most commonly, it is understood as the attainment of the path of a stream-enterer.[18] The experience of gaining the *dhamma*-eye is not simply a mundane recognition of the four noble truths; it is a full comprehension which results in the awareness that 'whatever has the nature of arising, all that has the nature of ending.'[19] This knowledge is understood to constitute at least the status of a stream-enterer.

Dhammacakkhu is also defined with reference to other kinds of vision or eyes. The commentary on the *Saḷāyatana-saṃyutta* ('Sayings on the Six Sense-spheres') explains *cakkhu* (eye) as twofold: the vision of knowledge (*ñāṇacakkhu*) and the physical eye (*maṃsacakkhu*).[20] The first vision of knowledge consists of five further kinds of 'eyes' or 'visions': the eye of a Buddha (*buddhacakkhu*), the *dhamma*-eye (*dhammacakkhu*), the eye [that can see] everywhere (*samantacakkhu*), the divine eye (*dibbacakkhu*), and the eye of wisdom (*paññācakkhu*). The Buddha-eye is defined as the 'knowledge of inclinations and dispositions' (*āsayānusayañāṇaṃ*) and the 'knowledge of the senses and inclinations of others' (*indriyaparopariyatti-ñāṇaṃ*). It is said, the commentary reads, that the Buddha surveyed the world with the vision of a Buddha.[21] The *dhamma*-eye is defined as the first three paths and the first three fruits.[22] *Samantacakkhu*, an eye [that can see] everywhere, is explained as omniscience. The divine-eye (*dibbacakkhu*) is explained as knowledge gained by a pervading light (*ālokapharaṇena uppannan ñāṇaṃ*), and the eye of wisdom (*paññācakkhu*) is clarified as knowledge according to the division of the four noble truths (*catusacca-paricchedakañāṇaṃ*). The second physical eye consists of the constituent parts of the eye (*sasambhāracakkhu*) and the colors of the eye (*pasādacakkhu*). The *dhamma*-eye refers to one kind of knowledge among these others: that of the path, understood in these enlightenment stories in terms of some combination of the first three paths and fruits.

Having developed the eye of *dhamma* in the third set of enlightenment stories, Yasa's mother is described as one 'who had seen *dhamma*, mastered *dhamma*, known *dhamma*, was immersed in *dhamma*, who was free from doubt, who had dispelled uncertainty, and who had gained complete confidence, not dependent upon others for the teachings of the teacher.'[23] As the explanation of how the *dhamma* eye arises is always the same, so too is this description of what the audience experiences. The *dhamma* that Yasa's mother saw, reached, knew, and plunged into is understood in the commentaries as the *dhamma* that is known by means of hearing the four noble truths. The remaining events in these enlightenment stories consist of some type of request for acceptance into the order (the third segment above), and in some of the enlightenment stories the Buddha gives a second talk (the fourth segment), by means of which the audience is able to eliminate the corruptions. The *Mahāvagga* usually notes this accomplishment by recording their new status as *arahat*s (the fifth segment), but not always.

The grammatical form of the four noble truths in these passages that describe how the first followers of the Buddha gained their knowledge is distinct. Norman enumerated three 'mnemonic' sets in which the four noble truths appear, in which there is a brief mention of the teaching that serves simply to remind the hearer of the four noble truths. In these formulaic passages found in the *Mahāvagga*, the four noble truths appear as *dukkhaṃ samudayaṃ nirodhaṃ maggaṃ*; they are not described as 'fourfold,' 'noble,' or 'truths,' as in the sets Norman identifies.[24]

One variation in this sequence of enlightenment stories is found in the story of the thirty friends: there is no mention of a group of thirty new *bhikkhu*s who have eliminated the corruptions, nor does the episode conclude with the observation that 'now there are so-and-so many enlightened ones in the world.' The would-be ordinands simply ask the Buddha for both acceptance (*pabbajā*) and ordination (*upasampadā*) into the order; they receive both and are welcomed.[25] This is the first time that the Buddha accepts followers into the order when they have not eliminated the corruptions and, therefore, are not yet *arahat*s. The four noble truths are the means by which the *dhamma*-eye arises, but are they *not* the means by which the corruptions are eliminated. When taken with the earlier conversions of Yāsa's father, mother, and former wife, this episode emphasizes that hearing the four noble truths and cultivating the *dhamma*-eye is separate from extinguishing the corruptions.

A second variation is that in the enlightenment of the leaders of the ascetics and their followers, there is no mention of the four noble truths. After convincing Kassapa of Uruvelā of his powers and of the fact that he was fully enlightened, the Buddha accepted the leaders of the ascetics and their followers into the order, with the phrase that we have noted above: 'Come, *bhikkhus*, *dhamma* is spoken well, live as a *brahmacariya* to bring about a proper ending to pain.'[26] Furthermore, the ascetics and their followers eliminate the corruptions while listening to the Buddha's 'Discourse on Burning' (*Ādittapariyāya*).[27] But, there is no mention of the graduated talk, the four noble truths, or the *dhamma* eye (*dhammacakkhu*) as in the previous sequences. This absence of the four noble truths is a foreshadowing of the wholesale disappearance of the four truths later on in the *Mahāvagga*, after the awakening of Sāriputta and Moggallāna.

The final enlightenment story is that of Sāriputta and Moggallāna. The narrative of how these two renouncers became enlightened and followers of the Buddha is divided in the Theravāda canon. The sequence found in the *Mahāvagga* describes how Sāriputta and Moggallāna became followers of the Buddha, but a *sutta* in the *Majjhima-nikāya* explains how Sāriputta eliminated the corruptions. The most significant variation in the *Mahāvagga* sequence of enlightenment stories is that Sāriputta and Moggallāna both cultivate the *dhamma*-eye upon hearing followers of the Buddha describe what the Buddha had realized. They do not hear about the four noble truths, nor do they receive their teaching from the Buddha himself. Even though the Buddha is aware that Sāriputta and Moggallāna are about to approach him, and tells his *bhikkhus* that they will be leaders among his followers, he does not teach them *dhamma* directly. In the narrative of the *Mahāvagga*, the Buddha has already enjoined his followers to teach before he meets Sāriputta and Moggallāna, and their experience of being taught by Assaji is the result of the growing pool of those followers who have been asked by the Buddha to spread his teachings. It is worth examining Sāriputta's and Moggallāna's story in greater detail to see how the narrative differs from the earlier enlightenment stories in the *Mahāvagga*.

The sequence begins with a description of how Sāriputta and Moggallāna were in staying Rājagaha with two-hundred and fifty other followers of the recluse Sañjaya. They had made an agreement between the two of them that the one who first attained enlightenment should announce it to the other. Sāriputta saw Assaji, one of the Buddha's first five followers, on his alms-rounds and realized that he was one of the perfected ones in the world. After Assaji had completed his rounds, Sāriputta approached him and asked him whose *dhamma* he taught. Assaji told him that he followed the Buddha; when asked what doctrine the Buddha taught, Assaji told Sāriputta that he could only provide a short explanation of its fundamental meaning. Assaji told Sāriputta that:

> The *tathāgata* has told the cause of those things which arise from a cause, [and] that which is their ending; the great recluse has such a teaching.[28]

Upon hearing those lines, Sāriputta developed the *dhamma*-eye, which is described with the usual formula. Sāriputta responded that 'if this indeed is *dhamma*, you have penetrated as far as the sorrowless path, unseen, neglected for countless eons.'[29]

The story continues: Sāriputta left Assaji and met Moggallāna, who recognized that his friend had attained the goal which they both sought. Sāriputta agreed that he had, indeed, attained the state that does not die and told Moggallāna what had transpired with Assaji. When Sāriputta repeated the lines that summarized the Buddha's teachings, Moggallāna too developed the *dhamma*-eye and realized that 'whatever has the nature of arising, that has nature of ending.'[30] They returned to their two-hundred and fifty companions and told them that they were going to the Buddha. Sañjaya asked them not to go, but they left despite his requests. As Sāriputta and Moggallāna approached the Buddha with their company, the Buddha told his followers that these two friends would be significant leaders among his followers.

> The Blessed One saw Sāriputta and Moggallāna coming from a distance, and, seeing them, said to the *bhikkhus*: '*Bhikkhus*, these two friends, Kolita and Upatissa, are coming. This respected pair will become my most valuable pair.' While, in the deep sphere of knowledge, they reached the freedom in which attachments are destroyed, the Buddha explained about them in the Bamboo Grove: 'These two friends, Kolita and Upatissa, are coming. This respected pair will become my most valuable pair.'[31]

After Sāriputta and Moggallāna arrived, they asked the Buddha for acceptance into the order and were received with the standard reply: 'Come, *bhikkhus*, *dhamma* is taught well, live as a *brahmacariya* to bring about a proper ending of pain.' The narrative is concluded with the now-familiar phrase: 'So this was the ordination of these venerable ones.'[32] All of the pieces of the enlightenment narratives are here, although with notable differences.

Sāriputta gains his experience of the *dhamma*-eye upon hearing a talk from Assaji and not from the Buddha. This is the first instance in the *Mahāvagga* of a follower of the Buddha who is taught by another follower, despite the Buddha's injunction that his disciples teach the *dhamma*. In turn, Sāriputta teaches Moggallāna. As noted above, the *Mahāvagga* sequence does not describe how Sāriputta and Moggallāna were able to eliminate the corruptions: the story of how Sāriputta became an *arahat* is told in detail in the *Dīghanakha-sutta*.[33] That *sutta* describes how Sāriputta listened to the Buddha's talk to Aggivessana on the kinds of feelings – pleasant, unpleasant, and neither – and how an instructed follower turns away from such feelings and thus understands that birth is destroyed.[34] Sāriputta eliminated the corruptions while overhearing this talk, and

Dīghanakha cultivated the *dhamma*-eye. But the *Mahāvagga* does not tell the story.

The *dhamma*-eye arises in Sāriputta and Moggallāna in response to Assaji's discourse which Sāriputta repeats to Moggallāna. The content of that discourse simply points the way to the Buddha's teachings. The four noble truths are not mentioned, nor is any other specific doctrine. The graduated talk (*anupubbikathā*) given by the Buddha is not given by Assaji or Sāriputta. A talk on *dhamma* (*dhammadesanā*) is the term used in the Buddha's conversion narratives; here, Assaji is described as giving a *dhammapariyāya* which Horner translates as 'terse expression of *dhamma*.'[35] *Pariyāya* and *desanā* are used interchangeably at various points in the *Nikāyas*, and the substitution here is not surprising.[36] Horner's translation draws attention to the brevity of Assaji's teaching of the Buddha's *dhamma*, but the term *pariyāya*, independent of this passage, does not seem to denote a summary or a paraphrase. Instead, Assaji's abbreviated teaching is characteristic of a changing pedagogical pattern. Despite the change in the standard formula, the teachings still catalyze the emergence of the *dhamma*-eye in both Sāriputta and Moggallāna.

The Sāriputta and Moggallāna sequence contains two significant departures from the previously established pattern. First, the Buddha does not teach his soon-to-be students. Second, the catalyst for the arising of the *dhamma*-eye is a summary of the Buddha's teachings – not a graduated talk culminating in the four noble truths. In fact, the four noble truths and other specific doctrines are mentioned only once more in the remainder of the *Khandakas*.[37] The specific set of teachings that has characterized the first section of the *Mahāvagga* begins to recede from the foreground of the pedagogical structure just as the Buddha sets up a formal pedagogical structure for the order. Other mentions of the four noble truths in the *Vinaya-piṭaka* show that they are taught by the Buddha in much the same way as they are taught in the *Nikāya* passages which identify the four noble truths as a symbol of the Buddha's larger *dhamma*.[38] Unlike the passages in the *Nikāyas*, in their capacity as a symbol for the Buddha's teachings and for attainment of the first of the four stages of the path, the four noble truths are shown as taught by teachers other than the Buddha. These passages that consistently display the four noble truths at the center of a set pedagogical and soteriological pattern give way in the *Mahāvagga* to the more pragmatic concerns of how to govern the community, and the four noble truths are no longer central.

In the *Sutta-piṭaka*

Just as Koṇḍañña, the first follower of the Buddha, sets the pattern for the awakening of Yasa and others in the *Mahāvagga*, so too does Koṇḍañña provide the example for entry into the path that recurs at least in a half-dozen other points throughout the *Nikāyas*. The audience changes, and the concrete situation varies, but the passage remains virtually the same in every occurrence. The standard unit is taken here from the *Upāli-sutta* in the *Majjhima-nikāya*, and it is identical to the description of Yasa's enlightenment.

> Then the Blessed One gave a graduated talk to the householder Upāli, that is, he gave a talk on alms, a talk on virtue, and a talk on heaven; he explained the dangers, depravity and defilment of sensual pleasures, and the advantages of release. When the Blessed One knew that Upāli's mind was ready, tender, free from the hindrances, happy, and devoted, then he gave a standard *dhamma*-talk of the Buddhas: pain, origin, ending, and the path. Just as a clean cloth with all black spots removed will readily become dirty, so too, as the householder Upāli (sat) in the very same seat, the *dhamma* vision, dustless and stainless, arose in him: whatever has the nature of arising, all that has the nature of ending. [He] said to the Blessed One: 'Now, sir, I must go. There is much to be done.' 'Householder, now you must do what is appropriate.'[39]

The *sutta* begins with a conversation between the Buddha and Dīghatapassin the Nigaṇṭhā in Pāvārika's Mango Grove in Nāḷanda. Dīghatapassin leaves after the Buddha establishes the positions of the debate, and Upāli is sent by Nātaputta to persuade the Buddha that the Jain position is correct. After the Buddha points out the inconsistencies in his argument, Upāli asks the Buddha for refuge. He asks the Buddha three times for acceptance as a lay follower; and, after examining his motivations and agreeing to give alms to the Jains, he is accepted. The Buddha, realizing that Upāli was prepared for a graduated talk (*anupubbikathā*), spoke to him and gave the series of talks which culminated in the four noble truths. Just like Koṇḍañña, Upāli developed the *dhamma*-eye and realized that 'whatever has the nature of arising has the nature of ending.' The remainder of the *sutta* details the uproar in the Jain community, and Upāli's proclamation that he is now a follower of the Buddha.

In the *suttas* that contain the *dhammacakkhu* version of awakening and of the path, the Buddha addresses brahmans, householders, and renouncers.[40] These men become lay followers or disciples; no women are converted by the preaching of the four noble truths in the *Sutta-piṭaka* (as opposed to the *Mahāvagga* account). The Buddha is not the only Buddha who converts followers with the teaching of the four noble truths. In the *Mahāpadāna-sutta*, Buddha Vipassin accepts a brahman's son and a prince as disciples after they see *dhamma* by means of the four noble truths.[41] In the same *sutta*, Vipassin converts two groups of eighty-four thousand followers with the same graduated talk (*anupubbikathā*). The episodes are each described exactly as in the *Upāli-sutta*. The Buddha – either Gautama or Vipassin – gives a graduated talk on giving, virtue, the heavens, and on the dangers of attachment, realizes that his audience is ready and accepting, and gives a standard talk on *dhamma* praised by Buddhas (i.e., the four noble truths); and, the *dhamma*-eye arises in the audience, just as a clean cloth easily takes up dirt. These passages establish a relationship between the four noble truths as the content of the Buddha's talks, the cultivation of the *dhamma*-eye, and, as the commentaries explain, the attainment of the path as a stream-winner (see Table 5.2). The two cases in which those who have cultivated the *dhamma*-eye become ordained as *bhikkhus* follow the pattern of the *Mahāvagga* by destroying the corruptions after hearing a second talk on *dhamma* and thus becoming *arahats*.

The *dhamma*-eye is almost always found in relation to the graduated talk, but there are exceptions. The first is the *Dhammacakkappavattana-sutta* itself, where Koṇḍañña cultivates the *dhamma*-eye after hearing the Buddha talk on the four noble truths and his experience of enlightenment. The second exception is found in the *Mahāvagga*, where Vappa, Bhaddiya, Mahānāma, and Assaji experience the *dhamma*-eye in the same way as Koṇḍañña. The third example is found in the story of how Rāhula eliminated the corruptions. The Buddha realized that Rāhula had an understanding of *dhamma* and decided to teach him to destroy the corruptions (*āsavā*). He did so, and as Rāhula eradicated them (according to the same phrases found in the *Mahāvagga* and elsewhere), the *devas* who were listening to this exchange developed the *dhamma*-eye.[42] A fourth exception is the experience of Dīghanakha, who cultivates the *dhamma*-eye by overhearing a talk that the Buddha was giving to someone else on turning away from the three kinds of feelings (pleasant, unpleasant, and those that are neither).[43] In all of these cases, however, causing the *dhamma*-eye to arise means that the one who has had the experience of the vision of *dhamma* has, at a minimum, entered the path as a stream-winner. These citations show that developing a vision of *dhamma* is not always linked to a graduated talk. With the exception of Rāhula's story, however, the *dhamma* vision is always associated with the four noble truths.

In contrast, teaching the four noble truths is not always associated with the *dhamma*-eye, as one passage where the Buddha teaches the four noble truths to Verañjā the Brahman shows. The four noble truths are taught as part of the three watches and Verañjā does not have the eye of *dhamma*, but he does become an *upāsako*.[44] When we look at the sequence of the three watches (where the Buddha understood the four noble truths in the last watch of the night), we see that that the sequence of the three watches is never associated with the development of the *dhamma*-eye (recall Table 2.1 in Chapter Two). These exceptions emphasize that the four noble truths were standarized in a sequence of events that were thought to produce an experience which resulted in the attainment of the first stage of

Table 5.2 The Four Truths and the *Dhamma*-eye in the *Nikāyas*

	Teacher	Audience	Teaching	Result
Upāli-sutta (M I 371–387)	Buddha	Upāli the householder	graduated talk (*anupubbikathā*) and the four truths (mnemonic set (d))	*dhamma*-eye *upāsako*
Brahmāyu-sutta (M II 133–147)	Buddha	Brahmāyu the brahman	graduated talk four truths	*dhamma*-eye *upāsako*
Ambaṭṭha-sutta (D I 87–110)	Buddha	Kūtadanta the brahman	graduated talk four truths	*dhamma*-eye *upāsako*
Mahāpadāna-sutta (D II 1–54)	Vipassin	Khaṇḍa Tissa	graduated talk four truths	*dhamma*-eye *bhikkhus* *arahats* after a second *dhamma* talk
A IV 186–188	Buddha	Sīha	graduated talk four truths	*dhamma*-eye (no status given)
A IV 209 A IV 213	Buddha	Ugga of Vesāli Ugga of Hatthigāma	graduated truths four truths	*dhamma*-eye *upāsako*
Dhammacakka-ppavattana-sutta (S V 420)	Buddha	Koṇḍañña Vappa Bhaddiya Mahānāma Assaji	four truths (introduction set) (enlightenment set) (gerundive set)	*dhamma*-eye *bhikkhus* *arahats* after a second *dhamma* talk

the path and an understanding of *dhamma* which the commentaries explained in terms of the four noble truths. This experience of enlightenment that resulted from knowledge of the four noble truths did not involve the elimination of the corruptions; as we have seen, the corruptions are only destroyed while listening to a second *dhamma* talk given by a Buddha or another qualified teacher, and it is only with the destruction of the corruptions that one attains the status of an *arahat*. Cultivating the *dhammacakkhu* introduces a follower to the path; understanding the four noble truths in this path sequence does not lead to the highest attainment of an *arahat*.

These passages show that listening to talks of the Buddha are understood in the canon to produce an experience of release from the saṃsāric realm through the acquisition of knowledge of the four noble truths. Why, the texts ask, should we listen to the Buddha? Because he knows and has experienced the very things that he teaches, because they are logical, and because they are convincing. The Buddha's actions (*adhisīlaṃ*) are also shown to be consistent with his teachings.[45] Other teachers lack this consistency and should not be followed. The authority of the four noble truths, the canon and commentaries assert, lies in the Buddha's own experience and realization of the four noble truths. The *Dhammacakkappavattana-sutta* exemplifies this conception of the power of the Buddha's teaching and the centrality of the four noble truths in their symbolic role. The following sections examine the many places in the *Nikāya*s where the four noble truths are taught in relation to other teachings, and in which the four noble truths are regarded as propositions about reality and not as symbols.[46]

The Four Noble Truths, the Corruptions, and the Path

In contrast to the passages discussed thus far in this chapter, where the four noble truths are set in relation to other teachings – where they function as propositions – they operate differently within the structure of the path. Put simply, the four noble truths are the means by which the corruptions are destroyed, according to the model of the *Sāmaññaphala-sutta*. Within this structure, the four noble truths appear in the company of the eight stages of *jhāna*ic meditation, the development of the transpersonal powers of the divine eye (*dibbacakkhu*), and they are the means to destroy the corruptions and thereby attain the status of an *arahat*, although the passages rarely make that claim explicit.

In the *Sāmaññaphala-sutta*, the Buddha describes the benefits of the life of a recluse to King Ajātasattu of Magadha. Recognizing the impediments of a householder's life, a recluse goes forth from the home into the homeless state (*agārasmā anagāriyaṃ pabbajati*).[47] Such a person lives according to the virtues (*sīlaṃ*);[48] and, in preparation for *jhān*ic meditation, s/he guards the senses by being mindful, aware, and in control of the senses. Such a person is content and chooses a quiet spot away from distractions to undertake the preparatory stages for *jhānic* meditation, which culminates with clearing the mind of doubt and worry. The recluse then enters the first, second, and third *jhānas*, and, finally, the fourth *jhāna*. The descriptions of these stages are the same as those introduced in Chapter Two, when they appear in the context of the *Bhayabherava-sutta*.

Following the attainment of the four stages of the *jhānas*, the recluse then cultivates the six higher knowledges (*abhiññā*), the first of which is the eight transpersonal or psychic powers (*iddhis*):[49] (i) to take on one or many bodies, (ii) to be visible or invisible, (iii) to walk through solid walls or ground as if they were space, (iv) to walk on water as if on solid ground, (v) to travel through the air, and (vi) to travel through the sky cross-legged, and (vii) to touch the sun and moon, 'things of great *iddhi* and things of great power,' and (viii) he is able to ascend with his body as far as the Brahmā worlds. The remaining higher knowledges (*abhiññā*) are: (2) the divine ear, which provides the ability to hear sounds nearby or far away, (3) the ability to know the minds of others, (4) the ability to know one's own past births, (5) the ability to know the previous births of others, and (6) the ability to know the future births of others by virtue of the divine eye (*dibbena cakkhunā*).

With a calm heart, a recluse directs one's practice toward knowing the destruction of the corruptions (*āsavānaṃ khayañāṇāya*):

> He fully comprehends 'this is pain,' he fully comprehends 'this is the arising of pain,' he fully comprehends 'this is the ending of pain,' [and] he fully comprehends 'this is the way to the ending of pain;' he fully comprehends 'these are the corruptions,' he fully comprehends 'this is the arising of the corruptions,' he fully comprehends 'this is the ending of the corruptions,' [and] he fully comprehends 'this is the way to the ending of the corruptions.'[50]

In this way, the recluse is set free from the three corruptions: the corruption of desire (*kāmāsavā*), the corruption of becoming (*bhavāsavā*), and the corruption of ignorance (*avijjāsavā*). And, as we might anticipate, King Ajātasattu requests and receives acceptance as a lay follower of the Buddha. There is an interesting end to the *sutta* that bears on the analysis of the *dhammacakkhu*. The Buddha addresses his *bhikkhus* after the king has left, telling them that the king was deeply affected by his talk, and had the king not put his father to death, he would have cultivated the *dhammacakkhu* upon hearing the Buddha talk.[51]

This sequence is a common structure of the path that is found throughout the *Dīgha-* and *Majjhima-nikāyas*, and most versions are fairly consistent with the *Sāmaññanaphala-sutta*. Joy Manné has identified this model as a 'hypothetical case history.'[52] She separates the steps in this sequence into several stages: Stage I 'The Prerequisites'; Stage II 'The Cultivation of the Mind'; Stage III 'Transcending the Mind'; Stage IV 'Developing the Transpersonal Powers'; and Stage V 'Liberation.'[53] The four *jhāna* levels appear in Stage III, and the four noble truths appear in Stage V, in the form of the passage quoted above.

The features of the formulaic relationship between the *jhāna*s, the four truths, and the elimination of the *āsavā*s include the same descriptions, the appearance of the four noble truths in their basic set, and an agreement with passages discussed earlier in Chapter Two in which the Buddha attains enlightenment during the third and last watch of the night by eliminating the *āsavā*s according to the four noble truths.[54] There are a surprisingly large number of *sutta*s in which this sequence occurs, including the first thirteen *sutta*s of the *Dīgha-nikāya* and at least seven *sutta*s from the *Majjhima-nikāya*.[55] This sequence that links the four levels of *jhāni*c meditation, the four noble truths, and the elimination of three corruptions (*āsavā*) is different in structure as well as grammar than the story told in the *Dhammacakkappavattana-sutta*.

Unlike the appearance of the four truths in the *dhammacakkhu* passages, the four noble truths have the grammatical form of the basic set in the sequence of the *jhāna*s, four truths, and elimination of the corruptions. That is, each of the four terms is declined according to its proper gender and has the correct pronoun. Remember here that Norman argues that the basic set is the earliest form in which the four noble truths appear because it has the correct endings. Therefore, the fact that the four noble truths appear in the basic set in the sequence of the four *jhāna*s, but in the introduction, enlightenment, and gerundival sets in the *Dhammacakkappavattana-sutta* might suggest that the four noble truths were incorporated into the *Dhammacakkappavattana-sutta* after they were introduced into the canon through other *sutta*s – namely those that contain the sequence of the four *jhāna*s, the four noble truths, and the elimination of the corruptions.

Based on other sources of evidence, Bronkhorst and Schmithausen have shown that the passages in which the four noble truths lead to an experience of liberating insight are not 'the original account of enlightenment.'[56] Building on Bareau's suggestion that the corruptions (*āsavā*) were added to the passage at a later date, Bronkhorst suggests that the four noble truths do not fit in this passage for a logical reason.[57] It makes sense, he writes, to presume that knowledge of the four noble truths is necessary before one embarks on the path to the ending of pain – it does not follow that knowledge of the four truths should come at the end of the path, as it does in this passage. Bronkhorst hypothesizes that the four noble truths were actually substituted for the notion of insight or wisdom (*paññā*) in these formulaic passages.[58] If this is the case, the grammatical form of the four noble truths in this passage indicates that the four noble truths were introduced into what became the canonical writings first in relation to attaining the *jhāni*c states and to the eradication of the *āsavā*, and later in the context of the Buddha's biographies, such as the *Dhammacakkappa-vattana-sutta*.

The four noble truths in the *Sāmaññaphala-sutta* and its parallels are the means by which a practitioner may destroy the corruptions and thereby become an *arahat*. This role of the four noble truths contrasts directly with the assertion in other *sutta*s where hearing the four noble truths leads to the cultivation of the *dhammacakkhu*, not to the eradication of the corruptions. In the *dhammacakkhu* passages, a practitioner must hear a second *dhamma* talk in order to eliminate the corruptions and become an *arahat*. I am aware of only one point in the commentaries where the *dhamma*-eye defined in terms of eliminating the corruptions.[59] It appears that there are two models of the path – one based on the cultivation of the *dhammacakkhu* and another based on attaining the *jhāna*s, realizing the four noble truths, and then eliminating the *āsavā* by analyzing them according to the four truths. These two models offer two different attainments: one that leads a follower to the first level of the path (*sotāpanno* or stream-enterer) and one that enables a practitioner to attain the status of an *arahat* – although those attainments are stated not in the *sutta*s themselves but in the commentaries.[60] These two distinct models of path attainments reflect the different roles of the four noble truths: as a symbol, the four noble truths lead to the acquisition of a vision of *dhamma* and at least to the status of a stream-enterer; as a proposition, the four noble truths are the means by which a practitioner eliminates the corruptions and becomes an *arahat*.[61]

These two models may also be a legacy of the historical process of remembering what the Buddha taught. Schmithausen and Bronkhorst show that the passages in which knowledge of the four truths lead one to eliminate the corruptions do not reflect the earliest descriptions of enlightenment. Norman has shown that the grammatical forms of the four noble truths in the *Dhammacakkappavattana-sutta* indicate that the teaching is an addition to the earliest versions of the *sutta*. What we emerge with is a tentative conclusion that the four noble truths were first conceptualized as related to the highest form of enlightenment: the attainments of an *arahat*. Perhaps as the teaching became more thoroughly dispersed throughout the teachings, they became more logically associated to the beginning of the path and the means to cultivate the *dhammacakku*. Bronkhorst suggests that it was perhaps the personal attention of the Buddha's teachings that was of more assistance to his followers than the specific items of doctrine that he taught. He suggests that the scene portrayed in the *Ariyapariyesana-sutta* (where the Buddha taught the first three followers while the other two went for food and then taught the next two while the first went for food) appears 'to preserve the idea of how the early monks conceived what the Buddha's instruction had been like.'[62]

However, this appeal to the Buddha's personal attention as the critical factor in the attainments of the Buddha's followers does not analyze sufficiently the pedagogical models that surround these two outlines of soteriological attainments associated with the four noble truths.

Teaching the Four Noble Truths

It might be logical to suppose that there are different pedagogical models for how to teach and learn the truths if knowing the four noble truths leads, at different points in the canon, to different levels of path attainment. Indeed, we will see that this is the case. However, the evidence is less clearly defined than that which we have surveyed so far. Since most studies of Buddhist doctrine presume that doctrines express a predominantly theoretical concern that is often divorced from more practical concerns, it is useful to explore what the Theravāda canon says about how doctrines are taught – and specifically how the four noble truths are taught and learned for the purpose of attaining the path.

The single difference between how the four noble truths are taught in their role as a symbol and in their role as a proposition of doctrine is that as a symbol, the four noble truths are taught with a single pedagogical formula. They are part of the graduated talk and they are the substance of a talk that is 'praised by Buddhas,' which results in the acquisition of the *dhamma*-eye. In these standarized teachings of the graduated talk and the *dhamma* talk praised by Buddhas, there is a carefully delineated relationship: hearing the graduated talk and the talk praised by Buddhas which contains the four noble truths produces the *dhamma*-eye, that is defined by the commentaries as entry into the path at least as a stream-enterer.

The commentaries carefully define *anupubbikathā* and *buddhānaṃ sāmukkaṃsikā dhammadesanā*, and these terms are perhaps the most narrowly defined pedagogical terms in the canon. According to Buddhaghosa, talks on giving, virtue, heaven, the dangers of sensual pleasures, and the advantages in being free of them, all belong to the class of graduated discourse (*anupubbikathā*), which refers to the fact that the four topics, giving (*dānaṃ*), virtue (*sīlaṃ*), heaven (*saggo*), and the path (*maggo*), are each discussed in turn, one immediately following the other.[63] A standard *dhamma*-talk, however, is less fixed in content. *Dhammadesanā* is generally taken as a exposition or discourse on the *dhamma* or simply as a talk or sermon.[64] But the rest of the phrase, the adjective *sāmukkaṃsikā* and *buddhānaṃ* in the genetive plural, modifies *dhammadesanā* to refer to a *dhamma*-talk praised by all Buddhas – throughout the cosmic span of time.[65] 'Graduated discourse' (*anupubbikathā*) and 'a *dhamma* talk praised by Buddhas' (*buddhānaṃ sāmukkaṃsikā dhammadesanā*) are two technical terms used to describe the content of the Buddha's teachings, and are used consistently in those passages that contain references to the the four noble truths in their symbolic function.

The consistency in what kind of talks are used to teach the four noble truths as a symbol extends to who teaches the four noble truths. The canon tell us that Sāriputta is known for his ability to teach the four noble truths and, generally, he is the only other teacher besides the Buddha who is considered capable to teach the four noble truths. The *Saccavibhaṅga-sutta* uses a number of terms to describe how the wheel of *dhamma* was turned: the wheel was a proclamation (*ācikkhanā*), a teaching (*desanā*), a disclosure (*paññāpanā*), an establishing (*paṭṭhapanā*), an opening up (*vivaraṇā*), analyzing (*vibhajanā*), and making clear (*uttānīkamma*).[66] Some of these terms appear in only a few places, such as disclosure (*paññāpanā*).[67] Others are used frequently and interchangeably: teaching (*desanā*) and speak (*bhāsati*) are two common examples. Sāriputta is often the teacher in the passages which contain these terms; the Buddha explains that Sāriputta is able to teach the four noble truths, and thus the audience should listen to him.[68] There is no discernable difference between terms that are used to describe the act of teaching in *sutta*s where the Buddha speaks and those where Sāriputta is the teacher. Some of these terms also appear in *sutta*s which describe the teachings of other teachers, such as Pūraṇa Kassapa or Uddaka Rāmaputta.[69]

In the *sutta*s that contain descriptions of how would-be followers of the Buddha cultivate the *dhamma* eye (the stories of enlightenment), the Buddha and Sāriputta are the only teachers who give the graduated talk and the talk praised by Buddhas. There are no cases in which a practitioner is able to cultivate the *dhamma* eye and thus gain entry into the path by learning the four noble truths in their relationship to other teachings. The result of this observation is that the canon has recorded two patterns for how practitioners might learn the four noble truths that are differentiated in terms of time. After the Buddha's death and after Sāriputta's death, there are no examples of followers cultivating the *dhamma* eye by hearing a graduated talk or a talk praised by Buddhas. The only way that a follower of the Buddha can learn the four noble truths after the Buddha's *parinibbāna* is by learning them as propositions, and within a broad range of teaching styles and practices.

Where the four truths are taught within the context of the *jhāna*s and the *āsavā* and in other teachings, they are characterized by a variety of terms that are remarkable only for their diversity, in contrast to the narrowly defined terms found in relation to the cultivation of the *dhammacakkhu* through the four truths. The Theravāda canon uses a number of terms to denote the acts of teaching, and uses other terms to denote the kinds of talks given. The list includes: discourse (*veyyākaraṇa*),[70] to advise and instruct (*ovadati* and *anusāsati*),[71] to teach *dhamma* (*dhamma deseti*),[72] discourse (*pariyāya*),[73] to declare (*pavakkhati*),[74] to make clear (*paṭibhāti*),[75] to proclaim (*pavedeti*),[76] talk on *dhamma* (*dhammakathā*),[77] and to explain (*vyākaroti*).[78] The list of terms appears, therefore, to refer to any act of teaching *dhamma* and does not vary according to the teacher. Taken together, these terms describe a broadly defined pedagogy for teaching in the *Nikāya*s.

Dhamma is taught in the *sutta*s in a variety of forms which range from a simple talk delivered to a general audience by the Buddha or another follower to an extended question and answer session with a single listener. In a comparative study of the Chinese *Madhyama Āgama* and the Pāli *Majjhima-nikāya*, Minh Chau has found eight different contexts in which *dhamma* is taught: (1) for no apparent reason, (2) to correct wrong views, (3) followers elaborate upon a brief statement given by the Buddha, (4) to counter views held by non-Buddhists, (5) to followers, (6) to lay followers, (7) for discussion among *bhikkhu*s, and (8) talks given by followers.[79] Manné suggests that debates were the most significant context in which teachings on path attainments were given, although she does not pursue the particular terms used in those debates.[80] The words which describe the genre of the teachings reveal a range of genres, which include a graduated talk (*anupubbikathā*), discourse (*veyyākaraṇa*), and method (*pariyāya*).[81] These terms are not used consistently to refer to one kind of teaching, and so they cannot be taken as well-defined signifiers for specific genres. They are roughly synonymous in the *Nikāya*s, with the exception of the graduated talks that refer to a series of graduated talks on giving, morality, heaven, and the four noble truths. These terms and this pedagogy are presumed by the canonical tradition and thus provide a pedagogical framework for the four noble truths as they appear within the networks of the Buddha's doctrines.

A passage found in the *Aṅguttara-nikāya* provides some insight into teaching *dhamma*. In this story, the Buddha asks a householder named Ugga of Vesāli to describe the 'eight marvelous and wonderful qualities' that he possesses.[82] Ugga of Vesāli is properly modest, but he says that his first quality was approaching the Buddha and listening to him. His second quality was taking refuge in the Buddha, *dhamma*, and the *saṅgha* (after developing the *dhamma*-eye while hearing the Buddha's graduated talk and the four noble truths); his third was seeing that his daughters and wife were cared for; the four quality was sharing his wealth impartially; the fifth was serving a *bhikkhu* appropriately; the sixth was listening to the *dhamma* talks of a *bhikkhu* attentively and, in turn, preaching *dhamma* to that *bhikkhu* if a talk was not forthcoming from the *bhikkhu*; the seventh quality was not taking pride in the fact that *deva*s spoke to him; and the eighth was that he had eliminated the five lower fetters (*saṃyojanāni*). The sixth quality – listening attentively and preaching to a *bhikkhu* if the need arises – shows that teaching *dhamma* was not always the prerogative of *bhikkhu*s and provides some insight into the broader context for the formulaic teaching of the four noble truths that lies outside the Buddha's graduated talk and his *dhamma* talk praised by Buddhas.

In the monastic community described in the Pāli canon, the teachings are passed down orally from the Buddha to his followers and from elders to novices. The doctrines are memorized, recited, and reflected upon; the mode of discourse is a dialogue of questions and answers. The fundamental purpose of the community is the cessation of suffering through the attainment of *nibbāna*; and, all knowledge and instruction is directed toward that end. The teachings are grouped into collections often governed by length or by number of items in a given list. Such organization aids memory and recitation; indeed, the commentaries count the size of a collection of sayings in recitations (*bhāṇavāra*).[83] These recitations consist of two-hundred and fifty stanzas, each with thirty-two syllables; each stanza has four feet of eight syllables.[84] The tradition was handed down orally, from teacher to student. The elders were respected for the collections of sayings they knew, and for their ability to train students.

With regard to specific types of knowledge, *bhikkhus* and *bhikkhunīs* are enjoined to listen and question the elders carefully, and to memorize and contemplate the sayings and stories diligently.[85] The tradition is handed down orally, from mouth to ear, but not simply memorized and repeated. A monk is taught to ask questions about the purpose of a teaching and its meaning, and thus to resolve his doubts about obscure points. For example,

> Here, monks, from time to time a monk frequents those monks of broad knowledge, who are versed in the sayings, who know the lists thoroughly, who know the discipline and summaries by heart. He inquires of them and questions them: 'How is this, sirs? What is the meaning of this?' Those noble ones then open up to him what was sealed, make clear what was obscure, and remove doubt regarding occasions of doubt.[86]

Within this exchange of questions and answers, the elders are those who have mastered the teachings. They hold 'summaries' (*dhamma*), 'discipline' (*vinaya*), and the 'lists' (*mātikā*) in trust for the future and pass them on to those who diligently study them.[87]

There are other lists of what genres are appropriate for a *bhikkhu* or *bhikkhunī* to learn. These genres are somewhat problematic in the canonical literature because they are not used consistently and we do not have clear evidence for the literature that was thought to comprise each genre.[88] Nonetheless, this passage from the *Aṅguttara-nikāya* provides a detailed description of what a *bhikkhu* is to know:

> Consider, revered Sāriputta, a *bhikkhu* who masters *dhamma*, the sayings (*suttā*), mixed prose and verse (*geyyā*), exposition (*veyyākaraṇā*), verse (*gāthā*), utterances (*udānā*), 'that which is said' (*itivut-*

> *taka*), birth stories (*jātakā*), wonders (*abbhutadhammā*), *vedallā*; as learned, as mastered, he teaches other *dhammā* in detail; as learned, as mastered, he makes others say it in detail; as learned, as mastered, he reflects and ponders over it in his heart, he pores over it mindfully. He spends Vas wherever revered elders reside, [those *bhikkhus*] of broad knowledge, who are versed in the sayings, who know the lists thoroughly, who know the discipline and summaries by heart. He inquires of them and questions them: 'How is this, sirs? What is the meaning of this?' Those noble ones then open up to him what was sealed, make clear what was obscure, and remove uncertainty regarding things in doubt.[89]

Alongside these nine genres, other *suttas* explain that the *dhamma* will last only if those who know the *dhamma*, *vinaya*, and *mātikās* carefully and dutifully pass on the texts and do not 'cut it down at the root.'[90] The duty of a monk, as it is described in these passages, is to ask questions of those elders who know the traditions: to inquire, interrogate, and learn. Such a duty shows that the authority of the tradition rested in the knowledge of elders who were well acquainted with the *dhamma*, *vinaya*, and *mātikā*.[91]

There are two passages in the *Suttavibhaṅga* and the *Bhikkhunīvibhaṅga* of the *Vinaya-piṭaka* which indicate that *abhidhamma*, and not necessarily the *Abhidhamma-piṭaka*, was a unique genre. *Abhidhamma* is first found in company with *suttanta* and *vinaya* in the *Vinaya-piṭaka*.[92]

> 'Might ask a question' means that it is an offense requiring expiation if, having received permission regarding the *suttas*, she asks about *abhidhamma* or discipline. It is an offense requiring expiation if, having received permission regarding discipline, she asks about the *suttas* or *abhidhamma*. It is an offense requiring expiation if, having received permission regarding *abhidhamma*, she asks about the *suttas* or discipline.[93]

The first passage is straightforward: a *bhikkhunī* must receive permission to discuss certain texts with a *bhikkhu*, and if she deviates from the topic in question, she commits an offense which requires expiation. The passage indicates that a *bhikkhunī* should be aware of the distinctions between the genres, and not confuse the different kinds of texts that one should know.[94]

The second passage appears to be unique in the canon because 'verses' (*gāthā*) are joined with the more familiar triad of *sutta*, *abhidhamma*, and *vinaya*.[95]

> It is not an offense if one who is mad or is the first to commit an offense, and does not wish to insult [discipline], says 'Come, thoroughly learn the *suttas*, or verses, or *abhidhamma*, and after that you will master discipline.'[96]

This is one of the few points in the canon where 'verses' (*gāthā*) refer to a distinct body of material which is to be learned. The quartet in this verse is distinctive, although all four genres belong to the set of nine *aṅga*s. The interesting point about this passage is the implication that one can *not* master discipline through the *sutta*s, *abhidhamma*, or *gāthā*s; although, if one's intentions are correct, it is no great error to say so. This statement indicates that one should study all four genres in order to learn them thoroughly, and that they are not equally interchangeable. This passage thus lends further support to the distinction between the genres of *sutta*, *abhidhamma*, and *vinaya*.

Abhidhamma is one form of discourse within this monastic community that is designed to produced path attainment which has established practices and definitions that define it as a distinctive discourse. The Theravāda canon contains formulaic descriptions of the proper attitude and role of *abhidhamma* within Buddhist life. For example, the following passage is found throughout the canon: 'And furthermore, friends, [this] *bhikkhu* loves *dhamma*, is pleasant in conversation, and rejoices greatly in *abhidhamma* and *abhivinaya*' (*puna ca paraṃ āvuso bhikkhu dhamma-kāmo hoti piya-samudāhāro abhidhamme abhivanaye uḷāra-pāmujjo*).[97] This phrase appears among a list of ten protections, which includes such items as living in accord with the self-control prescribed in the *Vinaya-piṭaka*, remembering what one has learned, being mindful and endowed with insight. The textual evidence examined in the following section shows that the Theravāda canon considered *abhidhamma* analysis to have an established and respected place within the pedagogy of the *saṅgha*.

The role of *abhidhamma* in this community was not necessarily to develop abstract theory, as Gethin points out, but rather to distill the essence of *dhamma* by elucidating the principles by which the cosmos was understood to develop, change, unfold, and evolve. Gethin writes that the compilers of the *abhidhamma* lists 'were primarily concerned to distinguish states and processes of mind on the basis of actual observation, rather than to construct an abstract theoretical system as such.'[98] The form of that discourse is denaturalized, but the substance of that discourse is concrete and specific. The principles of *dhamma* are extracted insofar as the specific relationships between states (*dhammā*) and mental processes are described in detail. Knowledge of these lists and this type of analysis is understood by the Theravāda canon as a noteworthy and essential feature of a *bhikkhu* within the monastic community.

Discussions of *abhidhammakathā* provide further insights into the pedagogical method of *abhidhamma* and, by comparison, other pedagogical methods. The term *abhidhammakathā* appears in three passages throughout the *Sutta*- and *Vinaya-piṭaka*s and should first be understood as one of several kinds of *kathā* (talks). For example, *dhammakathā*, or talks on *dhamma*, are said to 'rouse, incite and delight' audiences, and are defined as one of the highest jewels in the *Mahāmaṅgala-sutta.*[99] There is also a standarized list of ten kinds of *kathā*, which appears six times throughout the *Sutta-piṭaka.*[100] Here, in the *Mahāsuññata-sutta* the Buddha explains to Ānanda how a *bhikkhu* should develop concentration and awareness.

> But, Ānanda, regarding talk that is austere [and] an aid to setting the heart free, and which leads to complete indifference (with the world), detachment, stopping, calm, higher knowledge, enlightenment and nibbāna; that is, talk about wanting few things, contentment, solitude, seclusion, vigor, virtue, concentration, wisdom, freedom, and talk about the knowledge and vision of freedom – one thinks, 'This is how I will speak.'[101]

Thinking about these kinds of talks, the Buddha says, enables a *bhikkhu* to develop consciousness with regard to talk that is [both] austere (*kathā abhisallekhikā*) and an aid to setting the heart free. The goal is the acquisition of the happiness of renunciation, solitude, calm, and enlightenment.[102] Different kinds of *dhammakathā* are distinguished according to topic, as with the *anupubbikā dhammadesanā* (graduated *dhamma* talks). Little mention is made of the method according to which *dhammakathā* (talks), *sākacchā* (conversations), or *desanā* (talks) are conducted. The one exception is an exchange between a *bhikkhu* named Puṇṇiya and the Buddha on the conditions necessary for a *tathāgata* to preach the *dhamma.*[103] In comparison to these kinds of *dhammakathā* which are ordered according to topic, *abhidhammakathā* is defined according to the method of inquiry.

The best known *sutta* which illustrates *abhidhammakathā* is the *Mahāgosiṅga-sutta*, cited by Buddhaghosa in the commentary to the first book of the *Abhidhamma-piṭaka.*[104] The Buddha and his followers were gathered in Gosiṅga, and a group of followers went to Sāriputta to hear a talk on the *dhamma*. But, as they approached, Sāriputta turned to Ānanda and asked him what kinds of *bhikkhu* would best illumine the beautiful grove of sāl trees in which they are seated. Ānanda responded that a *bhikkhu* who has heard much, remembers what he has heard, and teaches what he has heard would best illumine the sāl-wood. The question is then asked of Revata, Anuruddha, Mahākassapa, and Moggallāna. Moggallāna answered:

> In regard to this, friend Sāriputta, two *bhikkhus* speak about *abhidhamma*. They ask each other questions, answer the questions each has asked and do not fail, and their talk on *dhamma* moves forward. By a *bhikkhu* such as this, friend Sāriputta, would the Gosiṅga sāl-wood be illumined.[105]

This explicit question-and-answer format for *abhidhamma* is also reflected in the passage cited above, where a *bhikkhu* dwelling in the forest was instructed to study *abhidhamma* because he should be able to answer questions on *abhidhamma*.[106] Likewise, a *bhikkhu* who cannot answer *abhidhamma* questions but who knows the four truths is compared to a horse which possesses speed but is not beautiful.[107] Finally, the *Kinti-sutta* explains how there may be a difference of opinion regarding *abhidhamma* among a well-ordered and harmonious community.[108] The passage from the *Mahāgosiṅga-sutta* suggests that *abhidhamma* talk enhances one's ability to speak on *dhamma*: in the exchange of *abhidhamma* question and answers, 'their talk on *dhamma* moves forward.' The commentary on the *Mahāgosiṅga-sutta* says that one who does not know *abhidhamma* confuses his own words with the words of others and does not know what others have said.[109] The *abhidhamma* method, then, is an exchange of questions and answers between two knowledgeable *bhikkhus*, who may not always agree, which enhances *dhammakathā*.

This description of *abhidhamma* method as a means to enhance one's ability to speak on *dhamma* is supported by Buddhaghosa in his commentary on the *Dhammasaṅgaṇī*:

> And tradition has it that only those *bhikkhus* who know *abhidhamma* are true teachers of *dhamma*; the rest, though they speak on the *dhamma* do not speak on [*abhidhamma*]. Why? In speaking on the *dhamma*, they confuse the different kinds of *kamma* and the results, the distinction between matter and the different kinds of states. The students of *abhidhamma* do not thus get confused; hence a *bhikkhu* who knows *abhidhamma*, whether he teaches the *dhamma* or not will be able to answer questions whenever asked. He alone, therefore, is a true teacher of the *dhamma*.[110]

Buddhaghosa cites the *Mahagosiṅga-sutta* as his authority for his position. In the commentaries, the *abhidhamma* method consisted of a question-and-answer exchange, a form of debate among equals which has the capacity to clarify one's understanding and teaching of *dhamma*.

Who engaged in *abhidhamma* debates? An exchange in the *Aṅguttara-nikāya* shows that there were clear distinctions made between those *bhikkhus* who were capable of discussing *abhidhamma* and those who were not.[111] A number of elders had returned from alms-gathering and were discussing *abhidhamma* in the hall. From time to time, a *bhikkhu* named Citta Hatthisāriputta interrupted their talk.[112] Finally, Mahākoṭṭhita asked him to stop interrupting and to wait until the talk was over. Citta's friends defended him, saying that Citta was a wise man who was just as able to speak on *abhidhamma* as the elders. Koṭṭhita explained, in turn, that Citta was like those *bhikkhus* who are quite learned and accomplished when in the company of the Buddha and the *saṅgha*, but who eventually return to the life of a householder when they enter the company of lay men and women, kings, ministers and so on. And before long, the story runs, Citta left the order. Some time later, Citta's friends approached the Buddha with Citta's situation, and the Buddha responded that Citta would soon return to the *saṅgha* and again take up the robes. Although the story ends happily for Citta, the turn of events after Citta's interruptions appear to justify Koṭṭhita's censure of Citta. Not only is Koṭṭhita recognized as a master of logical analysis, but in the *Mahāvedalla-sutta* he and Sāriputta exchanged opinions in a style very like the question-and-answer format described in the *Mahāgosiṅga-sutta* above. Koṭṭhita's authority seems to be rooted in his own ability to engage in *abhidhamma* debates, and thus his sanction of Citta (justified or not) demonstrates that not all *bhikkhus* were regarded as equally capable of participating in *abhidhammakathā*, although the standards are not made explicit. Koṭṭhita's comments show that the elders or *theras* were versed in *abhidhamma* analysis.[113]

Another passage in the *Aṅguttara-nikāya* sheds more light on the qualifications that a *bhikkhu* must possess to understand *abhidhamma*. The passage explains that *bhikkhus* who have not developed the body, virtue, mind, and insight will not understand the meaning of *abhidhamma*. This reference supports the point of Citta's story, that not all *bhikkhus* are equally capable of speaking on *abhidhamma*. In this passage, however, *abhidhamma* is paired with *vedalla*, and the meaning of that pairing is unclear. *Vedalla* is one of the nine styles or genres (*navaṅga*), a list which was briefly introduced above. The sentence reads:

> Again, *bhikkhus*, *bhikkhus* who have not developed body, virtue, mind or wisdom, those recluses who have not developed body, virtue, mind or wisdom will not develop when giving a talk on *abhidhamma* or on the *vedalla*, will not fully understand, falling into a dark state. Therefore, *bhikkhus*, corrupt discipline comes from corrupt *dhamma*; from corrupt *dhamma* comes corrupt discipline.[114]

The commentary on this passage defines *abhidhamma* as *uttamadhamma* (higher *dhamma*), and *vedalla* as *vedapaṭisaṃyuttaṃ ñāṇa-missaka-kathaṃ* (a mixed talk on knowledge related to the Vedas).[115] Buddhaghosa has defined *vedalla* as *suttas* in the form of questions 'asked through repeated attainment of delight and understanding' (*vedañ ca tuṭṭhiñ ca laddhā laddhā pucchitasuttantā vedallan ti veditabbam*).[116] Despite this gloss, the meaning of *vedalla* is too uncertain to attach any clear pedagogical method to the term.[117] The last sentence of this passage confirms that correct teachings on *abhidhamma* enhance one's understanding of *dhamma* and discipline – a point made in the *Mahāgosiṅga-sutta* above.

These passages in which *abhidhammakathā* appears show that the right to participate in an *abhidhammakathā* generally belonged to the elders and that there may have been specific qualities associated with one who could conduct an *abhidhammakathā*. Those qualities which an elder was said to possess are related to the four discriminations (of meaning, *dhamma*, language, and intelligence). The passages cited above show that *abhidhamma* pedagogy was practiced by elders who were judged to be capable of discussing the topics denoted by the term *abhidhamma*. Agreement was not always necessary among the elders, but mastery of the material appeared to be a prerequisite. Other *bhikkhus* should know *abhidhamma* in order to make other points of *dhamma* clear. *Abhidhammakathā*, then, is a form of discourse that is passed on through questions and answers, which is carried out among elders, and with which younger *bhikkhus* should acquaint themselves.

Conclusions

At the beginning of this chapter, I quoted from I. B. Horner's book *Buddhist Theory of Man Perfected* that she published in 1936. One of the points that she argued was that the compound 'worthy true things' (*ariyasaccāni*) did not always refer to the four noble truths, as we have been using the term throughout this study. Drawing on commentarial material, Horner suggested that in an early period of Buddhism the term 'noble truths' referred to the four paths, or to what she called 'the four Ways.' She also suggested that the 'noble truths' may have been a reference to the four foundations of mindfulness. Horner's argument reflects an concern with the history of early Buddhism that was characteristic of scholarship on Buddhism during the 1920s and 1930s, and historical hypotheses such as hers have since been recognized as insoluble at best. Nonetheless, Horner's observation that the 'noble truths' might refer to the four paths or to the four foundations of mindfulness is grounded in a close reading of where the compound is defined in the canon and commentaries and where it is not. It was not the point in this chapter to support Horner's argument that the 'four worthy true things' sometimes referred to the four paths and sometimes referred to other teachings. Nonetheless, her underlying analysis is correct: the relationship between the four noble truths and the path is not always laid out clearly in the Theravāda canon or commentaries. The four noble truths are linked in two distinctly different ways to the four paths; and, furthermore, there are different pedagogical models that reflect the different relationships between the four noble truths and the fourfold path. The existence of and differences between these two models may lie in the historical development of the various Buddhist canons.

Hearing a graduated talk (*anupubbikathā*) and the *dhamma* talks praised by Buddhas (the four noble truths) produces the *dhammacakkhu* which denotes entry into the first level of the path in certain listeners who are able to hear. In those passages, the structure of the path is clear: it is the fourfold path that begins with entry into the stream. The set of pedagogical techniques is equally clear: those who are able to hear understand in some fashion the truth of what the Buddha has taught and realize what he realized for themselves. The symbolic function of the four noble truths appears to be the crucial element in this pattern. The four noble truths, when applied to the corruptions as a doctrinal proposition, are the means by which the corruptions are eliminated; the destruction of the corruptions is the feature that marks one as an *arahat*. While the fourfold path remains the same in both models, knowledge of the four truths produces different attainments, depending on how they are learned and applied.

There are two roles of the four noble truths at work in these descriptions of how the teachings of the Buddha are to be learned. The four noble truths function symbolically because the Theravāda tradition has recorded that the four truths have the ability to catalyze knowledge of the path. This is not a feature that is characteristic only of the four noble truths; for example, Buddhaghosa tells us that the Buddha recited a passage from the *Dhammapada* that enabled a certain woman from Śrāvatī to become a stream-winner.[118] The significance of the capacity of the four noble truths to produce knowledge of the path lies in the ability of the Buddha to catalyze path knowledge by speaking. This is not a pedagogical practice available to all – certainly not in contemporary times – but it is a central theme throughout the canon and commentaries.

In contrast, when the four noble truths appear as a proposition in the *Sutta-piṭaka*, knowledge of the four truths enables one to eliminate the corruptions and thus to become an *arahat*. This is the clearest model in which knowledge of the four noble truths can be said to produce measurable progress along the path. There are other claims in the *Sutta-piṭaka*, such as the statement that the four noble truths lead to *nibbāna*, but these claims are not accompanied by precise explanations of how this knowledge leads one closer to *nibbāna*. In the *Vibhaṅga* of the *Abhidhamma-piṭaka* the fourth truth – the path – has three possible definitions: it is eightfold, fivefold, or is without any limbs at all, consisting only of the entry into the first *jhāna*. Entry into the first *jhāna* leads to the elimination of the factors that cause pain to arise. The set of relationships between the *jhāna*s, the four noble truths, and the elimination of the corruptions that we first encountered in the *Sutta-piṭaka* appears to run through the *Abhidhamma-piṭaka* as well.

Notes

1 Isaline Blew Horner, *The Early Buddhist Theory of Man Perfected: A study of the Arahan Concept and of the Implications of the of the Aim to Perfection in Religious Life* (London: Routledge & Kegan Paul, 1936; Amsterdam: Philo Press, 1975), 34.

2 George D. Bond, 'The Gradual Path as a Hermeneutical Approach to the *Dhamma*,' in *Buddhist Hermeneutics*, ed. Donald S. Lopez, Jr., Studies in East Asian Buddhism 6 (Honolulu: University of Hawaii Press, 1988), 29–45.

3 Joy Manné describes the situation: 'Particular processes lead to defined states or stages of attainment. The texts have a large variety of ways of presenting these processes, states and stages. Several schemas of stages exist side by side. No convincing mapping of one schema to the other, however, nor any discussion of the relationships between schemas is provided. One problem with which we are faced, therefore, is that of the relationship between these various systems of stages and sequences of states and processes.' Joy Manné, 'Case Histories from the Pāli Canon I: The Sāmaññnaphala Sutta Hypothetical Case History *or* How to be Sure to Win a Debate,' *Journal of the Pāli Text Society* 21 (1995): 4.
4 Buswell, Jr. and Gimello, *Paths to Liberation*, 6.
5 Buswell, Jr. and Gimello, *Paths to Liberation*, 4.
6 Vin I 18–21
7 Vin I 21, where the Buddha enjoins his new followers to 'walk and teach *dhamma* out of compassion for the world, gods, and humans.'
8 Vin I 23
9 The bracketed phrases are those which vary according to the particular groups. This passage is found at Vin I 15–16, 18, 19, 20, 23, 37; only last two lines at Vin I 40, 42.
10 Vin I 16, 18, 19, 20, 23–24, 37. The first time this sentence appears is in the description of Yasa's mother's awakening.
11 Vin I 17, 19, 20, 24, 33–34, 43
12 Vin I 14, 19, 20, 35
13 Vin I 18, 19, 20, 24
14 Sp V 971 (on Vin I 23)
15 Spk II 392 (on S IV 107). See Joy Manné, 'Case Histories from the Pāli Canon II: *Sotātapanna*, *Sakadādāmin*, *Anāgāmin*, *Arahat* – The Four Stages Case History *or* Spiritual Materialism and the Need for Tangible Results,' *Journal of the Pāli Text Society* 21 (1995): 40–42 for her introduction and overview of the sources.
16 Ps III 92 (on M I 380). The commentaıy explains that *dhammacakkhu* refers to the three paths in the *Brahmāyu-sutta* (M II 133–147) and to the eradications of the corruptions in the *Cūḷarāhulovāda-sutta* (M III 277–280). In this *sutta*, however, it denotes the attainment of a stream-winner (Ps III 92). The commentary on the *Cūḷarāhulovāda-sutta* (M III 277–280) also explains that: (a) in the *Upāli-sutta* (M I 371–387) and in the *Dīghanakha-sutta* (M I 497–501), *dhammacakkhu* means the path of a stream-winner, (b) in the the *Brāhmayu-sutta*, it refers to the three fruits, but (c) in the *Cūḷarāhulovāda-sutta*, *dhammacakkhu* refers to the four paths and the fruits (Ps V 99). Sp V 971 (on V I 16) defines *dhammacakkhu* as the first three paths, as does Sv I 237 (on D I 87), Sv II 467 (on D II 38), Spk I 200 (on S I 137), and Spk IV 354 (on S IV 1).
17 Ps III 92 (on M I 380)
18 Mp II 356 (on A I 242); Mp IV 102 (on A IV 186); Spk II 392 (on S IV 107); Ps III 92 (on M I 380); Ps V 99 (on M III 277ff.); Sv I 237 (on D I 86)
19 This phrase is found at the conclusion to the passages in which *dhammacakkhu* appears, and the commentary on D I 110 makes the connection explicit: *Dhammacakkhun ti idha sotāpattimaggo adhippeto. Tassa uppatti-ākāra-dassanattham̱ yam kiñci samudaya-dhammam̱ sabban tam̱ nirodhadhammam ti āha* (Sv I 278).
20 Spk IV 354; the same distinction without the explanation at Spk II 323.
21 The commentary refers to D II 38 with this verse (Spk IV 354).
22 Other references to passages in which these terms occur are all from the *Mahāvagga*: *dhammacakkhu* (Vin I 16), *samantacakkhu* (Vin I 5), *dibbacakkhu* (Vin I 8), and *paññācakkhu* (Vin I 11) (Spk IV 354, on S IV 1).

23 Vin I 16–17
24 Norman, 'The Four Noble Truths,' 213.
25 Vin I 24
26 Vin I 33–34
27 Vin I 34–35
28 Vin I 40
29 Vin I 40
30 Vin I 41
31 Vin I 42
32 Vin I 43
33 M I 497–501
34 The same reference to an 'instructed disciple' who turns away from feelings is also found in the *Cūḷarāhulovāda-sutta*, but there the subject is the *indriyāni*. Rāhula and Sāriputta both become *arahat*s by listening to this talk. See M III 279–280.
35 *Book of the Discipline*, 4:53
36 Buddhaghosa glosses *pariyāya* as *vāra* (turn, course), *desanā* (instruction), and *kāraṇa* (cause or reason) at Sv I 36. The distinction between *pariyāya* and *nippariyāya* is a technical one in *Abhidhamma* literature that refers to a difference between conventional and direct ways of analyzing and explaining. Here *pariyāya* should be taken as synonymous with *desanā*.
37 The four truths are found at strikingly few other points in the *Vinaya-piṭaka* (Vin II 155ff., III 2, 3–5). On Vin III 2, see Holt, *Discipline*, 72ff.
38 The four truths appear at Vin III 3–6 and at Vin II 155ff. The first passage is a dialogue with Verañjā the Brahman, to whom the Buddha describes his enlightenment. The Buddha says that he eliminated the corruptions during the third watch of the night by understanding them according to the four truths. Verañjā does not experience a vision of *dhamma* upon hearing this talk, but he does become an *upāsaka*. See Table 2.1 for a comparison of this story as it appears in the *Aṅguttara-nikāya* with other versions of the Buddha's teachings and the cultivation of a vision of *dhamma*. The second passage where the four truths appear in the *Vinaya-piṭaka* is also found in the *Mahāparinibbāna-sutta* (D II 90–91). Here, the Buddha explains that it is by not understanding the four truths that rebirth continues.
39 M I 379–380
40 M I 371–387 (*Upāli-sutta*); M II 133–147 (*Brahmāyu-sutta*); D I 87–110 (*Ambaṭṭha-sutta*); D I 127–148 (*Kūṭadanta-sutta*); D II 1–54 (*Mahāpadāna-sutta*); A IV 187–188; A IV 209 and 213; A IV 177–178; cf. S V 420 (*Dhammacakkappavattana-sutta*)
41 D II 1–54
42 M III 277–280. See Table 5.1 for the phrases used to describe the elimination of the corruptions and the attainment of the level of an *arahat*.
43 *Dīghanakha-sutta* (M III 497–501). It is interesting that the phrases in this *sutta* parallel those found in the story of Rāhula's elimination of the corruptions (*Cūḷarāhulavād-sutta*) where the *deva*s also develop a vision of *dhamma*. Both *sutta*s use the technique of showing how an instructed follower turns away from whatever the Buddha is addressing, and both result in a listener destroying the corruptions (Rāhula and Sāriputta) and in other listeners developing a vision of *dhamma* (the *deva*s and Dīghanakha).
44 A IV 177–179; Vin III 3–5
45 M II 1–22
46 The four noble truths come to function as rules for determining the word of the Buddha in the postcanonical Pāli tradition. See Bond, *Word of the Buddha*,

34–99. As a symbol, the four noble truths occupied such a central position in the textual tradition that they generated the very rules by which the teachings were judged to be teachings of the Buddha. These may be defined as 'governing doctrines' in Christian's scheme; see William Christian, *Doctrines of Religious Communities* (New Haven: Yale University Press, 1987).

47 D I 63

48 The list is also found in the *Brahmajāla-sutta* (D I 4–13), beginning with injunctions not to kill; not to take what is not given; to give up unchaste sexual behavior; and not to lie, slander, or gossip. There are three descriptions of the *sīlaṃ*, the short, middle, and long.

49 These are a stock list of eight or ten powers. Other citations may be found at D I 212; D II 87, 213; D III 112, 281; S II 121; S V 264, 303; A I 170, 255; A III 17, 28, 82, 425; and A V 199. See Gethin's helpful discussion of the *iddhis*, particularly in relation to the *iddhipādas*. Gethin, *The Buddhist Path*, 82–83, 97–103. Gethin cites two useful articles on this topic: H. W. French, 'The concept of *iddhi* in Early Buddhist Thought,' *Pāli Buddhist Review* 2 (1977): 42–77 and Luis O. Gomez, 'The Bodhisattva as Wonder Worker,' in *Prajñāpāramitā and Related Systems*, ed. L. Lancaster (Berkeley: University of California Press, 1977), 221–261.

50 D I 83–84

51 *Khatāyaṃ bhikkhave rājā, upahatāyaṃ bhikkhave rājā. Sacāyaṃ bhikkhave rājā pitaraṃ dhammikaṃ dhammarājānaṃ jīvīta na voropessatha, imasmiṃ yeva āsane virajaṃ vītamalaṃ dhammacakkhuṃ uppajjissathāti* (D I 86).

52 Manné, 'Case Histories I,' 1–34 and 'Case Histories II,' 35–128.

53 This is based on the *Majjhima-nikāya* version, and it is substantially the same as that found in the *Dīgha-nikāya*. See Manné, 'Case Histories I,' 9–13 and 20–26 for her discussion of models from both *Nikāyas*. She is mistaken in her claim that Stage IV includes the development of the *dhammacakkhu*; the *suttas* she cites do not contain the *dhammacakkhu* (*dhamma* eye or vision) – but they do contain the *dibbacakkhu* (divine eye).

54 *Bhayabherava-sutta* (M I 23); *Mahāsaccaka-sutta* (M I 249); *Chabbisodhana-sutta* (M III 36); *Suttavibhaṅga* (Vin III 5); A I 107, 165, II 211, III 93, IV 177–179; *Sāmaññaphala-sutta* (D I 83–84); and Pp 60.

55 D I 83–84 (*Sāmaññaphala-sutta*); D I 110 (*Ambaṭṭha-sutta*); D I 124 (*Soṇanaṇḍa-sutta*); D I 148 (*Kūṭadanta-sutta*); D I 158 (*Mahālī-sutta*); D I 159–160 (*Jāliya-sutta*); D I 174 (*Kassapa-sīhanāda-sutta*); D I 209 (*Subha-sutta*); D I 215 (*Kevaddha-sutta*); and D I 233 (*Lohicca-sutta*). D I 191 (*Poṭṭhapāda-sutta*) and D I 235–253 (*Tevijja-sutta*) have only the formula for the *jhānas*; the four noble truths and/or the *āsavā* are not explictly mentioned, but it is clear that the *jhāna* sequence is based on the *Sāmaññaphala-sutta*. In the *Majjhima-nikāya*, the *suttas* include: M I 183 (*Cūḷahatthipadopama-sutta*); M I 270 (*Mahātaṇhāsaṅkhya-sutta*); M I 348 (*Kandaraka-sutta*); M I 522 (*Sandaka-sutta*); M II 227 (*Devadaha-sutta*); M III 36 (*Chabbisodhana-sutta*); and M III 136 (*Dantabhūmi-sutta*). Other references include A II 208–211 and A V 204–209. The four noble truths are also found in relation to the *jhānas* and the *āsavā* at: M I 23 (*Bhayabherava-sutta*); M I 62 (*Satipaṭṭhāna-sutta*); M I 249 (*Mahāsaccaka-sutta*); A I 165–167; A II 36 and 211; A III 93; A IV 177–179; and It 105. The *Puggalapaññati* also contains a reference to the four noble truths and the *āsavā* (Pp 60).

56 Bronkhorst, *Two Traditions*, 103 and Schmithausen, 'On some aspects,' 205.

57 Bronkhorst cites Bareau, *Recherches*, 1:87. Bronkhorst, *Two Traditions*, 103.

58 Bronkhorst, *Two Traditions*, 104–108.

59 Ps III 92 (on M I 380)

60 Manné provides an excellent discussion of the four levels of path attainment, and she illustrates that there are sufficient variations on the fourfold schema that prohibits us from taking them at face value. She suggests that the four levels of the stream-enterer, once-returner, non-returner, and *arahat* served – and continue to serve – as a systematizing and organizing structure, not as consistent phenomenological descriptions of actual attainments. She suggests too that the earliest strata of these four attainments consisted only of the first and the last: that of the *sotāpanno* and the *arahat*. See Manné, 'Case Histories II,' 117ff.

61 For a more extensive discussion of these paths, see Bronkhort, *Two Traditions*, 102–111 and Schmithausen, 'On Some Aspects,' 202–211.

62 Bronkhorst, *Two Traditions*, 110.

63 Sv I 277. Buddhaghosa also gives *dīpana* (explanation or commentary) as a synonym for *anupubbikathā*. The Buddha gives Ānanda a talk on how to give a good *dhamma*-talk at A III 184, and teaching an *anupubbikathā* is the first instruction given. Peter Masefield translates *anupubbikathā* as progressive talk, but this is not specific enough. Peter Masefield, *Divine Revelation in Pali Buddhism* (Colombo: The Sri Lanka Institute of Traditional Studies, 1986), 164–170. (Masefield's Table 4 'Recorded Instances of Conversion' requires additional verification, particularly in reference to the points at which the *dhammacakkhu* appears in what he identifies as conversion stories.)

64 A IV 337f lists eight conditions which must come to pass for a Tathāgata to talk on the *dhamma*, i.e., to give a *dhammadesanā*. Among them are the willingness to hear, question, and test, together with knowing (in both letter and spirit) the truths of the lessons heard. At A II 182 the Buddha rebukes Upaka for using abusive language because he (the Buddha) had preached against that in 'endless variations of word, syllable and *dhamma*-teachings of a Tathāgata.'

65 PED, s.v. *sāmukkaṃsika*; BHSD, s.v., *sāmutkarṣika*.

66 M III 248

67 M III 17, 248; S III 59

68 *Saccavibhaṅga-sutta* (M III 248)

69 M I 164–166, II 3; D I 82–83

70 *Dhammacakkappavattana-sutta* (S V 423)

71 *Ariyapariyesana-sutta* (M I 173). *Ovadati* is usually found in combination with *anusāsati*, but *anusāsati* often stands alone. See P.E.D., s.v. *ovadati, anusāsati*

72 *Mahāsaccaka-sutta* (M I 249); *Ariyapariyesana-sutta* (M I 168); *Mahāpadāna-sutta* (D II 32–34)

73 *Sammādiṭṭhi-sutta* (M I 48); *nibbedhikapariyāya, dhammapariyāya* (A III 410)

74 D III 272

75 M I 46

76 *Ariyapariyesana-sutta* (M I 166)

77 *Ariyapariyesana-sutta* (M I 161)

78 D III 137

79 Thich Minh Chau, *The Chinese Madhyama Āgama and the Pāli Majjhima-nikāya: A Comparative Study* (Saigon: Saigon Institute of Higher Buddhist Studies, 1964), 56–78.

80 Manné, 'Case Histories II.' For an analysis of later forms of preaching, see Reverend Mahinda Deegalle, *Bana: Buddhist Preaching in Sir Lanka* (Ph. D. diss., University of Chicago, 1995).

81 *Pariyāya*, in this context, means discussion or discourse.

82 A IV 207–209

83 Gethin, 'The *Mātikās*,' 156.

84 As 6; see also Vin I 14, II 247.

85 For example, on *dhamma*, *vinaya*, and *mātikā*, see D II 125; A I 117; II 147; III 179, 361; A V 15–16; M I 223; Vin V 86.

86 A I 117

87 The same phrase (*abbu-ssuto āgatāgamo dhamma-dharo vinaya-dharo mātikā-dharo*) also appears at D II 125; M I 221–223; A II 147, 169, 170, III 179–180, 361–62, V 15–16, 349–353. Gethin notes that there is a Vinaya version of this phrase which adds 'mature, skilled, intelligent, conscientious, concerned, devoted to the training' (Vin I 119, 127, 337, 339, Vin II 8, 98, 229). Gethin, 'The *Mātikās*,' 169, n. 33.

88 This list is often interpreted as denoting different genres in the canon; however, it is much less specific than that. At best, it is a list of literary styles which may be found in the canon, which do not refer to specific *sutta*s or canonical texts. Lamotte discusses the seven classifications of the Buddha's Word, which includes the nine *aṅga*s, and concludes that '[o]f the seven classifications, only one, that of the three Baskets, is of real interest and corresponds to a true division of the writings. . . . the other six classifications . . . are of little more than theoretical value and consist rather of mental view.' Specifically regarding the *navaṅga*s, he says that they are a list of the literary styles in the canonical writings. Lamotte, HIB, 141, 143–145.

89 A III 361

90 A II 147, III 179

91 cf. D II 125; A II 167–170.

92 Vin IV 344

93 Vin IV 344

94 On whether *abhidhamma* refers to the *Abhidhamma-piṭaka*, Oldenberg argued in the introduction to his edition of the *Vinaya-piṭaka* that this verse was indisputable evidence for the existence of an *Abhidhamma-piṭaka*. Horner is far more tentative in her support of Oldenberg's argument, but she finally acknowledges that 'he may be right.' The reason she agrees, she wrote, is that this is the only triad in the canon where *abhidhamma*, *suttanta*, and *vinaya* are found. These three terms are not accompanied by *gāthā* (as they are at Vin I 144), by *abhivinaya*, or *mātikā*. Oldenberg and Horner were interested in this question in order to determine when the *Abhidhamma-piṭaka* may have been collected. My interest here is structural. *Vinaya-piṭakaṃ*, ed. Hermann Oldenberg (London: Pāli Text Society, 1969), 1:xii, n. 2.; I. B. Horner, 'Abhidhamma, Abhivinaya' *The Indian Historical Quarterly* 17 (no. 3):308.

95 Vin IV 144

96 Vin IV 144

97 D III 267

98 Gethin, 'The *Mātikās*,' 165.

99 Sn 266; M I 145–151, 176, 244

100 M III 113, 115; A 117–118; A IV 352; A V 67; Ud 36. Each passage is framed differently, but the list of ten kinds of *kathā* is identical. M III 112–113 also describes a number of undesirable kinds of *kathā*, including *tiracchānakathā* (worldly or low talk, i.e., gossip) and so on. On these kinds of talk, see Horner's cross references in her translation of the *Suttavibhaṅga*. *Book of the Discipline*, 3:82–83

101 M III 113. The first clause of this passage is also a formula. The phrase *ekantanibbidāya virāgāya . . . nibbānāya saṃvattati* is found at D I 189; S V 82, 179, 255, 361; A III 83, IV 143, and V 216.

102 M III 110

103 A IV 336f. Lists eight conditions which must be met for a *tathāgata* to preach *dhamma*. A V 154 lists ten conditions. The commentaries on both passages do not mention Puṇṇiya's identity or add anything to the content of the verses.

104 As 28–29

105 M I 214

106 M I 472

107 A I 288

108 M II 239

109 Ps II 256

110 As 29

111 A III 392

112 Citta Hatthisāriputta is also mentioned in the *Poṭṭhapāda-sutta* as a friend of Poṭṭhapāda's, and the commentary on that passage explained that the *abhidhammakathā* was held between Moggallāna and Koṭṭhita (D I 190, 199; Sv 379). The commentary explains *abhidhammakathaṃ* as *abhidhammamissakaṃ kathaṃ*, a talk mixed with *abhidhamma*. *Therā*s are glossed as *karaṇatthe sāmivacanaṃ therehi bhikkhūhi saddhin ti attho; yā ca therānaṃ abhidhammakathā, taṃ ayam 'pi kathetuṃ sakkotīti attho* (Mp III 401, on A III 392).

113 A III 113 describes the things that an elder should know; among them are the four kinds of discrimination (*paṭisambhidā*): *Pañcahi bhikkhave dhammehi samannāgato thero bhikkhu sabrahmacārīnaṃ piyo ca hoti manāpo ca garu ca bhāvanīyo ca. Katamehi pañcahi? Atthapaṭisambhidāpatto hoti, dhammapaṭisambhidhāpatto hoti, niruttipaṭisambhidhāpatto hoti, paṭibhānapaṭisambhidāpatto hoti, yāni tāni sabrahmacārīnaṃ uccāvacāni kiṃkaraṇīyāni tattha dakkho hoti analaso tatrupāyāya vīmaṃsāya samannāgato alaṃ kātuṃ alaṃ saṃvidhātuṃ.* (*Bhikkhus*, an elder endowed with five qualities is dear to his fellow *bhikkhus*, is pleasant, esteemed and is to be cultivated. Which five? He is a master of analyzing meanings (*attha*), causal relations (*dhammā*), grammatical analysis (*nirutti*), intellect (*paṭibhāna*), and he is skilled and energetic toward those various duties which are to be completed by fellow *bhikkhus*, possessing knowledge of all kinds of ways, ready to do and get them done.) The first four items are four kinds of discrimination (*paṭisambhidā*). The Buddhist Hybrid Sanskrit equivalent is *pratisaṃvid*, and Norman has shown that the *-v-* and *-bh-* alternation is an unusual dialectical shift. This variation makes it difficult, he writes, to determine the meaning that the two words may once have shared. Elsewhere, he states that the meaning of *paṭisambhidā* is uniquely Buddhist and does not derive from Brāhmanical Hinduism. Norman, *Collected Papers*, 4:52, 86, 271.

Sāriputta is said to have developed these four kinds of discrimination quickly (A II 160), and those who master them are said to 'quickly attain the stable state' – *nibbāna* (A III 120). It is difficult to establish a precise meaning for *atthapaṭisambhidā*. *Atthapaṭisambhidā* is also defined as the knowledge of effects (*hetuphale ñāṇa*), as opposed to *dhammapaṭisambhidā* which is explained as the knowledge of causes (*hetumhi ñāṇa*) (Vibh 293). Since *niruttipaṭisambhidā* is defined as 'knowledge of phrases' (*abhilāpe ñāṇa*), it is particularly difficult to clarify the meaning of *atthapaṭisambhidā* (Vibh 294). The PED explains that *nirutti* is one of the six *vedāṅgas*, or six Vedic 'sciences' which refers to grammatical analysis, but Edgerton says that *nirukti* means explanation of the meaning of a word, which is not necessarily etymological (PED, s.v. *nirutti*; BHSG, s.v. *nirukti*). Norman has translated *nirutti-* as interpretation. See K. R. Norman, *Elders' Verses* (*Theragāthā*) (London: Pāli

Text Society, 1969), 1:265. *Paṭibhānapaṭisambhidā* appears as *paṭibhāna-sambhidā* in the *Vibhaṅga* definitions, and it is explained as 'knowledge about knowledge' (*ñāṇesu ñāṇa*) (Vibh 293f). Ñāṇamoli translates the four discriminations as: discrimination of meaning (*atthapaṭisambhidā*), of Law (*dhammapaṭisambhidā*), of language (*niruttipaṭi-sambhidā*), and of intelligence (*paṭibhānapaṭisambhidā*). See *The Dispeller of Delusion (Sammohavinodanī)*, 2 vols., trans. Bhikkhu Ñāṇamoli (London: Pāli Text Society, 1987), 2:126–139. Despite the fact that it is difficult to define each of the discriminations precisely, each of these four kinds of discrimination was considered to be a quality that elders should cultivate.

114 A III 107

115 Mp III 271. Elsewhere, *abhidhammakathaṃ* is defined as a mixed talk (*missakaṃ kathaṃ*) (Mp III 401).

116 As 26. The structure of *laddhā laddhā* is unusual; at Steven Collins's suggestion, I have taken it here as repeated for emphasis.

117 Jayawickrama writes that the term *vetullavāda* in Sri Lanka denoted Mahāyāna teachings; Collins suggests that *vedalla* is a variant of *vetulla-piṭaka* and that *vedalla* means Mahāyāna teachings (e.g., Mp III 160). Lamotte follows Buddhaghosa, but he also notes that *vaitulya* or *vaipulya* carry the sense of 'incomparable' or 'extent.' Buddhaghosa understood *vedalla* to refer to some pedagogical method which involved questions (As 26). *Vedalla* probably refers to Mahāyāna teachings, but the evidence for Buddhaghosa's interpretation of the term is unclear. *Vedalla* probably does not refer to a particular pedagogical technique. Collins, 'Pāli Canon,' 98, n. 32, n. 40; Lamotte, HIB, 144; and *Kathāvatthuppakaraṇa-aṭṭhakathā*, xvii.

118 Mp I 356–360

CHAPTER SIX

Studies of the Four Noble Truths in Europe and the United States

Led by curiosity, or invited by the allurements of science, Europeans have, during the past half-century, devoted not a little of their time to unlocking the rich stores of Oriental literature.[1]

James de Alwis (1850)

The European Discovery of the Four Noble Truths

Officials of colonial governments in South Asia, both military and civilian, provided the earliest depictions of Buddhism outside of Asia. Their descriptions were soon followed by accounts written by missionaries and scholars in Sri Lanka, Thailand, Burma and Tibet that portrayed the religious traditions that were identified as Buddhism. One of the earlier portraits of Buddhism was provided by Captain Mahony, the author of an article on the doctrines of the Buddha that was published in 1801.[2] Mahony wrote: 'The religion of Bhooddha, as far as I have had any insight into it, seems to be founded in a mild and simple morality. Bhooddha has taken for his principles, wisdom, justice, and benevolence, from which principles emanate Ten Commandments, held by his followers as the true and only rule of conduct. He places them under three heads, thought, word, and deed.' Mahony provides Sinhalese and Pāli translations for these terms: wisdom (*buddha*), justice (*dharma*), benevolence (*saṅgha*); and thought (*manneshet*), word (*vāca*), and deed (*kaya*).[3] The article is devoted to Buddhist cosmology in the main, with a short discussion of the relationship between Buddhism and Hinduism. It was not until the systematic study of Pāli and Buddhist texts developed on the Continent that the four noble truths were recognized as one of the Buddha's teachings; it was not until the 1850s that the four noble truths became a familiar part of discussions of Buddhism in Europe and the United States.[4]

References to the four noble truths before the middle of the nineteenth century were scattered.[5] There is one elusive reference to the four noble truths in Francis Buchanan-Hamilton's English translation of one of a collection of three treatises called 'A Short View of the Religion of Godama' that was published in 1799.[6] Gautama is described as the 'only true and pure god . . . who can bestow *Nieban* [*nibbāna*],' and the text explains that those who observe *sila* will obtain *Nieban* through successive transmigrations and will be relieved from the 'four known miseries, namely, weight, old age, disease, and death.'[7] This phrase, as we have seen, is one of the most common definitions of the first noble truth that appears throughout the canon and commentaries. There is no fuller discussion of the four noble truths in Buchanan-Hamilton's article, and only in retrospect may this ambiguous reference be taken as an early indication of an awareness of the doctrine of the four noble truths in European or American studies of Buddhism.

The earliest description of the four noble truths that I have found in a European language was published in 1835, in an article by John Armour that contains an abridged translation of a Sinhalese text that outlined the features of Buddhism. Armour explained that the Sinhalese tract was composed in 1826 by the then-late Kitelagama Dewamitta Terunnanse ('one of the most learned of the Buddhist priests in this part of the country') at the behest of Sir S. Sawyers, who was the Judicial Commissioner of Kandy at that time. Of Sawyers, Armour wrote that he 'was desirous of forming a correct view of the genuine tenets of Buddhism . . . for the efficient discharge of the official control with which he was at that time invested over the national Church Establishment [i.e., Buddhism].'[8] The Sinhalese text is entitled *Jinapāwachanālankāre*, which Armour described as an outline of the tenets of Buddhism. The piece covers central Buddhist teachings, including the four noble truths. After the description of each of the truths, Kitelagama Dewamitta Thera explained that:

> the individual who has comprehended the four *satya*s, or truths, and utterly extinguished in himself the principles of evil [i.e., the corruptions (*āsavā*)] is not to be compared to a Sangwarti Dewa or conventional god (a sovereign constituted or appointed by his subjects) nor to an Utpatti Deva, or one born a god (in the Diwa Lokas), for he is superior to both, he is a Wisuddhi Dewiyo, being pre-eminently pure; as being adored by Brahmaya, and the gods, he is Brahmati-Brahma and Dewāti-Dewa – as knowing all this he is Sargwajnya (omniscient); and as having destroyed the principles of evil [*āsavā*] and attained *perfection of knowledge, Awabodha*, he is *Buddha* [italics in original].[9]

What is noteworthy about this description is the association between the four truths and the attainments of an individual who has thoroughly comprehended them: such a person has eliminated the corruptions (*āsavā*) and is thus fully enlightened – a purified god. This interpretation of the attainments of one who has understood the four noble truths reflects the second model of the path described in the previous chapter, in which knowing the *āsavā* according to the four truths leads to their destruction and thus to the status of an *arahat*. This is the earliest discussion of the four truths to be made available to a European audience in the nineteenth century. This description is also significant for its focus on the attainments that one may expect from knowing the four truths. This article on the 'tenets of Buddhism' was published in Sri Lanka and was thus accessible to Europeans in Sri Lanka, but it probably did not have a broader audience throughout western Europe.[10]

The four noble truths first appeared in print in Europe through translations of Buddhist texts, predominately in the the work of Eugène Burnouf (1801–1852). Burnouf was born in 1801, studied at l'école des Chartres, and, in 1832, began teaching Sanskrit at the Collége de france in the chair first established and occupied by Léonard de Chézy in 1814. Burnouf's *Introduction à l'histoire du bouddhisme indien* appeared in 1844, at a time when an increasing number of Buddhist texts were being translated into European languages. Some of the sources that Burnouf used for his *Introduction* contained brief mentions of the four noble truths, and Burnouf compiled these references as sources for his discussion of the doctrine.[11] While he was familiar with the few sources available from the Pāli canon in the 1830s, the bulk of Burnouf's material on the four noble truths came from Tibetan materials. Burnouf cited an overview of the *Lalita-vistara* published by Alexander Csoma Körösi in 1836 as his source for the four noble truths.[12]

Burnouf had collated the primary references for the four noble truths available in Buddhist Sanskrit literature by 1844, but there were no references to the doctrine in the Pāli canonical literature. Burnouf cited George Turnour's 1837 translation of the *Mahāvaṃsa*, but that text makes no mention of the four noble truths; Burnouf did, however, draw information on the four paths of the stream-winner, once-returner, non-returner, and *arahat* from the *Mahāvaṃsa*.[13] Even though the four noble truths in the Pāli sources were included in translations by Methodist missionary Daniel J. Gogerly, who translated the *Mahāsatipaṭṭhāna-*, *Saccavibhaṅga-*, and *Dhammacakkappavattana-sutta*s as well as other *sutta*s as early as 1837, it is unlikely that Burnouf had access to these materials because Gogerly's collected writings did not appear in a collected volume in Europe until much later.[14] Similarly, Reverend Robert Spence Hardy's two books on Buddhism that were standard readings in the field until early in the twentieth century did not appear until 1853 and 1866; Hardy's first articles appeared in the first volumes of the *Journal of the Ceylon Branch of the Royal Asiatic Society* in 1846.[15] The lack of Pāli sources for the four noble truths at the time of Burnouf's work meant that his discussion of the four noble truths was based largely on the Tibetan sources that he identified as products of 'northern' schools of Buddhism. Burnouf's familiarity with the Pāli texts nonetheless provided the foundation for an interpretation of the doctrine that would soon be drawn from both the 'northern' and the 'southern' schools of Buddhism.[16]

Burnouf's substantive analysis of the four noble truths was based on the Buddhist Sanksrit *Avadāna-śataka*, *Divyāvadāna*, and the *Sumāgadhāvadāna*, as well as the *Lalita-vistara* and the *Mahāvastu*.[17] The four noble truths appeared in Burnouf's *Introduction* within the context of his translations of the Sanskrit texts. While Burnouf's comments occupy only a few pages, they consolidated the basic information on the doctrine. The four noble truths appeared in the *Introduction* embedded in the section on the *Vinaya*, in an analysis of the structure of the *saṅgha*. Burnouf's comments are worth citing in full:

> It is certain, according to these legends, that the teaching of Śākya acted more or less rapidly, depending on whether those who received it were more or less prepared for it, with the result that, in a short period, a *religieux* could acquire a knowledge that was deeper and a saintliness that was more perfect than that of those who had been in the Order long before him. Moreover, the knowledge of the truths taught by Śākya had its degrees, and, in all likelihood, the one who had grasped them all was considered to be superior to one who had stopped along the way.[18]

Burnouf extended his examination of the act of the Buddha's teaching of the four noble truths by translating a passage from the *Avadāna-śataka* which explains that the Buddha knows the disposition of those who listen to his teaching so that he can teach them *dharma* and the four noble truths. The text explains that those who understand the four noble truths receive the fruits of the four stages of the path, which are the stream-winner, the once-returner, the non-returner and the *arhant*.[19]

Burnouf realized that the passages revealed a close relationship between the Buddha and his audience, and he analyzed the function of the four noble truths within the context of the act of the Buddha's teaching, in which the Buddha knows what his audience is capable of understanding. He acknowledged that the sources recognized two groups of people: those who were able to understand and act according to the four noble truths were the *ārya*s, or noble ones, who stood opposed to those who did not comprehend the four truths.

> First, the four noble truths are the fundamental axiom which serve as a basic Buddhist doctrine, to know that pain exists, that is is common to everything that comes into the world, that it is important to free oneself of it; in brief, that it is by knowledge alone that one can do it in a manner that will bring about deliverance. Those who comprehend these truths and who conform their conduct to them

> are called *Âryas* or venerables, in contrast to ordinary men (*prĭbthag djana*) who have not reflected upon these important subjects.[20]

Much of Burnouf's discussion following this statement is devoted to an analysis of the *āryas*, or noble ones, and he established that the four stages of the path was found in both the Sanskrit and Pāli texts.

Burnouf consulted a variety of sources that were based on the Theravāda tradition for his study. He cited Adoniram Judson's *Burman Dictionary*, a grammar and dictionary written by Methodist missionary Benjamin Clough, and George Turnour's translation of the *Mahāvaṃsa* as support for the existence of the four stages of path attainment in the Pāli tradition (even though Burnouf did not identify specific passages from the Pāli canon for the four noble truths themselves).[21] Adoniram Judson (1788–1850) was a Congregationalist who became a Baptist missionary. He arrived with his wife Ann Haseltine Judson (1789–1826) in Burma in 1814; their daughter, Abby Ann Judson (1835–1902), turned to Buddhism in the guise of Spiritualism as a religious faith.[22] Benjamin Clough's dictionary was supervised by Bartholomew Guṇasékara of the British Colonial Secretary's Office and remained a scarce but valuable resource for scholars interested in Pāli sources in Sri Lanka; it has been reprinted in recent years.[23] By 1830, Clough had defined the Sinhalese word *chatussatya* as 'the four chief truths connected with religions; viz. 1, that sorrow is connected with existence in every state: 2, that men are attached to existence only by sensual desire; 3, the means conducing to the complete subjugation of the passions: 4, the state preparatory to Nirváṇa, in which the passions are subjected, and every attachment to a continuance of existence destroyed.' He had also defined *saccavedita* as 'arrived at the knowledge of the four great truths, as a Rahat [*arahat*].'[24] George Turnour was a member of the Ceylon Civil Service, and his translation of the *Mahāvaṃsa* was published serially in 1837 and 1838.[25] These resources provided Burnouf with the evidence to draw comparisons between the Pāli and Buddhist Sanskrit sources for a comprehensive discussion of Buddhist literature.

Burnouf's work catalyzed interest in Buddhism in the United States as well as Europe; Edward Elbridge Salisbury (1814–1901) presented a synopsis of Burnouf's *Introduction* entitled 'Memoir on the History of Buddhism' at the first annual meeting of the American Oriental Society in May of 1844; a paper on Burnouf's findings later appeared in the *Journal of the American Oriental Society* (1849).[26] Salisbury was a Congregationalist and taught Arabic and Sanskrit at Yale University from 1841–1854.[27] Salisbury studied with Burnouf in France and taught his successor at Yale, William Dwight Whitney (1827–1894). Whitney, in turn, trained Charles Rockwell Lanman (1840–1941), who graduated from Harvard University. Lanman tutored Henry Clarke Warren (1854–1899), who wrote *Buddhism in Translations* (1896), in which he discussed the four noble truths as the framework for all of the Buddha's teachings.[28] Despite the contributions of early writings by American missionaries to South and Southeast Asia, most substantive scholarship on the four noble truths has been done in Europe, although Burnouf's work and the studies of later Buddhologists were well known in the United States.[29]

The Four Noble Truths: A Rational Doctrine (1856–1877)

The four noble truths emerged as a distinctive element of Buddhism in Europe during the 1850s, based largely on Burnouf's documentation of the four noble truths. Subsequent studies of Buddhism often failed to understand the advantages of Burnouf's comparative approach, extracting the four noble truths from his broader survey of Buddhist literature. The four noble truths became evidence that was used to support a particular image of the Buddha in the scholarship of the 1850s and 1860s. Speaking in 1856 to the Academy of Science in Berlin, Albrecht Weber was one of the first scholars to explicitly describe the Buddha as a social reformer, as a leader who brought new teachings to everyone, without distinction of caste, class, or lineage. Weber had translated the *Dhammapada* into German, some of the *Jātaka*s (stories of the Buddha's previous lives), and was a scholar not only of Buddhism but of the larger body of Indian literature. Weber described the Buddha in the following way:

> The greatness of the founder of Buddhism did not consist, as is wrongly thought, in this doctrine that the brahmans taught before him, which he only accepted to perhaps give it a new speculative direction; it exists entirely in the fashion that he gave the teaching to proclaim the common human rights in a time and for a people where they were absolutely unrecognized. Until now all theories of this genre had been expressed only in the solitude of the forest, in the schools of brahmans, or, at the very most, in the presence of some curious kings to instruct them; all other communication was forbidden under threat of punishment of the greatest curse, until the man who took the name *Buddha*, that is to say, Awakening, in the enthusiasm of his heart, in his firm conviction of the truth that he announced and in his profound compassion for those who did not know, he addressed all people, without distinction of rank, race or condition, went from one place to another, preaching everywhere in the popular language – open to all, great and small, brahmans and untouchables, rich and poor – the way of truth that he had to give joyously, and teaching that each individual was in the position of saving himself and by his own effort.[30]

Weber painted a compelling portrait of a reformer who taught to all people what had only been reserved for the elect in the Brahmanic system. Each individual, Weber announced, was capable of knowing the truth in order to be delivered from rebirth. The truth that the Buddha taught, according to Weber, was fourfold: 'I. Suffering is inseparable from existence; II. Birth in the world is the cause of passions from a prior existence; III. The suppression of passions is therefore the only way to stop future rebirths and, as a result, suffering; IV. The means to overcome the obstacles which are opposed to that suppression.'[31] The French translator of Weber's address, F. Baudry, provided a citation for Burnouf as the source for the four truths.[32] As soon became the case in the writings during the rest of the decade and into the early 1860s, Burnouf's close textual studies of Buddhist sources became the evidence used by other scholars to argue for one portrait of the Buddha and Buddhism over others. The use of the four noble truths as evidence in these controversies served to loose the doctrine from its moorings in particular Buddhist texts and also severed the connections between the four noble truths and the act of the Buddha's teaching first established by Burnouf.

Weber's selection of the four noble truths ought to be viewed against the background of the debates over the nature of nirvāṇa that erupted in the 1850s and 1860s. Students of Burnouf argued about what the doctrine of nirvāṇa meant and who, in the history of Buddhism, originally taught the doctrine; Burnouf's scholarship on Buddhism provided the basis for the conclusions that scholars were to draw in their debates over the nature of Buddhism during the decade following Burnouf's death in 1852.[33] Briefly, the debates surrounded the proper interpretation of nirvāṇa; if it was understood as annihilation, why would people aspire to it? The four noble truths became used as evidence in debates that focused on the heroic character of the Buddha and on the role of the Buddha's teachings in the historical development of Buddhism and other Indian schools.[34] The four noble truths were used as evidence of the Buddha's 'common sense,' in opposition to the perceived illogic of the doctrine of nirvāṇa.

The dispute over the nature of the Buddha's teachings was sparked by the popular book *Le Bouddha et sa religion* by Jules Barthélemy Saint-Hilaire.[35] Specifically, Barthélemy Saint-Hilaire asked whether the Buddha had actually taught such a nonsensical doctrine as nirvāṇa. Jean Baptise François Obry and others concluded that, in fact, the doctrine of nirvāṇa was not taught by the Buddha and thus could be rejected because it went against the 'common sense' of humanity. In the argument over the meaning and origin of the doctrine of nirvāṇa, the four noble truths were often offered as a teaching which was more central to the Buddha's teachings than nirvāṇa, as Weber did.[36] Another part of the argument adduced in this debate over the Buddha's teachings was the appeal of the Buddha's doctrines to the masses. If the Buddha was a social reformer, these scholars reasoned, his teachings had to attract the masses as well as his disciples -- and the four noble truths were considered by these scholars to be much more appealing than the doctrine of nirvāṇa. These arguments, even though they were substantively rejected by later scholars of Buddhism, set the parameters for the interpretation of the Buddha's doctrines and the four noble truths in two ways. First, they drew attention to the fact that the Buddhist tradition remembers the four noble truths as the first sermon of the Buddha, who was now portrayed as a social and democratic reformer. Second, they argued that the four noble truths were more appealing than the doctrine of nirvāṇa.

Against the larger debate over the meanings of nirvāṇa, then, the supposed 'practical dimension' of the doctrine of the four noble truths appealed to Albrecht Weber. He saw the four noble truths, particularly the fourth, as the expression of a reformer who was focused upon the salvation of all human beings. It is interesting to note that Weber emphasized the fourth truth – the path – while Victorians as a whole focused on the first as an expression of pessimism; it was far more common to take the four noble truths as an entire group, as the rest of this chapter shows.[37] Weber chose the teaching of the four noble truths as the Buddha's central doctrine because his erroneous interpretion of nirvāṇa led him to conclude that the doctrine of nirvāṇa diverged sharply from the Buddha's compassionate approach to individuals.[38] In Weber's construction of Buddhist history, he argued that the more abstract goal of nirvāṇa was 'aberrant' among the Buddha's teachings. The different teachings of the Buddha, Weber wrote, resulted in two distinct groups of the Buddha's followers: the 'religious' who followed the teachings to a 'final deliverance' (nirvāṇa) and the laity, who were to follow the practical virtues for a better rebirth, to whom the four noble truths appealed.[39]

Weber's interpretation of the four noble truths as the teaching of the laity diverges rather sharply from Burnouf's reading, even though Weber relied on Burnouf's work. Burnouf wrote that the *Ārya*s (noble ones) were those who had comprehended the four noble truths, in comparison to the 'ordinary man' who had not.[40] According to Weber, and in contrast to Burnouf, the four noble truths were to be seen as the concrete expression of the Buddha's democratic and social reforms of the Brahmanical traditions, for the masses of lay Buddhists, and thus ought to be considered as the most significant of the Buddha's doctrines. During the 1850s and 1860s, other discussions of the four noble truths emerged in the debate over what nirvāṇa meant and who taught it.

Barthélemy Saint-Hilaire had catalyzed the debate over the definition of nirvāṇa by arguing that nirvāṇa should be understood as annihilation.[41] He concluded that the doctrine of nirvāṇa, which he wrongly interpreted as annihilation, was taught not by the Buddha but by later scholastics within the Buddhist tradition. Barthélemy Saint-Hilaire studied Sanskrit informally with Burnouf and was an accomplished Sanskritist. His book, *Le Bouddha et sa religion*, was first published in 1860, appeared in a third edition in 1862, and was translated into English in 1895. While his arguments were ultimately indefensible because they were based on a flawed understanding of nirvāṇa, Barthélemy Saint-Hilaire both shared the image of the Buddha as a compassionate reformer and contributed to the popularity of the four noble truths as the central teaching of the Buddha. Although the Buddha did not invent the whole of his teachings, Barthélemy Saint-Hilaire wrote: 'he completed the doctrine of the school and he divulged it for the salvation of humanity, that his great heart had been seized by compassion. . . .'[42] And, within that compassionate act of teaching, the Buddha delivered a message which Barthélemy Saint-Hilaire characterized as 'moral Buddhism.' Barthélemy Saint-Hilaire then listed the teachings that, in his opinion, comprised the Buddha's message: the four noble truths, the ten precepts (*sīlaṃ*), and the six perfections (*pāramitā*).[43] Of the most important teaching, the four noble truths, he wrote: 'The first theory that presents itself, and which, in due order must indeed precede all the others, is that of the four Noble Truths (*âryâni satyâni*). It was known to all Buddhists, and was adopted in the south and east, as well as in the north, in Ceylon, Burma, Pegu, Siam and China, exactly as it was in Nepaul and Tibet.'[44] He concluded that the four noble truths, the precepts, and the six perfections were the actual teachings of the Buddha and that the doctrine of nirvāṇa was taught by later scholars of the Buddhist tradition. Barthélemy Saint-Hilaire argued that the four noble truths, the precepts, and the perfections, were the teachings that the Buddha used to persuade the masses of the truth of his message. Describing the Buddha's appeal, he wrote:

> He [i.e., the Buddha] calls to himself men of all castes and the totality of creatures, from the highest of the gods to the most degraded of beings; he exhorts them to embrace the Law that he exposes to them; he charms them with his discourses; he sometimes astonishes them with his supernatural power; he never thinks to constrain them.[45]

Like Albrecht Weber, Barthélemy Saint-Hilaire rejected nirvāṇa as a later addition to Buddhism in favor of other teachings, and the four noble truths were at the top of his new list. The image of the Buddha as a moral reformer was more consistent with the compassionate teaching of the four noble truths than the 'illogical' doctrine of nirvāṇa. This image persisted throughout the ensuing debates of the 1860s.

Jules Mohl, J. B. F. Obry, Philippe Édouard Foucaux, and F. Max Müller were among the scholars who argued with Barthélemy Saint-Hilaire's position on nirvāṇa. While the intellectual merits of their critiques varied widely, each of these men took issue with Barthélemy Saint-Hilaire's intepretation of nirvāṇa as annihilation. At the same time, each writer retained the image of the Buddha as a moral reformer, although only a few of these scholars referred to the four noble truths as the evidence of the Buddha's moral teachings. Jules Mohl was the secretary of the Société asiatique in 1860, and professor of Persian at the Collége de france. He wrote that it was easier to believe that later followers constructed 'interpretations which [were] contrary to the primitive doctrine' of the founder than it was '... to believe that a great man like the Buddha preached a metaphysics which would have contradicted his moral theory.'[46] J. B. F. Obry, on the other hand, rejected the interpretation of nirvāṇa as annihilation on the basis of the 'good sense' of the Buddhist peoples. 'Is it not to malign the good sense of the Buddhist peoples – who, if they are not exactly like us, are, after all, our own brothers, . . . is it not to do injury to all humanity to pose this strange proposition as an article of Buddhist faith: for twenty-five centuries the faithful and fervent ascetics are forced to practice the rigorous discipline of their master in order to be rewarded with nothingness!'[47] Foucaux, who translated the *Lalita-vistara* into French, raised the issue of the textual sources: how could Barthélemy Saint-Hilaire be certain that nirvāṇa was annihilation in the 'Buddha's pure doctrine' when the teachings were not recorded for two and a half centuries after the Buddha's death?[48] While each man offered a different resolution to the problem of what nirvāṇa meant, the Buddha as a moral reformer was at the center of their sketches of the early Buddhist community and the four noble truths were used occasionally as evidence in support of the Buddha's implied moral and social advances.[49]

In 1864, Foucaux argued that the greatness of the Buddha did not lie in his doctrines, but in his reforms of the Brahmanical tradition. Albrecht Weber had already made the same point in 1856. Foucaux detailed the reforms of the Buddha, which included erasing the role of caste in his new religion, incorporating women into his order, and abolishing the minutiae of ritual detail required by Brahmins. 'To say it all in a few words,' he wrote, 'this is the doctrine of Buddha . . . a school of philosophy has become a religion rivaling the religion of brahmanism. It is probably in this that we should see the cause of the implacable persecution that chased the Buddhists from India.'[50] Obry concurred with this position, writing passionately that, while the Brahmanical tradition offered salvation to a few, the Buddha offered a 'law of grace for all.'[51] Neither Foucaux nor Obry drew attention to the four noble truths in their responses to Barthélemy Saint-Hilaire, perhaps because the image of the Buddha as a moral reformer is one point on which they all agreed. Foucaux found little significance in the four noble truths, despite the fact that he published a French translation and an edition of the Tibetan *Lalita-vistara* which contains the doctrine.[52] Despite Burnouf's detailed textual study of the four noble truths and the history of Buddhism, interpretations of Buddhism offered by the scholars who followed him were never so closely tied to the texts. The doctrine of the four noble truths fit neatly into the portrait of the

Buddha as a moral reformer in a way that nirvāṇa never could, perhaps for the very reason that Albrecht Weber first turned to the doctrine: the four noble truths were seen to offer a practical solution for the masses who followed the Buddha instead of the complex and unimaginable goal of nirvāṇa that the renouncers sought.[53] This interpretation of the four noble truths belonged to European interpretations of the Buddha and his teachings, apparently independent of any new textual sources until the 1870s.

In his response to Barthélemy Saint-Hilaire, F. Max Müller held that the most significant element of the Buddhist reform was its social and moral code – not its metaphysical theories. 'That moral code, taken by itself, is one of the most perfect the world has ever known,' he wrote. 'On this point all testimonies from hostile and from friendly quarters agree.'[54] Even though Müller's studies had little in common with Obry's sometimes ill-reasoned writings, Müller argued, like Obry, that the Buddha's common sense dictated the rejection of philosophical notions in the texts.[55]

> If we may argue from human nature, such as we find it at all times and in all countries, we confess that we cannot bring ourselves to believe that the reformer of India, the teacher of so perfect a code of morality, the young prince who gave up all he had in order to help those whom he saw afflicted in mind, body, or estate, should have cared much about speculations which he knew would either be misunderstood, or not understood at all, by those whom he wished to benefit; that he should have thrown away one of the most powerful weapons in the hand of every religious teacher, the belief in a future life, and should not have seen that, if this life was sooner or later to end in nothing, it was hardly worth the trouble which he took to himself, or the sacrifices which he imposed on his disciples.[56]

When Müller discussed the place of doctrine in relationship to the Buddhist canon and the person of the Buddha, the doctrine that occupied his attention was nirvāṇa.[57] Like Foucaux and Obry, Müller made only a passing reference to the four noble truths, yet he noted the significance of the Buddha's first sermon in his biography of the Buddha.[58] Müller based his study of the Buddha's life on Barthélemy Saint-Hilaire's study of the *Lalita-vistara*; and, while he sharply critiqued Barthélemy Saint-Hilaire's definition of nirvāṇa and his assessment of Buddhism, Müller still shared the familiar portrayal of the Buddha as a social and moral reformer. For Barthélemy Saint-Hilaire, his supporters, and his critics, the Buddha's teachings were less important than his reforms of the Brahmanical system.[59] In their rejection of the doctrine of nirvāṇa, these scholars focused on the Buddha's character as a reformer and on other doctrines, including, at times, the four noble truths. The arguments over who the Buddha was led to different constructions of what the Buddha taught; Burnouf's close attention to the texts was neglected during the two decades that followed the publication of the *Introduction*.

Hippolyte Adolphus Taine wrote a review of Köppen's *Die Religion des Buddha und ihre Enstehung* that appeared serially in the *Journal des débats* in March of 1864. Taine was a French critic and philosopher who taught at the École des beaux-arts from 1864 until 1883. He was fundamentally liberal in his outlook; he sought a scientific basis for history and philosophy throughout his career. Taine was not widely recognized as a scholar of Buddhism, and his interest in the Buddha reveals more of the popular appeal of the Buddha and his teachings. Nonetheless, Taine was well-read in the field: he consulted Hardy's *Manual of Buddhism* and *Eastern Monachism*, Burnouf's *Lotus de la bonne loi* and *Introduction à l'histoire du Bouddhisme*, Foucaux's *Ryga-tcher-rol-pa*, Wilson's translation of the *Rig Veda*, Stanislas Julien's *Les Pèlerins bouddhistes*, and Colebrook and Lassen's *Indische Alterthumskunde*.[60] Taine was also cited by scholars of Buddhism; F. I. Shcherbatskoi appealed to him in his argument that the doctrine of Buddhism was fundamentally philosophical.[61] Taine retold the story of the Buddha's own enlightenment in his survey of Buddhism and made this comment:

> He recalled his previous births and those of all creatures; he embraced the immense and innumerable worlds with a single glance; he seized the infinite chain of all effects and causes; he pierced through the misleading appearance of becoming and being, discovered the void (le nèant) which is the true substance of things, and attained the supreme doctrine that leads to salvation.[62]

Not surprisingly, the next sentence reads: 'The four truths make up this doctrine.' Taine described the four noble truths and what he called the 'philosophic way.' There is another way, he said, one that is more popular. This second way is also rooted in the Buddha's teaching that all is suffering. 'In his idea of suffering, there is the idea of suffering of others; at the base of his dreariness there is *compassion*. Here there is the single word, the new good that will relieve and console all of those who are miserable; this may be reached by all of weak or desperate hearts. [italics in original]'[63] For Taine, the four noble truths were the salvific message of the Buddha. He dismissed the debates over the meanings of nirvāṇa in a footnote that simply notes the various interpretations.[64] The Buddha's compassion, in Taine's characterization, eliminated caste barriers, and we begin to see how the reforms of the Buddha that Albrecht Weber and others had described as political were understood as, and perhaps transformed into, moral reforms. Within a construction of the Buddha as a moral reformer, the four noble truths stood as the representation of the Buddha's compassion and thus his moral teachings.

The Essence of the Buddha's Teachings? (1858–1877)

While the meaning of *nibbāna*, who the Buddha was, and what the Buddha taught were the central questions among the debating European scholars of Buddhism in the 1850s and 1860s, other studies done by missionaries and scholars who had resided in Theravāda countries stood outside the the *nibbāna* arguments and offered a slightly different view of Buddhism – which sometimes included the four noble truths and sometimes did not. Bishop Paul Ambrose Bigandet (1813–1894) was the Vicar-Apostolic of Ava and Pegu. He published a study of Buddhism in 1858 that was based on sources that he had received in Burma; the book went through four editions by 1912. The book is entitled *The Life or Legend of Gaudama: The Buddha of the Burmese.*[65] The first edition of Bigandet's book consisted of a translation of the *Malālaṅkāravatthu*, while the second edition (1866) was supplemented with portions of the *Tathāgata-udāna*. Bigandet was of the opinion that these two texts were Burmese translations of Pāli works; but, more recently Heinz Braun has identified these texts as examples of religious stories in Burmese prose.[66] Even though Bigandet confused the two texts, particularly in the chronology of the Buddha, his book is useful for his description of the features of Buddhism and the four noble truths. Bigandet wrote a series of articles at the end of the translation. In a discussion of meditation, he began with a focus on human suffering: 'The root of all human miseries is ignorance. . . . It is the dark but lofty barrier that encircles all beings and retains them within the vortex of endless existences; it is the cause of all existences, and of all those illusions to which beings are miserably subjected; it causes those continual changes which take place in the production of all beings.'[67] The Buddha, Bigandet continued, discovered this cause and 'procure[d] a remedy': science or knowledge. Bigandet placed two doctrines of the Buddha at the center of Buddhism, the doctrine of *paṭiccasamupāda* (dependent arising) and the four noble truths, although he devoted little space to the details of either doctrine. Not surprisingly, perhaps, the majority of his comments were devoted to explaining the paths to *nibbāna*, even though he wrote that 'the important theory of the twelve *Nidānas*, or causes and effects, . . . with the four sublime truths, constitutes the very essence of the [Buddha's] system.'[68]

James de Alwis was a Sri Lankan scholar of Sinhalese literature whose publications included two lectures collectively entitled 'Buddhism: Its Origins, History and Doctrines; Its Scriptures and their language, the Pāli.' The lectures appeared first in the *Colombo Observer* in 1862 and were reprinted in the *Journal of the Pāli Text Society* in 1883. De Alwis provided an overview of Buddhism in Sri Lanka and made no mention of the four noble truths; he argued that the doctrines of *nibbāna*, *brahmacariya*, and no-self (*anattā*) were the significant teachings.[69] While de Alwis's lectures appeared in 1862, later than Gogerly and Hardy's writings, it is striking that de Alwis, a scholar of Sinhalese literature, and Gogerly and Hardy, Methodist missionaries in Sri Lanka, paid so little attention to the four noble truths.[70] Arguments that favored the centrality of the four noble truths appear to have been constructed in Europe, with the possible exception of Bigandet's study, and reflect the larger question of who the Buddha was and what he taught. Burnouf's comparative approach to Buddhist textual sources, which provided the first substantive study of the four noble truths, had yet to be emulated. The four noble truths were regarded either as a central doctrine of the Buddha or as if they were were not significant at all, as d'Alwis implies.

The Wheel of the Law, Buddhism illustrated from Siamese Sources was published in London in 1871 and written by Henry Alabaster, who was an interpreter of the British government in Siam and a member of the Royal Asiatic Society. Alabaster used the symbol of the wheel to signify the interdependence of cause-and-effect that he identified as the essence of Buddhism. The book has three parts. The first is a revised version of Alabaster's earlier essay 'Modern Buddhist,' where he offers the 'ideas of an eminent Siamese nobleman on his own and other religions' to a European audience. This nobleman was Chao Phya Thipakon, who Alabaster said was 'better known to foreigners as Chao Phya Phraklang;' he was a minister of foreign affairs in Siam from 1856 until 1869. Chao Phya Thipakon was versed in science and wrote a book entitled the 'Kitchanukit' on his speculations about Buddhism and other religions. Alabaster tells us that Thipakon's own purpose was to educate, and thus Alabaster paraphrased his remarks as the first section of Alabaster's own book. The second part is a life of the Buddha, translated from the Thai *Pathomma Somphothiyan* (*Pathamasambodhi*), translated by Alabaster as the 'Initiation, or First Festival of Perfect Wisdom.'[71] The third section is a discussion of the 'Phrabat, or Siamese Footprint of the Buddha,' which Alabaster calls 'a curious and gross superstition [that] offers a very thorough contrast to the ideas of the 'Modern Buddhist'.' Alabaster considered his book to be devoted primarily to a comparison of Buddhism with other religions.

The four noble truths appear in a section which summarizes many of the world's religions in a few paragraphs; the title of this section is 'The Modern Buddhist.' Thipakon, as Alabaster relates it, said: 'The teaching of the Buddha does not go back to the origin of life, but treats of that which already exists, showing that ignorance of the four truths in the cause of continued existence (in transmigration).' The four truths are defined, and he concluded: 'Such was the teaching of Buddha.'[72] Relying upon Thipakon, Alabaster identified the four noble truths as a central, perhaps the most readily summarized, teaching of Buddhism, although a number of other teachings are discussed throughout the remainder of the book. The other mention of the four noble truths in Alabaster's book is a footnote to a reference in the life of the Buddha, translated from the *Pathamasambodhi*.

The text describes the actions of the Buddha at his birth, saying that he stood and made a number of declarations. At that time, the passage explains that 'the sick were healed; signifying that he would attain the knowledge of the four pre-eminent truths.'[73] The four truths, Alabaster noted, were the four noble truths.

Alabaster wrote that the Thai were 'hazy' on precisely what the fourth truth was, and he was one of very few scholars to notice that there are a range of possible meanings for the fourth noble truth. While the eightfold path is the standard explanation, the relationship with the four paths and the four fruits, as we saw in Chapter Five, obscures the definition of the last truth. Alabaster offered three possible explanations for the fourth truth: (1) the four 'ways and four fruits' of the stream-winner, once-returner, non-returner, and arahat; (2) the eightfold path; and (3) the four 'paths' in which the passions are gradually eliminated. (The third explanation appears elsewhere in the same text.) Alabaster's explanation is quite similar to Burnouf's discussion, although not as rigorously examined; and, it is the first analysis of the doctrine since Burnouf's comments in 1844 that is not used explicitly in support of a particularly European portrait of the Buddha as a moral reformer. Instead, Alabaster's discussion of the four truths was framed by Thipakon's comments that reflected Thai sentiments of the time, and by the Thai Buddhist textual tradition.

The study of Buddhism and Buddhist doctrines – including the four noble truths – shifted in the late 1870s. J. W. de Jong takes the year 1877 as the point when additional Pāli and Buddhist Sanskrit texts were being edited and made available.[74] The emphasis on the Buddha as a reformer gradually grew less with the return to the textual sources then made possible by new resources. In 1872, I. P. Minaev published a Pāli grammar which was translated into French and English. The first Pāli-English dictionary, *A Dictionary of the Pāli Language* by Robert Caesar Childers, appeared in 1875.[75] The establishment of the Pāli Text Society, in 1881, consolidated the study and translation of the Pāli texts.[76] Hermann Oldenberg's translation of the *Vinaya-piṭaka*, with the *Mahāvagga*'s description of the Buddha's realization and teaching of the four noble truths, was published in 1881.

With the rapidly expanding body of Buddhist literature translated into European languages, the characterization of the Buddha as a reformer declined in Europe, but did not disappear entirely. The four noble truths were still used as evidence to show that the Buddha was a social and moral reformer, but such popular portrayals of the Buddha were less common than in the 1850s and 1860s. For example, T. W. Rhys Davids and Oldenberg both acknowledged the Buddha as a reformer, but Oldenberg replaced the focus on the Buddha's social reforms with an emphasis on the doctrines of salvation; Rhys Davids replaced the focus on the Buddha's social reforms by highlighting the Buddha's ethical teachings. Scholars who wrote in the second half of the nineteenth century also recognized a shift in scholarship on Buddhism. Of Émile Senart's book *Essai sur la légende du Buddha*, Auguste Barth wrote in 1881 that Senart 'goes a little too far in his mythic explanations; but, after this book, [there] can no longer be any idea of writing the life of the Buddha, as it is given, for instance, in the work of Barthélemy Saint-Hilaire. . . .'[77] At the end of the century, La Vallée Poussin dismissed several popular hypotheses about the Buddha, among which was the view that the Buddha was an 'agent for a social and religious revolution.'[78] Scholarship in the 1880s self-consciously moved beyond the arguments found among some of the academic and popular writings on Buddhism of the 1850s and 1860s, although Burnouf's work still commanded attention. Scholars recognized that the straightforward portrait of the Buddha as a social, political, or moral reformer was no longer justifiable; instead, the Buddha's innovations were cast as those of salvation.

The Four Noble Truths as Vehicles of Salvation (1877–1926)

One of the central approaches that emerged within the study of Buddhism in the 1870s and 1880s was the search for the historical development of the various schools of Buddhism described in the texts. Léon Feer published an extensive study of the different versions of the *Dhammacakkappavattana-sutta* and sought to locate the emergence of the *sutta* within the eighteen schools of Hīnayāna Buddhism. The list of the different schools of Buddhism had been translated and discussed by Stanislaus Julien in 1859 and by Vasile'ev in 1860, as Feer cited.[79] This material provided a framework for Feer's investigation of the different versions of the *sutta*. In his introduction to the study, Feer noted that little research had been done on such a central thesis within Buddhism. He referred to Spence Hardy's *Manual of Buddhism* and his *Legends and Theories of Buddhism*, Burnouf's work, Foucaux's translation of the *Lalitavistara*, and noted that Gogerly's writings were largely unavailable to European scholars.

Feer identified four sources for the four noble truths: Pāli Tibetan, Tibetan, Sanskrit, and Sanskrit Tibetan. The Pāli Tibetan group included the Pāli material from the Theravāda canon that was also found in the Tibetan canon.[80] Feer's approach was the same as Burnouf's approach; namely, to study the different versions of the teaching that were available from sources of the northern and southern schools. Unlike Burnouf, however, Feer had the actual texts available to him, either in translation or in the original languages. He suggested the possibility that the four noble truths emerged into Buddhist literature through *vinaya* collections, based on comparisons between the versions found in *sūtra* collections and those found in the *vinaya*. Feer offered parallel translations of the

Dharmacakra-sūtra found in the Tibetan canon and the *Dharmacakra-pravartana-sūtra* found in both the Tibetan canon and the Theravāda canon, and went on to analyze extensively the various segments found in both versions. Many of the specific points he made reappear in later studies of the four noble truths. Feer's conclusion located the different versions of the teaching among the different schools, and he tenatively suggested that the version of the *sūtra* in the Theravāda canon may have been the earliest of all of the versions.[81]

Although Feer's study employed a historicist approach, his close reading of the different versions of the four noble truths were not widely cited by scholars who incorporated discussions of the four noble truths into their own readings of the historical development of Buddhism. The desire to describe the historical development of Buddhism that developed during the late 1870s and 1880s was accompanied by disagreements over the significance of the mythological dimensions of the stories about the Buddha. At one end of the spectrum, although not as extreme as Hendrik Kern, was Senart; his *Essai sur le légende du Buddha* was first published between 1873 and 1875 in the *Journal asiatique* and revised in 1882. Once the mythological elements of the sources were identified, Senart suggested, the historical facts would remain. Senart went further to argue that the mythological elements found in the sources that described the Buddha's life formed a pattern within the history of Indian religions. Senart used the method of historical mythology, in comparison to comparative mythology, to suggest that, while there may have been a man called the Buddha, he was not the Buddha of whom the Buddhist tradition speaks.[82]

At the other end of the spectrum, Oldenberg published one of the most widely read books on Buddhism, *Buddha: sein Leben, seiner Lehre, seine Gemeinde*, in 1881, which was translated into English in the following year. For Oldenberg, the Buddha was a historical figure whose existence could be gleaned from the evidence of the Theravāda canon; he disagreed with Senart's conclusions about the significance of the mythological dimensions of the Buddha's life.[83] Oldenberg shared with T. W. Rhys Davids a desire to discover the history of the Buddha within the stories found in the texts of the Pāli sources. Both scholars affirmed the historical reliability of Pāli canon as well as the possibility of finding a historical basis for the stories about the Buddha. Oldenberg described the Buddha as a man who was revered as the source of all that is holy and true, and who lives within the memories of Buddhists today: 'And this master is not regarded as a wise man of the dim past, but people think of him as of a man, who has lived in a not very remote past.'[84]

T. W. Rhys Davids saw value in the myths that surrounded the Buddha; he wrote that they were 'the only embodiment possible, under these conditions, of some of the noblest feelings that have ever moved the world.'[85] Even though he recognized the sentiments revealed in the myths of the Buddha,

Rhys Davids, like Oldenberg, considered the Buddha to be a historical figure.[86] The life of the Buddha was to be gathered carefully from the Theravāda sources just like the task of reconstructing the life of Christ from the synoptic Gospels.[87] Oldenberg and Rhys Davids sought to sift the kernels of historical truth from the myths about the Buddha while still recognizing some significance in the myths, although they could not agree with Senart's argument.[88] Ananda Wickremeratne suggests that Rhys Davids saw the comparative approach to history as the means to a fuller understanding of unfamiliar cultures and a more comprehensive view of humanity itself.[89]

T. W. Rhys Davids set himself apart from the earlier position that the Buddha was a social reformer by arguing that most important contribution of the Buddha was not in his social reforms but in his doctrines, particularly in the doctrine of 'no-self' (*anattā*). Rhys Davids presented his position at the Hibbert Lectures in 1882: 'What I venture to submit to you is merely that it is this new departure, this ignoring of the soul which is the most important fact in the comparative study of Buddhism.'[90] T. W. Rhys Davids held that the Buddha was anti-philosophical; in this attention to the doctrines of the Buddha, we see that Rhys Davids (as well as Oldenberg) continued to make the same distinction that the earlier scholars made in the debate over the doctrine of nirvāṇa: a distinction between the Buddha's doctrines and the more philosophical teachings of larger Buddhist tradition. The influence of the doctrines attributed to the Buddha was significant for Rhys Davids: 'For the first time in the history of the world, [Buddhism] proclaimed a salvation which each man could gain for himself, in this world, during this life, without the least reference to God or to gods, either great or small.'[91] Throughout his career, T. W. Rhys Davids grounded his work in his conviction that the transformative contributions of the Buddha lay in his teachings that were designed to lead men and women to salvation.[92]

Wandering students and teachers sought the Buddha's teaching, Rhys Davids explained; he pointed out that the career of a wandering teacher was open to anyone, including women.[93] At this time in the history of Buddhism, Rhys Davids contended, the ideas of the soul were changing among the elite, if not among the masses, and after the hypothesis of a world soul (*paramātman*) was reached, all that the Buddha had left to do was entirely reject the soul theory. The mark of the Buddha's transformations lay, according to Rhys Davids, in his rejection of the idea of the soul that characterized the Brahmanic traditions. In short, it was the Buddha's new doctrines that signaled his reforms.

> For though Gotama was highly trained in the current systems of philosophy, he studied them only, like Hume, to show their unreliability. And he taught that dabbling in metaphysics and speculation was a hindrance, not a help, to that inward growth which was the only thing he held to be worth striving for.[94]

The Buddha, Rhys Davids explained, retained the doctrine of former and future lives but changed those doctrines definitively by detaching them from the soul theory to which they had been attached previously.[95] This transformation of the soul theory was the locus of the Buddha's doctrine in Rhys Davids' writings. He explored the four noble truths as they appeared in the *Dhammacakkappavattana-sutta*, citing Foucaux's translation of the *Lalita-vistara* and his own translation of the *Dhammacakkappavattana-sutta* as the sources of this doctrine.[96] In the chapter entitled 'Essential Doctrines,' Rhys Davids covered the aggregates (Sanskrit *skandhas*), thirst (Sanskrit *tṛṣṇa*), *karma*, and nirvāṇa. He discussed the four noble truths, like Burnouf, in the context of the fourfold path of the stream-winner, once-returner, non-returner and *arahat*, concluding the section with a brief but comprehensive survey of the literature on nirvāṇa.[97] In Rhys Davids's studies, the four noble truths were a doctrine integral to other teachings of the Buddha on salvation.

In an article which appeared in *The Fortnightly Review* entitled 'Buddha's First Sermon,' T. W. Rhys Davids praised the Buddha's first talk at greater length. That sermon, he wrote, 'presents to us in a few short and pithy sentences the very essence of that remarkable system which has had so profound an influence on the religious history of so large a portion of the human race.'[98] A substantial portion of this article on the four noble truths is directed at dispelling the popular and Orientalist impression that Buddhism is a pessimistic philosophy. Rhys Davids asserts that the Buddha was 'the mightiest thinker India has produced' and that he taught 'a scheme of salvation without any of the rites, any of the ceremonies, any of the charms, any of the various creeds, any of the priestly powers, without even any of the gods in whom men so love to trust.'[99] The significance of the four noble truths, Rhys Davids asserted, lay in the content as well as in the fact that the four noble truths were the substance of his first sermon; he referred to the *Dhammacakkappavattana-sutta* in the *Saṃyutta-nikāya*. After providing a translation and an explanation of the *Sutta*, Rhys Davids concluded that the Buddha's first sermon 'marked a great advance on the systems of salvation supported by its principal opponents in India' and that its primary contribution was historical. The historical importance of the four noble truths for Rhys Davids rested in the observation that the Buddha was part of the history of human ideas, that he was part of the emergence of a 'new system in which man was to work out his own salvation.'[100] Where earlier scholars like Albrecht Weber, Barthélemy Saint-Hilaire, and others emphasized the Buddha's social reforms first and then included the four noble truths, T. W. Rhys Davids gave primary attention to the four noble truths as the first teaching of the Buddha. The Buddha was no less a reformer in Rhys Davids' work, but the content of the Buddha's reforms lay in his teachings, rather than the area of social or political change.

Using an argument that was similar to that of T. W. Rhys Davids and others of the last two decades of the nineteenth century, Oldenberg found the genius of the Buddha not in his social reforms but in his teachings on salvation. The Buddha, for Oldenberg, was a religious leader *par excellence* as we can see from the following description of the Buddha's religious experience:

> The coming of such a turning-point in Buddha's inner life corresponds much too closely with what in all times similar natures have actually experienced under similar conditions, for us not to be inclined to believe in such an occurrence. In the most widely different periods of history the notion of a revolution or change of the whole man perfecting in one moment meets us in many forms: a day and hour it must be possible to determine, in which the unsaved and unenlightened becomes a saved and enlightened man: and if men hope and look for such a sudden, and probably also violent breaking through of the soul to the light, they realize it in fact. Within the Christian Church we have the Methodists especially, but not they alone, who bear testimony to this. . . . A flash of thought, a sudden excitement of warm emotion or vivid imagination, or a moment of tranquil breathing time following on times of internal strife, is metamorphosed for them into that opening of the heart, or that call by divine omnipotence, for which they were consciously or unconsciously waiting, and which is sufficient to give a new turn to their whole life.[101]

This moment of inspiration was the goal of the followers of the Buddha who had renounced home, family, and the world. The Buddha's triumph, his attainment of salvation that he taught to his followers, was real for Oldenberg because it was an experience found throughout the history of human religious experience. For Oldenberg, the Buddha was a religious as well as social reformer such as India had never seen before.

Rhys Davids and Oldenberg differed on the question of whether Buddhism was a religion of pessimism. Where Rhys Davids sought to dispell that notion, Oldenberg did not: 'The four noble truths give expression to Buddhist pessimism in its characteristic singularity.'[102] Despite the pessimistic tone that he ascribed to the doctrine, Oldenberg recognized that the doctrine of the four noble truths was at the center of the Buddha's teachings. The teachings of the Buddha were not philosophy, Oldenberg wrote:

> It does not purport to be a philosophy, which inquires into the ultimate grounds of things, unfolds to thought the breadths and depths of the universe. It addresses itself to man plunged in sorrow, and, while it teaches him to understand his sorrow, it shows him the

> way to exterminate it, root and all. This is the only problem with which Buddhist thought is concerned.[103]

Within his characterization of the Buddha as one who brought a new form of salvation, Oldenberg places the four noble truths as the paradigmatic expression of the central problem of pain.

Like earlier scholars, T. W. Rhys Davids and Oldenberg appropriately located the Buddha's doctrines within the life of the Buddha and as evidence of his insight as a religious leader. These scholars argued, implicitly and explicitly, that the doctrines taught by the Buddha were the vehicle for salvation and that the four noble truths are the most succint expression of the Buddha's teachings on salvation. Both Rhys Davids and Oldenberg assign the general category of doctrines the same place in their conceptions of Buddhism, although the four noble truths are not cast as the only fundamental teaching of the Buddha. Where Rhys Davids focused on the doctrine of no-self and simultaneously recognized the centrality of the four noble truths, Oldenberg took a broader approach by placing the entire category of salvation at the center of the Buddha's teaching, which naturally embraced the four noble truths. Although the Buddha was not seen primarily as a social or political reformer by the end of the Victorian era, the four noble truths were understood to be an integral – if not the most important – part of the teachings of a reformist Buddha, who transformed the possibilities for human salvation, if not the social or political spheres of human action.

Auguste Barth shared Rhys Davids' and Oldenberg's historicist method, although he was also inclined toward Senart's interpretation of the Buddha, as he indicated in *The Religions of India*: 'We have only legendary data, deeply infected with mythical elements, in regard to the life of the remarkable man who, towards the close of the sixth century before our era, laid the foundations of a religious system which, under a form more or less altered, constitutes, even in our own day, the faith of more than a third of the inhabitants of the globe.'[104] For Barth, the Theravāda sources held the greatest 'chance of finding the echo of [the Buddha's] word, although he found the doctrines encumbered by a 'formalism and scholasticism' in which there were 'sparks . . . but never flame.'[105] Barth wrote that the Buddha's doctrine was confined to the question of salvation, the scheme of which was to be found in the four noble truths which led to nirvāṇa. He followed a short definition of the four noble truths with a more extensive discussion of the 'conditions of existence' as shown in the theory of the *nidāna*s and the aggregates (*skandha*s). In discussing the four noble truths and then the twelvefold chain of dependent arising, Barth followed the pattern of the Buddha's enlightenment experience contained in the *Mahāvagga*.

Barth's short sketch of Buddhism in *The Religions of India*, which regards Buddhism as significant primarily in its relations to the religions of

India, is noteworthy here for two reasons. First, he discussed the doctrine of the four noble truths in a way that is not closely tied to a particular image of the Buddha. Like Senart, Barth did not argue strongly for the historical truth of the Buddha's life and experiences. He examined the Buddha's teachings apart from the historical question of the person of the Buddha. Second, his use of the four noble truths, the theory of the *nidāna*s, and the aggregates displayed a pattern shared by T. W. Rhys Davids, Oldenberg, and others. In contrast to the argument of Albrecht Weber in the 1850s, who suggested that the four noble truths were in tension with the teachings on nirvāṇa, Barth, Rhys Davids, and Oldenberg recognized the four noble truths as part of a larger set of teachings which led to nirvāṇa.

Hendrick Kern proposed a slightly different explanation for the four noble truths when he introduced the use of a medical model for the doctrine. Kern's book on the history of Buddhism in India appeared in Dutch in 1882 and 1884, was translated into German by Hermann Jacobi in the same years, and was published nearly twenty years later in French. Kern concluded that the Buddha was a solar god and that *that* Buddha, not the Buddha of the historical elements of the canon, was the true Buddha 'in an ideal sense.'[106] Kern first introduced the four noble truths in his biography of the Buddha, using the *Mahāvagga* of the *Vinaya-piṭaka* and the *Lalita-vistara*. His discussion of the doctrine was similar to Barth's insofar as he first presented the four noble truths and then turned to the *nidāna*s, although the imagery that followed his mention of these doctrines reflects his larger argument that the Buddha was a representation of a solar deity: 'At the first rays of the sun, he had acquired omniscience, he had become the Buddha (enlightened), and this event gave rise to a cry of jublication throughout the universe. . . .'[107] Kern explained in a footnote that the four noble truths were borrowed from medical terminology which first establishes the malady, the cause, the cure and then provides the medical measures necessary to eradicate the illness. He cited the *Lalita-vistara* as his authority.[108]

Kern's appeal to medicine as a source for the structure of the four noble truths became quite popular, and it has persisted throughout the twentieth century. The appeal to a medical analysis as a source for the four noble truths appears in such diverse sources as Heinrich Zimmer's *Philosophies of India*[109] and more recently in a 1992 Paris edition of *Vogue*.[110] In 1957, G. C. Pande provided a thorough review of the evidence in support of his argument for a medical 'archetype' for the four noble truths.[111] Despite the popularity of the argument, however, there is not sufficient historical evidence to conclude that the Buddha deliberately drew upon a clearly defined medical model for his fourfold analysis of human pain.[112] The medical metaphor was used extensively by the Buddhist tradition, as well as the Vedānta, Yoga, and Nyāya schools, but there is no explicit medical model for the analysis found in the four noble truths. With his structural approach to the biography of the Buddha, Kern referred to the Buddha's title 'Master of Medicine' (*vaidyarāja*) that appears in the *Lalita-vistara* as evidence that the the four noble truths were based on a medical diagnosis, but the analogy has no historical foundation. The medical terminology introduced by Kern has been one of the most common explanations for the origin of the doctrine of the four noble truths, despite the lack of support for the explanation.

By the end of the nineteenth century, the four noble truths were widely recognized as one of the most important teachings of the Buddha, sometimes in combination with other doctrines and sometimes not – much like their appearance in the Theravāda canon. In 1889, for example, Monier Monier-Williams identified the four noble truths as the fundamental teaching of the Buddha along with dependent arising (Sanskrit *pratītyasamutpāda*).[113] Like others, Monier-Williams linked the four noble truths to the reforms of the Buddha and shared with other scholars in the rejection of the rituals that then-contemporary Buddhists practiced in Asia.[114] After the turn of the century, H. C. Warren placed the four noble truths in an equally central position: '. . . wisdom, or the intellectual discipline, lies in the mastery of the four truths, of dependent arising . . . and of much else besides, but above all in the application of the three characteristics to the elements of being.'[115] There was an increase in the understanding of the Buddhist texts – Theravādan as well as Hīnayāna and Mahāyāna – at the end of the nineteenth century. A more refined understanding of the complexity of Buddhism emerged at the turn of the century. In the works of the late nineteenth century, which sought to represent the intricate nature of the whole of Buddhism, it was rare to find the four noble truths represented as the single most important expression of the Buddha's teachings; they are more commonly paired with at least one other teaching. Be that as it may, the four noble truths had become known as one of the most significant teachings of the Buddha by the end of the nineteenth century; and, among popular circles, the four noble truths continued to support a particular characterization of the Buddha as evidence of his salvific, if no longer political, reforms. Such widespread popularity of the four noble truths is striking when compared to its relative absence in the first writings on Buddhism which appeared in the first half of the century.

At the end of the nineteenth century and into the twentieth, Louis de la Vallée Poussin provided a different answer to the broad question of what Buddhism was, together with a slightly different interpretation of the four noble truths. Buddhism was, he wrote, 'a discipline of salvation' which 'cannot be exactly described either as philosophies or as religions.'[116] As a discipline, Buddhism was a body 'of doctrines and practices' which were designed for ascetics only and as 'personal or individualistic.'[117] The character of the Buddha was of less significance in La Vallée Poussin's studies than the nature of Buddhism as a discipline of salvation, particularly a discipline of yoga. The Buddha was significant as the source of truth, for he was the one who discovered 'the most celebrated among the Indian paths of salvation.' All good sayings and teachings came from the Buddha, said La Vallée Poussin, and there was no hope for salvation unless one takes refuge in the Buddha.[118] La Vallèe Poussin enjoined his audience to read the life history of the Buddha, but he suggested that even though it bears every mark of authenticity, one should remember that the Indians are 'wonderful storytellers.'[119] For La Vallée Poussin, the middle way was the fundamental teaching, and the Buddha was the one who discovered that way. The way to salvation was the teaching of Śākyamuni and avoiding the extremes; as La Vallèe Poussin wrote, 'the right way to extinguish the fire [of desire] is the intellectual method . . . coupled with a moderate asceticism.'[120] La Vallée Poussin's way to nirvāṇa was not simply the four noble truths or the eightfold path. The path itself depends on asceticism and 'getting away from desire;' and, it is composed of three parts: faith (*śraddhā*), sight (*darśana*), and cultivation (*bhāvanā*). Although La Vallée Poussin identified the path with the enlightenment of the Buddha and the *Dhammacakkappavattana-sutta*, the four noble truths themselves were less significant than the larger path.

The question of what the Buddha's teaching were remained an important one, but the answers that La Vallée Poussin gave were broader in scope and in detail than those of the previous fifty years. He was a student of Sylvain Levi; he pursued the connection between Buddhism and yoga that was first introduced by Kern and developed further by Senart.[121] While La Vallée Poussin did not identify the four noble truths as a direct legacy of yoga (as Senart did), he nonetheless located the four noble truths differently than his predecessors did within his overview of Buddhism.[122] In *The Way to Nirvāṇa*, La Vallée Poussin's 1917 Hibbert Lectures at Manchester College, the four noble truths appear in the sixth of as many lectures, following lectures on the Buddhist soul, *karma*, transmigration and nirvāṇa. La Vallée Poussin was one of few scholars to draw attention to the threefold training of the four noble truths that the Buddha explains in the *Dhammacakkappavattana-sutta*.[123] He explained that the four noble truths are linked first to the path and to the training necessary to attain the path, not to the person of the Buddha. La Vallée Poussin's discussion of the four noble truths recalls the early work of Eugène Burnouf, who discussed the four noble truths in the context of those who had attained the path. La Vallée Poussin placed the four noble truths within a larger structure of Buddhism that reflected the systematic nature of Buddhism – it was a discipline and a body of doctrines and practices that owed much to the yoga that preceded it.

The four noble truths, through the scholarship of La Vallée Poussin and others, came to occupy a central position in Max Weber's writings on Buddhism. His essays on Hinduism and Buddhism that appear in his posthumously published work, *The Religions of India: The Sociology of Hinduism and Buddhism*, were first printed in the *Archiv für Sozialwissenschaft und Sozialpolitik* in 1916 and 1917. Weber referred to a variety of scholars, including Oldenberg, T. W. Rhys Davids, C. A. Foley, Senart, Kern and La Vallée Poussin. Weber described ancient Buddhism as a specifically 'unpolitical and anti-political status religion' and as a religious 'technology' of 'wandering and intellectually-schooled mendicant monks.' Like all Indian philosophy and theology, it is a 'salvation theology,' he wrote, 'if one is to use the name 'religion' for an ethical movement without a deity and without a cult.'[124] In Weber's writings on Buddhism, the central figures were renouncers who were engaged in the attainment of salvation, an endeavor which consisted in the acquisition of knowledge and the refinement of one's intellectual abilities. The doctrine of Buddhist soteriology, Weber wrote, consisted of the four noble truths and the eightfold path.

The search for salvation – nirvāṇa – was a purely individual act according to Weber; and, such a search is one type of religious experience within Weber's larger study of the sociology of human exchange. Weber called Buddhism the 'most radical form of salvation-striving conceivable' because of the emphasis on the role of the individual.[125] His study was a sociology of rational action, in which action 'in the sense of subjectively understandable orientation of behavior exists only as the behavior of one or more individual human beings.'[126] The individuals Weber found in early Buddhism came from the upper strata of society and, as followers of the Buddha, had no interest in changing the social order. He characterized these men as renouncers who were completely indifferent to the world; men whose energy was directed wholly toward escape and release from the everyday world.[127] Buddhist soteriology, which he identified as the four noble truths and the eightfold path, rejected absolutely 'any form of inner worldly motivation to conduct or rational purpose in nature.'[128] Salvation in Buddhism, argued Weber, consisted of knowledge attained by individuals; and, because Buddhist renouncers pursued knowledge and the mind, they were agents of a type of rational action.[129]

Did the Buddha Teach the Four Noble Truths? (1927–1980)

By the middle of the twentieth century, there were several positions on the historicity of the four noble truths in Buddhist traditions. One group of scholars, which included E. J. Thomas, Nalinaksha Dutt, M. Winternitz, and B. C. Law, identified the four noble truths as one of the original teachings of the Buddha. E. J. Thomas, writing in 1927, recounted the passages from the *Sutta-piṭaka*, the *Lalita-vistara*, and the *Mahāvastu* in which the four noble truths appear as an integral part of the biography of the Buddha.[130] In 1930, Dutt stated that Hīnayāna and Mahāyāna had no disagreement on whether the Buddha preached the four noble truths.[131] In 1933, Winternitz wrote that we may 'without laying ourselves open to the charge of credulousness' accept that the Buddha himself gave the famous sermon of Banaras on the four noble truths and the eightfold path.[132] The evidence that Winternitz adduced is based upon the work that Burnouf and others did to show that the four noble truths were found in Buddhist Sanskrit texts as well as the Pāli canon. In 1937, B. C. Law wrote that the four noble truths were 'regarded as the quintessence of Buddhism as propounded by the Master himself.'[133]

Other scholars, including Caroline Augusta Foley, F. I. Shcherbatskoi, and I. B. Horner, disagreed with this position – for varying reasons. Foley argued that the four noble truths had been edited: 'But there clearly has been a reduction of a discourse, remembered in *these* words by one listener, in *those* words by another, to a fixed wording. Not of the whole discourse, but of just those sayings which *came to appeal most forcibly to the monk:* Ill, and riddance of Ill. And I hold this may well have happened in Gotama's lifetime, and sometimes in a wording and with an emphasis of which he may not have approved.'[134] Her use of italics emphasized that she found the four noble truths to be a 'monkish gloss' – probably not for lay use – unlike the rest of the *Dhammacakkappavattana-sutta* which, she wrote, 'is for Everyman.'[135] Shcherbatskoi had a different criticism to make of the claim that the four noble truths belonged to the Buddha alone. In 1927, Shcherbatskoi noted that the meaning of the four noble truths 'changes according to the content which is put into them, according to what is understood under phenomenal life (*duḥkha*) and under extinction (nirvāṇa).'[136] The evidence for his argument is the observation that the formula of the four noble truths appears in non-Buddhist texts, including the *Yogabhāṣya* and the *Nyāyabhāṣya*. On the other hand, in his characterization of the first of three stages of Buddhist philosophy, Shcherbatskoi wrote that 'the whole doctrine is summarized in the formula of the so-called four 'truths' or four principles of the Saint. . . .'[137]

In 1935, Isaline Blew Horner suggested that the four noble truths did not necessarily refer to the Buddha's talk on pain. As noted in Chapter Five, in *The Early Buddhist Theory of Man Perfected*, she argued that the 'four worthy true things,' as she translated *ariyasaccāni*, did not always refer to the four items of pain, arising, ending, and the way.[138] Sometimes the 'four worthy true things,' she suggested, referred to the 'four Ways' which are the four paths (*magga*) of the stream-enterer, the once-returner, the non-returner and the *arahat*, as well as the accompanying fruits (*phalāni*). Horner's larger argument in this work was to demonstrate that early Buddhism was distinguished into two strands; one of which was the original body of teachings of the Buddha, 'primitive Śākya,' and a second of which was 'dominated by monkdom.'[139] The first strata had much more in common with Upaniṣadic and Mahāyāna thought, she suggested, than is usually considered. Within this original core of teachings, Horner argued that the 'four worthy true things' had two possible meanings: the four ways (*magga*) and the four uprisings of mindfulness (*satipaṭṭhānā*). '. . . [B]oth these meanings became all but lost to view when Ill and the escape from it had grown to be the all-absorbing and predominating interest.'[140] While the theory of an original or primitive Buddhism has been largely rejected in contemporary scholarship, Horner's observations on the four noble truths indicate a shift in scholarship on the doctrine. She returned to the textual sources, to the commentary on the *Majjhima-nikāya* and the *Kuddaka-pāṭha*, to examine how the four noble truths appear in the text. The relationships she identified do fall into a well established set of relationships that link the four noble truths with other Buddhist teachings; these relationships were analyzed above in Chapter Three. Horner's close attention to the canonical and postcanonical sources raised a new question about the four noble truths themselves.[141]

Horner's larger argument about 'primitive Buddhism' reflects debates on dating the Pāli canon that dominated the decades between 1920 and 1960. Writing at approximately the same time as Horner, in the 1920s and 1930s, Foley's point regarding the historical emergence of the four noble truths was similar to Horner's: the four noble truths did not belong to the earliest strata of Buddhist teachings. Despite these criticisms of the position, the commonly-held conclusion in the first half of the current century was that the four noble truths represented an early strata of Buddhist teachings.

Even such scholars as Louis Renou, Étienne Lamotte, and Hajime Nakamura share this position. Renou suggests that the four noble truths encompass all of the Buddha's doctrines, and organized his discussion of Buddhist doctrine with reference to the four noble truths in *L'Inde classique*. In 1953, Renou wrote:

> The description of Buddhist doctrines organizes itself quite naturally according to the four truths. The Buddhist representation of the state of things in the world is that upon which the first truth is based: pain. This representation is a cosmology with regard to nature, [and] it is a physiology and a psychology with regard to beings. The theory of the interplay of things is what leads to the second truth: the origin of pain. The definition of conditions of the cessation of pain deriving from the notion of its origins constitutes the third truth: the cessation of pain. Finally, the technique of realization of these conditions reveals the fourth truth, the path to stopping pain, and includes the entire process of salvation, from the entry into the stream to the final extinction.[142]

Étienne Lamotte also cited the four noble truths within the traditional biographies of the Buddha and, similar to Renou, used them as a structural framework for all of the Buddha's teachings.

In 1948, Lamotte placed the four noble truths in the first of five identifiable stages of the Buddha's biography: those fragments of the biography which were incorporated into the *sūtra*s.[143]

> With this brief sketch we have tried to show how hte legend of Buddha gradually took shape, through successive revisions and additions. To the extent that one can discover a chronology in a literaure which repeats itself incessantly, the disciples of Gautama took an interest first in the psychological crisis which made Śākyamuni an enlightened one, in his last days, then in the miracles of his birth . . . .[144]

In his discussion of the the *Dhammacakkappavattana-sutta* in *Histoire du bouddhisme indien* (1958), Lamotte provided a summary and an extended discussion of the Buddha's teachings using the four noble truths as a framework. Under the subheading of the 'Truth of Suffering,' he laid out the aggregates (*khandā*), the sense spheres (*āyatanā*), the elements (*dhātu*), and *saṃsāra*. Dependent arising (*paṭiccasamuppāda*) is explained under the second truth; nirvāṇa under the third; and the eightfold path (*attāṅgika maggo*) in its three divisions together with the four stages of attainment under the four truth.[145] This method of explaining the four noble truths was also employed by Hajime Nakamura in his *Indian Buddhism: A Survey with Bibliographical Notes* (1980). Nakamura identifies the four noble truths as '[p]robably the first systematized teaching' in the development of Buddhist thought and points out that the *Dhammacakkappavattana-sutta* is known throughout the Buddhist world.[146] The construction of the four noble truths as central to the architectural design of Buddhist ideas in the work of Renou, Lamotte, and Nakamura is much like the construction of a historically early date for the emergence of the four noble truths in the works of Law and Thomas.

There have been more recent studies that explore various aspects of the four noble truths that we have encountered throughout the analysis of the previous chapters. K. R. Norman's analysis of the grammatical anomalies, Bronkhorst's inquiry into traditions of meditation in India, and Schmithausen's sharp investigation of the nature of liberating insight avoid the reductionism of previous studies by focusing on detailed and specific questions. In certain ways, the work of these scholars draws on the spirit of Burnouf's early scholarship by placing the four noble truths in a context and by exploring the detailed relationships between the versions of the teaching.

Conclusions

When James de Alwis acknowledged the efforts of European scholars toward 'unlocking the rich stores of Oriental literature' in a paper that he read before the Ceylon Branch of the Royal Asiatic Society on August 13, 1850, he did so with a full awareness of the cultural and literary chasms that separated the British who governed Sri Lanka and Sinhalese Buddhists. De Alwis translated the *Sidatsangarava*, a grammer of the Sinhalese language that was probably composed in the fourteenth century, in no small part to induce the British to learn Sinhalese and also to display the wealth of Sinhalese literature before speakers of English.[147] As others scholars have discussed, the study of Buddhism in Europe and the United States emerged within the geographical and cultural spaces that were created by colonizing governments of European countries to bridge the distance between the countries of South, Southeast, and East Asia and Europe.[148] The study of language, literature, and religion was an integral part of the colonialization; Bernard Cohen has illustrated how the emergence of comparative philology in the late eighteenth century created the power for 'the practitioner to classify, bound, and control variety and difference.'[149] Well aware of this phenomenon even as he participated in it, de Alwis sought to introduce the Sinhalese literary tradition to the British in part to provide redress for the imbalance of power that existed between the governors and the governed in Sri Lanka.[150]

It is important to realize that the study of Buddhism, and thus these studies of the four noble truths, developed within this colonialist paradigm. In the interests of moving toward an interpretation of the four noble truths that is more firmly grounded in the history of the Theravāda tradition, there are several points that emerge in this survey. The first is the persistent desire of many scholars of Buddhism to cast the four noble truths as the most important teaching of the Buddha, if not the entirety of Buddhism itself. In part, this is a reflection of the position of the four noble truths within the Theravāda canon itself as the subject of the *Dhammacakkappavattana-sutta*. It is likely that the emergence of the four noble truths in postcanonical Theravāda literature, as a measure to determine what should be accepted as the 'word of the Buddha' (*buddhavacana*), derives from the same interpretation of the four noble truths as the subject of the Buddha's first talk on *dhamma*.[151] Yet, there is a difference between how the four noble truths are regarded within European and American studies of Buddhism and how they are placed in postcanonical and contemporary Theravāda Buddhism.

In studies of the four noble truths done outside of countries that are primarily Buddhist in religious practice the reading audience is frequently unaware of the variety of teachings contained in Buddhist literature and/or of the various practices that are integral to Buddhist identities. As students who are introduced more thoroughly to Buddhism often relate, it is difficult at first to gain a sense of how the teachings of the Buddha are interrelated and connected. However, even in the face of the multitude of discourses, teachings, analyses, and admonitions that are recorded in the Theravāda canon, the four noble truths have emerged consistently as one of the most accessible teachings of the Buddha. Rhetorically, then, the four noble truths are a teaching that is understood readily by those outside Buddhist traditions. It is in this spirit that Walpola Rahula used the four noble truths as the framework for his book, *What the Buddha Taught*, which is one of the most widely used texts for the introduction of Buddhism to non-Buddhists in the last half of the twentieth century. However, we must analyze the accessibility of the four noble truths to non-Buddhist audiences at the same time as we acknowledge that one of the central tools of colonizing governments was control of language and thereby of texts – particularly religious texts.

When we do so, it is a quick step to arrive at the observation that there is a great deal of power vested in the four noble truths when they are identified as the most significant teaching of the Buddha. In other words, if the British gained a measure of control over the colonized countries of India and Sri Lanka through classifying the languages, translating literature, and explaining, for example, Buddhism to the 'civilized' world, the language and terms used to 'interpret' Buddhism become bounded and shaped by the very power that fueled colonialist enterprises. In short, the four noble truths have become an integral part of, if not a significant vehicle for, the hegemonic structures of colonialism.

How did the four noble truths serve as such a vehicle? They have functioned as a conduit of a colonialist hegemony in a variety of ways: Albrecht Weber, Barthélemy Saint-Hilaire, and others in Europe in the 1850s and 1860s cast the four noble truths as the logical alternative to the nonsensical teaching of nirvāṇa that were more easily grasped by the masses; during the same period Bigandet in Burma and Alabaster in Thailand placed them at the center of Buddhism; Hermann Oldenberg, T. W. Rhys Davids, Barth, Kern, Warren, Max Weber, and (to a lesser extent) Louis de la Vallée Poussin each portrayed the four noble truths as a central vehicle for the Buddha's salvation in the world; Winternitz, Law, Thomas, and Dutt considered them to be one of the original teachings of the Buddha; Renou, Lamotte, and Nakamura have each argued that the four truths are the foundation for all of the Buddha's teachings. While the particular shape of the vessel that the four noble truths have been asked to fill has changed throughout the decades since the 1830s, each time a scholar has positioned the four noble truths as the most, or even as one of the two or three most, important teaching(s) of the Buddha, it has been to reduce the four noble truths to a teaching that is accessible, pliable, and therefore readily appropriated by non-Buddhists.

This survey has demonstrated that not each and every European or American scholar of Buddhism has claimed that the four noble truths were the most important teaching of the Buddha. The scholars who did *not* identify the four noble truths as the most important teaching of the Buddha are significant because they offer us alternative ways of looking at the four noble truths. In review, these scholars are: Kitelagama Dewamitta Thera, in his 1826 tract on the tenets of Buddhism (translated by Armour in 1835); Burnouf, in his 1844 study of the literature of Indian Buddhism; de Alwis, Gogerly, and Hardy, all writing in Sri Lanka in the 1840s, 50s, and 60s; Foley, Horner, and Shcherbatskoi, each suggesting that the four truths were not sufficiently defined within the canonical tradition to be attributed to a single historical period; and, most recently, Norman, who has untangled the grammatical puzzles of the teaching; Schmithausen, and Bronkhorst, each of whom conclude that the four noble truths were not part of the earliest strata of the *Dhammacakkappavattana-sutta*.

If none of these scholars placed the four noble truths at the center, either alone or in combination with other teachings of the Buddha, it is worth explaining how they did frame the four noble truths. These scholars explicitly placed the four noble truths into one of two settings. Burnouf, Feer, Foley, Horner, Shcherbatskoi, Bronkhorst, Schmithausen, and Norman located the four truths in a fuller reading of the Theravāda canon and the larger context of South Asian literature. Kitelagama Devamitta Thera, de Alwis, Gogerly, and Hardy located the teaching within an experience of Buddhism as practiced in a contemporary setting. With the exception of de Alwis, each of these authors suggests a more complex reading of the four noble truths than those who locate the teaching as the key or as a crucial element within a grand scheme of Buddhism. This is the methodological conclusion that I draw from the studies discussed in this chapter: that it is to the complexities of the four noble truths, to the multiple and different contexts in which it appears, that we should look for our intepretations, instead of to the simple and seemingly straightforward explanations.

Notes

1 James de Alwis, *A Survey of Sinhala Literature (Being an Introduction to a Translation of the Sidat Sangarāva)*, Lithograph Edition, Ceylon National Museums Translation Series (Colombo: Department of National Museums, 1966), ix. The original edition was entitled *The Sidath Sangarawa, a Grammar of the Singhalese Language, Translated into English with Introduction, Notes, and Appendices*, and was published in 1852. De Alwis gives the date of June 18, 1851 for the dedication of his book to Sir George William Anderson, Governor of Ceylon. De Alwis provided the following description to his Introduction: 'A paper, being 'A brief sketch of the history of the Singhalese language,' read before the Ceylon Branch of the Royal Asiatic Society on the 13th August, 1850' (ix).

2 The four noble truths do not appear in these early descriptions of Buddhism. For the most part, the accounts focused on cosmology, rituals, and purportedly 'demonic practices.' For example, see Captain Robert Percival, *An Account of the Island of Ceylon, Containing its History, Geography, Natural History, with the Manners and Customs of its various Inhabitants to which is added the Journal of an Embassy to the Court of Candy*, 2nd ed. (London: C. & R. Baldwin, 1805), 210–231. Percival arrived in Sri Lanka with the Eighteenth or Royal Irish Regiment 'shortly after its capture' by the British (which was in

1796). Percival's book includes a chapter on the 'Religion of the Ceylonese' which is devoted to a discussion of temples, priests (by which he means *bhikkhus*), so-called demon-worship, and predestination (which is the teaching of *karma/kamma*). Similarly, Major Jonathan Forbes with the 78th Highlanders wrote a volume that was in its second edition in 1841, in which he writes that 'all religions must have some points in common; and by founding arguments on these, learned and ingenious men have attempted to assimilate the mild and tolerant Buddhist with the haughty Brahmins, – he who denounced caste, and those who exist by it alone; the amiable sage with the ambitious conqueror, – Gautama with Sesotris, – the being who threatens warlike kings, and whose first commandment is, 'From the meannest insect up to man, thou shalt not kill,' with him whose life was spent in wars and carnage' (205). This desire to separate Buddhism from the 'haughty Brahmin' is reflective of a theme that emerged more fully in the middle of the nineteenth century. Major Jonathan Forbes, *Eleven Years in Ceylon: Comprising Sketches of the Field Sports and Natural History of that Colony and an Account of its History and Antiquities*, 2nd ed. revised and corrected, 2 vols. (London: Richard Bentley, 1841). One of the earliest accounts of Buddhism in Sri Lanka was written by Portuguese Captain John Ribeyro, who arrived in Ceylon in 1640. His book was dedicated on January 8, 1685. His comments on Buddhism are condemning even as they are useful for their brief descriptions. There are various translations of this from the Portuguese; and, in one edition published in 1847, the Methodist missionary Reverend Daniel Gogerly added a chapter on Buddhism in an Appendix. Jean Ribiero, *History of Ceilão with Notes from De Barros, De Conto and Antonio Bocarro*, trans. P. E. Peiris (Galle, Sri Lanka: Albion Press, n.d.). (The translator of this edition, P. E. Peiris, was a district judge in Kalutara under the British.) See also John Ribeyro, *History of Ceylon Presented by Captain John Ribeyro to the King of Portugal in 1685, Translated from the Portuguese by the Abbé Le Grand. Re-translated from the French edition with an Appendix Containing Illustrative of the Past and Present Condition of the Island*, trans. George Lee (Ceylon: Ceylon Government Press, 1847), 264–273.

3 Captain [William C.?] Mahony, 'On Singhala, or Ceylon, and the Doctrines of Bhooddha; from the Books of the Singhalais,' *Asiatik Researches* 7 (1801): 32–56.

4 For the emergence of the study of Buddhist texts, see J. W. de Jong, 'A Brief History of Buddhist Studies,' *The Eastern Buddhist* 7 no. 1 (1974): 66; see also William Pruitt, 'References to Pāli in 17th century French Books,' *Journal of the Pāli Text Society* 11 (1987):121–131.

5 Philip Almond argues that these scattered references are characteristic of all early studies of Buddhism prior to the 'creation of Buddhism' in the 1830s. See Almond, *British Discovery*, 9–14.

6 Francis Buchanan-Hamilton, 'On the Religion and Literature of the Burmas,' *Asiatik Researches* 6 (1799): 265. The author explains that the Buddha's teachings are known as *sammadeitti* (*sammādiṭṭhi*, 'right views'), defines *dana* (alms) and *bavana* (*bhavanā*, 'meditation'), and enjoins those who will read this text – the English, Dutch, Armenians, and others – to take this text, 'faithfully to transcribe its contents, and diligently to act according to the precepts therein contained' (273).

7 Buchanan-Hamilton, 'On the Religion,' 271 and 266.

8 John Armour 'Essay on Buddhism,' *The Ceylon Almanac and Compendium of Useful Information* 3 (1835): 208. Armour himself was a district judge of Tangalle, on the southern coast of Sri Lanka; Captain Forbes notes that Armour

was recognized as the leading Sinhalese and English scholar at that time in Sri Lanka. Forbes, *Eleven Years in Ceylon*, 2:198.

9 Armour, 'An Essay on Buddhism,' 224.

10 I have found only one citation to this article in work on the four noble truths or on Buddhism that is available outside of Sri Lanka; Forbes mentions the work in his *Eleven Years in Ceylon*.

11 One of Burnouf's earlier works was a Pāli grammar done with Christian Lassen (1800–1876) that was published in 1826, the *Essai sur le Pāli*. In the introduction to this work, Burnouf and Lassen provided an overview of the study of Pāli and works translated from Pāli sources through 1826. Eugène Burnouf and Chr. Lassen, *Essai sur le Pāli ou langue sacrée de la presqu'île au-delà du Gange* (Paris: Dondey-Dupreé, 1826), 1–19. Among the Pāli sources they discussed were translations made by La Loubère of the life of Devadatta and excerpts from the *Pātimokkha*, as well as the three texts from Sangermano translated and published in English by Francis Buchanan-Hamilton. In a pamphlet written as a supplement to *Essai sur le Pāli* in 1827 entitled *Observations grammaticales sur quelques passages de l'essai sur le Pāli*, Burnouf and Lassen discussed Edward Upham's then-forthcoming edition of the *Mahāvaṃsa* and the Pāli dictionary *Abhidhānappadīpikā* edited by J. P. Abel-Rémusat. See Burnouf and Lassen, *Observations grammaticales sur quelques passages de l'essai sur le Pāli* (Paris: Dondey-Dupré, 1827), 6, n. 1 and 8. Upham's translations of the Mahāvaṃsa appeared in 1833. See Edward Upham, *The Mahāvansi, The Rājā-Ratnācari, and the Rājā-Vali, forming the Sacred and Historical Books of Ceylon*, 3 vols. (London: Parbury, Allen and Co., 1833). Upham includes letters from Alexander Johnston, who received the Mahāvaṃsa manuscripts from Buddhist *bhikkhus*, and Reverend W. B. Fox, a Wesleyan missionary. Fox reviewed the translations made by Johnston's staff (who were Sri Lankan scholars) and was named by Johnston 'the best European Pāli and Singhalese scholar at present' (Upham, *Mahāvansi*, 1:x). In 1829, Upham had published *The History and Doctrine of Budhism, popularly illustrated, with notices of the Kappooism, or Demon Worship, and the Bali, or Planetary Incantations, of Ceylon* (London: Ackermann, 1829). See an anonymous synopsis of the work in *The Oriental Herald* 21 no. 64 (1829): 93–103. On the Sri Lankan contributions to the translations of Pāli Buddhist texts from 1861–1942, see Ananda W. P. Gurugé, *From the Living Fountains of Buddhism* (Colombo: Ministry of Cultural Affairs, 1984). For a more detailed discussion of these early translations, see J. W. de Jong, *A Brief History*, 58–76. De Jong does not mention Edward Upham's publication of the *Mahāvaṃsa*.

12 Burnouf's citation in his *Introduction* gives the date of Csoma Körösi's article as 1832, but the volume in which the article actually appeared was published in 1836. Alexander Csoma Körösi, 'Notices on the Life of Shakya, extracted from the Tibetan Authorities,' *Asiatik Researches* 20 (1836): 285–317. The four noble truths are simply introduced as the substance of what the Buddha realized during his enlightenment experience (Csoma Körösi, *Notices on the Life*, 294). For Burnouf's reference to Csoma Körösi, see Eugène Burnouf, *Introduction à l'histoire du bouddhisme indien* (Paris: Imprimerie royale, 1844; 2nd edition, Paris: Maissonneuve, 1876), 569.

13 George Turnour, 'An Examination of the Pāli Buddhistical Annals,' Parts 1–6, *Journal of the Asiatic Society of Bengal* vol. 6, pt. 2, no. 67 (July 1837): 501–528; no. 69 (September 1837): 713–737; vol. 7, pt. 2, no. 80 (August 1838): 686–701; no. 81 (September 1838): 789–817; no. 83 (November

1838): 919–939; no. 84 (December 1838): 998–1014. For Burnouf's citation of Turnour, see Burnouf, *Introduction*, 261.

14 Auguste Barth, writing in 1880–1881, noted that Gogerly's works were 'now so very scarce' and indicated that some of the Pāli texts that Gogerly had translated had passed into Grimblot's collection. Auguste Barth, *The Religions of India*, trans. J. Wood (London: Trübner & Co., 1882), 107, n. 1. For a description of Grimblot's collection, see Jules Barthélemy Saint-Hilaire, 'Du Bouddhisme et de sa littérature à Ceylan: Collection de M. Grimblot, consul de France à Ceylan,' *Journal des savants* 1866:43–96, 100–116, and 151–166. For Gogerly's writings, see Arthur Stanley Bishop, *Ceylon Buddhism being the Collected Writings of Daniel John Gogerly* (London: Kegan Paul, Trench, Trübner & Co., 1908). For a brief description of Gogerly and Hardy, see Gurugé, *Living Fountains*, lxxx–lxxxi.

15 Robert Spence Hardy, *A Manual of Buddhism in its Modern Development* (1853; Varanasi: Chowkhamba Sanskrit Series, 1967); and *Legends and Theories of the Buddhists* (London: Williams & Norgate, 1866). See also Gurugé, *Living Fountains*, lxxx.

16 Burnouf's *Introduction à l'histoire du bouddhisme indien* was the first systematic study of the texts brought to Europe by Brian Houghton Hodgson from Nepal, with comparisons with the Pāli sources from Sri Lanka, Burma and Thailand. In the *Introduction*, Burnouf analyzed the texts of the 'northern school' in detail, and his plans were to compare the texts from the Sanskrit sources to those in Pāli, a task that was left uncompleted at the time of his death. When he died on May 28, 1852, he was working on an essay entitled 'Comparaison de quelques texts sancrites et pâlis.' For his own discussions of his comparative approach, see two of Burnouf's letters sent to Theodore Benfy (April 9, 1841 and April 30, 182) in Eugène Burnouf, *Choix de lettres d'Eugène Burnouf, 1825–1852*, ed. Laura Burnouf Delisle (Paris: H. Champion, 1891), 326ff. and 346; Burnouf, *Introduction*, xxxvii, 23–27, 65–66, n. 1 and 512–524; and finally, see Jules Barthélemy Saint-Hilaire's comments in 'Notice sur le travaux de M. Eugène Burnouf,' in Burnouf, *Introduction*, xxii.

17 Burnouf, *Introduction*, 569.

18 Burnouf, *Introduction*, 258. The French that I have translated here as 'knowledge' is 'science,' and could just as well be translated as the English 'science.' However, because the French means either science or knowledge, and because the notion that the Buddha's truths were a technology of salvation emerged much later in the writings of Max Weber, I have chosen 'knowledge' as the English translation. The translations from French and German that follow in this chapter are my own.

19 The passage from the *Avadāna-śataka* is also found in the *Divyāvadāna* and the *Sumāgadhāvadāna*. Burnouf, *Introduction*, 258, n. 1. In the 'Additions and Corrections,' Burnouf provides another citation for the four noble truths from the *Mahāvastu*, which he attributes to the Mahāsāṅghikas. He compared this fragment to the *Lalita-vistara* and found that the doctrine was the same. See Bournouf, *Introduction*, 569.

20 Burnouf, *Introduction*, 259.

21 Burnouf, *Introduction*, 259, n. 3, 260, n. 1 and 261, n. 3. The full references for Burnouf's sources are: Adoniram Judson, *A Dictionary of the Burman Language, with Explanations in English* (Calcutta: Baptist Mission Press, 1826); Benjamin Clough, *A Compendious Pāli Grammar with a Copious Vocabulary in the Same Language* (Colombo: Wesleyan Mission Press, 1924);

and George Turnour, 'An Examination.' See J. W. de Jong, *A Brief History*, 58–76, although de Jong does not discuss Judson's work.

22 Tweed, *American Encounter*, 5, 45, 171, n. 9.

23 Gurugé, *Living Fountains*, 61.

24 Benjamin Clough, *A Sinhalese-English Dictionary*, 2nd ed. (1830; Colombo: Wesleyan Mission Press, 1892), s.v. *chatussatya, saccavedita*.

25 Gurugé, *Living Fountains*, lxviii; and Turnour, 'An Examination.'

26 Edward Eldridge Salisbury, 'Memoir on the History of Buddhism,' *Journal of the American Oriental Society* 1 (1843–1849): 81–135 and 'M. Burnouf on the History of Buddhism in India,' *Journal of the American Oriental Society* 1 (1843–1849): 275–298.

27 Tweed, *American Encounter*, xix and 30.

28 Henry Clarke Warren, *Buddhism in Translations*, Harvard Oriental Series, vol. 3 (1896; Cambridge: Harvard University, 1906), 3:282.

29 For a discussion of American missionaries and their writings, see Tweed, *American Encounter*, 1–47.

30 Albrecht Weber, 'Über den Buddhismus [Ein Vortrag im Berliner Wissenschaftlichen verein, Gerhalten am 1. Marz 1856],' *Indische Skizzen* (Berlin: Dummlers, 1857), 46–47.

31 Weber, 'Über den Buddhismus,' 48.

32 Albrecht Weber, 'Le Bouddhisme,' trans. F. Baudry, *Revue germanique* 4:142–160. The reference is to Burnouf, *Introduction*, 629, and it is accurate: Burnouf provided an addendum to his text on page 629 in the 1844 edition of the *Introduction* in which he discussed the four noble truths. The addendum is exactly the same in the 1876 edition, although the pagination differs in the two editions.

33 See Lacôte's useful survey of French scholarship on Indian traditions for a fuller discussion of Burnouf's role in the field of Indian studies. Félix Lacôte, 'L'indianisme,' *Société asiatique: livre du centenaire* (1922): 219–249.

34 Review articles of the 1850s and 1860s and notes in the published works show that these men recognized their indebtedness to Burnouf and to each other. One example of the close-knit character of the circle in which these arguments were formed is found in a review by Philippe Foucaux of Obry's response to Barthélemy Saint-Hilaire, where Foucaux directly critiqued Barthélemy Saint-Hilaire's use of Burnouf while supporting several of Obry's own points. Philippe Édouard Foucaux, *Doctrine des bouddhistes sur le nirvāna* (Paris: Benjamin Duprat, 1864), 4.

35 Barth described Barthélemy Saint-Hilaire's book as the 'first rank' among popular works on Buddhism. Barth, *Religions of India*, 104, n. 1; Jules Barthélemy Saint-Hilaire, *Le Bouddha et sa religion*, 3d ed. (1860; Paris: Didier, 1862); *The Buddha and His Religion*, trans. Laura Ensor (London: George Routledge, 1895).

36 Weber, 'Über den Buddhismus,' 48. See also Barthélemy Saint-Hilaire, J. F. Obry, P. E. Foucaux and Max Müller, discussed below.

37 Almond suggests that the theme of suffering appealed to Victorians interpreters of Buddhism; this is an intriguing possibility that requires a more detailed study of the role of pessimism and suffering in British thought. See Almond, *British Discovery*, 81.

38 For a discussion of Weber's interpretation of nirvāṇa, see Guy Richard Welbon, *Buddhist Nirvāṇa and Its Western Interpreters* (Chicago: University of Chicago Press, 1968), 64–66. Essentially Weber wrote that Buddhist nirvāṇa was the same as Brahmanical notions of release insofar as they both sought release. Weber, 'Über den Buddhismus,' 46 and 50.

39 Weber, 'Über den Buddhismus,' 52.
40 Burnouf, *Introduction*, 259.
41 The interpretation of nirvāṇa as annihilation was at the center of the debate over the meaning of the term. Barthélemy Saint-Hilaire was not the first to offer this interpretation. In 1799 Francis Buchanan-Hamilton wrote that annihilation was not the correct translation of nirvāṇa, Buchanan-Hamilton, 'On the Religion,' 267. For a more extended discussion, see de Jong, *A Brief History*, 68–79.
42 Barthélemy Saint-Hilaire, *Le Bouddha*, viii.
43 Barthélemy Saint-Hilaire, *Le Bouddha*, 81–88.
44 Barthélemy Saint-Hilaire, *Le Bouddha*, 81.
45 Barthélemy Saint-Hilaire, *Le Bouddha*, 94. This passage is not difficult to render into English, but there is one word which requires a note. Barthélemy Saint-Hilaire's French clause 'il les charme par ses discours' loses a bit in my translation as 'he charms them with his discourses.' 'Charme' in French carries a stronger sense of allure than 'to charm' does in English; put differently, 'charme' has a hint of 'to cast a spell' that the English 'to charm' lacks.
46 Jules Mohl, 'Rapport sur les travaux du conseil de la Société asiatique, pendant l'année 1860–61, fait à la séance annuelle de la Société le 29 juin 1861,' *Journal asiatique*, 5e série, 18 (1861): 119–120.
47 J. B. F. Obry, *Du Nirvâna bouddhique en réponse à M. Barthélemy Saint-Hilaire* [Academy of Ameins 14 and 28 March, 1863] (Paris: Auguste Durand, 1863), 15–16.
48 Foucaux, *Doctrine des bouddhistes*, 2 and 27.
49 For an analysis of these different definitions of nirvāṇa, see Welbon, *Buddhist Nirvāṇa*, 79–100.
50 Foucaux, *Doctrine des bouddhistes*, 6–8.
51 Obry, *Du Nirvâna bouddhique*, 24.
52 Philippe Édouard Foucaux, *Rgya Tch'er rol pa, ou développement des jeux*, 2 vols. (Paris: Benjamin Duprat, 1847–1848).
53 Among these scholars who sought to reinterpret the Buddha's teachings to reflect a particular portrait of the Buddha were those who both admired and denigrated Buddhism, in part – but not always – because of the relationship between Buddhism and Christianity. For example, Ernst Eitel considered the Buddha to be a reformer with 'undoubted originality,' yet Eitel ultimately rejected the teachings of the Buddha. Even though the Buddha was cast in a positive light as a political, social, or moral reformer, many of these scholars dismissed the content of the doctrines they sought to understand – but not all of those who disagreed with the teachings of Buddhism did so on the basis of their allegiance to Christianity. Barthélemy Saint-Hilaire was liberal and sought to replace the claims of religion with a scientific basis; Taine was the editor of the *Journal des débats*, a journal known for its liberal and humanistic tone. On the other hand, Derôme and Deschamps rejected the claims of Buddhism because they did not compare favorably to Christianity, along with Eitel. Eitel was identified as having 'a wide reputation as a zealous and accomplished Missionary' in an 1871 review of his book, *Buddhism: Its Historical, Theoretical, and Popular Aspects in Three Lectures*. Eitel was known for other writings on Chinese Buddhism, although he was critiqued at the time for his series of lectures on Buddhism for (what we call today) his ethnocentrism. Eitel's work, however, followed the pattern established in the previous decade: he located the four noble truths at the center of the Buddha's teaching at one point and explains that the doctrine of transmigration was the key to the Buddha's

system at another. Eitel had a distinct distaste for these doctrines, and like most scholars of this period, he both inherited and contributed to the Orientalist representation of Buddhism: while the doctrine of transmigration may be frightful to descendents of Western nations, he wrote, '[t]here may be rather something attractive in it for many.' And again: 'It is a different thing for the sons of hot climates, with the indolent Hindoo, with the sedentary Chinaman. To him life itself has no particular fascination. . . . The clever founder of Buddhism, Shakyamuni himself, knew this well, and therefore he made this dogma of the soul's transmigration the very centre of his system, and daily he preached it, and daily his fanatic followers spread this doctrine farther and farther.' Ernest J. Eitel, *Buddhism: Its Historical, Theoretical and Popular Aspects*, 2nd ed. (London: Trübner & Co., 1873), 56. Within this account of Buddhism that simultaneously praised and damned the Orient, Eitel placed the four noble truths at the heart of the doctrines of all the schools of Buddhism: 'All start from the so-called four truths (Aryâsatyâni) or the idea that misery is a necessary attribute of sentient existence, that the accumulation of misery is caused by desire, that the extinction of desire is possible and that there is a path that leads to that extinction.' In Eitel's arrangement of the Buddha's teachings, the four noble truths were followed with a discussion of the aggregates (Sanskrit *skandhas*), dependent arising (Sanskrit *pratītyasamutpāda*), and, finally, nirvāṇa. See Eitel, *Buddhism*, 10 and 65. Thomas Watters (the author of *On Yuan Chwang's Travels in India* published after his death from his notes on Hsüan-tsang's Hsi-yü-chi) was one of Eitel's critics. Watters noted Eitel's failure to maintain his impartiality: 'Mr. Eitel extols Buddhism in a certain sense, but it is plain that he does not like it, and that he regards it as a bane in the world . . . .' Thomas Watters, 'Mr. Eitel's Three Lectures on Buddhism,' *The Chinese Recorder* 4 (August 1871): 64. Eitel's work shows that the four noble truths were cast as central teachings of the Buddha by those who disliked Buddhism in ways that were very similar to those used by writers who were more favorably disposed toward Buddhism; the pattern that defined the four noble truths as the most important teaching of the Buddha was well established by the 1870s.

54 Friedrich Max Müller, *Selected Essays on Language, Mythology, and Religion*, vol. 2 (London: Longman's, Green & Co., 1881), 207.

55 Müller presented a more comprehensive rationale for his conclusions in the introduction to his translations of the *Dhammapada*. Beginning with the question of whether it is possible to distinguish between Buddhism and the personal teachings of the Buddha, he stated that 'in general, all honest inquirers must oppose a No to this question, and confess that it is useless to try to cast a glance beyond the boundaries of the Buddhist canon.' Müller wanted to push this further: 'If it happens that on certain points we find in different parts of the canon, not only doctrines differing from each other, but plainly contradictory to each other, it follows, surely that one only of these can have belonged to the Buddha personally. In such a case, therefore, I belive we have a right to choose, and I believe that we shall be justified in accepting that view as the original one, the one peculiar to the Buddha himself, which harmonizes *least* with the later system of orthodox Buddhism [italics in original].' On the basis of this, Müller rejected the definition of nirvāṇa as nihilism. F. Max Müller, *Buddha's Dhammapada or 'Path of Virtue'* (London: Trübner & Co., 1870), xxvii–xxix.

56 Müller, *Selected Essays*, 222–223.

57 Müller, *Selected Essays*, 302–304.

58 Müller, *Selected Essays*, 201.

59 Other authors who wrote in the 1860s supported Barthélemy Saint-Hilaire's interpretation of nirvāṇa as annihilation; the four noble truths were more central in these writings and the doctrine was still linked to the inferred moral reforms of the Buddha. There were a number of articles on the relative merits of Buddhism and Christianity in the popular journals of Europe at this time. For example, l'Abbé Auguste F. Deschamps and Derôme wrote about the relationship between Christianity and Buddhism, and both readily accepted the idea that nirvāṇa meant annihilation. Barthélemy Saint-Hilaire's argument was taken at face value and subsumed into a portrait of the Buddha as a reformer – whose central teaching was the four noble truths. In 1861, Deschamps described the four noble truths as the fundamental teaching of the Buddha. A member of the Société Asiatique and an author of a book on Buddhism and Christianity, Deschamps depicted the Buddha as the one who had reformed the Brahmanical tradition and 'who preached salvation to all!' Auguste F. Deschamps, *Les Origines du bouddhisme, vues nouvelle pour servir aux travaux de l'apologétique chrètienne* (Paris: Benjamin Duprat, 1861), 12; see also *Journal asiatique* 18 (July 1861): 144. Deschamps wrote that the four noble truths were the fundamental truths and teachings of Śākyamuni. Deschamps, *Les origines*, 23–24. Deschamps made an effort to explain that one need not be intimately familiar with Indian philosophy to understand the four noble truths. After detailing the four noble truths, he compared them to Job's struggle, seeking to illustrate what he saw as the fundamental insight of Buddhism that life is suffering. Deschamps, *Les origines*, 24. Four years later, Derôme put forth a similar argument. In a joint review of Vasili'ev *Der Buddhismus, seine Dogmen, Geschichte und Literatur* and Barthélemy Saint-Hilaire's book, Derôme wrote that Buddhism was quite similar to Christianity insofar as the Buddha's teachings contained both a political and a moral revolution. Vasily Vasil'ev, *Der Buddhismus, seine Dogmen, Geschichte und Literatur* (Saint Petersbourg: Kaiserliche Akademie der Wissenschaften, 1860); L. Derôme, 'Le Bouddhisme et la critique des idées religieuses en Occident,' *Revue Contemporaine* [1865]: 314–351 in *Vignaud Pamphlets: Buddhism* (University of Michigan Graduate Library, Ann Arbor). Derôme explained that the theory of suffering rests at the base of Buddhist doctrine. Derôme, 'Le Bouddhisme,' 324–325. While Derôme and Deschamps both accepted the doctrine of nirvāṇa as the goal of the Buddha's teachings, they focused on the apparent moral lesson of the four noble truths that 'life is suffering.' These French authors echoed the Victorian theme of Buddhism as a pessimistic religion of suffering and placed the four noble truths at the heart of that conception.

60 H[ipppolyte Adolphe] Taine, 'Le Bouddhisme, *Die Religion des Buddha und ihre Entstehung*, par M. Koeppen,' *Journal de débats* 3 March 1864, n. 1.

61 See Shcherbatskoi, 'The Doctrine,' 894–896.

62 Taine, '*Le Bouddhisme*,' 4 March 1864.

63 Taine, 'Le Bouddhisme,' 4 March 1864.

64 Taine, 'Le Bouddhisme,' 4 March 1864, n. 2.

65 Paul Ambrose Bigandet, *The Life or Legend of Gaudama: The Buddha of the Burmese*, 2nd enlarged edition (1858; London: Kegan Paul, Trench & Trübner & Co., 1866), 203. The book was issued in four editions by 1911 (1858, 1866, 1880, 1911) and was most recently reprinted in Varanasi in 1979. For a short discussion of Bigandet's work, see Hallisey, 'Roads Taken,' 40.

66 Heinz Braun, 'The Buddhist Era in the *Mālālaṅkāravatthu*,' *The Dating of the Historical Buddha*, ed. Heinz Bechert (Göttingen: Vandenhoeck & Ruprecht, 1991), 47–48.

67 Bigandet, *The Life*, 203.
68 Bigandet, *The Life*, xv–xvi.
69 James de Alwis, 'Buddhism: Its Origin, History, and Doctrines; Its Scriptures and their language, the Pāli,' *Journal of the Pāli Text Society* 1 (1883): 1–39.
70 De Alwis makes his reasons for providing a survey of the Sinhalese literary tradition clear in the following dedication: 'During the proceedings in one of the state prosecutions in 1848, it was elicited in evidence, that there were, in this comparatively small Island, many natives who had never seen an Englishman. This, doubtless, is to the people a source of regret, and may, under peculiar circumstances, prove to be a serious grievance: but how much greater must be the vexation and annoyance to thousands to know, that the majority of those whom they *do* see, and with whom they hold official discourse, do not understand the Singhalese, and cannot correctly interpret the language of their complaints, or the expression of their grievances? – and how often, indeed, does an ignorance of the native character, the habits and feelings of the people (all of which spring as it were from their language), induce Europeans to act in a manner hostile to the general interests of the Island?' See De Alwis, *Survey*, vi. The events of 1848 to which he refers were riots that took place in Colombo, Matale, and Kurunegala, in protest against a new set of taxes imposed by the British: 'the shop-tax, the gun-tax, the dog-tax, and the Road Ordinance, all of which bore heavily on the local population, chiefly, the peasants.' For a discussion of the riots of 1848 and the quote on the taxes cited above, see K. M. de Silva, ed., *Letters on Ceylon 1846–1850, The Administration of Viscount Torrington and the 'Rebellion' of 1848 – The Private Correspondence of the Third Earl Grey (Secretary of State for the Colonies 1846–1852) and Viscount Torrington* (Kandy and Colombo: K. V. G. de Silva & Sons, 1965), 5.
71 The author and date of composition of this text are unknown, although it is likely that it was written earlier than the 17th century. The various fragments were compiled into a complete text in 1845 by Krom Somdet Phra Paramānujit Jinnorot, the head of Wat Jetuphon, at the request of Rāma III. It is not surprising that Alabaster would have had access to this life of the Buddha during his time in Thailand. See H. Saddhātissa, 'Pāli Literature of Thailand,' in *Buddhist Studies in Honour of I. B. Horner*, ed. L. Cousins, A. Kunst, and K. R. Norman (Boston and Holland: D. Reidel Publishing Co., 1974), 218.
72 Henry Alabaster, *The Wheel of the Law, Buddhism Illustrated from the Siamese Sources* (London: Trübner & Co., 1871), 32.
73 Alabaster, *The Wheel of the Law*, 104.
74 De Jong, *A Brief History*, 76.
75 See J. W. de Jong for a discussion of the translation of Buddhist manuscripts during this period. See de Jong, *A Brief History*, 71f. Gurugé has an extensive discussion of Subhuti Nakaya Thera's contributions to Childers' dictionary based on correspondence. See Gurugé, *Living Fountains*, 3–40.
76 For a short history of the Pāli Text Society, see K. R. Norman, 'The Pāli Text Society, 1881–1981,' in *Collected Papers*, 2:194–199.
77 Barth, *The Religions of India*, 107 n. 2.
78 Louis de la Vallée Poussin, *Bouddhisme: Études et matériaux* (London: Luzac & Co., 1898), 21.
79 Feer, 'Études bouddhiques,' 463, n. 1 and 2.
80 Feer, 'Études bouddhiques,' 350–351.
81 Feer, 'Études bouddhiques,' 462–472.

82 For Senart's argument, see Émile Charles Marie Senart, *Essai sur la légende du Buddha son charactère et ses origines*, 2nd edition (Paris: Ernest Leroux, 1882), 442–463; for his methodological comments, see xi-xii; see also É. Senart, 'Origines Bouddhiques,' *Musée Guimet Annales: Bibliothèque de vulgarisation* 25 (1907): 115–158. De Jong's discussion of this exchange is also useful; see de Jong 'A Brief History,' 7 no. 1 (1974): 78–83.
83 For Oldenberg's objections to Senart, see Hermann Oldenberg, *Buddha: His Life, His Doctrine, His Order*, trans. William Hoey (1881; Delhi: Indological Book House, 1971), 74.
84 Oldenberg, *Buddha*, 75.
85 T. W. Rhys Davids, 'Buddhism and Christianity,' *The International Quarterly* 7 (1903): 13.
86 For an interesting discussion of T. W. Rhys David's biography of the Buddha, see Hallisey, 'Roads Taken,' 34–38.
87 Oldenberg, *Buddha*, 78f.; T. W. Rhys Davids, 'Buddhism and Christianity,' 1–13.
88 Senart said little about the four noble truths, although he discussed the significance of the *dhammacakṣus* and the eightfold path in 'Bouddhisme et Yoga,' 355. In his discussion of these two doctrines, he anticipated La Vallée Poussin's treatment of the four noble truths as an integral part of a fundamentally yogic system of salvation. See Émile Senart, 'Bouddhisme et Yoga,' *Revue de l'histoire des religions* 42 (1900): 355. For a very useful overview of the debates over the question of history and mythology in studies of Buddhism, see J. W. de Jong, 'The Study of Buddhism: Problems and Perspectives,' in *Buddhist Studies*, ed. Gregory Schopen (China: Asian Humanities Press, 1979), 23–26.
89 Ananda Wickremeratne, *The Genesis of An Orientalist: Thomas William Rhys Davids and Buddhism in Sri Lanka* (Delhi: Motilal Banarsidass, 1984), 162ff.
90 T. W. Rhys Davids, *Lectures on the Origin and Growth of Religion* (New York: G. P. Putnam's Sons, 1882), 30.
91 Rhys Davids, *Lectures*, 29.
92 In a comparison of Buddhism and Christianity, Rhys Davids wrote that Buddhism was different from other Indian schools in only three things: 'the emancipation from the soul-theory, the Noble (or perhaps Aryan) Eightfold Path, and the manner in which these two ideas were made to dominate the whole system. . . .' Rhys Davids, 'Buddhism and Christianity,' 10.
93 T. W. Rhys Davids, *Buddhist India* (New York: G. P. Putnam's Sons, 1903), 246–247.
94 Rhys Davids, *Buddhist India*, 256–257.
95 Rhys Davids, *Lectures*, 13, 87–88.
96 T. W. Rhys Davids, *Buddhism: Being a Sketch of the Life and Teachings of Gautama, the Buddha* (London: Society for Promoting Christian Knowledge, 1899), 48, n. 1; see also T. W. Rhys Davids, *Buddhist Suttas* (Oxford: Clarendon Books, 1881).
97 Rhys Davids, *Buddhism*, 106.
98 Rhys Davids, 'Buddha's First Sermon,' *The Fortnightly Review* 39 (1879): 899.
99 Rhys Davids, 'Buddha's First Sermon,' 901.
100 Rhys Davids, 'Buddha's First Sermon,' 909–910.
101 Oldenberg, *Buddha*, 109f.
102 Oldenberg, *Buddha*, 212.
103 Oldenberg, *Buddha*, 205.
104 Barth, *The Religions of India*, 105.

105 Barth, *The Religions of India*, 108.
106 Henrick Kern, *A Manual of Indian Buddhism* (Delhi: Indological Book House, 1968), 12. See also Hendrick Kern, *Histoire du bouddhisme dans l'Inde*, 2 vols., trans. Gédéon Huet (Paris: Ernest Leroux, 1901), 2:19–20. See de Jong's comments on Kern in 'The Study of Buddhism,' 23–24.
107 Kern, *Histoire du bouddhisme*, 1:79.
108 Kern, *Histoire du bouddhisme*, 1:216, n. 2 and 247.
109 The summary of the origins of Buddhism which appeared in Zimmer's posthumously published volume, *Philosophies of India*, reflects Kern's insight that the Buddha was a physician. The *Philosophies of India* was edited and, at certain points, written by Joseph Campbell, who used Zimmer's notes from a series of lectures that he gave at Columbia University in the spring of 1942. Zimmer fell ill five weeks after the lectures in 1942 and was thus unable to complete his projected volume. Campbell explained that the chapters on Buddhism were fairly complete, unlike later portions of the manuscript, and were easily edited. Concerning the four noble truths, Zimmer wrote: '. . . the teaching of the Enlightened One . . . was presented as therapy, a treatment or cure, for those strong enough to follow it – a method and a process of healing. . . . Following the procedure of the physician of his day inspecting a patient, the Buddha makes four statements concerning the case of man. These are the so-called 'Four Noble Truths' which constitute the heart and kernel of his doctrine. . . . The Buddha's thoroughgoing treatment is guaranteed to eradicate the cause of the sickly spell and dream of ignorance, and thus to make possible the attainment of a state of serene, awakened perfection. No philosophical explanation of man or the universe is required, only this spiritual physician's program of psycho-dietetics.' Heinrich R. Zimmer, *Philosophies of India* (Princeton: Bollingen Foundation, 1951), 266–269.
110 The entire issue of the December 1992/January 1993 Paris edition of *Vogue* was devoted to the Dalai Lama, and one of the articles is entitled 'Quand le maître des médecines est Bouddha.' Although the article is about Bhaiṣajya-guru, the Tibetan Medicine Buddha, the author relies on the assertion that the four noble truths are based on a medical model to relate the Tibetan tradition to early Buddhist teachings. Fernand Meyer, 'Quand le maître des médecines est Bouddha,' *Vogue (Paris)* No. 732 (December 1992-January 1993): 174 and 290.
111 Govind Chandra Pande, *Studies in the Origins of Buddhism* (Allahabad: University of Allahabad, 1957), 398–399.
112 Wilhelm Halbfass, *Tradition and Reflection: Explorations in Indian Thought* (Albany: State University of New York Press, 1991), 242–249; and Kenneth G. Zysk, *Asceticism and Healing in Ancient India* (Oxford: Oxford University Press, 1991), 38ff.
113 Monier Monier-Williams, *Buddhism, in its Connexions with Brāhmanism and Hinduism* (London: John Murray, 1889), 42, 56, 99–102.
114 This mixture of acceptance and rejection of different aspects of Buddhism was characteristic of Orientalism; see Almond for a further discussion. Barthélemy Saint-Hilaire and Hardy both soundly rejected the governments of Asia and the influence of Buddhism on politics. See Barthélemy Saint Hilaire, 149; Robert Spence Hardy, *The British Government and the Idolatry of Ceylon* (London: Crofts & Blenkarn, 1841), 45–46.
115 Henry Clarke Warren, *Buddhism in Translation*, Harvard Oriental Series, vol. 3 (1896; Cambridge: Harvard University, 1906), 282.

116 Louis de la Vallée Poussin, *The Way to Nirvāṇa: Six Lectures on Ancient Buddhism as a Discipline of Salvation* (Cambridge, 1917; Delhi: Sri Satguru Publications, 1982), 4. See also Louis de la Vallée Poussin, *Nirvāṇa* (Paris: Gabriel Beauchesne, 1925); *Le dogme et la philosophie du bouddhisme*, Études sur l'histoire des religions, vol. 6. (Paris: Gabriel Beauchesne, 1930); and 'Musilā et Nārada: Le chemin du nirvana,' *Mélanges chinois et bouddhiques* 5 (1937): 189–222.

117 La Vallée Poussin, *The Way*, 4.

118 La Vallée Poussin, *The Way*, 106 and 153; Louis de La Vallée Poussin, *Bouddhisme: Opinions sur l'histoire de la dogmatique* (Paris: Gabriel Beauchesne, 1909), 132.

119 La Vallée Poussin, *The Way*, 144, n. 1.

120 La Vallée Poussin, *The Way*, 147 and 151.

121 For La Vallée Poussin's relationship with Senart, see Étienne Lamotte, 'Notice sur Louis de La Vallée Poussin,' *Annuaire de l'Academie royale des sciences, des lettres et des beaux-arts* 131 (1965): 145–168. For Senart's discussion of the yogic dimensions of the Buddha, see Senart, 'Origines Bouddhiques,' 145–158; see also Émile Senart, 'Bouddhisme et yoga,' *Revue de l'histoire des religions* 42 (1900): 345–365 and 'Nirvāṇa,' *Album Kern: opstellen geschreven te eere van Dr. H. Kern* (Leiden: E. J. Brill, 1903): 101–104. See de Jong's discussion in *A Brief History*, 86–88; 96–98 and his comments on La Vallée Poussin in a review of Welbon's *The Buddhist Nirvāṇa and Its Western Interpreters*. De Jong, 'Review of *The Buddhist Nirvāṇa*,' 399–400.

122 Senart discusses the four noble truths and the *dhammacakkhu* as inspired by the practices of yoga: 'The *dharmacakṣus*, 'the eye of the Law,' which marks the perception of religious truths, is in the same way certainly a metaphor, inspired by the supernatural power which the practice of *samādhi* was supposed to develop in the yogi; likewise, the Buddhist truth appears superimposed on the presumably ancient edifice of the magic faculties.' Senart, 'Bouddhisme et yoga,' 355.

123 La Vallée Poussin, *The Way*, 151.

124 Max Weber, *The Religion of India: The Sociology of Hinduism and Buddhism*, trans. and ed. H. Gerth and D. Martindale (Glencoe, IL: The Free Press, 1958), 206.

125 Weber, *Religions of India*, 206.

126 Max Weber, *Economy and Society: An Outline of Interpretive Sociology*, ed. Guenther Roth and Claus Wittich (Berkeley: University of California Press, 1978), 1:13.

127 Weber, *Religions of India*, 227.

128 Weber, *Religions of India*, 222.

129 It is perhaps important to recall that Weber was not primarily a historian. He was a sociologist who sought to identify ideal types of rational activity, predominantly economic activity. Weber never intended that his studies be taken as history, though he drew upon authoritative secondary studies of Buddhism that dominated the late nineteenth and early twentieth centuries. He distinguished the sociological enterprise and history: the sociological enterprise 'seeks to formulate type concepts and generalized uniformities of empirical process,' where history is 'oriented to the causal analysis and explanation of individual actions, structures and personalities possessing cultural significance.' Weber, *Economy and Society*, 1:19. Although both sociology and history share the same kind of empirical data, the goals of each enterprise are different, and there are significant differences between La Vallée Poussin's and Weber's studies.

130 Edward J. Thomas, *The Life of Buddha as Legend and History* (London: Routledge, Kegan & Paul, 1927); see also Edward J. Thomas, *History of Buddhist Thought* (New York: Barnes & Noble, 1951), 13 and 42.

131 Nalinaksha Dutt, *Aspects of Mahāyāna Buddhism and its Relation to Hinayāna* (London: Luzac & Co., 1930), 49.

132 M[oriz] Winternitz, *A History of Indian Literature*, 2 vols. (Calcutta: University of Calcutta, 1933), 2:2.

133 Bimala Churn Law, *Concepts of Buddhism* (Leiden: Kern Institute, 1937), 27.

134 C. A. F. Rhys Davids, 'Buddhism and the Negative,' *Journal of the Pāli Text Society* 1924–1927:245.

135 She makes this point in a book review: 'It is significant that the first sermon, with the exception of the fourfold stereotyped phrase for the Goal – probably a monkish gloss – is *not a gospel for the monk alone*. It is for Everyman [italics in original].' C. A. F. Rhys Davids, 'Review,' *Bulletin of the Oriental Society* 6 (1930–1932): 356.

136 F[edor] I[ppolitovich] Shcherbatskoi, *The Conception of Buddhist Nirvāṇa*, Revised & Enlarged edition (Leningrad: Academy of Sciences of the USSR, 1927; Varanasi: Bharatiya Vidya Prakashan, [1968?]), 27–28. See also his dismissal of A. B. Keith's assertion that the four noble truths were an original teaching of the Buddha. Shcherbatskoi, 'Doctrine of the Buddha,' 892.

137 F. I. Shcherbatskoi, *Buddhist Logic*, 2 vols. (1930–1932; New Delhi: Oriental Books Reprint Corporation, 1984), 7.

138 Horner, *Early Buddhist Theory*, 34.

139 Horner, *Early Buddhist Theory*, 26.

140 Horner, *Early Buddhist Theory*, 37.

141 For a useful discussion of Horner and her work, see R. E. and C. W. Iggleden, 'Isaline Blew Horner: A Biographical Sketch,' in *Buddhist Studies in Honour of I. B. Horner*, ed. L. Cousins, A. Kunst, and K. R. Norman (Dordrecht, Holland and Boston: D. Reidel Publishing Co., 1974), 1–8.

142 Louis Renou and Jean Filliozat, *L'Inde classique: manuel des études indiennes* (1953; Paris: École Française d'Extrême-Orient, 1985), 2:519.

143 Étienne Lamotte, 'La lêgende du Buddha,' *Revue de l'histoire des religions* 134 (1947–1948): 37–71.

144 Lamotte, 'La lêgende,' 70f.

145 Lamotte, HIB, 23–47.

146 Hajime Nakamura, *Indian Buddhism: A Survey with Bibliographical Notes* (Japan: Kansei University of Foreign Studies, 1980), 66 and 38. Nakamura provides extensive notes to research done on the four noble truths in Japan.

147 De Alwis, *Survey*, clxxxiii. He attributes the grammar to the period of Parakrama Bahu IV (1319–1347) and quotes from Turnour on the reign of Parakrama Bahu IV on the bottom of this page.

148 Generally, see Almond, Tweed, and Lopez, Jr., *Curators of the Buddha* for their discussions of Orientalism and the impact of colonialism on studies of Buddhism.

149 Bernard S. Cohen, *Colonialism and Its Forms of Knowledge: The British in India* (Princeton: Princeton University Press, 1996), 55.

150 That de Alwis did so by advocating a position that has grown into the Sinhalese nationalist movement is comprehensible, but the price for these arguments has been paid in the deaths of thousands of Sri Lankans since 1983. His work anticipated the Sinhalese nationalist movement by a full century, but we can still see arguments that have now become integral to

current Buddhist chauvinism in Sri Lanka, such as references to Malabar 'usurpation' of 'the Sinhalese throne' and the Malabar destruction of the Sinhalese language: 'few indeed are the works that escaped the fury of the Malabars . . . . This was the third act of the kind; but alas! it was not the last.' De Alwis, *Survey*, clxvii.

151 Bond, *Word of the Buddha*, 34–99.

CHAPTER SEVEN

Symbols, Propositions, and Religious Experiences

This is how Buddhism is a religion: in default of gods, it admits the existence of sacred things, namely, the four noble truths and the practices derived from them.

Emile Durkheim (1912)[1]

Symbols and Direct Experiences

This final chapter begins with the observation is that the categories of symbol and doctrinal propositions have been employed as if they consisted of two kinds of religious experiences that were perceived to be distinct from each other by scholars of religion in the early part of this century. Symbols were thought to represent a certain kind of direct, sensuous, and immediate experience that transcended the normal parameters of daily life. Theorists who sought to define the origins of this experience did not all agree in their precise definitions of symbol, but they were consistent in their descriptions of symbols as bearers of a direct and immediate experience. In contrast, philosophy was considered to be embedded in the logical propositions of doctrines that were understood to be the focus of certain beliefs. Definitions of symbols were contructed within the larger question of the origin of religions. Theories on the origin of religion were proposed by such scholars as Robertson Smith, J. G. Frazer, E. B. Tylor, Emile Durkheim, Lucien Lévy-Bruhl and others; all of these scholars operated within a framework that distinguished the experiences of primitive cultures from those of civilized cultures, although they made this distinction in different ways.

Lévy-Bruhl was the author of one of the more popular and influential theories put forth as an explanation for the thinking of primitive cultures. He suggested that 'primitives' had turned their back on what they recognized as logical thinking; then, he identified the thinking of these 'primitive cultures' as pre-logical. Lévy-Bruhl began with collective representations, by which he meant the intellectual grasping of the idea of an object. Where 'we' distinguish between the particular elements of the representation and the 'essential relation to the object which it makes known to us,' 'primitives' make so such distinction. 'They' cannot separate 'ideas or images of objects by themselves apart from the emotions and passions which evoke these ideas or are evoked by them.'[2] Briefly, Lévy-Bruhl defined the pre-logic of 'primitives' as mystical, lacking in discursive analysis, indifferent to secondary causes, lacking reflection, and consisting of direct experience.

> At the very moment when he perceives what is presented to his senses, the primitive represents to himself the mystic force which is manifesting itself thus. He does not 'infer' the one from the other any more than we 'infer' the meaning of a word from the sound in our ears. . . . It is not a process accomplished in two succeeding moments, it takes place all at once. In this sense, then, preconnections amount to intuitions.[3]

The pre-logical mind is mystical because the 'primitive' immediately perceives a power acting outside of his own and thus gives 'implicit faith in *the presence and agency* of powers which are invisible and inaccessible to the senses. . . .'[4] Lévy-Bruhl's mystical mind of the 'primitive' is radically different than the logical mind of 'civilized man.' What appear as concepts to a 'civilized' culture appear as objects to a 'primitive' culture; to try to assimilate 'their' thinking to 'our' thought would 'despoil them of what there is in them that is elementally concrete, emotional, and vital.'[5]

Lévy-Bruhl did not often use the term symbol, but the thinking that he has defined as pre-logical has been taken by scholars who followed him as a description of the kind of thinking associated with symbols. That pre-logical thought is opposed to logical and conceptual analysis is evident even in this brief look at Lévy-Bruhl's ideas. Lévy-Bruhl's romanticized pre-logical mind – rich in emotion, concrete, and immediate – is perhaps a step beyond Frazer's contempt for 'primitives'. Frazer found little of value in symbolism – which he characterized as 'the decorous though transparent veil which a refined age loves to throw over its own ignorance of the past.'[6] Lévy-Bruhl both reified and segregated the pre-logical from the logical mind, forming two distinct models which he considered to accurately describe two kinds of thinking.

Writing in the same period as Lévy-Bruhl, Durkheim sought not to separate these two kinds of thinking but rather to draw them together on an evolutionary continuum. The origin of religion, he argued, was also the origin of logical thought. In his analysis of totems and the clan as the crucial context out of which religion emerges, Durkheim assigned a central role to symbols. The catalyst that produces religious experiences, and thus religion, he explained at length, was the totem which came to embody a particular emotional experience for a group of people. In Durkheim's theory, a totem is an animal, plant, or object that serves as an emblem for the identity of the clan insofar as it is the vehicle for a set of deeply felt emotions that are attached to the totem.

> In fact, it is a well-known law that the sentiments aroused in us by something spontaneously attach themselves to the symbol which represents them. . . . This transference of sentiments comes simply from the fact that the idea of a thing and the idea of its symbol are closely united in our minds; the result is that the emotions provoked by the one extend contagiously to the other. But this contagion, which takes place in every case to a certain degree, is much more complete and more marked when the symbol is something simple, definite and easily representable, while the thing itself, owing to its dimensions, the number of its parts and the complexity of their arrangement, is difficult to hold in the mind.[7]

Durkheim shifted the locus of the discussion to the interactions between a totemic symbol and the group of people who share a certain emotional experience. The clan, he wrote, 'awakens within [its members] the idea of external forces which dominate them and exalt them. . . .'[8] The intensely felt emotion that is conveyed by a symbol is simply the totality of the clan, projected beyond the clan and its members and experienced as something that comes from beyond them. For Durkheim, the origin of religion thus lies in the dynamics of the clan itself through the mediation of the totemic symbol.

Durkheim explained that the significant features of a symbol are its simplicity, concreteness, and forcefulness in conveying the emotions collectively experienced by an assembly of people.

> The sentiments experienced fix themselves upon it [i.e., the symbol] for it is the only concrete object upon which they can fix themselves. It [i.e., the symbol] continues to bring them to mind and to evoke them after the assembly has dissolved, for it survives the assembly, being carved upon the instruments of the cult, upon the sides of rocks, upon bucklers, etc. By it, the emotions experienced are perpetually sustained and revived. Everything happens just as if they inspired them directly.[9]

He explains that a symbol functions because it is simple, not complex; concrete, not abstract; and the bearer of emotions as well as ideas. Beyond the symbol, emotional experience is passed on through rituals; and, in the end, 'religious force is nothing other than the collective and anonymous force of the clan.'[10] This religious force is the same for magic and religion; and, he suggested, it was the origin for what we now call logic.[11] For Durkheim, the origin of religion lay in a collectively-felt, intense experience whose immediacy and direct experience was transferred and embodied in a symbol.

Durkheim explained logic in both civilized and primitive cultures with reference to the experiences of a group – not with reference to a pre-logical mind. Even though he argued that the origins of logic lay in the origins of religions and did not pose two different kinds of thinking as did Lévy-Bruhl, Durkheim's work is still characterized by a distinction between experiences that are direct and emotional (and projected onto symbols) and those which are reflective and conceptual. Durkheim was aware of these two categorizations of experience, and he used these categories to classify the various theories of the origin of religion.

> The theorists who have undertaken to explain religion in rational terms have generally seen in it before all else a system of ideas, corresponding to some determined object. This object has been conceived in a multitude of ways: nature, the infinite, the unknowable, the ideal, etc.; but these differences matter but little. In any case, it was the conceptions and beliefs which were considered as the essential elements of religions. . . .
>
> But the believers, the men who lead the religious life and have a direct sensation of what it really is, object to this way of regarding it, saying that it does not correspond to their daily experience. In fact, they feel that the real function of religion is not to make us think, to enrich our knowledge, nor to add to the conceptions which we owe to science others of another origin and another character, but rather, it is to make us act, to aid us to live. The believer who has communicated with his god is not merely a man who sees new truths of which the unbeliever is ignorant; he is a man who is *stronger.* He feels within him more force, either to endure the trials of existence, or to conquer them. It is as though he were raised above the miseries of the world, because he is raised above his condition as a mere man; he believes that he is saved from evil, under whatever form he may conceive this evil.[12]

Wilhelm Schmidt was to later characterize these two approaches as the intellectualist and the emotionalist; E. E. Evans-Pritchard used Schmidt's terms as a framework for his Sir D. Owen Evans Lectures at the University College of Wales that he delivered in the spring of 1962 (and which were published a few years later as *Theories of Primitive Religions*).[13]

Lévy-Bruhl and Durkheim arranged these two sorts of experience – the direct and emotional, and the logical and more philosophical – in different ways. Lévy-Bruhl's distinction was on the basis of culture; pre-logical and logical thinking existed for him at the same point in time in different parts of the world. Durkheim distinguished them in evolutionary terms within which the origin of religion – an intense, direct, and emotional experience felt collectively within a clan – gave rise to conceptual analysis. Despite the very different theories of these two scholars, the distinction between logic and direct experience, or the intellect and emotion (as Schmidt put it) was fundamental for both scholars.

In his conclusion to *Elementary Forms of the Religious Life* Durkheim laid out his analysis of how religion gave rise to philosophical analysis. He explained first that his theories of the role of the clan incorporated both 'intellectual' theories of the origin of religion and 'emotional' theories by showing how an ideal is necessary for all societies and how the roots of scientific thought lie in the origins of religion. Then he suggested that 'there is something eternal in religion: it is the cult and the faith.' One of his final propositions was that religions will always have a dimension of speculation which cannot be replaced by science.[14]

Durkheim explained in greater detail how logic has its roots in the origins of religion, or as he rephrased his own question, 'what has been able to make social life so important a source for the logical life?'[15] He pointed out that 'logical thought is made up of concepts.' To explain the role of society in the production of logic is to understand that logical concepts are not restricted to general concepts. The difference is one of degree; concepts are both general and particular. Therefore, he concluded,

> the concept must be defined by other characteristics. It is opposed to sensual representations of every order – sensations, perceptions, or images – by the following properties.[16]

These properties are, first, sensual representations in perpetual flux where the concept is outside time and change – 'language is something fixed; it changes but very slowly and consequently it is the same with the conceptual system which it expresses.[17] Second, the concept is universal 'or at least capable of becoming so.' Sensuous experiences, by definition, are not.

Durkheim brought his discussion back to his touchstone argument: the 'nature of the concept, thus defined, bespeaks its origin. If it is common to all, it is the work of the community.'[18] He continued his argument by suggesting that concepts were collective representations – in much the same way that Lévy-Bruhl sought to show how 'primitive peoples' grasped collective representations (with the pre-logical mentality). The part that logical thought has in a society is revealed only after an individual within a group has recognized the 'intellectual kingdom in which he participates' apart from his own private ideas, sensations, or images.[19]

> This is possible only from the moment when, above the fugitive conceptions which they owe to sensuous experience, men have succeeded in conceiving a whole world of stable ideas, the common ground of all intelligences. In fact, logical thinking is always impersonal thinking, and is also thought *sub species Æternitatis* – as though for all time. Impersonality and stability are the two characteristics of truth.[20]

By the end of the conclusion to *Elementary Forms of the Religious Life*, Durkheim had established an argument for the emergence of conceptions and logical thinking. An outline of his argument follows.

First, logical thinking has its origins in the origin of religion – that collective experience of the clan that is projected onto a totemic symbol. Second, logical thinking and propositions are concepts, and concepts are distinguished from sensuous experiences. Concepts are timeless, while sensuous experiences fluctuate and shift with time; concepts are universal, while sensuous experiences are particular. Finally, he concluded that the two characteristics of concepts – impersonality and stability – are also those of truth. In the opening pages of his conclusion, Durkheim had identified already the two types of theories of the origin of religion: those that sought to explain the emergence of religions in rational terms and those that recognized that from the inside out, from the experiences of practitioners, religion is a direct experience intended to influence the way humans act and live in the world. He united these two approaches into a single theory that identified the origins of logical thinking in the process by which a clan 'awakens within [its members] the idea of external forces which dominate them and exalt them. . . .' Having united the emotional and the logical in a way that other scholars did not (Lévy-Bruhl's pre-logical and logical mind are eternally separated from each other), Durkheim's approach was a step forward. But, the separation of emotion and logic remained, encapsulated in the symbol and in logical propositions – even as he linked them sequentially within the evolution of a society.

We should recall here Catherine Bell's observation that in studies of ritual, thought has been separated from action; I extended this observation in Chapter One to include studies of Buddhism. In these studies of the origin of religions, it appears that emotion has been set apart from logical thinking. The challenge here is to begin to put these categories of human experience back together; first, in order to highlight thinking and feeling with respect to the four noble truths, we should *retain* the categories of proposition and symbol in order to avoid conflating these two kinds of experience, and second, place both into a context of acting. This is, in the end, what the category of *sammādiṭṭhi* requires.

Contemporary Theories of Symbols and Propositions

In contemporary theories of symbols, the category assigned to symbol still represents that which is considered to be not logical. Logical propositions continue to serve as evidence of the presence of rationality. While Paul Ricoeur's analysis of metaphor and symbol are more nuanced and refined than earlier theories of symbol, the distinction between experiences that are direct and immediate *versus* logical thought is still fundamental. The same is true of Dan Sperber's analysis of symbols. Sperber provides us with a useful framework to answer the question that should be answered in a conclusion to such a study as this: what does it mean to say that (a) the four noble truths are a symbol, (b) they are propositions of doctrine, and (c) they are both?

Paul Ricoeur gives us a clear description of the relationship between human experience, symbol, and speculative thought in the introduction to *The Symbolism of Evil.*

> If, then, we begin with the interpretation of living experience, we must not lose sight of the fact that that experience is abstract, in spite of its lifelike appearance; it is abstract because it is separated from the totality of meaning from which we detach it for didactic purposes. We must not forget, either, that this experience is never immediate; it can be expressed only by means of the primary symbolisms that prepare the way for its treatment in myths and speculation.[21]

We can gain a sense of what Ricoeur means by 'symbol' by looking at his definition – and without venturing too far into his analysis of an authentic symbol (with its three moments of the cosmic, oneiric, and poetic). Ricoeur offers a series of 'increasingly close approximations' as a way of grasping the essence of a symbol. The first is the recognition that a symbol is, indeed, a sign and that therefore it communications a meaning. He next constricts the boundary cast around the definition of a symbol as a sign by suggesting that a symbol 'conceals in its aim a double intentionality.'[22]

Ricoeur's double intentionality defines two meanings, the literal and the more opaque; 'this opacity constitutes the depth of the symbol which . . . is inexhaustible.'[23] The link between the literal and symbolic meanings is the analogy, which is not based necessarily on simple likeness or similarity. The analogy which ties the two meanings of a symbol together is 'a movement of the primary meaning which makes us participate in the latent meaning and thus assimilates us to that which is symbolized without our being able to master the similitude intellectually.'[24] Ricoeur continues to refine what he means by symbol, drawing distinctions between symbol and allegory and symbol and symbolic logic. For our purposes here, it is sufficient to understand Ricoeur's explanation of the relationship that exists between experience, symbol, and speculation: symbols makes human experiences possible by virtue of their 'analogical meanings that are spontaneously formed and immediately significant;' myths and other forms of speculative thought follow upon symbols insofar as myths are symbols that function in the context of a narrative that is rooted in a particular time and space.[25]

There is one more feature of Ricoeur's conception of symbol that requires attention: the depth and power that symbols have by virtue of their ability to take us beyond the surface of language. In his essay 'Metaphor and Symbol,' Ricoeur explains that one difficulty attendant upon the conception of symbol is that a symbol has two dimensions of discourse: one that is linguistic and one that is not. These two dimensions are the same as the two meanings introduced above in the previous paragraph, and in the same way that the literal meaning assimilates us to the latent or opaque meaning of the symbol, so too does Ricoeur state that 'a symbol always refers its linguistic element to something else.'[26] The literal meaning of a symbol is the linguistic component of a symbol, and the latent meaning is the component that is not linguistic. There is something in a symbol, Ricoeur suggests, that 'does not correspond to a metaphor and, because of this fact, resists any linguistic, semantic, or logical transcription.'[27] The dimension of a symbol that resists such analysis is its opacity: 'This opacity of a symbol is related to the rootedness of symbols in areas of our experience that are open to different methods of investigation,' such as psychoanalysis, poetic analysis, and so on.[28] Ricoeur concludes his essay with this contrast between metaphor and symbol:

> The symbol is bound in a way that the metaphor is not. Symbols have roots. Symbols plunge us into the shadowy experience of power. Metaphors are just the linguistic surface of symbols, and they owe their power to relate the semantic surface to the presemantic surface in the depth of human experience to the two-dimensional structure of the symbol.[29]

The power of a symbol for Ricoeur lies in its opacity – in its ability to refer the linguistic element to 'something else,' the meaning that lies beneath the literal meaning. This second dimension of a symbol lies beyond the intellect, takes us into areas of human experience that lie beyond linguistic, semantic, or logical analysis. Ricoeur does equate the symbol with emotional experience, but he shifts the relationship. Where Durkheim explained that logic had its origins in the same communal experiences as religion, Ricoeur places experience – direct and immediate experience – beyond the capacity of human knowing at all. Symbols, however, are the vehicles by which we can come to know human experience, and symbols are also the means by which experience is the subject of myth and speculation. We see a similar progression from experience to speculation in Durkheim and Ricoeur, but Ricoeur draws a line that Durkheim does not. Ricoeur makes clear that experience itself can never be known; it lies entirely beyond language. For him, experience is never direct or immediate: it is always mediated by symbols. Symbols have this capacity for mediation precisely because they have a dual nature and dual meanings: one that is linguistic and one that escapes linguistic, semantical, and logical analysis. Even though Ricoeur explains that experience itself cannot be known, the fact that symbols get us closer to knowing experience than logic makes his distinction between experience and language comparable to Durkheim's theory. For Ricoeur, the dimension of a symbol that evades logic is precisely what gives the symbol its power.

In *Rethinking Symbolism* Dan Sperber's analysis of how symbols work defines more precisely how symbols operate in contrast to what Ricoeur calls logical analysis. He begins with a provocative suggestion that the 'criterion of irrationality' in the work of Frazer, Lévy-Bruhl, and others has circumscribed contemporary discussions of symbolism.[30] Sperber shows his readers in his opening comments how the 'criteria of irrationality' might work in a field study. Casting himself as an anthropologist, he suggests that he would use the category of symbolic activity in the field to define that activity whose rationale he does not understand. Or, in his own words, 'I note then as symbolic all activity where the means put into play seem to be clearly disproportionate to the explicit or implicit end, whether this end be knowledge, communication, or production. . . .'[31] In short, activity defined as symbolic is that activity whose logic escapes us.

Faced with this observation, Sperber lays out three possibilities:

> . . . either the criterion of irrationality is worthless and thinking we are delimiting the field of symbolism we are only gathering the bric-à-brac of our ignorance; or else, as mystical minds would have it, the criterion of irrationality is the right one, and symbolism is not open to scientific investigation; or else the criterion of irrationality delimits symbolism – albeit approximately – without defining it, which will require explanation.[32]

Sperber's comparison to mystic minds in this sentence is not accidental. Just as one of the defining characteristics of magic and magicians is a logic of the emotions – not of the head – so too one of the central characteristics of mysticism is a logic that defies our intelligibility. Sperber illustrates how the lack of intelligibility is the feature that would lead him as an anthropologist to define an activity as symbolic providing us with a captivating example of how it is that the criteria of irrationality delimits symbolism – without defining it.

In the remainder of his book, Sperber shares Ricoeur's observation that at least some dimension of symbols elude a logical analysis.[33] Sperber explains that the symbolic mechanism operates alongside the conceptual mechanism. The conceptual mechanism is the mechanism by which humans define and comprehend the world through a process of testing statements that contain new knowledge against statements of encyclopedic knowledge and statements of semantic knowledge contained in one's active memory. Encyclopedic knowledge consists of statements that can be definitively verified or falsified; semantic statements are analytic statements that convey items of semantic knowledge, which is knowledge about the categories into which we classify the world. When faced with a new statement, the conceptual mechanism compares the new statement to encyclopedic statements in the active memory by invoking other encyclopedic statements about the world that we know to be right or wrong, and the process enables us to verify the new encyclopedic statement. Semantic statements are verified or falsified in a similar way. Sperber suggests that symbolic statements become identified as symbolic when the conceptual mechanism fails. If a given statement cannot be verified by other encyclopedic or semantic knowledge that one has in one's memory, yet if it evokes other associations that do not allow one to dismiss the statement as illogical, the statement is symbolic and operates according to the symbolic mechanism – not the conceptual. He suggests that one of the paradoxes of symbolic knowledge is that it cannot be falsified; and, therefore, such statements involve a mechanism that operates differently than the conceptual – thus, his explication of the symbolic mechanism.[34] The symbolic mechanism is a universal mechanism that operates within a particular culture and that generates endless individual interpretations.

The symbolic mechanism works by putting a symbolic statement in quotation marks, thus distinguishing the statement from the territory demarcated by the conceptual mechanism and distinguishing the statement from encyclopedic statements, which must be verified or falsified. For example, Sperber suggests that this principle explains how it is that we know that $e = mc^2$ is valid without knowing exactly how $e = mc^2$ is true, because most of us are not physicists.[35]

> By taking it [i.e., a statement] in quotes, he treats it symbolically. We could give more examples and show that for many Marxists, Freudians or structuralists, their doctrine functions symbolically. They take its theses to be true without knowing exactly what they imply. Empirical counter arguments, in so far as they concern themselves with them, lead them not to reject these theses, but to modify their import.[36]

Putting a statement in quotation marks indicates a statement to be a statement of symbolic knowledge. Doing so means that one does not subject the statement in quotes to the same process of verification or falsification to which one subjects statements of encyclopedic knowledge. Other forms of verifibility are put into action.

Sperber suggests there are two aspects of symbolic processing that verify symbols: focalization and evocation. Focalization is the process by which the focus of attention is shifted away from the statements containing the new information to the unfulfilled conceptual conditions, which are in turn compared against a new background of passive memory instead of the active memory that contains encyclopedic statements.[37] (The 'conceptual conditions' are unfulfilled if the new information cannot be made relevant through auxiliary statements that link the statement with new information to statements in one's active memory.) The process of comparing the statement with new information against the information contained in one's passive memory is evocation. Processing a statement with new information involves comparing the new statement against other encyclopedic statements in active memory; the statement with new information invokes the appropriate encyclopedic statements. If there are no appropriate encyclopedic statements to invoke, the symbolic mechanism shifts attention to the unfulfilled conceptual conditions and evokes other statements from one's passive memory. In other words, memory is a constructive process. The act of evocation seeks to reconstruct the background information that, had it been available in active memory, would have allowed one to process the statement as an encyclopedic statement, not as a symbolic statement.[38]

Sperber describes this somewhat technical process more dynamically in the following paragraph.

> The cyclical movement of cultural symbolism might seem absurd if it were not precisely for the constructive character of remembering. Indeed, it is not a question here of the endless quest for an impossible solution, but rather of a repeated work of re-organization of the encyclopedic memory. Each new evocation brings about a different reconstruction of old representations, weaves new links among them, integrates into the field of symbolism new information brought to it by daily life; the same rituals are enacted, but with new actors; the same myths are told, but in a changing universe, and to individuals whose social position, whose relationships with others, and whose experiences have changed.[39]

Sperber began his book by asserting that the criteria of irrationality has circumscribed our understandings of symbol, but without defining it. We should be able to see how it is that the criteria of irrationality has set the parameters of our understanding of symbols: symbols are, in one sense, those statements that cannot be logically understood. This is the same point that Ricoeur makes: there is a dimension to symbols that defies logic and reaches into the depths of human experience.

Sperber provides a way for understanding how symbols work. Symbols evoke, they are interpreted differently by any number of individuals within a single culture and across cultures, and yet they are constrained by the process of focalization. As he explains,

> It is therefore not a question of discovering the meaning of symbolic representations but, on the contrary, of inventing a relevance and a place in memory for them despite the failure in this respect of the conceptual categories of meaning.[40]

There are not, in the end, 'two contradictory interpretations – the one constant and universal, the other variable and appropriate to each society; they have a universal focal structure and a variable evocational field.'[41] This observation is what distinguishes Sperber's remarks on how symbols work from Ricoeur's theory: there are not two dimensions inherent to symbols themselves, but rather there is a symbolic mechanism that is characteristic of humans which allows us to classify certain statements not according to our encyclopedic but according to our passive memory.[42]

If we attribute to symbols the two dimensions of discourse (the literal and the opaque), we are faced with the difficulty of sketching out how each dimension evokes meaning in any given setting. In Ricoeur's terms, determining the literal meaning is relatively straightforward in a particular cultural context. Determining how one knows what the opacity of a symbol means, again in Ricoeur's terms, is deliberately and necessarily obscured. However tantalizing or provocative the opaque dimension appears to be, our inability to define *how* a symbol means something in a sense that 'lies beyond' the literal dimension requires that we consider everything that 'lies beyond' any and each cultural context as roughly synonymous or equivalent. In other words, by positing literal (rational) and opaque (irrational) dimensions to symbols, we limit the parameters of logical analysis to what we know according to an encyclopedic type of knowledge at the expense of knowing with any precision the type of perception that both Durkheim and Ricoeur considered to be particularly close to experience itself. As Sperber points out, not being able to define the opaque dimension means that we place it outside the possibility of knowing at all. In the study of religions, we usually refer to this dimension as the sacred; the problem with this approach is that anything that 'lies beyond' the literal dimension of a symbol is commonly taken as a reference to a universal and unchanging 'sacred' thus blurring the distinctiveness of what a tradition identifies as ultimately real. At the very least, employing classical theories of symbol without exploring them means that we replicate the separation of thought and experience (both of which are then set apart from actions). Sperber's symbolic mechanism moves us beyond this impasse but still permits us to distinguish between the different experiences of logically assessing the truth claims of a proposition and the evocation of symbols.

The Four Noble Truths: As Symbols, Propositions, and *Sammādiṭṭhi*

When I suggest that the four noble truths are a symbol I deliberately invoke a certain set of assumptions about experience and logic that have traditionally demarcated what the word symbol means in contemporary discourse. The theoretical question of the origins of religions determines the shape of the definitions that we generally attribute to the categories of symbol and logical propositions. As I discussed briefly in the conclusion to Chapter Two, this distinction is the same one that Derrick Bell makes in his dialogue with Mr. Jesse B. Semple: 'The fact is, most people in those neighborhoods we drove through, tryin' to live decent and they do it in part by living on symbols. Religious symbols, freedom symbols, legal symbols, and now holiday symbols. They are all but worthless at the bank, but sometimes black folks don't try to cash them there. Know what I mean?'[43]

The categories of symbol and logical propositions carry with them certain assumptions about the relationship between experience and language. Both Durkheim and Ricoeur have argued that experience gives rise to logical analysis (Durkheim) and speculation (Ricouer). Even though Ricoeur carefully places any direct knowledge of a experience beyond our limits of knowing in any way, he shares Durkheim's conviction that experience, when made known to humans through the medium of a symbol and then through myths, gives rise to philosophical analysis. Ricoeur goes much further than Durkheim does in explaining how a symbol functions; and he does not share Durkheim's insistence that religion is a product of the group experience of a clan. Nonetheless, their arguments are similar insofar as they provide an explanation for the relationship between human experience and thought.

Sperber has a slightly different approach to the issue, insofar as he omits the question of direct experience and deals only with how humans know what we know about the world through conceptual and symbolic mechanisms. In his outline of how a theory of symbols might work, he delineates precisely how symbolic knowledge works in tandem with encyclopedic and semantic knowledge by coming into operation when the conceptual mechanism fails. Although symbolic knowledge does not give rise to encyclopedic knowledge in Sperber's theory, there is still a classification of human experience that he places beyond the boundaries of the conceptual mechanism: the passive memory that contains the statements evoked by the symbolic mechanism. Durkheim, Ricoeur, and Sperber all distinguish a particular kind of human experience from logical analysis (Durkheim), speculation (Ricoeur), or the conceptual mechanism (Sperber). Whether that experience is the direct and immediate experience of the clan (Durkheim), is beyond any direct knowledge (Ricoeur), or is the experience that we have in dreams (Sperber), these scholars each explain, in different ways, that humans have their most direct access to such experiences through symbols and that the rules of logic do not apply to symbols.

When we compare how scholars of religions in Europe and the United States have divided human experience into that which is direct and immediate (symbolic) on the one hand and distanced and reflective (philosophical) on the other to the category of *sammādiṭṭhi* as examined in the first chapter, the incongruity of these conceptual maps becomes apparent. J. Z. Smith has observed that scholars of religion should 'reflect on and play with the necessary incongruity of our maps before we set out on a voyage of discovery to chart the worlds of other men.'[44] This discussion of what the categories of symbol and logic have meant for scholars of religions in the past one hundred and seventy years has been such a reflection. In turn, we must look at what it means to say that the four noble truths are symbols or propositions, and then turn to what it means to say that they are right view.

I wish to suggest in these final pages that the classical categories of symbol and doctrinal propositions both fail to embrace the full range of meanings associated with the four noble truths, largely because the category of right views does not distinguish between thought and action in the same way. On the other hand, the category of right views does not provide us with the tools to distinguish closely between statements that function evocatively (symbolically) and those that function as rational claims of truth (propositionally). In the end, all three categories are necessary to fully understand the breadth of the four noble truths as accurately as possible.

As symbols

Durkheim referred to the symbolic function of the four noble truths in his quote that I used as the epigraph at the start of this chapter:

> This is how Buddhism is a religion: in default of gods, it admits the existence of sacred things, namely, the four noble truths and the practices derived from them.[45]

Durkheim understood the essence of Buddhism to be its doctrines and the practices derived from them. These doctrines were revealed by the Buddha, he explained; but, once they were made known, the Buddha was no longer as significant as the teachings. 'From that moment [i.e., of revelation] he [i.e., the Buddha] ceased to be a factor necessary to the religious life. The practice of the four holy truths would be possible, even if the memory of him who revealed him were completely obliterated.'[46] What is sacred in Durkheim's theories is the teachings of the Buddha, not the Buddha. The sacred for Durkheim means that which is set apart from the profane, and the classification of all things into either sacred or profane is absolute: 'The sacred thing is *par excellence* that which the profane should not touch, and cannot touch with impunity.'[47] Religious beliefs represent that which is sacred; and, as we have already seen, Durkheim understands the sacred to be that which first emerges in the collective experience of an intense emotional experience that is then projected upon a symbol. In short, the sacred, like symbols, represents a direct and immediate emotional experience.

However, the experience that is evoked in the memory of the Theravāda canon by the four noble truths when they function as a symbol is not a generic religious experience. It is a specific experience of enlightenment, that is, attaining the first of four paths to *nibbāna*. The four noble truths are not simply a symbol that refers us to an experience that lies beyond the grasp of logic, as they would be if we applied Ricoeur's theory of symbols.

We need to use the category of symbol judiciously, not simply as shorthand for a particular emotional or immediate experience. To say that the four noble truths are a symbol is not to say that they are pre-logical, that they are the product of an intense collectively-felt emotional experience, or that they point us to a dimension that lies beyond the logical. This is where Sperber is most useful. His explanation of the symbolic mechanism permits us to understand that when the four noble truths function symbolically, their encyclopedic relationship to other statements of doctrine is suspended, and they evoke other associations in the culturally defined memory recorded in the Theravāda canon.

When one understands the four noble truths to be the first teaching of the Buddha and the most important teaching of the Buddha, one does so not because the four noble truths were actually the first teaching or because they are literally the most important teaching of Buddhism. We have seen that the four noble truths were probably not the first teaching; Norman and others have shown that they were inserted into the *dhamma* talk that was said to be the first talk of the Buddha. We have also seen that the four noble truths are not the most important teaching of the Buddha because they are not set explicitly and consistently as such in relation to other doctrinal propositions. When one understands the four noble truths to be the first and most important teaching of the Buddha, the explicit truth value as encyclopaedic statements of the four noble truths is not the source of their authority. When the four noble truths appear as a symbol, their authority resides in their capacity to evoke a certain set of associations that are rooted first in the Theravāda canon and commentaries and, secondly, in the larger Theravāda historical tradition. What the symbol of the four noble truths evokes is the possibility of an actual experience of enlightenment that is called to mind when one considers the four noble truths to be the first teaching of the Buddha. It is the evocative capacity of the four noble truths that sets them apart as a symbol and the memory of the Theravāda canon that provides the paths by which other symbolic statements are recalled.

As propositions

What does it mean to say that the four noble truths are also propositions of doctrine? Paul Griffiths proposes that any potential statement of doctrine should meet the following criteria to qualify as a primary doctrine:

1. Being taken by its community to possess to a greater degree than any of its known competitors whatever property or properties the community thinks of as making doctrine-candidates acceptable in their spheres of relevance – or, if the property controlling acceptability does not, for some community, admit of degrees (as may be the case

for truth), then the doctrine-candidate must have it in the eyes of the community, and its known competitors must lack it.

2. Being taken by its community to be of significance for its religious life.
3. Being taken by its community to be binding upon its members.[48]

If we apply these criteria to the four noble truths, we should be able to decide whether it is a primary doctrine or not. Griffiths' criteria specify the requirements that will allow us to put the four noble truths into the category of semantic knowledge (as Sperber discusses it).

The appearance – or insertion – of the four noble truths into the *Dhammacakkappavattana-sutta* and throughout the canon is evidence that the Theravāda community considered the four noble truths to be *the* word of the Buddha, *dhamma par excellence*. The consistency of the commentaries on this point provides further support for this conclusion. Second, they are important for the religious life – but this aspect requires more attention than I have given it here. They are important to the path, even though the four noble truths are placed at two rather distinct points on the path (resulting in the attainment of a stream-winner or an *arahat*); the four noble truths were remembered in the *Mahāvagga* of the *Vinaya-piṭaka* as the means by which the first thousand or so members of the *saṅgha* gained access to the path as stream-winners. Are they important for the contemporary religious life? In some cases they are, and in other cases they are not. The problem with a clear answer to this criteria is what one uses as a definition of community.[49] Finally, Griffiths suggests that a primary doctrine must be taken to be binding upon its members. The four noble truths are taken to be binding, but not as clearly as we might like to see. Insofar as a Buddhist is identified as one who takes refuge in the Buddha, *dhamma*, and *saṅgha*, and because the four noble truths are a common definition of *dhamma*, they might be said to be binding upon the community. But applying these criteria to the four noble truths leaves us with a sense of having left something out. While these criteria provide us with the necessary definitional parameters for a primary doctrine, the fact that the four noble truths do not precisely meet Griffiths' criteria indicates that we have not yet understood adequately what it means to say that the four noble truths are a proposition of doctrine.

As a logical proposition, we should understand that the four noble truths are first of all, claims about experience: pain, arising, ending, and the practices that lead to its ending. As a primary doctrine, the four noble truths are considered to be true. Does this mean that one can verify the truth of the four noble truths by 'practicing' the four noble truths according to the Theravāda canon? Not consistently. There are certain points which have a clear 'practice' of the four noble truths: the *Mahāsatipaṭṭhana-sutta* explains that mindfulness can be practiced according to the four noble truths. What one is supposed to do with the four noble truths – what their practices are – is not defined consistently throughout the canon. Out of all of the different doctrines that are linked with the four noble truths within the network of the Buddha's teaching, the most coherent statement of how the four noble truths lead to the eradication of pain is in the model of the path that shows the four noble truths as the means by which the corruptions.are eliminated and thus the final means by which one becomes an *arahat.* Is knowing the four noble truths the only way to end pain? Certainly not. They are not the only means to *nibbāna.* When they are taught as a way to *nibbāna* and they are set in relation to other teachings, such as dependent origination there are no explicit references to how one attains awakening. The general claim that knowledge of the four noble truths leads to *nibbāna* is broad and descriptive, not prescriptive. As a proposition of doctrine, the four noble truths are claims about experience, but there is only one formulation of the path through which the four noble truths are consistently shown to produce an experience of enlightenment that is accessible to those who live after the Buddha's *parinibbāna*: that is, by eliminating the corruptions through a knowledge of the four noble truths.

As right views

The claims that are made for *sammādiṭṭhi* are not nearly as clear cut as those of Durkheim, Ricoeur, Sperber or Griffiths. We are not comparing the same sort of texts or discourses. Further, these scholars seek to describe how symbols and doctrines function in relationship to experience and logic, while the category of right view by definition makes claims about cultivating a particular kind of experience: the experience of *nibbāna.* Moreover, *sammādiṭṭhi* is articulated within a set of religious and psychological claims about the self and the world that are different from the claims that under ie the explanations that Durkheim, Ricoeur, Sperber, and Griffiths propose. Taking into account the distance in time, space, and religious claims separating these two approaches to experience, the proposals of the scholars make an explicit distinction between thought and experience that the category of *sammādiṭṭhi* does not take up in detail.

We have sen that there are claims that one's views and actions are more important in determining one's future rebirths than one's emotional state in one's current life. Similarly, understanding *sammādiṭṭhi* requires both bodily and mental effort. There are also levels of understanding *sammādiṭṭhi*, as Collins has proposed: first is the recognition that right view is a worthy thing to know; second is knowing right view in the terms of Buddhist doctrine; and, the third is knowing right view. as liberating insight. To know right view in the third sense is not generally considered by the Theravāda tradition to be possible unless one cultivates that knowledge within the context of the *saṅgha*. That is, to cultivate such knowledge means doing so within a particular pedagogical setting that, ideally, allows one to direct all of one's actions, thoughts, and behaviors toward learning right view.[50] In that setting, right views are soteriologically efficacious as a teaching that requires both intellectual and practical assent and commitment. The four noble truths are readily understood as a right view within this context.

However, the heuristic descriptions of *sammādiṭṭhi* do not provide sufficient detail to explain how it is that the four noble truths play such different roles throughout the canon. We have seen the different claims for the efficacy of the four noble truths when they are taught by the Buddha and when they are taught simply as one doctrine among others. In the first, they lead to the attainments of a stream-winner. In the second, and only in certain cases within their capacity as a proposition, they lead one to eliminate the corruptions and thus to become an *arahat*. The four noble truths evoke the recollection of the Buddha's enlightenment within the memory of the Theravāda tradition, and also represent the possibility of enlightenment for anyone. I should note that the Theravāda tradition does not appear to be bothered by these apparently contradictory claims. The four noble truths are both propositions and symbols, but at different points. In short, the category of *sammādiṭṭhi* does not provide an explanation for what I have identified as the symbolic or the doctrinal functions of the four noble truths.

The Theravāda canon claims that the four noble truths, as propositions, were considered to be the means by which the corruptions are eliminated, thus the means by which one attained the status of an *arahat*. We saw that other doctrinal claims were more abstract, such as the statement that the four noble truths led to an experience of *nibbāna*; they should be understood as descriptive propositions, not as particular prescriptions for a particular kind of practice. As a right view, the four noble truths should be understood to be propositions that are capable of leading one to a transformative experience within a disciplined lifestyle oriented toward cultivating such a transformation. Within the same context, the four noble truths are also a symbol of the possibility of liberation. As an efficacious right view, the four noble truths embrace both functions.

There is still a question of whether or not the four noble truths constitute liberating insight in the earliest strata of Theravāda tradition. Bronkhorst and Schmithausen claim that they do not.[51] The teaching of the four noble truths, we have seen, were not present in the oldest versions of certain *sutta*s. They were added at a relatively early date, but were not present in the first versions of the *Dhammacakkappavattana-sutta*. The variations of that *sutta* led Bareau, Bronkhorst, and Schmithausen to their conclusions that the four noble truths were not linked to the eradication of the *āsavā*s in the earliest layers of Buddhist teachings. Bronkhorst cites the illogic of placing the four noble truths at the end of one's progress along the path as another reason that the four noble truths were not considered to be among the earliest of definitions liberating insight. Nonetheless, the Theravāda tradition did incorporate the four noble truths as one of its central teachings by claiming them as *sammādiṭṭhi*.

I have suggested that we should seek first to understand the role of the four noble truths with the tools of historical analysis. The evidence we have indicates that the four noble truths were not the first teaching; nor is it likely that they were a teaching of the Buddha, if we postulate that he was a man who lived sometime between the fifth and third centuries B.C.E. But if I suggest that the four noble truths are not the legacy of a particular religious experience which may have actually occurred in history, is that to undercut their authority as the word of the Buddha or their authority as a symbol of the Buddha's enlightenment? No, for the simple reason that the authority of the four noble truths, as an evocative symbol of a specific experience, does not rely upon the truth or falsehood of the four noble truths and other encyclopedic statements within history. The authority of the four noble truths does not rely upon the historical claim that they were in fact the first teaching of the Buddha. The authority of the four noble truths as a symbol relies, in the end, upon the memory of the Theravāda Buddhist tradition as recorded in the Theravāda canon.

The point at which the category of *diṭṭhi* diverges from doctrine lies in the fullest sense of right view as liberating insight. In both senses of proposition and symbol, the four noble truths are properly understood as teachings that lead to liberation. They lead to that liberation in two distinct ways, only one of which corresponds to our contemporary definition of proposition: when knowledge of the four noble truths leads to *nibbāna* by eliminating the corruptions. This is the context in which we should treat the four noble truths as encyclopedic statements and therefore as a proposition of doctrine. Regardless of the earliest relationship between the actual experience of eradicating of the corruptions and the actual experience of knowing the four noble truths, the Theravāda tradition has remembered and claimed that the four noble truths function as propositions in relation to the corruptions. The same structure of the path underlies most of the discussions of the four noble truths in the *Abhidhamma-piṭaka*, and thus the four noble truths should also be understood as propositions in that context. At all other points in the canon, the four noble truths are significant not because they are a doctrine but because they are a symbol. The reason why the four noble truths are a unique teaching in the Theravāda canon is because they are both a symbol and a proposition of doctrine. To reformulate Durkheim's observation about the four noble truths, I would say that the four noble truths are truly set apart within the body of the Buddha's teachings, not because they are by definition sacred, but because they are both a symbol and a doctrine and transformative within the sphere of right view. As one doctrine among others, the four noble truths make explicit the structure within which one should seek enlightenment; as a symbol, the four noble truths evoke the possibility of enlightenment. As both, they occupy not only a central but a singular position within the Theravāda canon and tradition.

Notes

1 Emile Durkheim, *Les Formes élémentaires de la vie religieuse*, (1912; translated by Joseph Ward Swain as *The Elementary Forms of the Religious Life*, London: George Allen & Unwin, 1915; reprint, New York: The Free Press, 1965), 52.
2 Lucien Lévy-Bruhl, *Les Fonctions mentales dans les sociétés inférieures* (1910; translated as *How Natives Think* by Lilian A. Clare, with an introduction by Ruth L. Bunzel, 1926; New York: Washington Square Press, 1966), 23.
3 Lucien Lévy-Bruhl, *La Mentalité primitive*, (1922, translated as *Primitive Mentality* by Lilian A. Clare, London: George Allen & Unwin, Ltd., 1923; Boston: Beacon Press, 1966), 60. This book was in its fourteenth edition by 1947, to indicate its popularity.
4 Lévy-Bruhl, *Primitive Mentality*, 60.
5 Lévy-Bruhl, *Primitive Mentality*, 447.
6 James George Frazer, *Man, God, and Immortality: Thoughts on Human Progress* (New York: Macmillan Company, 1927), 306.
7 Durkheim, *Elementary Forms*, 251.
8 Durkheim, *Elementary Forms*, 251.
9 Durkheim, *Elementary Forms*, 252.
10 Durkheim, *Elementary Forms*, 253.
11 Durkheim, *Elementary Forms*, 267–270.
12 Durkheim, *Elementary Forms*, 463–464.
13 Wilhelm Schmidt, *The Origin and Growth of Religion*, trans. H. J. Rose (1930; New York: Dial Press, 1931); E[dward] E[van] Evans-Pritchard, *Theories of Primitive Religions* (Oxford: Clarendon Press, 1965), 4.
14 Durkheim, *Elementary Forms*, 478.
15 Durkheim, *Elementary Forms*, 480.
16 Durkheim, *Elementary Forms*, 481.
17 Durkheim, *Elementary Forms*, 481.
18 Durkheim, *Elementary Forms*, 482.
19 Durkheim, *Elementary Forms*, 485.
20 Durkheim, *Elementary Forms*, 484.
21 Ricoeur, *Symbolism of Evil*, 10.
22 Ricoeur, *Symbolism of Evil*, 15.
23 Ricoeur, *Symbolism of Evil*, 15.
24 Ricoeur, *Symbolism of Evil*, 16.
25 Ricoeur, *Symbolism of Evil*, 18.
26 Paul Ricoeur, *Interpretation Theory: Discourse and the Surplus of Meaning* (Fort Worth: Texas Christian University Press, 1976), 53–54.
27 Ricoeur, *Interpretation Theory*, 57.
28 Ricoeur, *Intepretation Theory*, 57.
29 Ricoeur, *Interpretation Theory*, 69.
30 Dan Sperber, *Rethinking Symbolism*, trans. Alice Morton, Cambridge Studies in Anthropology (Cambridge: Cambridge University Press, 1974), 1–16.
31 Sperber, *Rethinking Symbolism*, 4.
32 Sperber, *Rethinking Symbolism*, 4.

33 Where Sperber parts company from Ricoeur is in his suggestion that symbols do not mean anything – although they can be interpreted. Symbols do not mean anything because one of the central features of the symbolic mechanism is that they can be endlessly interpreted, by individuals who draw upon what he calls the 'cultural field of evocation.' Sperber, *Rethinking Symbolism*, 140.
34 Sperber, *Symbolism*, 98.
35 Sperber, *Symbolism*, 99.
36 Sperber, *Symbolism*, 101.
37 Sperber, *Symbolism*, 120–121.
38 Sperber, *Symbolism*, 127.
39 Sperber, *Symbolism*, 145.
40 Sperber, *Symbolism*, 113.
41 Sperber, *Symbolism*, 40.
42 There are weaknesses in Sperber's outline; he notes that he does not provide a theory of symbols in this volume. The role of passive memory is still unclear; he notes that the processes of focalization and evocation are similar to Freud's notions of displacement and condensation. Sperber, *Symbolism*, 123. What Sperber does in this book is to show us the parameters within which a theory of symbols might be developed. His distinction of conceptual mechanisms and symbolic mechanisms in terms of encyclopedic, semantic, and symbolic knowledge clarifies what has, at least for the last one hundred and fifty years, been presumed but not carefully delineated.
43 Bell, *Faces at the Bottom of the Well*, 24.
44 Jonathan Z. Smith, 'Map is Not Territory,' in *Map is Not Territory*, 309.
45 Durkheim, *Elementary Forms*, 52.
46 Durkheim, *Elementary Forms*, 47.
47 Durkheim, *Elementary Forms*, 55.
48 Griffiths, *On Being Buddha*, 6ff.
49 See, for example, the variations in contemporary practice described by George Bond in *Buddhist Revival*.
50 This approach is similar to what Pierre Hadot has called 'philosophy as a way of life,' by which he means that what we usually take to be philosophy (abstract and so on) was actually a way of life that required spiritual exercises designed to transform one's vision of the world. Arnold I. Davidson, 'Spiritual Exercises and Ancient Philosophy: An Introduction to Pierre Hadot,' *Critical Inquiry* 16 (Spring 1990): 475–505.
51 Bronkhorst and Schmithausen explicitly reject the claim that the four noble truths should be considered as an original definition of liberating insight. In this study, I am less interested in assessing the historical and logical evidence that leads them to their claims than in tracing how the Theravāda tradition has located the four noble truths and how the tradition has reconciled tensions that emerged historically with the introduction of the teaching into the tradition. See Bronkhorst, *Two Traditions*, 104–110 and Schmithausen, 'On Some Aspects,' 202–214.

GLOSSARY OF PĀLI TERMS

abhibhāyatanāni	stages of control over the sense spheres (eight); see *āyatanāni*
abhiññā	special, further, or higher knowledges (six)
akusala	unwholesome, wrong, bad, not meritorious
aṭṭhaṅgiko maggo	eightfold path
aṭṭhakathā	commentaries
anattā	no self
anāgamin	'non-returner'; the third stage of the fourfold path
arahat	the highest of four states within the fourfold path to enlightenment; one who attains this state will not be reborn again
ariya	noble, noble one (i.e., an *arahat*)
ariyapariyesana	noble quest or search
avijjā	ignorance
ayoniso manasikaroto	one who does not pay proper or careful attention
āhāro	sustenance or nutriment (four)
āloko	light, sight, look, splendor
āsavā	corruptions
āyatanāni	spheres of sense (six or twelve). The sense spheres are one of the classifications of sentient life in Theravāda Buddhism and are accompanied by six internal spheres (eye, ear, nose, tongue, body, and mind) and six external spheres (visible form, sound, odor, taste, tangible things, and things which may be sensed by the mind such as ideas and thoughts)
āvuso	friend (a form of address among equals)
avyākata	unexplained problems; ethically neutral
balāni	powers (five)
bhava	being or existence
bhavadiṭṭhi	the view that everything exists permanently
bhikkhu or *bhikkhunī*	monk or nun (respectively)
bojjhaṅgā	factors of awakening (seven)
buddhavacana	word(s) of the Buddha
cakkhuṃ	vision or eye
catuparivaṭṭaṃ	fourfold analysis
cetanā	will or volition
cittaṃ	mind or occasionally consciousness
dhātuyo	elements
diṭṭhi	view, point of view

diṭṭhigataṃ	holding, resorting, or going to views
diṭṭhisampadā	attached to views
dukkhaṃ	pain, suffering, unsatisfactoriness
dukkhanirodhogāminī paṭipadā	way leading to the ending of pain
iddhi	psychic or transpersonal powers (eight)
iddhipādā	bases of success (four)
indriyāni	sense faculties (five)
jarāmaraṇaṃ	old age and death
jhānāni	trance states of enstatic meditation (four)
jāti	birth
kasiṇāyatanāni	kasina spheres (ten) used in *jhān*ic meditation
kilesā	impurities or defilements
kāmā	sensual desire or desire for sensual pleasures
kāyo	body
kusala	good, right, wholesome, meritorious
laddhidiṭṭhi	theories and views
maggo	path
manas	mental organ or mind
manasikāro	attention
mettā	love, loving-kindness
micchādiṭṭhi	wrong view(s)
moha	delusion
ñāṇaṃ	knowledge or insight
nirodho	ending or cessation
nāmarūpaṃ	name and form
nīvaraṇāni	obstacles or hindrances
oḷārikaṃ	heavy, gross, or coarse matter
pabbajā	minor ordination, 'going forth' (cf. *upasampadā*)
paṭiccasamuppāda	dependent arising or co-dependent origination
paṭipadā	way, practice, means
paññā	wisdom
parinibbāna	entrance into nibbāna upon the dissolution of the physical body
phasso	contact
puggala	individual, person
sacca	truth
saddhā	faith or confidence
sakadāgāmin	'once returner,' the second stage of the fourfold path
samādhi	concentration through meditation
saṃkhārānaṃ	constructions (usually translated as formations)
sammappadhānā	right efforts (four)
sammādiṭṭhi	right view
sammāpaññā	right or proper wisdom
samudayo	arising or origin
saṃsāra	cycle and continuity of existence
saññā	recognitions or perceptions
santaṃ	calm
sassato	eternal
sati	mindfulness or awareness
satipaṭṭhānā	setting up of mindfulness (four)

saṃyojanāni	fetters, which include: adherence to rites and ceremonies (*sīlabbataparāmaso*) belief in a self (*sakkāyadiṭṭhi*) doubts (*vicikicchā*)
sāsana	teachings (collection of) or order
sīla	ethics, virtue, morality
sotāpanno	stream enterer or winner; first stage of the fourfold path
sukha	happiness or ease
sutta	discourse or text
taṇhā	craving or thirst
tipiṭaka	'three baskets' of the Theravāda Buddhist canon
ucchedavāda	annihilation or the theory of annihilation
upādānaṃ	grasping or attachment
upāsako	lay follower of the Buddha (male)
upāsikā	lay follower of the Buddha (female)
upasampadā	full or higher ordination
upekkhā	equanimity
vedanā	feeling
vibhaṅga	analysis
vibhava	non-existence or annihilation
vicāro	(sustained) deliberation
vijjā	knowledge
vimokhā	deliverances (eight)
viññaṇaṃ	consciouness
vipāko	result or consequence
vitakko	initial thought
yathābhūtaṃ	'just as it is'; in reality

BIBLIOGRAPHY

Primary Sources

Pāli and Sanskrit Texts

Aṅguttara-nikāya, 5 vols. Edited by Richard Morris and E. Hardy. 1885–1890. Reprint. London: Pāli Text Society, 1958–1961.

Apadāna of the Khuddaka-nikāya, 2 vols. Edited by Mary E. Lilley. London: Pāli Text Society, 1927.

Aṭṭhasālinī. Edited by Edward Müller. London: Pāli Text Society, 1897.

Dhammasaṅganī. Edited by Edward Müller. London: Pāli Text Society, 1885.

Dīgha-nikāya, 3 vols. Edited by T. W. Rhys Davids and J. Estlin Carpenter. 1889–1910. Reprint. London: Pāli Text Society, 1960.

Divyāvadana. Edited by P. L. Vaidya. Buddhist Sanskrit Texts, no. 20. Darbhanga: Mithila Institute, 1959.

Kathāvatthu, 2 vols. Edited by A. C. Taylor. London: Pāli Text Society, 1894–1897.

Kathāvatthuppakaraṇa-aṭṭhakathā. Edited by N. A. Jayawickrama. London: Pāli Text Society, 1979.

Lalitavistara, 2 vols. Edited by S. Lefmann. Halle a. S.: Verlag der Buchhandlung des Waisenhauses, 1902.

Mahāvastu, 3 vols. Edited by Émile Charlie Marie Senart. Paris: Imprimerie Nationale, 1882–1897. Reprint. Japan: Meicho-Fukyū-kai, 1977.

Majjhima-nikāya, 4 vols. Edited by V. Trenckner, Robert Chalmers and C. A. F. Rhys Davids. 1887–1925. Reprint. London: Pāli Text Society, 1948–1960.

Manorathapūraṇī, 5 vols. 2nd ed. Edited by Max Walleser and Hermann Kopp. London: Pāli Text Society, 1967–1973.

Mohavicchedanī Abhidhammamātikaṭṭhavaṇṇanā. Edited by A. P. Buddhadatta and A. K. Warder. London: Pāli Text Society, 1961.

Mūlamadhyamakakārikaḥ. Edited by J. W. de Jong. Adhyar: Adhyar Library and Research Centre, 1977.

Papañcasūdanī, 5 vols. Edited by J. H. Woods, D. Kosambi and I. B. Horner. 1922–1938. Reprint. London: Pāli Text Society, 1977–1979.

Puggalapaññatti. 2nd ed. Edited by Richard Morris. London: Pāli Text Society, 1972.

Samantapāsādikā, 5 vols. Edited by J. Takakusu and M. Nagai. 1924–1938. Reprint. London: Pāli Text Society, 1966–1975.

Saṃyutta-nikāya, 6 vols. Edited by M. Leon Feer and C. A. F. Rhys Davids. 1884–1904. Reprint. London: Pāli Text Society, 1960.

Gilgit Manuscript of the Saṃghabhedavastu Being the 17th and Last Section of the Vinaya of the Mūlasarvāstivādins, 3 vols. Edited by Raniero Gnoli. Rome: Instituto Italiano Per Il Medio Ed Estremo Oriente, 1977.

Sāratthappakāsinī, 3 vols. Edited F. L. Woodward. 1929–1937. Reprint. London: Pāli Text Society, 1977.

Sumaṅgalavilāsinī, 3 vols. Edited by T. W. Rhys Davids, J. Estlin Carpenter, and W. Stede. 1886–1932. Reprint. London: Pāli Text Society, 1968–1971.

Vibhaṅga. Edited by C. A. F. Rhys Davids. London: Pāli Text Society, 1904.

Vinayapiṭaka, 5 vols. Edited by H. Oldenberg. London: Pāli Text Society, 1879–1883.

Visuddhimagga. Edited by H. C. Warren and D. Kosambi. Harvard Oriental Series. Cambridge: Harvard University Press, 1950.

Yamaka, 2 vols. Edited by C. A. F. Rhys Davids. London: Pāli Text Society, 1911–1913.

English Translations

The Book of Analysis (Vibhaṅga). Translated by Paṭhamakyaw Ashin Tiṭṭhila. London: Pāli Text Society, 1969.

The Book of the Discipline (Vinayapiṭaka), 6 vols. Translated by I. B. Horner. 1938–1966. Reprint. London: Pāli Text Society, 1972–1975.

The Book of the Gradual Sayings (Aṅguttara-nikāya), 5 vols. Translated by F. L. Woodward. 1932–1936. Reprint. London: Pāli Text Society, 1972–1979.

The Book of Kindred Sayings (Saṃyutta-nikāya), 5 vols. Translated by C. A. F. Rhys Davids and F. L. Woodward. 1917–1930. Reprint. London: Pāli Text Society, 1973–1979.

A Buddhist Manual of Psychological Ethics (Dhammasaṅgaṇi). 3d ed. Translated by C. A. F. Rhys Davids. London: Pāli Text Society, 1974.

Conditional Relations (Paṭṭhāna). Translated by U Nārada. London: Pāli Text Society, 1969.

Designation of Human Types (Puggalapaññatti). Translated by Bimala Churn Law. 1922. Reprint. London: Pāli Text Society, 1979.

Dialogues of the Buddha (Dīgha-nikāya), 3 vols. Translated by T. W. and C. A. F. Rhys Davids. 1899–1921. Reprint. London: Pāli Text Society, 1977.

Discourse on Elements (Dhātukathā). Translated by U Nārada. 1962. Reprint. London: Pāli Text Society, 1977.

The Dispeller of Delusion (Sammohavinodanī), 2 vols. Translated by Bhikkhu Ñāṇamoli. London: Pāli Text Society, 1987.

The Elders' Verses (Theragāthā and Therīgāthā), 2 vols. Translated by K. R. Norman. London: Pāli Text Society, 1969–1971.

The Expositor (Aṭṭhasālinī), 2 vols. Translated by Pe Maung Tin. 1920–1921. Reprint. London: Pāli Text Society, 1976.

Further Dialogues of the Buddha (Majjhima-nikāya), 2 vols. Translated by Lord Chalmers. London: Pāli Text Society, 1926–1927.

Mahāvaṃsa: The Great Chronicle of Sri Lanka. Translated by Ananda W. P. Gurugé. Colombo: Associated Newspapers of Ceylon, 1989.

Middle Length Sayings (Majjhima-nikāya), 3 vols. Translated by I. B. Horner. 1954–1959. Reprint. London: Pāli Text Society, 1975–1977.

The Path of Purification. 2 vols. Translated by Bhikkhu Nyanamoli. Sri Lanka, 1956; Berkeley: Shambhala Press, 1976 .

Points of Controversy (Kathāvatthu). Translated by Shwe Zan Aung and Caroline A. F. Rhys Davids. 1915. Reprint. London: Pāli Text Society, 1979.

Secondary Sources

Abel-Rémusat, J. P. 'Notes sur quelques épithètes descriptives du Bouddha.' *Journal des savants* (October 1819): 25–633.

Ackerman, Robert. *J. G. Frazer: His Life and Work*. Cambridge: Cambridge University Press, 1987.

Adikaram, E. W. *Early History of Buddhism in Ceylon or State of Buddhism in Ceylon as Revealed by the Pāli Commentaries of the Fifth Century*. Colombo: M. D. Gunasena, 1946.

Adikari, A., ed. *Sambhasha: Maha Bodhi Centenary Commemorative Volume*. Sri Lanka: Ministry of Education and Higher Education, 1991.

Akira, Hirakawa. *History of Indian Buddhism*. Translated and edited by Paul Groner. Honolulu: University of Hawaii Press, 1990.

Alabaster, Henry. *The Wheel of the Law: Buddhism Illustrated from the Siamese Sources*. London: Trübner & Co., 1871.

Almond, Philip C. *The British Discovery of Buddhism*. Cambridge: Cambridge University Press, 1988.

Alwis, James de. 'Buddhism: Its Origins, History, and Doctrine; Its Scriptures and Their Language, the Pāli.' *Journal of the Pāli Text Society* 1 (1883): 1–39.

——. *A Survey of Sinhala Literature (Being an Introduction to a Translation of the Sidat Sangarāva)*. Original Title The Sidath Sangarawa, a Grammar of the Sinhalese Language, Translated into English with Introduction, Notes, and Appendices. Ceylon National Museums Translation Series. 1852; Colombo: Department of National Museums, 1966.

Armour, John. 'Essay on Buddhism.' *The Ceylon Almanac and Compendium of Useful Information* 3 (1835): 208–29.

Bareau, André. *Les premiers conciles bouddhiques*. Paris: École Française d'Extrême-Orient, 1955.

——. *Recherches sur la biographie du Buddha dans les Sūtrapiṭaka et les Vinayapiṭaka anciens*. 2 vols. Publications de l'Ecole Française d'Extrême-Orient, vol. 53 and 77. Paris: Ecole Française d'Extrême-Orient, 1963–70.

——. *Les sectes bouddhiques du petit véhicule*. Paris: École Françaíse d'Extrême-Oriente, 1955.

Barth, Auguste. *The Religions of India*. Translated by J. Wood. London: Trübner & Co., 1882.

Barthélemy Saint-Hilaire, Jules. *Le Bouddha et sa religion*. 3d ed. 1860; Paris: Didier, 1862.

——. *The Buddha and His Religion*. Translated by Laura Ensor. London: George Routledge, 1895.

——. 'Du Bouddhisme et de sa litérature à Ceylan: Collection de M. Grimblot, consul de France á Ceylan.' *Journal de savants* (1866): 43–96, 100–16, 151–66.

Barua, B. M. 'Pratītyasamutpāda as a Basic Concept of Buddhist Thought.' In *B. C. Law Volume*, vol. 1, 574–89. Calcutta: Bhandarker Oriental Research Institute, 1945.

Bechert, Heinz. *Dating of the Historical Buddha. 2 vols. Abhandlungen der Akadeie der Wissenschaften in Göttingen Philosogische-Historische Klasse Dritte Folge, Nrs. 189 and 194. Göttingen: Vandenhoeck & Ruprecht, 1991.*

——. 'The Importance of Aśoka's So-called Schism Edict.' In *Indological and Buddhist Studies: Volume in Honor of Professor J. W. de Jong on His Sixtieth Birthday*, 61–68. Canberra: Faculty of Asian Studies, 1982.

——. The Date of the Buddha Reconsidered. *Indologica Taurinensia* 10 (1982): 29–36.

——. 'A Remark on the Problem of the Date of Mahāvīrā.' *Indologica Taurinensia* 11 (1983): 287–90.

——. 'Remarks on the Date of the Historical Buddha.' *Buddhist Studies (Bukkyō Kenkyū)* 17 (1988): 97–117.

Bell, Derrick. *Faces at the Bottom of the Well: The Permanence of Racism*. New York: Basic Books, 1992.

Bigandet, Paul Ambrose. *The Life or Legend of Gaudama: The Buddha of the Burmese*. 2d ed. 1858; London: Kegan Paul, Trench & Trübner, 1866.

Bloch, Jules. *Les inscriptions d'Asoka*. Paris: Société d'édition 'Les Belles Lettres,' 1950.

Bond, George D. *The Buddhist Revival in Sri Lanka: Religious Tradition, Reinterpretation and Response*. Studies in Comparative Religion. Columbia: University of South Carolina Press, 1988.

——. 'The Gradual Path as a Hermeneutical Approach to the *dhamma*.' In *Buddhist Hermeneutics*, edited by Donald S. Lopez, Jr., 29–45. Studies in East Asian Buddhism, vol. 6. Honolulu: University of Hawaii Press, 1988.

——. *The Word of the Buddha: The Tipiṭaka and Its Interpretation in Theravāda Buddhism*. Sri Lanka: M. D. Gunasena, 1982.

Bourdieu, Pierre. *An Outline of a Theory of Practice*. Translated by Richard Nice. Cambridge: Cambridge University Press, 1977.

Braun, Heinz. 'The Buddhist Era in the *Mālālaṅkāravatthu*.' In *The Dating of the Historical Buddha*, edited by Heinz Bechert, 46–48. Göttingen: Vandenhoeck & Ruprecht, 1991.

Bronkhorst, Johannes. 'Dharma and Abhidharma.' *Bulletin of the School of Oriental and African Studies* 48, no. 2 (1985): 305–20.

——. *The Two Traditions of Meditation in Ancient India*. Delhi: Motilal Banarsidass, 1993.

Brough, John. "Thus Have I Heard . . ." *Bulletin of the School of Oriental and African Studies* 13, pt. 2 (1950): 416–26.

Buddhaghosa's Parables. Translated by Captain T. Rogers. Introduction by Friedrich Max Müller. London: Trübner & Co., 1870.

Buchanan-Hamilton, Francis. 'On the Religion and Literature of the Burmas.' *Asiatik Researches* 6 (1799): 136–308.

Buddhadatta, A. P. *English-Pāli Dictionary*. London: Pāli Text Society, 1970.

Burford, Grace. *Desire, Death and Goodness: The Conflict of Ultimate Values in Theravāda Buddhism*. New York: Peter Lang, 1991.

Burnouf, Eugène. *Introduction à l'histoire du buddhisme indien*. With a foreword by M. Barthélemy Saint-Hilaire. 2d ed. Bibliothèque Orientale, vol. 3. Paris: Imprimerie royale, 1844; Paris: Maisonneuve et Cie, 1876.

Burnouf, Eugène. *Choix de lettres d'Eugène Burnouf, 1825–1852*. Edited by Laura Burnouf Delisle. Paris: H. Champion, 1891.

Burnouf, Eugène, and Christian Lassen. *Essai sur le Pāli ou langue sacrée de la presqu'île au delà du Gange*. Paris: Dondey-Dupreé, 1826.

——. *Observations grammaticales sur quelques passages de l'essai sur le Pāli*. Paris: Dondey-Dupré, 1827.

Buswell, Robert E., Jr., and Robert M. Gimello. *Paths to Liberation: The Mārga and Its Transformations in Buddhist Thought*. Kuroda Institute Studies in East Asian Buddhism, vol. 7. Honolulu: University of Hawaii Press, 1992.

Carrithers, Michael. *The Forest Monks of Sri Lanka: An Anthropological and Historical Study*. Delhi: Oxford University Press, 1983.

Carrithers, Michael, Raymond Dawson, Humphrey Carpenter, and Michael Cook. *Founders of Faith*. Oxford: Oxford University Press, 1989.

Carter, John Ross. *Dhamma: Western Academic and Sinhalese Buddhist Interpretations – a Study of a Religious Concept*. Tokyo: The Hokuseido Press, 1978.

Chau, Thich Minh. *The Chinese Madhyama Āgama and the Pāli Majjhima-nikāya: A Comparative Study*. Saigon: Saigon Institute of Higher Buddhist Studies, 1964.

Christian, William A, Sr. *Doctrines of Religious Communities: A Philosophical Study*. New Haven: Yale University Press, 1987.

——. *Oppositions of Religious Doctrines: A Study in the Logic of Dialogue among Religions*. London: Macmillan, 1972.

Clough, Benjamin. *A Compendious Pāli Grammar with a Copious Vocabularly in the Same Language*. Colombo: Wesleyan Mission Press, 1925.

——. *A Sinhalese-English Dictionary*. 2d ed. 1830; Colombo: Wesleyan Mission Press, 1892.

Cohen, Bernard S. *Colonialism and Its Forms of Knowledge: The British in India*. Princeton: Princeton University Press, 1996.

Collins, Steven. 'On the Very Idea of the Pāli Canon.' *Journal of the Pāli Text Society* 15 (1990): 89–126.

——. *Nirvāṇa and Other Buddhist Felicities: Utopias of the Pāli Imaginaire*. Cambridge Studies in Religious Traditions, vol. 7. New York: Cambridge University Press, 1997.

——. *Selfless Persons: Imagery and Thought in Theravāda Buddhism*. Cambridge: Cambridge University Press, 1982.

Conze, Edward. *Buddhist Thought in India: Three Phases of Buddhist Philosophy*. Ann Arbor: University of Michigan Press, 1962.

Corless, Roger. 'The Chinese Life of Nāgārjuna.' In *Buddhism in Practice*, edited by Donald S. Lopez, Jr., 525–31. Princeton: University of Princeton Press, 1995.

Cousins, L. S. 'Buddhist Jhāna: Its Nature and Attainment According to the Buddhist Sources.' *Religion* 3 (1973): 115–131.

——. 'Pāli Oral Literature.' In *Buddhist Studies: Ancient and Modern*, edited by Philip Denwood and Alexander Piatagorsky, 1–11. Collected Papers on South Asia, no. 4. London: Curzon Press, 1983.

——. 'The Paṭṭhāna and the Development of the Theravādin Abhidhamma.' *Journal of the Pāli Text Society* 9 (1981): 22–46.

Cousins, L. S., A. Kunst, and K. R. Norman, eds. *Buddhist Studies in Honour of I. B. Horner*. Boston and Dordrecht: D. Reidel Publishing Co., 1974.

Cutler, Sally Mellick. 'The Pāli Apadāna Collection.' *Journal of the Pāli Text Society* 20 (1994): 1–42.

Davids, Caroline Augusta Foley Rhys. *The Birth of Indian Psychology and Its Development in Buddhism*. London: Luzac & Co., 1936.

——. 'Curious Omissions in the Pāli Canonical Lists.' *Journal of the Royal Asiatic Society of Great Britain and Ireland* (1935): 721–24.

——. *Gotama the Man*. London: Luzac & Co., 1928.

Davids, T. W. Rhys. 'Buddha's First Sermon.' *The Fortnightly Review* 39 (1879): 899–912.

——. 'Buddhism and Christianity.' *The International Quarterly* 7 (1903): 1–13.

——. *Buddhism: Being a Sketch of the Life and Teachings of Gautama the Buddha*. London: Society for Promoting Christian Knowledge, 1899.

——. *Buddhist India*. The Story of the Nations. New York: G. P. Putnam's Sons, 1903.

——. *Buddhist Suttas*. Oxford: Clarendon Books, 1881.

——. *Lectures on the Origin and Growth of Religion*. The Hibbert Lectures, 1881, New York: G. P. Putnam's Sons, 1882.

——. 'On Nirvāṇa and on the Buddhist Doctrines of the Groups, the Sanskāras, Karma and the Paths' *The Contemporary Review* 29 (1877): 249–70.

Davidson, Arnold I. 'Spiritual Exercises and Ancient Philosophy: An Introduction to Pierre Hadot.' *Critical Inquiry* 16 (Spring 1990): 475–505.

Deegalle, Mahinda, Ven. *Bana: Buddhist Preaching in Sri Lanka.* Ph.D. Diss.: University of Chicago, 1995.

de Bary, William Theodore, ed. *The Buddhist Tradition in India, China and Japan.* Collaborators Yoshito Hakeda and Philip Yampolsky. New York: Random House, 1969.

de Jong, J. W. 'Brief History of Buddhist Studies in Europe and America.' *Eastern Buddhist*, n.s. 7 (May 1974): 55–106; 7 (October 1974): 49–82. Reprinted as *A Brief History of Buddhist Studies in Europe and America.* Tokyo: Kosei, 1997.

——. 'Review of Hermann Oldenberg, 'Kleine Schriften'' *Indo-Iranian Journal* 12 (1970): 223–26.

——. 'The Study of Buddhism: Problems and Perspectives.' In *Buddhist Studies*, edited by Gregory Schopen, 23–26. China: Asian Humanities Press, 1979.

Deschamps, Auguste F. *Les origines du bouddhisme, vues nouvelles pour servir aux travaux de l'apologéteque chrètienne.* Paris: Benjamin Duprat, 1861.

Douglas, Mary. *Purity and Danger: An Analysis of Concepts of Pollution and Taboo.* 1966; London: Routledge and Kegan Paul, 1980.

Durkheim, Emile. *The Elementary Forms of the Religious Life.* Translated by Joseph Ward Swain. New York: Free Press, 1915; New York: Free Press, 1965.

Dutt, Nalinaksha. *Aspects of Mahāyāna Buddhism and Its Relation to Hinayāna.* London: Luzac & Co., 1930.

Dutt, Sukumar. *Buddhist Monks and Monasteries of India: Their History and Their Contributions to Indian Culture.* London: George Allen & Unwin, 1962; Delhi: Motilal Banarsidass, 1988.

Eitel, Ernst J. *Buddhism: Its Historical, Theoretical and Popular Aspects.* 2d ed. London: Trübner & Co., 1873.

Eliade, Mircea. 'Methodological Remarks on the Study of Religious Symbolism.' In *History of Religions: Essays in Methodology*, edited by Mircea Eliade and Joseph M. Kitagawa. Chicago: University of Chicago Press, 1959.

——. *Yoga: Immortality and Freedom.* Translated by Willard R. Trask. 2d ed. Bollingen Series, no. 66. 1958; Princeton: Princeton University Press, 1969.

Engler, John H. *Theravāda Buddhism Insight Meditation and an Object Relations Model of Therapeutic-developmental Change: A Clinical Case Study of an Ethnopsychiatric Tradition.* Ph.D. diss., 2 vols. Chicago: University of Chicago, 1983.

Evans-Pritchard, E. E. *Theories of Primitive Religion.* Oxford: Oxford University Press, Clarendon, 1965.

Feer, Léon. 'Études bouddhiques: Les quatre vérité et la prédication de Bènarés (Dharma-cakra-pravartanaṃ).' *Journal asiatique*, 6e série, 15 (1870): 345–472.

Forbes, Jonathan. *Eleven Years in Ceylon: Comprising Sketches of the Field Sports and Natural History of That Colony and an Account of Its History and Antiquities.* 2d ed. 2 vols. London: Richard Bentley, 1841.

Foucaux, Philippe Édouard. *Doctrine des bouddhistes sur le nirvāna.* Paris: Benjamin Duprat, 1864.

——. *Rgya Tch'er rol pa, ou Développement des jeux.* 2 vols. Paris: Benjamin Duprat, 1847–8.

Foucher, Alfred. *The Life of the Buddha According to the Ancient Texts and Monuments of India.* Paris: Payot, 1949; Middletown, CT: Wesleyan University Press, 1963.

Frauwallner, Eric. *The Earliest Vinaya and the Beginnings of Buddhist Literature.* Serie orientale Roma, no. 8. Rome: Instituto Italiano Per Il Medio Ed Estremo Oriente, 1956.

——. *Studies in Abhidharma Literature and the Origins of Buddhist Philosophical Systems.* Translated by Sophie Kidd Kidd. Albany: State University of New York Press, 1995.

Frazer, James George. *The Golden Bough: A Study in Magic and Religion.* Abridged Edition. New York: Macmillan, 1951.

——. *Man, God, and Immortality: Thoughts on Human Progress.* New York: Macmillan Company, 1927.

Geiger, Magdalene, and Wilhelm Geiger. *Pāli Dhamma, vernehmlich in der kanonischem Literatur.* Munich: Bavarian Academy of Science, 1920.

Geiger, Wilhelm. *Pāli Literature and Language.* Translated by Batakrishna Ghosh. 2d ed. Delhi: Oriental Books Reprint Corporation, 1968.

Gethin, Rupert M. L. *The Buddhist Path to Awakening: A Study of the Bodhipakkhiyā-dhammā.* Leiden: E. J. Brill, 1992.

——. 'The Mātikās: Memorization, Mindfulness, and the List.' In *In the Mirror of Memory: Reflections on Mindfulness and Remembrance in Indian and Tibetan Buddhism*, edited by Janet Gyatso, 149–72. Albany: State University of New York Press, 1992.

Gogerly, Daniel John. *Ceylon Buddhism Being the Collected Writings of Daniel John Gogerly.* 2 vols. London: Kegan Paul, Trench, Trübner & Co., 1908.

Gombrich, Richard F. *Theravada Buddhism.* London and New York: Routledge and Kegan Paul, 1988.

——. *Precept and Practice: Traditional Buddhism in the Rural Highlands of Ceylon.* Cambridge: Cambridge University Press, 1971.

Govinda, Lama Anagarika. *The Psychological Attitude of Early Buddhist Philosophy.* Delhi: Motilal Banarsidass, 1969.

Griffiths, Paul J. 'An Apology for Apologetics.' *Faith and Philosophy* 5 (October 1988): 399–420.

——. 'Buddhist Jhāna: A Form-critical Study.' *Religion* 13 (1983): 55–68.

——. 'Concentration or Insight: The Problematic of Theravāda Buddhist Meditation-theory.' *Journal of the American Academy of Religion* 44 (1981): 605–24.

——. 'Denaturalizing Discourse: Ābhidhārmikas, Propositionalists, and the Comparative Philosophy of Religion.' In *Myth and Philosophy*, edited by Frank E. Reynolds and David Tracy, 57–91. Albany: State University of New York Press, 1990.

——. 'The Doctrine of Buddhahood.' Chicago, n.d.

——. *Indian Buddhist Meditation-theory: History, Development and Systematization.* Ph.D. diss. Madison, Wis.: University of Wisconsin, 1983.

——. *On Being Buddha: The Classical Doctrine of Buddhahood.* Albany: State University of New York Press, 1994.

——. *On Being Mindless: Buddhist Meditation and the Mind-body Problem.* LaSalle, Ill.: Open Court Press, 2986.

Griffiths, Paul J., and John Keenan. *Realm of Awakening.* Oxford: Oxford University Press, 1989.

Guenther, H. V. *Philosophy and Psychology in the Abhidhamma.* Lucknow: Buddha Vihara, 1962.

Gunaratne, V. F. *The Four Noble Truths: Their Nature and Signficance.* Dona Alphina Ratnayake Trust Lecture on March 13, 1968. Colombo: The Public Trustee of Ceylon, 1968.

Gunawardana, R. A. L. H. *Robe and Plough: A Economic Interest in Early Medieval Sri Lanka*. Monographs for the Association for Asian Studies, no. 35. Tucson: University of Arizona Press, 1979.

Gurugé, Ananda W. P. *From the Living Fountains of Buddhism*. Colombo: Ministry of Cultural Affairs, 1984.

Halbfass, Wilhelm. *Tradition and Reflection: Explorations in Indian Thought*. Albany: State University of New York Press, 1991.

Hallisey, Charles. 'Apropos the Pāli Vinaya as a Historical Document.' *Journal of the Pāli Text Society* 15 (1990): 197–208.

——. 'In Defense of Rather Fragile and Local Achievement: Reflections on the Work of Guruḷugōmī,' in *Religion and Practical Reason: New Essays in the Comparative Philosophy of Religions*, edited by Frank E. Reynolds and David Tracy, 121–160. Albany: State University of New York, 1994.

——. 'Roads Taken and not Taken in the Study of Theravāda Buddhism.' In *Curators of the Buddha: The Study of Buddhism Under Colonialism*, edited by Donald S. Lopez, Jr., 31–61. Chicago: University of Chicago Press, 1995.

Hardy, Robert Spence. *The British Government and the Idolatry of Ceylon*. London: Crofts & Blenkarn, 1841.

——. *The Legends and Theories of the Buddhists*. London: Williams & Norgate, 1866.

——. *A Manual of Buddhism in Its Modern Development*. Chowkamba Sanskrit Series, vol. 56. 1853; Varanasi: Chowkamba Sanskrit Series Office, 1967.

Hazra, Kanai Lal. *History of Theravada Buddhism in Southeast Asia*. Delhi: Munshiram Manoharlal Publishers, 1981.

Hinüber, Oskar von. 'On the History of the Name of the Pāli Language.' In *Selected Papers on Pāli Studies*, edited by Oskar von Hinüber, 76–90. Oxford: Pāli Text Society, 1994.

——. 'On the Tradition of Pāli Texts in Early Sinhalese Buddhism.' In *Buddhism in Ceylon and Studies in Religious Syncretism in Buddhist Countries*, 48–57. Abhandlungen der Akademie der Wissenschaften in Göttingen Philologische-Historische Klasse, Dritte Folge, nr. 108. Göttingen: Vandenhoeck & Ruprecht, 1978.

——. 'Pāli as an Artificial Language.' *Indologica Taurinensia* 10 (1982): 133–140.

Holt, John C. *Discipline: The Canonical Buddhism of the Vinayapiṭaka*. Delhi: Motilal Banarsidass, 1983.

Horner, Isaline Blew. 'Abhidhamma, Abhivinaya.' *The Indian Historical Quarterly* 17 (September 1941): 291–310.

——. *The Early Buddhist Theory of Man Perfected: A Study of the Arahan Concept and of the Implications of the Aim to Perfection in Religious Life*. London: Routledge & Kegan Paul, 1936; Amsterdam: Philo Press, 1975.

——. *Women Under Primitive Buddhism: Laywomen and Almswomen*. London: G. Routledge & Sons, 1930.

Inden, Ronald. *Imagining India*. Cambridge: Blackwell, 1990.

Jayatilleke, J. N. *Early Buddhist Theory of Knowledge*. London: George Allen & Unwin, 1963.

Johansson, Rune E. A. *The Dynamic Psychology of Early Buddhism*. Scandinavian Institute of Asian Studies Monograph Series, no. 37. London: Curzon Press, 1979.

——. *The Psychology of Nirvāṇa*. London: George Allen and Unwin, 1969.

Judson, Adoniram. *A Dictionary of the Burman Language, with Explanations in English*. Calcutta: Baptist Mission Press, 1826.

Kalupahana, David J. *Buddhist Philosophy: A Historical Analysis*. Honolulu: University of Hawaii Press, 1976.

——. *Causality: The Central Philosophy of Budhism.* Honolulu: University of Hawaii Press, 1975.

Karunadasa, Y. *Buddhist Analysis of Matter.* Colombo: Department of Cultural Affairs, 1967.

Karunaratne, W. S. 'Unpublished Brāhmī Inscriptions of Ceylon.' *Epigraphia Zeylanica* 7 (1984).

Keith, A. Berriedale. *Buddhist Philosophy in India and Ceylon.* Oxford: Clarendon Press, 1923.

——. 'The Doctrine of the Buddha.' *Bulletin of the School of Oriental Studies* 6, pt. 2 (1930–2): 393–404.

Kern Hendrik. *Histoire du bouddhisme dans l'Inde.* 2 vols. Translated by Gédéon Huet. Paris: Ernest Leroux, 1901.

——. *Manual of Indian Buddhism.* Varanasi: Indological Book House, 1968.

King, Winston. *Theravāda Meditation: The Buddhist Transformation of Yoga.* University Park: Pennsylvania University State Press, 1980.

Körösi, Alexander Csoma. 'Notes on the Life of Shakya, Extracted from the Tibetan Authorities.' *Asiatik Researches* 20 (1836): 285–317.

La Vallée Poussin, Louis de. *Bouddhisme: études et matériaux.* London: Luzac & Co., 1898.

——. *Bouddhisme et religions de l'Inde.* Paris: Gabriel Beauchesne, 1912.

——. *Bouddhisme: opinions sur l'histoire de la dogmatique.* Paris: Gabriel Beauchesne, 1909.

——. 'The Buddhist Councils.' *The Indian Antiquary* 37 (1908): 1–106.

——. *Le dogme et la philosophie du bouddhisme.* Études sur l'histoire des religions, vol. 6. Paris: Gabriel Beauchesne, 1930.

——. 'Faith and Reason in Buddhism.' *Transactions of the Third International Congress for the History of Religions* 2 (1908): 32–43.

——. 'Musīla et Nārada: le chemin du nirvana.' *Melanges choinois et bouddhiques* 5 (1937): 189–222.

——. *Nirvāṇa.* Paris: Gabriel Beauchesne, 1925.

——. 'The Tantras.' Letter to the Editor. *Journal of the Royal Asiatic Society* (1899): 141–42.

——. *The Way to Nirvāṇa: Six Lectures on Ancient Buddhism as a Discipline of Salvation.* Cambridge: Cambridge University Press, 1917.

Lacôte, Felix. 'L'indianisme.' In *Société Asiatique: Livre Du Centenaire,* 219–49. Paris: Société Asiatique, 1922.

Lamotte, Étienne. *Histoire du boudhdisme indien, des origines à l'ére Śaka.* Bibliotèque du Musèon, vol. 43. English translation by Sara Webb Boin, *History of Indian Buddhism from the Origins to the Śaka Era.* Publications de l'Institut Orientaliste de Louvain, vol. 36. Louvain-la-Neuve: Institut Orientaliste, 1988.

——. 'Notice sur Louis de La Vallée Poussin.' *Annuaire de l'Academie royale des sciences, des lettres et des beaux-arts* 131 (1965): 145–68.

——. 'La légende du Buddha.' *Revue de l'histoire des religions* 134 (1947–8): 37–71.

——. 'Problems Concerning the Minor Canonical Texts.' Translated by Sara Boin Webb. In *Buddhist Studies in Honour of Hammalava Saddhātissa,* edited by Gatare Dhammapala, Richard Gombrich, and K. R. Norman, 148–58. University of Sri Jayewardenepura, 1984.

Law, Bimala Churn. *Concepts of Buddhism.* Leiden: Kern Institute, 1937.

——. 'Formulation of the Pratītyasamutpāda.' *Journal of the Royal Asiatic Society* (1937): 287–92.

——. *A History of Pali Literature*. 2 vols. 1933; Varanasi: Bharatiya Publishing House, 1974.

——. 'Influences of the Five Heretical Teachers on Jainism and Buddhism.' *Journal of the Asiatic Society of Bengal* 15 n.s. (1919): 134 ff.

——. *The Life and Work of Buddhaghosa*. Calcutta Oriental Series. Calcutta: Thacker, Spink & Co., 1923.

Lehmann, D. Edv. *Der Buddhismus*. Tübingen: J. C. B. Mohr, 1911.

Lévy-Bruhl, Lucien. *How Natives Think*. Translated by Lilian A. Clare. New York: Alfred A. Knopf, 1925; New York: Washington Square Press, 1966.

——. *Primitive Mentality*. Translated by Lilian A. Clare. New York: Macmillan, 1923; Boston: Beacon Press, 1966.

Lillie, Arthur. *India in Primitive Christianity*. London: Kegan Paul, Trench, Trübner & Co., 1909.

Lindbeck, George A. *The Nature of Doctrine: Religion and Theology in a Post-liberal Age*. Philadelphia: Westminster Press, 1984.

Lopez, Donald S. Jr., ed. *Buddhist Hermeneutics*. Studies in East Asian Buddhism. Honolulu: University of Hawaii Press, 1988.

Lovejoy, Arthur Oncken. 'The Buddhistic Technical Terms Upādāna and Upadisesa.' *Journal of the American Oriental Society* 19 (July 1898): 126–36.

Lovin, Robin W., Reynolds, and Frank E, eds. *Cosmogony and Ethical Order: New Studies in Comparative Ethics*. Chicago: University of Chicago Press, 1985.

McGovern, William Montgomery. *A Manual of Buddhist Philosophy*. Lucknow, India: Oriental Reprinters, 1976.

Macy, Joanna Rogers. *Interdependence: Mutual Causality in Early Buddhist Teachings and General Systems Theory*. Ph.D. diss. Syracuse: Syracuse University, 1978.

Mahony, [William C. ?]. 'On Sinhala, or Ceylon, and the Doctrines of Bhoddha, from the Books of the Sinhalais.' *Asiatik Researches* 7 (1801): 32–56.

Malalasekera, G. P. *The Pāli Literature of Ceylon*. London: Royal Asiatic Society of Great Britain and Ireland, 1928.

Malalgoda, Kitsiri. *Buddhism in Sinhalese Society, 1750–1900: A Study in Religious Revival and Change*. Berkeley: University of California Press, 1976.

Manné, Joy. 'Case Histories from the Pāli Canon I: The Sāmaññaphala Sutta Hypothetical Case History or How to Be Sure to Win a Debate.' *Journal of the Pāli Text Society* 21 (1995): 1–34.

——. 'Case Histories from the Pāli Canon II: *sotāpanna, sakadāmin, anāgāmin, arahat – the Four Stages Case History or Spiritual Materialism and the Need for Tangible Results.' Journal of the Pāli Text Society 21 (1995): 35–128.*

Masefield, Peter. *Divine Revelation in Pāli Buddhism*. Colombo: Sri Lanka Institute of Traditional Studies, 1986.

Masson-Oursel, Paul. 'Louis de La Vallée Poussin – Nécrologie.' *Journal asiatique* 230 (1938): 287–89.

Matthews, Bruce. *Craving and Salvation: A Study in Buddhist Soteriology*. Ontario: Wilfred Laurier Press, 1983.

Meyer, Ferdinand. 'Quand le maître des médecines est Bouddha.' *Vougue (Paris)*, no. 732 (December 1992/January 1993:174ff.

Mohl, Jules. 'Rapport sur les travaux du conseil de la Société asiatique, pendent l'année 1860–61, faint à la séance annuelle de la Société le 29 juin 1861.' *Journal asiatique*, 5e série, 18 (1861): 10–140.

Monier-Williams, Monier. *Buddhism, in Its Connexion with Brāhmanism and Hinduism and in Its Contrast with Christianity*. London: John Murray, 1889.

Mori, Sōdō. 'Chronology of the Sīhala Sources for the Pāli Commentaries.' *Buddhist Studies (Bukkyō Kenkyū)* 17 (1988): 119–67.

Morrell, Robert. 'Passage to India Denied: Zeami's Kasuga Ryūjin.' *Monumenta Nipponica: Studies in Japanese Culture* 37, no. 2 (1982): 179–200.

Müller, Friedrich Max. *Buddha's Dhammapada or 'Path of Virtue'*. London: Trübner & Co., 1870.

——. *Selected Essays on Language, Mythology, and Religion*. 2 vols. London: Longman's, Green, & Co., 1881.

Mus, Paul. *Barabudur: esquisse d'une histoire du Bouddhisme fondée sur la critique archéologique des textes*. 2 vols. With a preface by George Coedès. Hanoi: Imprimerie d'Extrême-Orient, 1935; Arno Press, 1978.

Nakamura, Hajime. 'The Theory of "Dependent Origination" in Its Incipient Stage.' In *Buddhist Studies in Honor of Walpola Rahula*, edited by Somaratna Balasooriya, 165–72. London: George Fraser, 1980.

Nakamura, Hakamura. *Indian Buddhism: A Survey with Bibliographical Notes*. Japan: Kansei University of Foreign Studies, 1980.

Nārada, Mahāthera. *A Manual of Abhidhamma (Abhidhammatthasangaha)*. 4th ed. 1956; Kandy: Buddhist Publication Society, 1980.

Nattier, Janice J., and Charles S. Prebish. 'Mahāsāṃghika Origins: The Beginnings of Buddhist Sectarianism.' *History of Religions* 16 (1977): 237–72.

Norman, K. R. *Collected Papers*. 6 vols. Oxford: Pāli Text Society, 1990-.

——. 'On the Role of Pāli in Early Sinhalese Buddhism.' In *Buddhism in Ceylon and Studies in Religious Syncretism*, edited by Heinz Bechert, 28–47. Abhandlungen der Akademie der Wissenschaften in Göttingen Philosogische-Historische Klasse, Dritte Folge, nr. 108. Göttingen: Vanderhoeck & Ruprecht, 1978.

——. *Pāli Literature, Including the Canonical Literature in Prakrit and Sanskrit of All the Hīnayāna Schools of Buddhism*. Vol. 7, fascicle 2 of *A History of Indian Liturature*. Wiesbaden: Otto Hararassowitz, 1983.

Nyanaponika, Thera. *Abhidhamma Studies: Researches in Buddhist Psychology*. 3d ed. Kandy: Buddhist Publication Society, 1976.

——. 'Anattā and Nibbāna.' *The Wheel* 11 (1971).

Nyanaponoka, Thera. *The Heart of Buddhist Meditation*. New York: The Citadel Press, 1962.

Nyanatiloka Mahāthera. *Guide Through the Abhidhammapiṭaka*. 4th ed. Kandy: 1938; Buddhist Publication Society, 1983.

Obry, J. B. F. *Du nirvâna bouddhique en réponse à M. Barthélemy Saint-Hilaire*. Paris: August Durand, 1863.

Oldenberg, Hermann. *Ancient India: Its Language and Religions*. Chicago: Open Court Publishing Company, 1896.

——. *Aus Indien und Iran*. Berlin: Wilhelm Herz, 1899.

——. *Buddha: His Life, His Doctrine, His Order*. Translated by William Hoey. 1881; Delhi: Indological Book House, 1971.

——. 'The Relations of the Religions of Ancient India to the Science of Religion.' *Congress of Arts and Sciences* 2 (1906): 467–80.

Panabokke, Gunaratne. *History of the Buddhist Sangha in India and Sri Lanka*. Kelaniya, Sri Lanka: Postgraduate Institute of Pali and Buddhist Studies Publications University of Kelaniya, 1993.

Pande, Govind Chandra. *Studies in the Origins of Buddhism*. Allahabad: University of Allabad, 1957.

Pelliott, Paul. 'Review of Thomas Watters' On Yuan Chwang's Travels in India.' *Bulletin de L'Ecole Française de Extrême-Orient* 5 (1905): 423–57.

Percival, Robert. *An Account of the Island of Ceylon, Containing Its History, Geography, Natural History, with the Manners and Customs of Its Various*

Inhabitants to Which is Added the Journal of an Embassy to the Court of Candy. 2d ed. London: C. & R. Baldwin, 1805.

Pischel, Richard. *Life and Doctrines of Buddha.* Translated by B. H. Kapadia. 1904; India: Dr. B. H. Kapadia, 1965.

Prebish, Charles S. 'A Review of Scholarship on the Buddhist Councils.' *Journal of Asian Studies* 33 (1974): 239–54.

Prinsep, James. 'On the Edicts of Piyadasi, or Asoka, the Buddhist Monarch of India, Preserved on the Girnar Rock in the Gujerat Peninsula, and on the Dhaulí Rock in Cuttack; with the Discovery of Ptolemy's Name Therein.' *Journal of the Asiatic Society of Bengal* 7 (March 1838): 219–82.

Pruitt, William. 'References to Pāli in 17th Century French Books.' *Journal of the Pāli Text Society* 11 (1987): 121–31.

Przyluski, Jean. 'Le nord-ouest de l'Inde dans le Vinaya des Mūla-Sarvāstivādins et les textes apparentés.' *Journal asiatique* 4 (1914).

Rahula, Telwatte Bhikkhu. *A Critical Study of the Mahāvastu.* Delhi: Motilal Banarsidass, 1978.

Rahula, Walpola. *What the Buddha Taught.* With a foreword by Paul Demieville. 1959; New York: Grove Press, 1974.

Read, Kay Almere. *Time and Sacrifice in the Aztec Cosmos.* Bloomington: Indiana University Press, 1998.

Renou, Louis. *Memorial Sylvain Lévi.* Paris: P. Hartmann, 1937.

——. *Religions of Ancient India.* London: University of London, 1953.

——. *Vedic India.* Translated by Philip Spratt. Classical India, vol. 3. 1947; Calcutta: Susil Gupta Private, 1957.

Renou, Louis, and Jean Filliozat. *L'Inde classique: manuel études indiennes.* 2 vols. 1953; Paris: École Française d'Extrême Orient, 1985.

Reynolds, Frank E. 'Multiple Cosmogonies and Ethics: The Case of Theravāda Buddhism.' In *Cosmogony and Ethical Order: New Studies in Comparative Ethics,* edited by Robin W. Lovin and Frank E. Reynolds, 203–24. 1985.

Reynolds, Frank E., and Mani B. Reynolds, trans. *Three Worlds According to King Ruang: A Thai Buddhist Cosmology.* Berkeley Buddhist Studies Series, no. 4. Berkeley: University of California Press, 1982.

Ribeyro, John. *History of Ceylon Presented by Captain John Ribeyro to the King of Portugal in 1685.* Translated by Abbé Le Grand and George Lee. Ceylon: Ceylon Government Press, 1847.

Ribiero, Jean. *History of Ceilão with Notes from De Barros, de Conto, and Antonio Bocarro.* Translated by P. E. Peiris. Galle, Sri Lanka: Albion Press, n.d.

Ricoeur, Paul. *Interpretation Theory: Discourse and the Surplus of Meaning.* Fort Worth: Texas Christian University Press, 1976.

——. 'The Symbol . . . Food for Thought.' *Philosophy Today* 4 (Fall 1960): 196–207.

——. *The Symbolism of Evil.* Translated by Emerson Buchanan. Boston: Beacon Press, 1967.

Roussel, Alfred. *Le bouddhisme primitif.* Paris: Pierre Téqui, Libraire-Éditeur, 1911.

Ruegg, David, and Lambert Schmidthausen, eds. *Earliest Buddhism and Madhyamaka.* Panels of the 7th World Sanskrit Conference (Kern Institute, Leiden: August 23–29, 1987), vol. 2. Leiden: E. J. Brill, 1990.

Sadaw, Ledi. 'Some Points in Buddhist Doctrine.' *Journal of the Pāli Text Society* 7 (1912–23): 115–63.

Saddhātissa, H. 'Pāli Literature of Thailand.' In *Buddhist Studies in Honour of I. B. Horner,* edited by L. S. Cousins, A. Kunst, and K. R. Norman. Boston: D. Reidel Publishing Co., 1974.

Salisbury, Edward Eldridge. 'M. Burnouf on the History of Buddhism in India.' *Journal of the American Oriental Society* 1 (1843–9): 275–98.

——. 'Memoir on the History of Buddhism.' *Journal of the American Oriental Society* 1 (1843–9): 81–135.

Schayer, Stanislaus. 'Pre-Aryan Elements in Indian Buddhism.' *Bulletin de L'Académie Polonaise Des Sciences et Des Lettres* (1934).

——. 'Pre-canonical Buddhism.' *Archiv Orientalni (Prague)* 7 (1935): 121–32.

Schmidt, Wilhelm. *The Origin and Growth of Religion.* Original Title of Work Ursprung und Werden der Religion. Translated by H. J. Rose. 1930; New York: Dial Press, 1931.

Schmithausen, Lambert. 'On some aspects of descriptions or theories of 'Liberating Insight' and 'Enlightenment' in Early Buddhism.' In *Studien zum Jainismus und Buddhismus: Gedenkschrift für Ludwig Alsdorf*, 199–250. Wiesbaden: F. Steiner, 1981.

——. 'On the Problem of the Relation of Spiritual Practice and Philosophical Theory in Buddhism.' In *German Scholars on India: Contributions to Indian Studies*, vol. 2, 235–50. Bombay: Nachiketa Publications, 1976.

Schopen, Gregory. *Bones, Stones, and Buddhist Monks: Collected Papers on the Archaeology, Epigraphy, and Texts of Monastic Buddhism in India.* Honolulu: University of Hawaii, 1997.

Schrader, F. Otto. 'On the Problem of Nirvāṇa.' *Journal of the Pāli Text Society* (1904–5): 157–70.

Schweitzer, Albert. *Indian Thought and Its Development.* Translated by Mrs. Charles E. B. Russell. New York: Henry Holt and Company, 1936.

Senart, Émile Charles Marie. 'Origines bouddhiques.' *Annales: Bibliothèque de vulgarisation* 25 (1907): 115–58. Paris: Musée Guimet Bibliothèque de Diffusion.

——. 'A propos de la théorie bouddhique des douze nidānas.' In *Recueil de travaux d'érudition offert á Mgr Charles de Harlez*, 281–97. Leiden: E. J. Brill, 1896.

——. 'Buddhisme et yoga.' *Revue de l'histoire des religions* 42 (1900): 345–65.

——. *Essai sur la légende du Buddha son charactère et ses origines.* 2d ed. Paris: Ernest Leroux, 1882.

——. 'Nirvāṇa.' In *Album Kern: opstellen geschreven te eere van Dr. H. Kern*, 101–04. Leiden: E. J. Brill, 1903.

Shcherbatskoi, Fedor Ippolitovich. *Buddhist Logic.* 2 vols. 1930–32; New Delhi: Oriental Books Reprint Corporation, 1984.

——. *The Central Conception of Buddhism and Meaning of the Term 'dharma'* London: Royal Asiatic Society, 1923.

——. 'The Doctrine of the Buddha.' *Bulletin of the School of Oriental Studies* 6 (1930–2): 867–96.

——. 'Review of *Nirvāna.*' *Bulletin of the School of Oriental Studies 4 (1926–8): 357–60.*

——. *The Conception of Buddhist Nirvāṇa.* Indo Iranian Reprints 6. Leningrad: Academy of Sciences of the USSR 1927; The Hague: Mouton and Co., 1965.

Silva, K. M. de. *Letters on Ceylon 1846–1850: The Administration of Viscount Torrington and the 'Rebellion' of 1848 – The Private Correspondence of the Third Earl Grey (Secretary of State for the Colonies 1846–1852) and Viscount Torrington.* Kandy and Colombo: K. V. G. de Silva & Sons, 1965.

Skilling, Peter. 'Theravadin Literature in Tibetan Translation.' *Journal of the Pāli Text Society* 19 (1993): 69–201.

Smith, Jonathan Z. *Imagining Religion: From Babylon to Jonestown.* Chicago studies in the history of Judaism. Chicago: University of Chicago Press, 1982.

——. *Map is not Territory: Studies in the History of Religions*. Studies in Judaism in Late Antiquity, vol. 23. Leiden: E. J. Brill, 1978.

Sperber, Dan. *Rethinking Symbolism*. Translated by Alice Morton. Cambridge Studies and Papers in Social Anthropology. Cambridge: Cambridge University Press, 1975.

Spiro, Melford E. *Buddhism and Society: A Great Tradition and Its Burmese Vicissitudes*. New York: Harper and Row, 1970.

Stalker, Susan C. *A Study of Dependent Origination: Vasubandhu, Buddhaghosa, and the Interpretation of Pratītyasamutpāda*. Ph. D. Diss. University of Pennsylvania, 1987.

Stargardt, Janice. 'The Oldest Known Pāli Texts, 5th–6th Century: Results of the Cambridge Symposium on the Pyu Golden Pāli Text from Śrī Kṣetra, 18–19 April 1995.' *Journal of the Pāli Text Society* 21 (1995): 199–213.

Strong, John. *The Experience of Buddhism: Sources and Interpretations*. Belmont, Calif.: Wadsworth Press, 1995.

Swearer, Donald K. 'Two Types of Saving Knowledge in the Pāli Suttas.' *Philosophy East and West* 22 (1972): 355–71.

Taine, Hippolyte Adolphe. 'Le Bouddhisme, *Die Religion Des Buddha und Ihre Entstehung par M. Koeppen.' Journal de débats, March 3, 4, 5, 6 1864.*

——. *Nouveaux essais de critique et d'histoire*. Paris: Librairie Hachette et Cie, 1905.

Takakusu, J. 'On the Abhidhamma Literature of the Sarvāstivādins.' *Journal of the Pāli Text Society* (1904–5): 67–146.

Tambiah, Stanley Jeyaraja. *The Buddhist Saints of the Forest and the Cult of the Amulets*. Cambridge Studies in Social Anthropology. Cambridge: Cambridge University Press, 1984.

——. *World Conqueror and World Renouncer.* Cambridge Studies in Social Anthropology, no. 15. Cambridge: Cambridge University Press, 1976.

Tatia, N. 'Paṭiccasamuppāda.' *Nava Nālandā Mahāvihara Research Publication* 1 (1957): 177–239.

Thapar, Romila. *Aśoka and the Decline of the Mauryas*. Oxford: Oxford University Press, 1961.

Thomas, Edward J. *History of Buddhist Thought*. New York: Barnes & Noble, 1951.

——. *The Life of the Buddha as Legend and History.* London: Routledge & Kegan Paul, 1927.

Turnour, George. 'An Examination of the Pāli Buddhistical Annals.' *Journal of the Asiatic Society of Bengal* 6, pt. 2 (July 1837): 501–528; 6, pt. 2 (September 1837): 713–737; 7, pt. 2 (August 1838): 686–701; 7, pt. 2 (September 1838): 789–817; 7, pt. 2 (November 1838): 919–939; 7, pt. 2 (December 1838): 998–1014.

Tweed, Thomas. *The American Encounter with Buddhism, 1844–1912: Victorian Culture and the Limits of Dissent*. Bloomington: Indiana University Press, 1992.

Upham, Edward, ed. *The Mahāvansi, the Rājā-Ratnācari, and the Rājā-Vali, Forming the Sacred and Historical Books of Ceylon*. 3 vols. London: Parbury, Allen & Co., 1833.

——. *The History and Doctrine of Buddhism, Popularly Illustrated, with Notices of the Kappooism, or Demon Worship, and the Bali, or Planetary Incantations, of Ceylon*. London: Ackermann, 1829.

Urubshurow, Victoria. 'Transformation of Religious Symbol in Indian Buddhism: Reflections on Method from a Reading of Mus's *Barabudur.' Numen 35, no. 2 (1988): 260–79.*

Van der Leeuw, Gerardus. *Religion in Essence and Manifestation.* 2 vols. 1933; London: George Allen & Unwin, 1963.
Vasile'ev, Vasiley. *Der Buddhismus, Seine Dogmen, Geschichte und Literatur.* Saint Petersbourg: Kaiserliche Akademie der Wissenschaften, 1860.
Verdu, Alfonso. *Early Buddhist Philosophy in the Light of the Four Noble Truths.* Delhi: Motilal Banarsidass, 1985.
Wach, Joachim. *Types of Religious Experience Christian and Non-Christian.* 1951; Chicago: University of Chicago Press, 1972.
Waldschmidt, Ernst. *Von Ceylon bis Turfan.* Göttingen: Vandenhoeck & Ruprecht, 1967.
Walters, Jonathan S. 'A Voice from the Silence: The Buddha's Mother's Story.' *History of Religions* 33 (1994): 358–79.
——. *Rethinking Buddhist Missions.* Ph.D. Diss.: University of Chicago, 1992.
Warder, A. K. 'Dharmas and Data.' *Journal of Indian Philosophy* 1 (1971): 272–95.
Warren, Henry Clarke. *Buddhism in Translations.* Harvard Oriental Series, vol. 3. 1896; Cambridge: Harvard University, 1906.
Watanabe, Fumimaro. *Philosophy and Its Development in the Nikāyas and Abhidhamma.* Delhi: Motilal Banarsidass, 1983.
Watters, Thomas, trans. *On Yuan Chwang's Travels in India, 629–645 A.D.* 2 vols. Edited by T. W. Rhys Davids. Oriental Translation Fund. London: Royal Asiatic Society, 1904–5.
——. 'Mr. Eitel's Three Lectures on Buddhism.' *The Chinese Recorder* 4 (August 1871).
Weber, Albrecht. 'Le Bouddhisme.' Translated by F. Baudry. *Revue germanique* 4:142–60.
——. *Indische Skizzen.* Berlin: Ferd. Dümmlers, 1857.
Weber, Max. *Economy and Society: An Outline of Interpretive Sociology.* Edited by Guenther Roth and Claus Wittich. Vol. 1. Berkeley: University of California Press, 1978.
——. *The Religion of India: The Sociology of Hinduism and Buddhism.* Edited and translated by Hans H. Gerth and Don Martindale. New York: Free Press, 1958.
——. *The Sociology of Religion.* Translated by Ephriam Rischoff. With an introduction by Talcott Parsons. Boston: Beacon Press, 1964.
Welbon, Guy Richard. *The Buddhist Nirvāṇa and Its Western Interpreters.* Chicago: University of Chicago Press, 1968.
Wickremeratne, Ananda. *The Genesis of an Orientalist: Thomas William Rhys Davids and Buddhism in Sri Lanka.* Delhi: Motilal Banarsidass, 1984.
Wilson, Liz. *Charming Cadavers: Horrific Figurations of the Feminine in Indian Buddhist Hagiographic Literature.* Chicago: University of Chicago Press, 1996.
Winternitz, Moriz. *A History of Indian Literature.* 2 vols. Calcutta: University of Calcutta, 1933.
Zimmer, Henrich. *Philosophies of India.* Edited by Joseph Campbell. Bollingen Series, vol. 26. Princeton: Princeton University Press, 1951.

INDEX